FOR HEARING PEOPLE ONLY

"Making the world a better place
for the next Deaf generation—
and for Deaf people now"

WARNING: This book is written from a Deaf viewpoint. You may find certain chapters or statements offensive. Please read this book with an open mind, and read the Introduction first.

A note on the cover photograph

Holly Marvin photographed 9-year-old Barney Santos of Managua, Nicaragua, during her 1996 visit to the Bluefields School, where a small community of deaf children and teens has been creating a new national sign language, a phenomenon that has received a measure of publicity and attracted interest from the academic and general communities. Marvin recalls that Barney was one of the first to learn Nicaraguan Sign Language. Her striking photographs of the Bluefields School project were originally published in the Spring 1996 issue of **Rutgers Magazine**, and reprinted in the December 1996 issue of **DEAF LIFE**. In this photo, Barney is making the letter "R."

Answers to Some of the
Most Commonly Asked Questions
About the Deaf Community,
its Culture, and the "Deaf Reality"

Third Edition
a newly-revised and expanded compilation
from the popular monthly magazine
DEAF LIFE

FOR HEARING PEOPLE ONLY

by
Matthew S. Moore
and Linda Levitan
Co-Editors-in-Chief
DEAF LIFE

With a foreword by Harlan Lane,
author of **When the Mind Hears: A History of the Deaf** and
The Mask of Benevolence: Disabling the Deaf Community

Deaf Life Press
a division of MSM Productions, Ltd.
Rochester, New York
2003

Cover photograph: Holly Marvin
Cover Design: Colin O'Brien
Illustrations: Michael Freeman
Manual-alphabet capitals: Tony Landon McGregor

Grateful acknowledgment is made to the following: Gallaudet University Press for permission to quote or cite passages from **American Sign Language: A Student Text** by Dennis Cokely and Charlotte Baker-Shenk; **Ben's Story: A Deaf Child's Right to Sign** by Lorraine Fletcher; **The Other Side of Silence** by Arden Neisser; **I Didn't Hear the Dragon Roar** by Frances M. Parsons; and **A Place of Their Own** by John Vickrey Van Cleve and Barry A. Crouch; to McGraw-Hill Company for permission to quote a passage from the **Gallaudet Encyclopedia of Deaf People and Deafness**; and to the following individuals whose letters, articles, or comments originally appeared in **DEAF LIFE**: David Anthony; Barb and John Boelter; Paulette R. Caswell; Duane King; Dr. Richard Nowell; Dr. Peter Seiler; Dr. Allen Sussman; and Dr. Sherman Wilcox. Quotations from **When the Mind Hears** by Harlan Lane are used by permission of the author.

Publisher's Cataloging in Publication Data
Moore, Matthew S., 1958-
Levitan, Linda J., 1951-

For hearing people only: answers to some of the most commonly asked questions about the Deaf community, its culture, and the "Deaf Reality" / Matthew S. Moore and Linda Levitan. With a foreword by Harlan Lane.

Bibliography: p.
Includes index.
ISBN 0-9634016-3-7 (paperback)
1. Deaf studies. 2. Deaf—Culture. 3. Deaf—United States—background. 4. Sign language. I. Title.

Library of Congress Control Number: 2001088213
Printed in the United States of America

The paper use in this publication meets the minimum requirements of American National Standard for Information Sciences—Permanence of Paper for Printed Library Materials, ANSI Z39.48-1984 ⊚

10 9 8 7 6 5 4 3 2
Third Edition

First Printing, January 2003
Second Printing, August 2003

For all hearing people
who want to better their understanding
of our community and our language,
and for all those, deaf and hearing,
who helped make this book possible.

For my mother, JoNelle, who sought out
the best education for me.
—MSM

For my mother and father,
in the hope that they will *finally* understand;
and for my good teachers, counselors, and friends.
—LL

And to the memory of all those deaf people
who died because of failed or inaccessible
communications, misunderstandings,
and ignorance on the part of society.

DEAF.com
Your Gateway to the Deaf Community
http://www.deaf.com/

Come and explore the exciting world
of the Deaf community! News, events, profiles,
controversies, resources, features for kids
and parents, chatroom . . . and more!

Foreword

I doubt whether people are more curious about anything in life than other people—especially other people with another culture. Imagine for a moment striking all discussion of how other groups act, think, socialize, and view the world from conversation, literature and the other arts (not to mention travel books); really, what would we talk about? How many of our sentences start something like: "Although the Germans . . ." "The thing about people from California . . ." "Despite the way Japanese people . . ." For many years, I resisted. French people, I said, are so different one to the next that I refuse to generalize. (Besides, the stereotypes were either adoring or totally damning and neither extreme was plausible.) But in the end I had to give in and generalize—I found I was being left out of too many conversations.

The trouble is, these descriptions of people with another culture are rarely unbiased and rarely well-informed. You are told that French people are unfriendly, Japanese self-effacing, Deaf clannish; what you are not told is: I feel more comfortable in familiar surroundings; I didn't know how to read the taxi meter; I had no idea how to begin politely; I couldn't communicate well enough to be interesting. (If only people said what they meant and meant what they said!) The problem, in my opinion, is that we have too much hasty and deceptive description of others and not enough self-description.

This is especially true for relatively invisible cultures like Deaf culture. How are outsiders to learn about it—to learn even the rudiments; for example, that there *is* such a culture? I think the members of the Deaf community may fail to appreciate how utterly unaware hearing people are of the existence of their culture. (The published remarks of some distinguished Deaf people denying that there is such a culture have not helped.) There is, after all, no Chinatown or

Little Italy of the Deaf. Until recently, the language of the Deaf community was not taught in our high schools and colleges. (That has changed dramatically but the language is still grudgingly granted second-class status in most schools.) Deaf culture is rarely portrayed in the media, as infrequently as Black, Native American or Gay culture was portrayed when I was a boy.

There is a special obstacle to hearing people's understanding of Deaf culture in particular. Whereas few Americans construct for themselves an image of Hispanic culture (for example) by extrapolating—by imagining themselves with mastery of their high-school Spanish and a meal ticket to Taco Bell—most Americans who are led to think about Deaf culture do construct their idea of the lives of Deaf people by extrapolating—by imagining themselves without hearing. Of course, a real difference in culture does not enter into this equation (only abrupt silence, a loss, not a gain) and so it is utterly useless to solve any problem that concerns culturally Deaf people. This acultural approach to Deaf culture leaves hearing people with only the concept of handicap to guide them.

Although we never tire of figuring out what the other person can't do, we are almost invariably wrong. Blacks, women and gays couldn't fight alongside straight white males; a deaf person could not be a major actress, lawyer, doctor. We underestimate human ingenuity—and thus ourselves. The same flexibility (miraculous plasticity, really) that fosters spoken languages in hearing people and signed languages in visual people, fosters novel solutions to many of life's challenges. Then, too, "can't" can be a self-fulfilling prophecy. The only clear human "can't" is—you can't figure out most of the time what someone very different from yourself can and cannot do.

Alas, uninformed guesses at what deafness must be like are frequently presented as authoritative by hearing people who stand to gain by such pronouncements. There is a vast literature on "the Deaf"—countless journals, books, texts, theses, etc. (I review it critically in my book, **The Mask of Benevolence: Disabling the Deaf Community**.) This is the record mostly of hearing people explaining their ideas about deafness to other hearing people. It has many false stereotypes; it suffers from ignorance of ASL and Deaf culture and Deaf history; it is as bad for what it fails to say (about Deaf art, for example) as for what it does say (about Deaf thought). It is about as useful as Europeans' explanations to each other about what Africans are really like. It is, however, more dangerous because it is presented as the product of social science research.

Hearing people's account of Deaf people is, then, very faulty, yet our government listens exclusively to hearing people in matters concerning Deaf people. Only hearing people at the Food and Drug Administration decided to approve cochlear implants for young deaf children (down to the age of two). Only hearing people at the National Institute on Deafness and Other Communication Disorders [*sic*] decide on what research should be conducted concerning the Deaf community, ASL, Deaf literacy, Deaf heredity, and much more. Only hearing people in the Department of Education refuse to provide ASL-using children with the special bilingual programs provided children from other language minorities.

So we need more self-description by Deaf people (among other cultural groups) and I think outsiders would ask for such descriptions more often if we were not so afraid of appearing the fool or of offending. There are two kinds of questions we are tempted to ask, if we only dared. The first kind satisfies our curiosity about obvious differences. I recall an African friend arriving in Boston at midnight on his first trip abroad. As we left the airport, we encountered a few other cars on the highway. "Where is everybody going?" he asked. A question of this first type addressed to Deaf people might be: Is there one universal sign language for Deaf people?

The second kind of question, harder to formulate (why haven't anthropologists helped us more here?), concerns carving an unfamiliar fowl at the joints. What are the revealing questions to ask? We want to know whether the other group, so startlingly different on the surface, doesn't really see the world much as we do and, if not, how its vision differs. Is there another (better?) way to conceive and manage intimacy? Decision making? Spirituality? Wealth? What constitutes achievement? Great art? A good life? These are the more interesting issues, but if we ask any questions at all we are more likely to ask the first kind, the easy ones. And perhaps, after all, those elementary matters need to be cleared up first.

Deaf people have long been trying to explain themselves to hearing people if we would only listen. The first published trace may be Pierre Desloges' well-known book, published in Paris in 1779, where he defends French Sign Language against the false claims of its detractors, hearing teachers who didn't know the least bit about it. The first traces of this self-description in America may be Laurent Clerc's public speeches throughout the northeastern United States, reprinted in the newspapers in 1816. Ever since, there has been a great tradition of Deaf self-description through art, drama, poetry, literature and nonfiction. Just a few examples of the latter are **The Silent Worker, A Deaf Adult Speaks Out, Deaf Heritage, DEAF LIFE** and now this book, **For Hearing People Only**.

In one sense the Deaf culture reflected in **For Hearing People Only** is unfamiliar—in another it is thoroughly familiar. Take language, for example. Sign Language is in an unfamiliar mode (visual and manual, not aural and oral) and it works in unexpected ways. But hearing people will find the puns, jokes, slang, highfalutin language, putdowns, tall tales and so on, familiar to them from their own language. Or, consider the Deaf club. In the neighborhood of Brooklyn where I grew up there were many ethnic clubs. For example, there was a Polish-American club over a nearby supermarket, its name stenciled in black on the windows. Many evenings when the subway brought me home from high school I looked across from the elevated station into the club and saw men in rolled-up shirtsleeves playing cards, thick plumes of purple smoke rising from their cigars. Sometimes I would pass them on the street as a handful would enter or leave the building. They had their own mysterious language, their own camaraderie—that much was clear. They had dances and parties, too (at those times, women were invited). I am reminded of all this on Las Vegas Night at the Boston Deaf Club.

For Hearing People Only contains the responses of the editors of **DEAF LIFE** to questions submitted by their hearing readers. Sincere questions deserve straight answers and that's what the reader will find here. Good common sense. Opinion backed by scholarship. Pride in Deaf culture. A sense of humor. The topics range over language (How do Deaf people learn ASL?), parenting (Is it better to be a hearing child of Deaf parents or a Deaf child of hearing parents?), history (Was Alexander Graham Bell as much of a villain as he appears to have been?), relations with hearing people (Why don't Deaf people trust them?)—and much, much more. How do hearing people come off in this Deaf cultural document? I have told how hearing people commonly describe Deaf people in unflattering terms—well, the compliment is returned! We are seen as woefully ignorant—prey to the most ridiculous beliefs: Deaf people can't drive well, shouldn't marry one another, they speak a universal language, read Braille, can't dance . . . In the last chapter Deaf readers sound off with gripes of their own about hearing people. They accuse us hearing people of having a low opinion of them and revealing it in our actions and our words. We rudely leave them out of conversation. We change our manner of speaking and exaggerate it when we learn someone is deaf, making lipreading more difficult. We expect Deaf people to perform on our terms and never we on theirs.

There is much for hearing people to learn here and much for us to reflect on. **For Hearing People Only** will interest anyone with a connection to Deaf people, of course—parents, teachers, co-workers, students of ASL, to name a few—but, more broadly, it will entertain and inform everyone who rejoices at the rich diversity of humankind and sees in its examination an opportunity to glimpse our essential humanity and to live a more considered life.

Harlan Lane

Acknowledgments

First of all, our profound thanks to those readers of **DEAF LIFE**, whether Deaf, deaf, hard-of-hearing, or hearing, who sent us their thoughtful and provocative questions—sometimes in multiples. (They have provided some of the answers as well.) In 1990, DeAnn Sampley sent us "the best" 10 questions she had collected from her class at Bakersfield College. (These are answered in Chapters 20, 29, 71, 79, 89, 104, 105, and 131; we haven't yet gotten around to answering the complicated tenth question.) We are grateful to the Laurent Clerc National Deaf Education Center (formerly known as the National Information Center on Deafness) at Gallaudet University for supplying resource information, contacts, articles, and answers to some of the questions.

Cindy Campbell, Dr. Harlan Lane, Robert F. Panara, Donn Patton, and Dr. Frank R. Turk generously gave of their time to read through the manuscript. Dr. Lane took time from an extraordinarily busy schedule to provide a foreword. We valued their comments, criticisms, and suggestions.

We extend our grateful thanks to Michael Freeman for his expressive and high-spirited illustrations, and to Charles F. Bancroft for his invaluable technical assistance. Incidentally, with the exception of Donn Patton, everyone associated with this book through the output stage (writing, editing, proofing, illustrations, and indexing) is Deaf.

Although we have done our utmost to ensure the accuracy of statements, quotes, and statistics cited herein, we recognize that a book of this sort is ultimately subjective. We take responsibility for any factual errors in this book.

Table of Contents

Over a decade of promoting Deaf Awareness

Over a decade of promoting Deaf Awareness

Over a decade of promoting Deaf Awareness

Over a decade of promoting Deaf Awareness

Introduction

To those of you who are unfamiliar with the book, and are taking their first glance at its contents, we say, "Welcome!"

This book is inspired by and written for people who have questions about Deaf culture, sign language, and Deaf life in general, and need a quick answer. It is not intended to be an in-depth excursion into a vast and complex subject, but it may provide accurate and provocative answers to at least some persistent questions. It is for "beginners." Our scope is necessarily limited; we want our answers to be as concise and accessible as possible to every reader, no matter how sketchy their background.

Each chapter is designed as an independent unit focusing on one topic. Although we have tried to keep repetition to a minimum, there is an inevitable amount of overlap. Certain facts, we found, needed to be restated.

We have written the monthly installments of "For Hearing People Only" in **DEAF LIFE**, and have compiled this book, with our families and friends in mind—as well as beginning students of ASL and the casual reader who's taking a peek into this subject for the first time. It can be used as a handy in-class or supplementary text in beginning ASL, Basic Sign Language, Deaf Studies, or Introduction to Deaf Culture classes.

Since its original publication in Fall 1992, **For Hearing People Only** has become Deaf Life Press's best-selling book, and a staple of college/university classes across the nation. We have sold thousands of copies to individual readers, and some of them have taken the time to share their responses with us and offer their feedback and criticisms. We wish to thank them for making the book part of their lives. Their feedback has enabled us to improve the text.

For Hearing People Only is written by two Deaf persons. One (MSM) is congenitally deaf, a native ASL signer, educated at a school for the deaf, and bilingual. The other (LL) is progressively deafened and has personally experienced being hearing, hard-of-hearing, moderately, *and* (currently) severely-deaf-on-the-left, profoundly-deaf-on-the-right—the whole shebang.

About the terminology used in this book: We wish to de-emphasize the concept of "deafness" and emphasize "the Deaf reality." Even such a seemingly neutral term as "deafness" can have a faintly negative connotation. There are two basic ways of looking at deafness: medically and culturally. The medical view sees deaf people in terms of deficit—patients with broken, wounded, diseased, malfunctioning, or disordered ears. The cultural view sees deaf people as whole persons. Medically speaking, a deaf person has a disability and needs auxiliary aids or surgical intervention to become more "normal." Culturally speaking, to be deaf is to be whole, and thus, "ethnically different" but every bit as "normal." We have a language; we have an identity; we have gifts. We often capitalize the "D" in "deaf" to emphasize this cultural affiliation and pride as members of a sign-language-using community. We use the word "deaf" with a small "d" in the broader sense—medically deaf, but not necessarily culturally-Deaf. Likewise, we will occasionally capitalize the "H" in "hearing" to emphasize the cultural aspect of the surrounding society, the hearing majority.

Why did we title this book **For Hearing People Only**? Hearing people—those with normal hearing—do not think of themselves as being "hearing people." They think of themselves as, well, people. They do not automatically think in terms of *being* "hearing." Now, imagine. You are the insiders. To you, we deaf people are the outsiders. You call us "deaf people." But we deaf people see non-deaf people as the outsiders—"hearing people." We are a minority with an ancient history of oppression. And oppression is signified by labels. It was Aristotle who first started labeling us "deaf and dumb." Thousands of years later, we are still struggling to free ourselves from that label. To deaf people, the non-deaf majority are labeled "hearing people." The labeled minority has its own label for the labeling majority. As a label, "hearing" can have negative or positive connotations, just as "deaf" does in common (Hearing) usage.

We hope that it makes our readers think about images—the image you have of deaf people, and the images deaf people have of you. It will, we also hope, shake some readers' minds up a bit. Our ultimate hope is that it broadens your perspective of human differences.

It can be said with reasonable certainty that Deaf people have a far better understanding of the majority ("Hearing") culture that surrounds them than hearing people have of Deaf culture. Deaf people can hardly fail to grasp it; they're bombarded with it from all sides from the time they're born. Not so with hearing people. The Deaf world has long been a closed community, an invisible walled city—an alien and mysterious place many people refused to concede existed at all. Many "Hearing" images of it have been highly distorted. Even today, we find an earthly abundance of misunderstandings, stereotypes, skewed perceptions, and just plain ignorance about deaf people. Books, newspapers, magazines, movies, plays, TV programs—all are powerful tools for shaping opinions, but all have served to perpetuate erroneous ideas about our culture, language, and our abilities as individuals.

We began monthly publication of **DEAF LIFE** in July 1988. From the beginning, we recognized the need to include an informative column written especially for our hearing readers—a palatable morsel of information offered in a way that respects their intelligence while tempting them away from prejudicial ways of thinking. It has become one of our most enduringly popular features—perhaps *the* most popular.

"Do you read lips?" "Don't all deaf people read lips?" "Do all deaf people use the same sign language?" "If you're deaf, how come you can talk?" "Can deaf people hear at all?" "Is sign language like Braille?" "Who invented sign language?" These are questions we've run into again and again. We've gotten them from children, teenagers, and adults of all manner of backgrounds—even our own parents. The prevalence of such questions emphasizes the need to educate everyone in at least a basic grasp of Deaf issues. All the questions in this book have been sent to us, asked directly of us, or are based on questions we've encountered (in books, for example). Individual readers have sent in a number of these questions—about communication, attitudes, Deaf history, medical aspects of deafness, education, and linguistic aspects of sign language. We've gotten some exceptionally good and difficult questions from a teacher at Bakersfield College in California who solicited questions from her 150 sign-language students and sent us the 10 best. Some questions, of course, are far more difficult than others to answer. We cherish them all and seek to give them the best answers we can. Some we have turned over to our readers, especially deaf ones. Our title notwithstanding, we know that deaf people read "HPO," and this book is for them, too.

Smart people can ask dumb questions, but "dumb" questions aren't necessarily dumb—and all questions deserve good answers. Those who ask questions are at least *thinking* about the subject, even momentarily; at least they're *asking*. The truly apathetic ones have no questions at all. They are our real problems. We hope that at least some of them may find their way to this book. With each step forward, each spurt of shared understanding and enlightenment, each tiny victory, we are constantly reminded that we still have a long distance to cover. **For Hearing People Only** is intended as a small contribution towards that effort.

If you are left with more questions than answers, feel free to share them with us! We will continue to publish our popular Q/A column in **DEAF LIFE**, and to revise and refine this book. As long as people ask questions about the Deaf community, we will try to meet that need.

And we wish you a rewarding excursion.

Matthew S. Moore
Linda Levitan
Co-Editors-in-Chief, **DEAF LIFE**
Rochester, New York
January 2003

Note on the Third Edition

HPO was originally published in Fall 1992 as a compilation of the first 48 installments of our popular Q/A feature from **DEAF LIFE**. The second edition was published in Fall 1993, with an additional 12 chapters (making a total of 60), and that edition has already gone through 14 printings.

This third edition incorporates the 60 new chapters published in **DEAF LIFE** from Fall 1993 (when the second edition was published) through Spring 2002. Older chapters have been checked for accuracy, and revised and expanded where needed. The book has been completely redesigned and re-illustrated. For the first time, a teacher's guide and student's workbook will be available. These will be revised periodically.

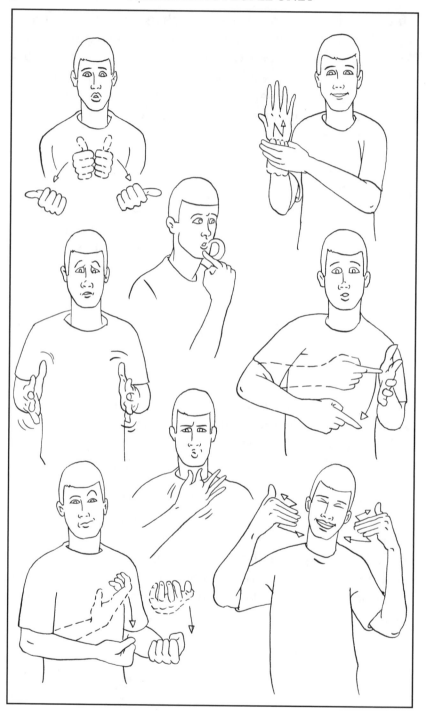

Chapter 1

What is ASL?

merican Sign Language (also called ASL or, inaccurately, "Ameslan") is not "bad English," "broken English," "short English," or *any* kind of English. Nor is it Morse Code, Braille, fingerspelling, or pantomime. ASL is a unique language with its own grammatical rules and syntax (sentence structure), and is every bit as precise, versatile, and subtle as English. In some ways, it's even more so.

It's easy enough to describe what ASL isn't. But there is no satisfactory definition of exactly what ASL *is*. Some deaf people maintain that there can be no universally acceptable, satisfactory-to-all definition of ASL; others claim that there is (or can be). This is a subject of some controversy. Where to draw the line between what's acceptable and unacceptable ASL? Every user seems to have a different opinion!

Historically, ASL had two major contributors: Laurent Clerc and the Vineyarders. Clerc (1785-1869) was the first deaf teacher of the deaf in the United States, and co-founder of the American School for the Deaf at Hartford, Connecticut, the first school of its kind here. "Old Hartford," as it was affectionately known, pioneered sign-based education for deaf people in the Western Hemisphere.

ASL has evolved from a blend of what's now called Old French Sign Language (brought here by Clerc) and Old American Sign Language, which has been traced to the "dialect" used in the communities of Chilmark and West Tisbury on Martha's Vineyard. Some sort of native sign language was being used there well over a century before Clerc arrived in Hartford. In these Vineyard communities, an unusually high incidence of hereditary deafness manifested itself for many generations. Not only did deaf and hearing residents use sign with each other, but hearing residents used it among themselves when no deaf people were around. Signing was as accepted and normal as speech. Recent research has broadened our understanding of the "Vineyard dialect" and its influence on the development of ASL.

ASL, then, is a hybrid of *langue des signes français* (LSF, otherwise known as French Sign Language or FSL) and an indigenous sign language. Many ASL signs were borrowed from LSF, but some have always been "American."

Young Vineyarders who attended "Old Hartford" brought their native sign-dialect with them, but picked up ASL at school, then brought back their acquired signs when they returned to the Vineyard, and used these "new" signs when communicating with others, who in turn picked them up. The "new" signs thus became part of the Vineyard dialect. This process is called "creolization"—a "subordinate" language picks up words and usages from a "dominant" language, which are gradually incorporated into the subordinate language.

At any rate, ASL has developed quite independently of English. Its structure and vocabulary owe nothing to English, or to British Sign Language. Just like any other modern, living and ever-changing language, ASL continues to evolve. Iconic (pictorial or mime-like) signs gradually become more concise, more abstract, more arbitrary. New signs are gradually introduced; old signs are altered or dropped. ASL possesses regional variations (dialects), slang, and fad expressions. There are also puns, wordplay (like handshape-rhymes), and plenty of creative humor. The ASL used by educated deaf persons will be quite different from that used by uneducated ones; both groups may find it difficult to communicate with each other. Every ASL user has a unique style of signing.

ASL has been the precious heritage of the Deaf community, whose users have nonetheless suffered from widespread prejudice in the Hearing world. Not so long ago, deaf children were discouraged (if not *prohibited*) from using ASL even in schools for the deaf, and adults were ashamed to be seen signing in public. They were made to feel that ASL was strictly inferior to English, and communicating in Sign was not socially acceptable. (Some "well-meaning" hearing teachers told their students that it was considered "animal-like.") Happily, we've made progress against such destructively ignorant attitudes, but sentiment against ASL still exists, and, in many situations, deaf children still are discouraged from making ASL their first language.

Linguists have only recently started to pay serious attention to ASL as a language, but ASL has already begun to enrich American culture through theater, poetry, song, sign mime, and storytelling. A new ASL literature-on-videotape/DVD is in the making. Even to those who don't understand it, ASL can be enthralling to watch. Its popularity is steadily increasing, and it has been (arguably) labeled the third most widely used language in the United States. It should be noted that no sufficiently hard statistics are available, so this assertion cannot really be proven, but there *is* a definite boom in the popularity of Beginning ASL classes in high schools and colleges, including community-college classes for laypeople. ASL is a beautiful, expressive, and colorful language that is finally beginning to get the respect it deserves.

Did you know that . . .

—people using ASL can communicate comfortably with each other across a football field—much farther than the loudest shout can carry!?

—sign language is so handy it's used in underwater communication?

—while whispering can be picked up by microscopic "bugging" devices, sign language is bug-proof? (CIA, take notice!)

—gorillas (and chimpanzees, less successfully) have been taught how to communicate in sign? (Paradoxically, people who support its use by primates may not favor its use by humans!)

How ASL and deaf education
began here
(a reasonably brief history)

Deaf people in the American colonies were using sign language long before 1817.

The history of ASL in the classroom begins in Hartford, Connecticut, in the early 19th century. Dr. Mason Fitch Cogswell, alumnus of Yale, a wealthy and respected physician, had a daughter, Alice (born 1805), who had been early-deafened by "spotted fever" (probably cerebrospinal meningitis). She was his favorite child. In those days, if you lived in the States and could afford it, you had two options: you sent your child overseas to the famous Braidwood Academy in Edinburgh, Scotland (which established English branches in London and Manchester), or hired a private tutor to teach your child to speak, read, and write. If you were poor, you could keep your children at home. Or send them to an asylum. (No education involved.)

Alice's parents could certainly have afforded to send her to the Braidwood school, but undoubtedly recoiled from the idea of shipping her off on the hazardous month-long voyage across the Atlantic Ocean to a foreign country for several years on end. Who could guarantee that they would ever see her again? But they could not find a qualified tutor for her. As for the other alternative—to have her institutionalized ("put away")—they refused to consider it. Alice was obviously bright, but her intellect was not developing normally. She had no real language. There had to be a better way.

Dr. Cogswell equipped himself with whatever books he could find on education of the deaf, including one written by the abbé Sicard, who headed the Institution Nationale des

Sourds-Muets de Naissance (National Institution for Congenital Deaf-Mutes) in Paris, France. So he knew something about the possibility of education in Sign.

Providentially, Cogswell's neighbors were the Gallaudets, a distinguished merchant family. Thomas Hopkins Gallaudet (b. 1787), also a graduate of Yale and a divinity student at Andover Theological Seminary, was home recuperating from his chronic ill-health. He happened to notice 9-year-old Alice Cogswell, still languageless, standing apart from the other children, unable to join in their play. For all his fundamentalist fire-and-brimstone tendencies, Gallaudet had a natural affinity for children and an immediate empathy for the languageless deaf girl. His own sickliness had excluded him from the rough-and-tumble play of childhood; he too had been forced to stand apart. He summoned her. That afternoon, he taught her to write the word HAT in the dirt with a stick. She enjoyed the game, and wanted to know the spelling of her own name. Confident that she understood, he discussed her situation with her father later that day. They agreed that Alice could and should be educated. Gallaudet could tutor her. But surely there were others like Alice! Why not start a school?

Most other wealthy parents of deaf children had been content to hire tutors for their own children. Dr. Cogswell's concern went beyond the plight of his daughter; he recognized the need for a school to serve all the deaf children of New England. They had a Constitutional right to an education. He shrewdly enlisted the aid of other wealthy citizens, some of whom also had deaf children. He had a census taken by Congregationalist ministers, which showed that there were 84 deaf persons in Connecticut alone—enough to warrant the establishment of a school. Finally, he convened a meeting of ten "city fathers," and Gallaudet was chosen to go to Europe and learn whatever he could about educating the deaf. He accepted eagerly. In just one evening, sufficient funds were raised for him to undertake the journey. The goal:

to establish a school in Hartford to serve all deaf people of the United States.

Gallaudet was not successful in getting assistance from the Braidwood Academy. As did other oralists of that time, the Braidwood family guarded their "secret" techniques jealously. They enjoyed a profitable monopoly on education of the deaf in the English-speaking world, and had no intention of giving away their methodology for free. Their terms required that Gallaudet stay 3 to 5 years to learn their method, and that the Braidwoods be paid a certain amount for each child educated thereby. "Monstrous" was how Gallaudet described these terms. He refused to sign any agreement.

Nor was he impressed with the progress of the students at the London academy.

Disgusted and disappointed, Gallaudet left the Braidwoods and went to a public demonstration given by the abbé Sicard in London. Waiting out the political turmoil then raging in France (he was not on good terms with Napoléon), the abbé was giving public lectures about the French method of educating the deaf and demonstrations of the intellectual abilities of two of his prize pupils, Jean Massieu and Laurent Clerc. (These lectures must have been conducted in English, so both Massieu and Clerc already knew how to write it.) The audience was invited to ask them questions—such as definitions of abstract concepts—which the abbé interpreted to the deaf men in Sign. Taking turns, they wrote their answers, in French and English, on a large slateboard propped on an easel. These answers were often witty, sometimes profound. Gallaudet was astounded.

Sicard invited Gallaudet to visit the French National Institute. Finally, in 1816, despairing of accomplishing anything in England, Gallaudet embarked for Paris. He was accorded a warm welcome at the Institute.

Even though he was given free access to all the classes, had private tutoring by Sicard and Massieu, and studied diligently, Gallaudet recognized that there was simply not enough time to master everything he needed to know to teach the deaf. Dwindling funds compelled him to book passage home. Clerc boldly volunteered to accompany him to the States to help set up the new school. This, of course, was not part of the original plan. Clerc had an adventurous streak. He was tired of being exploited, too. Although he was the Institute's finest teacher, Sicard had not seen fit to give him a commensurate salary. Although Sicard at first refused to let Clerc go, he finally relented, agreeing to loan Clerc for 3 years. He drew up an elaborate agreement to safeguard Clerc's religious rights as a Roman Catholic, and to ensure that he would be treated well in Hartford.

During their 51 days on board the *Mary Augusta*, Clerc taught Gallaudet the fine points of LSF, and Gallaudet tutored Clerc in English. (Clerc became an excellent writer in his second language. But—to contradict the commonly held assumption that Gallaudet taught Clerc English—he obviously *already* knew English when he met Gallaudet, and had probably learned it from Massieu, who compiled a French-English dictionary that Clerc took with him to Hartford.)

When Gallaudet and Clerc arrived in the States, they set about raising funds for the school. Gallaudet was a superb orator—and a persuasive one. Alice Cogswell had been placed in a nearby girls' school for the time being, and was barely literate. On arrival in Hartford, Clerc met Cogswell and Alice. There was great joy at their first meeting—the urbane, cultured, and brilliant Parisian gentleman and the child for whose sake he had come. Both deaf. Cogswell must have been mightily reassured. Gallaudet's bold gamble was to pay off, quite handsomely.

The American Asylum for the Instruction of Deaf and Dumb Persons opened in rented quarters in Hartford on April 15, 1817. Alice Cogswell was the first to enroll. Clerc and Gallaudet each taught classes. Sign language was used in class. Clerc used FSL, fingerspelling, and, for a time, the cumbersome "methodical signs" used in the French National

Institute classes, but soon found, to his dismay, that his students were "changing" his signs. What they were doing, of course, was adapting them to their preferences. A number of them already had their own way of signing—a background in native Sign, so to speak. Quite a few knew the Martha's Vineyard dialect. Ultimately, Clerc discarded the methodical signs, and ASL became more and more a distinct language, used inside and outside the classroom, although it really wasn't thought of as *a language* until William C. Stokoe subjected it to linguistic analysis 143 years later. It was simply called "sign(s)" or "deaf sign," or some other casual term. ASL was not taught as a subject in the class; it was employed as the medium of communication, along with written English. The school's goals were English literacy, industriousness, and Congregational-style morality.

The curriculum did *not* include speech training. It was considered unprofitable, a waste of time, as the majority of students would not derive enough benefit from it to make it worthwhile. A few "semi-mutes" (students who had lost their hearing after learning how to talk, or those with a moderate hearing loss) were given some articulation training, but aside from these, there was no attempt to teach speech skills. The emphasis was on education.

Clerc settled down to a busy and productive life in Hartford and largely spent the rest of his life there; he made only three visits to France. Gallaudet became supervisor of the institution. Underpaid and overworked, he was frequently in conflict with the school board. Both Clerc and Gallaudet married "Old Hartford" alumnae. In 1818, Clerc married Eliza Crocker Boardman, one of his first pupils. It was the first recorded Deaf marriage in the country. Soon afterwards, Gallaudet married Sophia Fowler, the future "queen of the Deaf community." Both marriages were happy. All the children were hearing, but the eldest and youngest Gallaudet children each continued their father's mission. The younger Thomas Gallaudet, an Episcopalian minister, established the first Deaf church in the States, St. Ann's. Edward Miner Gallaudet was the founder and first president of what is now Gallaudet University. They were native signers, and most likely learned ASL from their mother. Some of the descendants of Eliza and Laurent Clerc have likewise been involved in deaf education.

Although the name of the school—"American"—reflected the aim of serving the entire deaf population of the United States, it soon became evident that one school was not sufficient. As the U.S. population (hearing *and* deaf) grew, the need for more schools in other states likewise increased.

Two of the first Hartford pupils became teachers of the deaf, initiating an honored American tradition of the best deaf pupils becoming teachers of the deaf themselves. Old Hartford became a model for the establishment of dozens of other schools for the deaf—Fanwood (New York), Pennsylvania, Indiana, Kentucky—across the country. Schools for the deaf predated the formal establishment of public schools, and led to the establishment of Gallaudet University—the world's first (and still the only) liberal-arts college for the deaf. (It was named in memory of Thomas Hopkins Gallaudet.)

Within a remarkably short time, ASL-based education led to the formation of a real Deaf community, complete with clubs, churches, organizations, sports, and a flourishing Deaf press—periodicals originating from the printrooms of the schools for the deaf—affectionately known as the "Little Paper Family." The residential schools created a class of highly-educated, skilled deaf people who were, in fact, bilingual—fluent in sign, and articulate in written English. We call this the "Golden Age of Deaf Culture."

In 1850, Gallaudet and Clerc were honored at a convocation of all living Hartford alumni. (Dr. Cogswell and Alice had both died in 1830.) What a beautiful sight that was—the reunion of dozens of educated and skilled deaf citizens, alumni of Hartford! Gallaudet died the following year. Clerc lived long enough to witness the upsurge of oralism that threatened to undo everything he had labored to achieve.

▲ ▲ ▲

The Presidential connection

n June 1817, two months after its opening, President Monroe visited "Old Hartford" to give a speech. On that occasion, the pupils invented the sign for "president" that became standard usage in ASL.

    James Monroe was a tall, slim, ruggedly built man of unassuming appearance. On the occasion of his visit to Old Hartford, he wore a tricorn hat, which had long since gone out of fashion. A crowd of adults surrounded Monroe's slender figure, blocking him from the view of the eager pupils. One deaf boy climbed a tree to get a better look. His schoolmates asked him, "Can you see him?" "Yes," the boy signed, "there's his tricorn hat"—and he made a spontaneous sign for "tricorn hat" (squeezing both hands into fists while moving them outward and upward from the temples, in a single brisk motion) and pointed to where the President stood. The other pupils eagerly picked up and passed around the sign—"There's the President!" Thus the new sign for "president" was spontaneously created and adopted by the pupils of Old Hartford. It is still used today.

    In 1818, Laurent Clerc traveled to Washington, D.C., the nation's raw new capital, to request financial assistance for his school. He became the first deaf person to address the U.S. Congress, and received a thunderous ovation. Congress approved the grant. Afterwards, Clerc had some intriguing encounters with some of the nation's leaders. Speaker of the House Henry Clay remembered seeing Clerc at one of Sicard's public demonstrations in London. Clerc communicated with Clay by writing in French and English. And President Monroe, whom he met the next day, told Clerc that *he* had seen him carrying on an animated signed conversation with another deaf man (most likely Jean Massieu) in a Parisian café, during his stint as an assistant U.S. envoy to France. (Monroe had been in Paris in 1803, helping to negotiate the terms of the Louisiana Purchase, and happened to walk past the café, which was located near the National Institute.)

As he did with Henry Clay, Clerc communicated with President Monroe by writing. Monroe was probably the first U.S. President to have direct contact—and real communication—with a deaf person.

Key to illustrations on page 36

how?	spring
who?	
nervous	what?
curious	
confident	laughing

"Mother"

American Sign Language   Australian Sign Language

 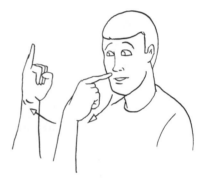

Spanish Sign Language   Japanese Sign Language

Gestuno
(International Sign Language)

"Man"   "Woman"

Chapter 2

Is there one sign language for all countries?

—Chaya Rozen, Rochester, New York

o more so than there is one spoken language for all countries! But everywhere you find deaf people, you will find sign language. The impulse to communicate is universal. For deaf people, the impulse to sign is universal. Deaf children not exposed to any standard sign language have invented their own sign systems—"home sign." Every national sign language, however, is different. In Europe, even within a single country, there can be tremendous variation from city to city, while American Sign Language, although possessing many regional dialects and "accents," is standardized enough to be easily understood by ASL users (an estimated 500,000 to 2 million, although no one really has accurate numbers) from coast to coast. So a Deaf Californian and a Deaf New Englander will have no difficulty understanding each other. ASL is also used in Canada, which extends its scope considerably.

As we've already noted, Deaf people in the States were using sign language long before Laurent Clerc, the first deaf educator in America, arrived from France, bringing French Sign Language with him. The native sign language of Chilmark and Tisbury, the Martha's Vineyard communities with an unusually high incidence of hereditary deafness, evolved from Old Kentish Sign Language, as the earliest deaf settlers came from the southeastern English county of Kent.

Although ASL was subsequently influenced by FSL (and thus has some recognizably French signs), many such borrowed signs have been modified over time. But while ASL belongs to the same family as FSL and Spanish Sign Language, which all have some signs in common ("baby," "book"), it is quite different from British Sign Language, which remained largely impervious to French influence. Nonetheless, the French National Institute (where Clerc trained and taught) sent its teachers to several countries, including Holland, Denmark, Spain, and Russia, so FSL left its mark on those sign languages too.

Scandinavian sign languages (e.g., Swedish Sign Language) form an important group, rich and vibrant, whose artistic possibilities have begun to be explored. Asian sign languages (e.g., Japanese Sign Language, Taiwanese Sign Language) differ from any European sign language. Each school for the deaf in Japan—and 11 of the 12 schools there are oral—has its own sign-language system, as used by the students. Some African sign languages are influenced by the native sign languages of missionaries. There are undoubtedly several complete and rich sign languages that have never been adequately studied or recognized. And in Nicaragua, for example, a new sign language is being created by deaf children.

Every different sign language reflects its own history, culture, and social mores. Thus (in most of these different sign languages) you will find completely different signs for universal concepts: "mother," "father," "boy," "girl," "day," "night," "tree," "water," "good," "bad," and so forth.* Each sign language may have a myriad of regional variations. And what is a perfectly acceptable sign in one language may turn out to be an obscenity in another!

But signers from one country seem to have less trouble establishing communication with signers from another than do their speaking counterparts. Deaf people can be inventive, even ingenious, in bridging language gaps! They improvise, using gestures, pantomime, expressions—whatever works—until they establish some sort of mutual comprehension, and build on that foundation.

"International sign language" does exist to some extent. An

"artificial" international vocabulary, "Gestuno," which functions as a kind of visual Esperanto, was developed in the mid-1970s by the World Federation of the Deaf's Commission on Unification of Signs. Gestuno hasn't really caught on—on an everyday level, at least. It *is* useful for international gatherings of Deaf people, where it's impractical to throng the stage with dozens of interpreters in everybody's native sign languages.

One such memorable occasion was the Gala Opening Performance at The DEAF WAY International Conference and Festival in Washington, D.C., on July 9, 1989. In preparation for the influx of several thousand Deaf people (some 5,500) from 76 nations, American Deaf performers were specially drilled in Gestuno, and used it to introduce acts and give simple communications to the audience—"Welcome, ladies and gentlemen;" "No smoking, please;" "No flash photography allowed at performances;" "I hope you enjoy our show." There was also an animated video in Gestuno. The signs used were as simple, logical, and universally recognizable as possible.

Since Gestuno was developed by a committee, it's not a real language. But Gestuno was partly based on ASL, which, as the world's most well-known and popular sign language, is the closest thing we have to a "universally" recognized one.

---

* In many spoken languages across the world, the word for *mother* begins with or contains the letter "m." For example: *mater* (Latin); *mama* (Italian); *mère* (French); *maman* (French vernacular); *madre* (Spanish); *maht* (Russian); *matka* (Polish); *Mutter* (German); *mor* (Danish, Swedish, Norwegian); *imma* (Hebrew); *umm* (Arabic). There is no "universal" sign-language equivalent to this similarity. But the signs for "mother" tend to be simple and easily formed, as befits a sign that is often the very first one a child learns.

Chapter 3

Is there any similarity between Braille and ASL?

one whatever, but you'd be surprised how many folks apparently think they're the same thing. Some hearing people have told us that when they first saw deaf people signing to each other, they immediately thought, "Oh, they're using Braille. They must be blind!" Why?

Blind people are visible to us in a way that the deaf aren't. Many blind people use special white canes; some also have guide dogs with distinctive harnesses. A blind person waiting to cross a traffic-congested street or boarding a city bus is immediately recognized as blind and quickly offered assistance—an arm while crossing the street, a front seat on the bus. (A very general statement, this.)

Deaf people, however, are not immediately recognizable as "deaf." There will be no telltale cane or (in most cases) dog, no dark glasses, nothing out of the ordinary except, perhaps, one or two hearing aids or a cochlear-implant cord, if they're visible at all. Thus, hearing people undoubtedly have very clear images of what blind people "look like," but no clear notion of how deaf people "look." Not until deaf people are seen communicating with each other in Sign (or a hearing stranger approaches, mumbles something to them, and gets no response or a gesture of incomprehension) are they identifiable as "Deaf."

In our culture, blindness has garnered more recognition and respect than deafness. We suspect that far more hearing schoolchildren know about Louis Braille than about Laurent Clerc. They may also have a clearer notion of Braille, a tactile code, than ASL, a visual language. Consequently, when they see native signers for the first time (and this is our wild guess), they associate signing with the language of the blind, not the language of the Deaf. Or they assume that most deaf people "know Braille."

Just for the record, Braille is not a language like ASL or English. It's a code, a way of translating "flat copy"—written and printed media—into a tactile form: raised dots in a matrix pattern read with the fingertips. Not all blind people read Braille (and it is by no means the only available code, or the easiest to learn). Many blind people find it indispensable, though, and a good number use Braille books, typewriters, notetaker punches, Telebraille machines, and Braille-printing computers with voice synthesizers, like the state-of-the-art Kurzweil Personal Reader. Braille has much more in common with Morse Code than with ASL. But Morse Code, unlike Braille, *can* be used to communicate directly with blind people (i.e., conversationally), by substituting taps and strokes for dots and dashes. It is thus—*very* roughly—equivalent to fingerspelling.*

Deaf-blind people use tactile signing and fingerspelling (either done directly in the palm, or in the usual front-of-body position and "read" with the fingertips) to converse with each other or with sighted Deaf people. They are extraordinarily adept at it. Blind hearing people (especially those who have attended combined schools for the deaf and the blind) may be skilled in this as well; fingerspelling is relatively easy to learn. But you will never see two people standing on the corner having a conversation "in Braille."

---

* Samuel F. B. Morse's second wife, Sarah Ann Griswold, was deaf. He communicated with her by "tapping out Morse code in her hands." See Harlan Lane, **When the Mind Hears**.

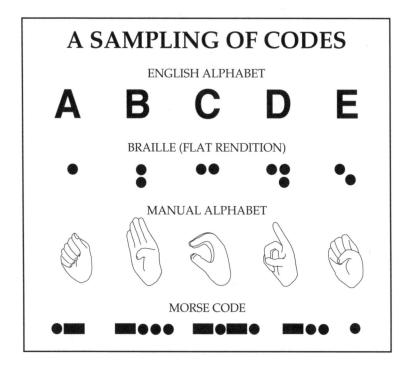

Chapter 4

Wasn't French Sign Language invented by the Abbé de l'Epée?

o. French Sign Language was invented by deaf people. It was the exclusive property of the French Deaf community, for there were a fairly large number of deaf people living in Paris in the 18th century. They may have been forced to the outer fringes of society, but they had the rudiments of a recognizable Deaf culture—namely, a language.

The abbé Charles-Michel de l'Epée (1712-1789) was a "neighborhood priest" whose involvement with deaf people began in the mid-1700s when he met twin deaf sisters whose mother begged him to teach them. (Another priest, the abbé Simon Vanin, had been working with them, teaching them moral concepts by means of engraved illustrations of the lives of the saints, but had died before they could make much progress.) Accordingly, Epée sought to instruct them. His original purpose was, of course, religious as well as humanitarian. He wanted to save deaf people's souls from damnation. To achieve salvation, deaf people had to understand the sacraments. They had to have access to education. But the Abbé first had to learn to communicate with the deaf.

He researched what available information there was on deaf education, and adapted the Spanish system of fingerspelling. More significantly, he was the first hearing person to go to the Deaf community, to learn its language, to let deaf people teach *him*. Ultimately, he founded the first successful school for deaf students in Paris, which became the Institution Nationale des Sourds-Muets (National Institute for Deaf-Mutes). It was the world's first free public school for the deaf. In his classes, he used signs from FSL with an added set of signs he *had* invented, *les signes méthodiques* ("methodical signs"), which represented aspects of French grammar that lacked equivalents in FSL. Erroneously, he assumed that FSL was a collection of "natural" signs lacking grammatical structure, and wished to remedy this supposed deficiency. The abbé's "methodical signs" were something of an early "Signed French" system. They were ugly and cumbersome, and his successors modified them—and later dropped them altogether. But the students used "pure" FSL in the dormitories—and so French Deaf culture began in earnest.

Previous educators of the deaf had imposed their sometimes ridiculous ideas, misguided philosophies, and erroneous notions about language onto their pupils, and never took into account the fact that deaf people already had a highly-developed *visual* means of communication. All the oralists tried to make their deaf pupils function as hearing persons. They all failed to do so. Epée approached deaf people with a more open mind. To paraphrase Harlan Lane's monumental history, **When the Mind Hears**, the Abbé was the first known educator who bothered to learn from the deaf themselves, and that is why, for all his own mistaken notions, he is remembered as a friend of deaf people.[1] His memory is revered by the French Deaf community, and is also honored by its American counterpart.[2]

The Abbé had nothing to do with the invention of sign language. Rather, he *recognized* the importance of sign language as the best way to communicate with and educate deaf people. And he *pioneered* its use in an institutional setting.

Epée's successor, the Abbé Roch-Ambroise Cucurron Sicard (1742-1822), wrote a two-volume treatise on deaf education, **Théorie des Signes** (1808). This book found its way into Dr. Mason Cogswell's library; Dr. Cogswell gave it to Thomas Hopkins Gallaudet, who had just met 9-year-old Alice Cogswell. Gallaudet studied it and ultimately adapted it for American use. During his sojourn in London, he met Sicard, and went to the National Institute in Paris to learn the method firsthand. The French approach—the use of the native sign language to teach the native written language—was known as the "silent" or "natural" method. In contrast to the oralists of that time, its proponents made no secret of it; they disseminated it, demonstrated it publicly, shared it with whomever wished to learn it, and trained teachers to establish free public schools for the deaf throughout Europe, including Russia. This French model in turn inspired the American model.

Sicard, who directed the Institute during and after the French Revolution, had a remarkable pupil, Jean Massieu, an erstwhile shepherd who became one of the first truly educated Deaf persons. And Massieu's pupil was the legendary Laurent Clerc, the first teacher of the deaf in the United States. Clerc brought FSL to the States, and to this day, American Sign Language shows a distinct French influence.

[1] "Still, it was the abbé de l'Epée, son of the king's architect, who first turned to the poor, despised, illiterate deaf and said, 'Teach me,' And this act of humility gained him everlasting glory. It is his true title to our gratitude, for in becoming the student of his pupils, in seeking to learn their signs, he equipped himself to educate them and to found the education of the deaf. For this reason, the deaf everywhere have always excused him for failing to see that the sign language of the French deaf community was a complete language in its own right, not merely a collection of signs, and did not need to be made to 'conform to clear rules'—French word order and word endings, to be transformed into 'manual French'—in order to serve as the vehicle for instructing the deaf."
    —Harlan Lane (writing as Laurent Clerc), **When the Mind Hears**, p. 63.

[2] On April 17, 1998, handsome new granite headstones for Laurent and Eliza Clerc were dedicated in Hartford's Spring Grove Cemetery. These replaced the original weather-scarred and vandalized marble stones. A delegation of seven French Deaf citizens came to participate in the ceremony. When a friend took them to visit St. Mary's School for the Deaf in Buffalo, New York, they were thrilled to see the statue of the Abbé de l'Epée that stands in front of the school. They went wild with joy at the sight of this tangible reminder of the Deaf community's esteem. They spent a half-hour there, running out into the street—and dodging traffic—with their cameras and videocams, taking frame after frame of photographs and video footage to show their friends back home.

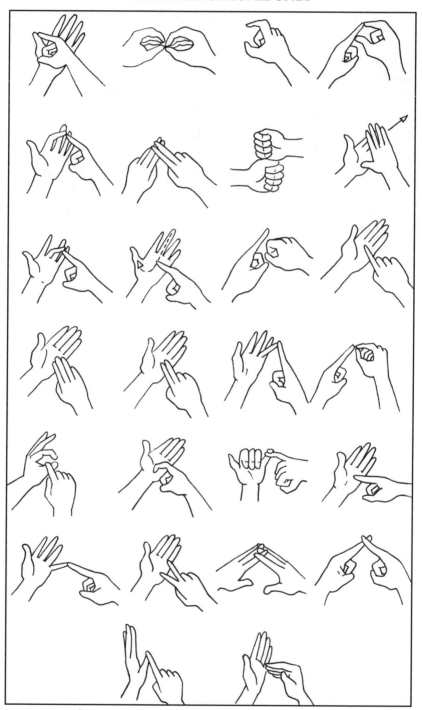

Chapter 5

Why isn't American Sign Language like British Sign Language?

ne very common misconception about ASL is that it must be similar to or derived from BSL, since American English derives from British English and, despite numerous differences in usage, the two spoken languages are essentially the same.

Is there any similarity between ASL and BSL? Not much. The two developed from completely different sources. BSL is the creation of members of the Deaf community in the British Isles, New Zealand, and Australia; ASL is an indigenous product influenced by French Sign Language, as brought to the States by Laurent Clerc.

In 1992, the British Deaf Association published a comprehensive (and, at 1084 pages, hefty) **Dictionary of British Sign Language/English**, with photographs of the signs organized by handshape, linguistic notations, detailed glosses, notes, and commentary. It's a must for any serious student of the language. In her introduction, Mary Brennan notes:

> The Republic of Ireland, the U.S.A. and the U.K. all share a common spoken language, English, but three quite separate and mutually unintelligible sign languages are used in these three countries. Sometimes, for historical reasons, there are closer links than might be expected between two different sign language communities. The fact that Thomas Gallaudet introduced the 'systematic sign system' developed by the Abbé de l'Epée into the United States in the eighteenth century [sic] means that today's American Sign Language has much closer links with French Sign Language (LSF) than with BSL. Similarly, because of the close political relationship (through the British Commonwealth) between Australia, New Zealand and Britain, the sign languages of these countries share many common features. Inevitably, languages change and adapt as they are affected by internal and external influences. Even when signs betray some historical

similarity, they tend to diverge over time. Because sign languages share a common modality, the visual-gestural modality, they may indeed share certain types of patterning. However, as with all living human languages, they are constantly subject to change and evolutionary processes.

One indirect link between ASL and BSL is the "Martha's Vineyard dialect." The history of the high-density Deaf population of Martha's Vineyard has been traced to a handful of settlers from a section of the Kentish district of England known as the Weald. Congenital deafness ran strong in these families, who intermarried and had an unusually high proportion of deaf offspring. A form of sign language used in Kent—"Old Kentish Sign Language"—was brought to Martha's Vineyard by these early deaf settlers. This evolved into the Vineyard dialect. Over the years, new signs were devised, incorporated, and used by both deaf and hearing natives. As previously noted, hearing Vineyarders even used it with each other when no deaf people were around.

Some deaf Vineyarders enrolled in the newly-established "Old Hartford," bringing with them their vigorous sign dialect, and this blended with Clerc's French Sign Language to become what we now call Old ASL. As for the original Vineyard dialect, it remained in use well into the 20th century. As the Deaf population declined and scattered, dying off, its use dwindled. But it wasn't entirely lost. Recent research has preserved some of the signs and stories—as recalled by elderly hearing Vineyarders—on videotape.*

So contemporary ASL is not entirely devoid of British influence. Otherwise, BSL and ASL, as Brennan notes, have maintained divergent paths.

Used by a skilled signer, BSL could at first glance be mistaken for ASL, except that it isn't "readable" to an ASL user who doesn't know BSL. As Brennan suggests, there are a few similarities between ASL and BSL (e.g., classifiers, facial grammar, and iconic signs), but some major differences.

For starters, BSL uses a two-handed manual alphabet (one of the few such still in use); ASL, like FSL, a one-handed version derived from the Spanish system. The British manual alphabet is more iconic than ours, more closely resembling the letters it represents, with the five vowels being indicated, in sequence, on the fingertips.

Some handshapes are found in one language but not the other. BSL employs one that has obscene or vulgar connotations in ASL, but is perfectly permissible in BSL.

Some signs—e.g., *ballpoint pen, Canada, clean, coat, fed up, letter/stamp, mirror/reflection, ocean, post* (on a bulletin board), and *pull*—are similar. But similar-looking signs can have entirely different meanings—the ASL sign for *electricity* or *battery* is made like the BSL sign for *Brussels*. The BSL sign for *definite* looks much like the ASL *stop*. *Dreadful* (BSL) looks rather like *spaghetti* (ASL); *divorce* (BSL) resembles *egg* (ASL). The ASL and BSL signs for *cat* resemble each other, but those for *squirrel* are different. Both languages use different signs for *ability, all right, brilliant, exam, family, medicine, praise,* and *week* (to cite a few).

Let it be said that BSL is a beautiful, expressive, and vivid language in its own right, and reflects the culture, struggle, and visual humor of the British Deaf community. It has its own integrity and power. Like ASL, BSL has been transmitted from child to child at residential schools, or from Deaf parents to their children. It has survived more than a century of oralist suppression. Efforts to gain greater recognition for BSL, empowerment for Deaf people, and to preserve residential schools, are ongoing. The parallels between the fortunes of the American and British Deaf communities—and their languages—are striking. Two languages—but a common experience.

* See Jamie Kageleiry's "The Island That Spoke By Hand," originally published in the March 1999 issue of **Yankee** and reprinted in the March 2002 issue of **DEAF LIFE**.

The British connection

To understand the development and workings of BSL, it helps to know something of the history of sign language in England and France. While France had a strong sign-language tradition, England had a rigorously oral one.

With the founding of the Institut National des Jeune Sourdes by the abbé de l'Epée, and due to the efforts of his successors, Paris became the world center of sign-language education, accepting students and training teachers from all over. Except England. As we've already noted, the Braidwood family maintained a profitable monopoly on deaf education in the British Isles. At least one wealthy American family—the Bollings of Virginia—sent their deaf children overseas to the Braidwood Academy.

For several generations, the Braidwood family, originally from Scotland, maintained their monopoly. They kept their methods of instruction a closely-guarded secret. Their approach appears to have utilized fingerspelling, and did not rely on physical punishment as an "incentive" (as it did with a number of other oralists).

The Braidwoods' attempt to found a satellite school in the United States failed because of the dissolute and unscrupulous character of John Braidwood the Younger, who was entrusted with a task he was unsuited for. Still, he was a prime reason why the Braidwoods refused to give Thomas Hopkins Gallaudet the timely assistance he requested when he visited them. They wanted to safeguard their monopoly. They wanted John Braidwood the Younger, and not some outsider, to establish and run the new American school.

In contrast to the Braidwoods, the French National Institute openly demonstrated and freely taught its methods to all those who were interested. It was the world's first free public school for the deaf. Epée was not interested in establishing a profitable monopoly, but in making education available to deaf children throughout Europe. This was a crucial distinction that changed the course of Deaf history.

When Gallaudet went to Paris and brought back Laurent Clerc, Clerc brought French Sign Language with him. He objected to the way his students at the Hartford Asylum were "mangling" his "beautiful French signs," but the process of evolution of ASL was already underway. Several of these students already used a form of old ASL—notably, the Vineyard dialect. Even so, an estimated 60% of contemporary ASL signs derive from FSL. Clerc's influence is still felt.

The fusion of FSL, the Martha's Vineyard dialect, and old ASL led to a rich and distinctly American form of sign (much as modern English derives much of its quirky power and color from the fusion of Norman/Romance and Saxon/Celtic/Germanic influences), creating a powerful, expressive, and flexible medium that lends itself to the artistic (poetry, theater, sign mime) as gracefully as the utilitarian (everyday conversational and instructional usage).

The British manual alphabet was invented by hearing teachers as an aid to oral education. (The more familiar one-handed manual alphabet, which originated in Spain, had a similar function, which is why some of the letters in both systems are iconic—they resemble their written counterparts.) In one early form, letters were indicated by pointing to the joints of the "base" hand and various locations in the palm. In today's alphabet, each of the 5 vowels is indicated, in sequence, by pointing to a fingertip—"a" on the thumb, "u" on the pinkie.

The history of the British Deaf community parallels ours. Deaf British people were undoubtedly using sign for ages. In the mid-1800s—around the time that Gallaudet University was founded and Deaf culture was at its peak here—British Deaf culture was flourishing. After the demise of the Braidwood Academy, sign-language-based education reigned—albeit briefly. Deaf teachers taught deaf children at residential schools. After the infamous Congress of Milan in 1880, the quality of British deaf education went downhill, and BSL went underground. Oralism became the rule, deaf teachers became an extinct species, and the century of oppression began.

The subsequent history of sign language in the British Deaf community is largely tragic. The chief center for the training of oralist teachers is the famous—or infamous—Manchester University, whose graduates have carried a peculiarly rigid "Manchester Method" oral approach to schools for the deaf throughout Africa and Asia.

Progress has been notably slow. Attitudes can be astonishingly (to us) backwards. The British press still uses the term "deaf and dumb." One Australian principal was quoted in 1990 as comparing the teaching of sign language to "hearing-impaired children" to child abuse. There are no counterparts, as yet, to the Hartford School, nor Gallaudet University, nor NTID—nor the National Theatre of the Deaf. Education of the deaf is still largely oral (and controlled by hearing administrators), although lately there have been signs that the stranglehold is being broken, and the British Deaf community is becoming more politicized. Only recently have Deaf people begun to reclaim their language and to push for greater rights. The British and Irish Deaf communities are still oppressed, but thanks to the visibility and influence of the American Deaf community and ASL advocates, efforts are being made to improve deaf education, legitimize sign language in schools, and gain official recognition for BSL and ISL.

Making headlines—and friends

The late Princess Diana was Patron of the BDA for several years, and contributed a much-appreciated foreword to the monumental **Dictionary**. Her visits to Deaf groups and schools were, of course, noted by the press. When she addressed a Deaf audience in BSL, she endeared herself to the nationwide Deaf community, whch responded with enthusiasm, gratitude, and love. She had been tutored in BSL by Liz Scott-Gibson, the daughter of Deaf parents, and, critics noted, Diana did a fine job with her signing. Her remarks were brief, but her signing was clear and confident.

Several ancestors of the present British royal family were deaf (notably Prince Philip's mother, Princess Alice of Battenberg, 1885-1969), and Queen Victoria is said to have learned sign language to communicate with her deaf relatives. Although Princess Diana was not the first or only royal patron of the BDA (Princess Anne has been a longtime patron, and Prince Andrew suceeded Diana as patron after she resigned her many patronages in 1994), she was probably the first of the modern royals to take the time and trouble to learn BSL. And she learned it willingly, because she wanted to address Deaf people in their own language. She knew something about the issues, too. She was scheduled to attend the opening of a new school for the deaf in September 1997, but her violent death on August 31 precluded those plans.

Representatives of the BDA, along with representatives from the other nonprofit organizations Diana had supported, attended her funeral at Westminster Abbey. An interpreter was stationed there.

The British Deaf community—and the U.S. Deaf community, too—still mourns her untimely death. She is, and will be, remembered as a friend of Deaf people.

Chapter 6

"Can you explain the sentence structure of ASL? Is it a result of its French background?"

I am presently enrolled at Gallaudet University in their beginning ASL course. Do you have or know of a text which can explain the sentence structure of ASL? I assume it's a result of its French background. At Gallaudet we haven't gotten into that as yet; we've been concentrating on gestures and signs for basics like numbers, colors, living quarters, alphabet, and shapes. I realize gestures play a major role in the language, but I've also noticed that questions are not in an English order.

—Roger Mindel, Wheaton, Maryland

he syntactical structure of ASL is not really due to a French origin. Yes, ASL *was* deeply influenced and enriched by FSL. The French influence is most evident in its vocabulary—some 60% of its signs are said to be borrowed from FSL. But ASL originated in the United States. In its oldest form, it existed well over a century before Laurent Clerc brought FSL to the States in 1817. Its syntax is peculiarly "American," and is logically "the way it is" because it's a true visual/spatial/gestural language—perfectly adapted to the needs of Deaf Americans who communicate visually. It owes nothing to English.[1]

Crudely speaking, in English you have a fairly pat syntactical structure—modifier-subject-verb-object (MSVO). Other combinations—SMVO, MSVO, SVOM, OVMS—are also possible. But ASL has a syntactical flexibility lacking in English.

The word order varies according to the emphasis—and the nuances of expression—a sort of visual-kinetic-poetic license that adds vividness to the simplest statement.[2] English is relatively dry, sequential. In ASL the entire body is used expressively to convey information. Spoken English uses a string of phonemes (sounds), words, and sentences. Period. ASL can expand the expression of each sign according to the signer's mood, feelings, or attitude. English cannot do that; it's much more limited. The expressive possibilities of ASL are virtually limitless. English is uni-dimensional; ASL multi-dimensional.

William Newell, a veteran ASL professor at NTID and an expert on the multiplicity of sign-language systems, explains the structure of ASL:

> The generally preferred order for ASL is OSV. A good example of this type of structure occurs in the sentence "A cup is on the table." Signed TABLE (which is the object) CUP (which is the subject) CL:B (non-dominant hand flat, palm down) with CL:C (dominant hand, palm to side) on top of CL:B (which is the verb).
>
> Since all sign languages stem from the same set of articulators (hands, face, body) and the same receivers (eyes), it would be safe to assume that their structures will share some common characteristics. Languages usually adapt to the articulators by which they are produced and received. It is not an accident that the frequency at which human speech is articulated matches exactly with the most sensitive range that the human ear can hear. Oral languages "match" the expression of language with the reception of language. Since sign languages are articulated in time and space (visually), it makes sense that they would use similar properties that would match how the eyes process information rather than how the "ears" process information. For example, extending the example above, if I asked you to draw the sentence as a picture, the "rules" of art would suggest that you should start with drawing the "table" (background) and then draw the cup on top of the table (foreground/detail). This "rule" of art matches exactly with how ASL is expressed. It is because they both are "visual" and therefore share common properties of how the eyes process information.

In ASL, information about nouns, subject, or object, is incorporated into directional verbs. Verbs are inflected in a way foreign to English. There are features like classifiers that are lacking in English. (Classifiers are also found in Navajo, a highly visual spoken language that, until recently, lacked a written form. ASL and Navajo use classifiers in the exact same way; their morphology (word formation) is similar. ASL is thus structurally closer to Navajo than to English![3]) And the face is used as a grammatical marker—as with questions and negatives. These are but a few aspects that make assimilation of ASL difficult even for motivated hearing people.

There have been numerous attempts to teach English to deaf students through Manually Coded English (MCE)—invented sign systems that depict English vocabulary and grammatical structure. Innumerable MCE systems have been devised to make it easier for native English speakers (hearing teachers) to teach English to native ASL users (i.e., deaf children). The best-known are SEE-1 (Seeing Essential English), SEE-2 (Signing Exact English), and Signed English. (Signed English is the simplest and most flexible of these systems.) They were developed in the late 1960s and early '70s for classroom use; SEE-1 and SEE-2 were both developed by deaf professors. Each MCE system has special signs for aspects of English grammar that are not found in ASL—prefixes like *un-* and *re-*, suffixes like *-ness* and *-ment*, participles (*-ing*), particles like *a*, *an*, and *the*, verbal past tense (*-ed*), etc. Many root signs are liberally borrowed from ASL, with these invented elements grafted onto them. While the signs may be taken from ASL, the syntax imposed on the signs is that of English. The effect is odd. When (as in the Morphemic Sign System) the signs are arranged to represent morphemes (the sounds of English syllables), the effect is grotesque.

That these MCE systems have generated considerable controversy in the Deaf community is evident. There is an ongoing dispute over just how useful these signed-English systems are, and how well they promote literacy skills in Deaf people. Many deaf people argue that they don't promote good language skills at all; they're confusing and unnatural. Which is not to say that they are useless. A number of deaf people believe that Signed English has its uses. Communicating with hearing people who don't know ASL is one such use. Learning the intricacies and quirks of English grammar is another.

Hearing people taking beginning sign-language classes usually learn Signed English (that is, ASL signs used in English word order). Deaf people tend to use a flexible, rough-and-ready mode, Pidgin Sign English (PSE), when communicating with hearing people—a signed form of English is easier for the hearing people to understand. Neither Signed English nor PSE are true languages. They are signed forms of communication. But while MCE systems are not considered part of the ASL continuum, Signed English and PSE are. (PSE could be considered a variant form of ASL.)

With ASL you have to abandon "English thinking" and think **visually**. It's not easy.

Here are some texts that can help explain the structure of ASL. (Also see the annotated bibliography in Oliver Sacks' **Seeing Voices** and the **Gallaudet Encyclopedia** entry on "Sign Languages.")

● Charlotte Baker-Shenk and Robin Battison, eds., **Sign Language and the Deaf Community: Essays in Honor of William C. Stokoe**. NAD, 1980. (A scholarly but readable *Festschrift*. Insights into Stokoe's revolutionary work; the recognition of ASL as a language; the differences between ASL, PSE, and Sign English; sign languages in other countries; the problem of deaf education.)
● Charlotte Baker-Shenk, **American Sign Language: a Look at its History, Structure, and Community**. Silver Spring: T.J. Publishers, 1978.
● Dennis Cokely and Charlotte Baker-Shenk, **American Sign Language: A Student Text** (3 vols.); **A Teacher's Resource Text** (2 vols.). Illus. Washington, D.C.: Gallaudet University Press, 1981.
● Tom Humphries, Carol Padden, and Terrence J. O'Rourke, **A Basic Course in American Sign Language**. Illus. Silver Spring: T.J. Publishers, 1980.

● Tom Humphries and Carol Padden, **Learning American Sign Language**. Paramus, NJ: Prentice-Hall PTR, 1992.
● Edward Klima and Ursula Bellugi, **The Signs of Language**. Illus. Boston: Harvard Univ. Press, 1979. (Advanced but fascinating reading.)
● Cheri Smith, Ella Mae Lentz, and Ken Mikos, **Signing Naturally** (Vista American Sign Language Series). Illus. San Diego: DawnSignPress, 1988.
● William C. Stokoe, **Sign Language Structure**, 1960; rpt., Silver Spring: Linstok Press. (A ground-breaking work, but it won't help beginners; it's much too technical.)
● William C. Stokoe, Dorothy C. Casterline, and Carl G. Croneberg, **A Dictionary of American Sign Language on Linguistic Principles**. Illus. 1965; rev. ed., Silver Spring: Linstok Press, 1976. (Advanced, technical reading.)
● Clayton Valli and Ceil Lucas, **Linguistics of American Sign Language: An Introduction**. Washington, D.C.: Gallaudet University Press.
● Ronnie Wilbur, **American Sign Language: Linguistic and Applied Dimensions**. Boston: Little, Brown, 1987.
● Sherman Wilcox and Phyllis Wilcox, **Learning to See: Teaching American Sign Language as a Second Language**. Washington, D.C.: Gallaudet University Press, 1997.

[1] Can a native ASL user understand a native FSL user? The answer is yes—given time to familiarize each other. Understanding doesn't come immediately, but there is *some* common linguistic ground.

[2] ASL certainly has grammatical rules. But it isn't accurate to say that the subject always comes first, or even "usually" or "often." The subject may be implied or dropped. What is true of ASL is not necessarily true of other sign languages; there is no universal parallel structure. In Spanish Sign Language and Japanese Sign Language, for example, the verb, not the subject, comes first.

[3] If not for the interest in Navajo, we might still be waiting for linguistic recognition of ASL. Navajo is a spoken language used by hearing people—and yet it has classifiers, just as ASL does. Navajo established a precedent for recognizing ASL as a full-fledged language. We are fortunate in that Navajo, as a native language, survived at all. Most other American Indian languages have vanished without being recorded.

Chapter 7

Is ASL a written language? (And can it be translated into written English?)

ince American Sign Language (ASL) is a purely visual/gestural language, it has no written form. (Only a relatively small percentage of spoken languages have written forms, for that matter.) Authors of ASL dictionaries and textbooks are therefore faced with the problem of "reproducing" in print a language that "cannot be written down"! As the introduction to Dennis Cokely and Charlotte Baker's first ASL textbook puts it:

> ASL is not a written language. This means that there are no newspapers, magazines, books, etc., written in ASL. Because ASL does not have a written form, we generally have to use English to write about ASL. This means using English words (called "glosses") when trying to translate the meaning of ASL signs and for trying to write down ASL sentences. [1]

Dr. William C. Stokoe, the pioneering researcher of ASL who did so much to gain linguistic respect for ASL as a distinct and living language, published the first ASL dictionary in 1965, for which he devised a set of useful linguistic symbols, showing at a glance the five parameters of each sign: handshape, palm orientation, location, movement, and repetition. Cokely and Baker's pioneering ASL textbooks (1980) utilize a code of symbols and abbreviations. As these books emphasize, the English words used to translate the meaning of the ASL sentences are an approximation—"glosses." Valerie Sutton publishes a bilingual newspaper, **The Sign Writer**, using an ASL-based pictographic code (stylized signs, movements, and facial grammar), the most ambitious attempt we've seen so far. A number of ASL-translation computer programs have been developed, and much experimental work done in this field. Sam Supalla, a Deaf professor and linguist in Arizona, has created a modified ASL-writing system and used it successfully to help young deaf children learn English.

But as far as rendering ASL in written form in a print medium, there are considerable difficulties. Outside of the areas of research and classrooms, no sign-writing system seems to be very wide use.

Even a good ASL dictionary—and there are some very attractive ones on the mass market for non-scholars—acknowledges its limitations. Although it will clearly illustrate a good number of common signs (with arrows and blur-lines to indicate movement or repetition), in reality, the gloss accompanying the illustration may depict only one possible meaning of the sign. ASL's vocabulary does not correspond to that of English, and its grammatical structure is quite different. One of the things that makes ASL so fascinating (and difficult to learn from scratch) is its subtlety. You can't get that from a dictionary; you have to experience it firsthand with skilled signers. Second best is a series of good video-tapes, films, or CD-ROMs—a visual medium—or multimedia program.

ASL is not a written language. In everyday usage, it is never written. It can, of course, be coded, glossed, or translated into English. But the gloss or text will only be an approximation of the ASL. Grammatically correct ASL can be rendered in grammatically correct English, but it loses something in translation—which is, of course, a universal problem.[2]

1 Dennis Cokely and Charlotte Baker-Shenk, **American Sign Language: a student text** (Units 1-9), "Note to the Student," x.

2 Consider the title of Marcel Proust's **À la recherche du temps perdu**. It is generally translated as **Remembrance of Things Past**—a phrase taken from Shakespeare's Sonnet 30—but a closer translation would be **In Search of Lost Time**. The opening sentence of the first volume, **Du côté de chez Swann (Swann's Way)**, reads in the original French: "Longtemps, je me suis couché de bonne heure." C.K. Scott Moncrieff's standard translation reads: "For a long time, I used to go to bed early." What gets lost is Proust's music—the languid cadence, the rhythm of the long, solemn vowels and consonants. The original is poetic; the translation is banal.

Chapter 8

How do deaf people learn sign language?

—Ephraim and David Salhanick, New Haven, Connecticut

hey learn it from each other. Until recently, American Sign Language was never formally taught to deaf children; the only ASL classes available were, ironically, for hearing college students. With the advent of the Bilingual-Bicultural approach to deaf education, and recognition of ASL as a foreign language by a number of states, the situation is changing.

From the beginning, deaf children who have deaf parents have always taught the other deaf kids ASL at residential schools. As Arden Neisser observes:

> [F]or close to a century, [sign language] was matter-of-factly ignored, despised and outlawed, neither taught nor tolerated in classrooms for the deaf. Teachers in the schools were completely unfamiliar with it, did not use it, and could not understand it. They were trained in oral methods. (...) Oral programs begin by teaching the children to make sounds, then words, one at a time. Deaf children who have been in oral kindergarten programs have learned, by age five, perhaps fifty words. At the same time, a child with normal hearing has a vocabulary of several thousand words; and a deaf child of deaf parents who has learned ASL as a first language has a vocabulary of several thousand signs. But most deaf children (around 90 percent) have hearing parents and enter school with no ASL and such a restricted knowledge of English that they are virtually without any functioning language at all. (...)
>
> It is estimated that 90 percent of deaf adults who were deaf as children use ASL, and most of them learned it at schools for the deaf—from each other. They simply signed behind their teachers' backs.[1] (...) ASL is said to be the only language in the world that is transmitted from child to child.[2]

Deaf children, newly arrived at school, are plunged into an ASL environment in the playgrounds, cafeteria, and (especially) the dorms. Even if signing is forbidden in class (e.g., Clarke School) or if Signed-English-only or a modified form of oralism like sign-supported speech is used there, deaf kids use ASL everywhere *outside* the classroom, total-immersion style. New kids pick it up quickly. Within a few months, they've become fluent, skillful signers, ASL their first language. When they grow up, many alumni marry another deaf person, a veteran ASL user. Most deaf parents (an estimated 90%) have hearing children. The 10% who have deaf children often send them to the residential schools, where they teach the other kids ASL. Thus ASL has been transmitted from generation to generation.

Deaf children of hearing parents with no prior exposure to ASL who meet ASL-fluent deaf children of deaf parents early in life are lucky, since they're able to pick up a language quickly—and this vital learning has often taken place entirely outside of the classroom!

Some deaf persons learn ASL later in life—on arrival at NTID, for example.[3] And they do very well. But the easiest way to become proficient in ASL is to achieve total immersion in it—living with Deaf people—or, second best, through everyday social contact with native ASL users. Third best is to associate with them regularly in the classroom or office. Fourth best is to learn it through an electronic medium such as video or CD-ROM.

It's certainly possible to learn ASL as an adult. Some late-deafened adults do so, enthusiastically, and do well. But it takes time, commitment, practice, good teachers, and the right attitude. (What worthwhile venture doesn't?) A real "amateur" attitude is to pant, "I want to become fluent overnight!" or sigh, "I'll never learn all this!"

We think it's significant that deaf kids, even those who had no previous exposure to ASL, pick it up so quickly . . . and cheaply, too! We know of no deaf child who has ever lamented, "I'll never be able to learn this!" They just go right ahead and do it.

Taking a course in "Basic Sign" is okay for starters, but not all sign-language classes are created equal! Videotapes of skilled native ASL users are good as a supplement, but real live person-to-person interaction is the best way—as all deaf kids know. There's just no substitute.

[1] Arden Neisser, **The Other Side of Silence: Sign Language and the Deaf Community in America** , p. 8.

[2] Neisser, p. 47.

[3] The National Technical Institute for the Deaf (NTID) is one of 8 colleges of Rochester Institute of Technology in Rochester, New York. It attracts deaf students from a wide variety of backgrounds—oral, ASL/signing, mainstreamed, and residential. Some NTID alumni never learn to sign—which is certainly possible, given the mainstream environment—but most do. There are three or so ASL-theater productions each year, interest groups, and unlimited socializing opportunities in and outside the residential halls.

NTID's mainstage theater is named in honor of Robert F. Panara, NTID's first deaf faculty member (specializing in literature) and founder of its Drama Club, which gradually evolved into a full-scale Performing Arts Program. Dr. Panara's long career includes stints at Fanwood and Gallaudet. He is also a notable baseball buff, and his extensive knowledge of Deaf history, personalities, and achievers is touched upon (albeit briefly) in this book.

Chapter 9

Can people who are deaf from birth appreciate jokes and puns that involve homonyms (sound-alike words)?

Here are a few examples of homonym (phonetic) humor:

Mini-skirt: wearing a peril. (Robert Kuranz)

Q. Why can't a bicycle stand by itself?
A: Because it's two-tired.

As one horse said to the other: "I can't remember your mane,
but your pace is familiar."

Q: What's round and purple and conquered the world?
A: Alexander the Grape.

okes like these that rely on homonyms (or puns, for that matter) are pretty much incomprehensible to many born-deaf people. To enjoy English word-play, you really need some degree of everyday immersion in English as a spoken language, *or* a top-notch bilingual education. Young hearing children love wordplay (the sillier the better), but then, a normal hearing 6-year-old already has a vocabulary of some 3,000 words and intuitively constructs grammatically correct sentences. A child born deaf grows up without that unconscious absorption of spoken English that all hearing English-speaking people take for granted. Far too many deaf children receive a strictly inferior education. They often start school without *any* real language at all! As a result, their English vocabulary tends to be quite limited and augmented slowly and painfully; according to the stereotypical and much-quoted pseudo-statistic on Deaf literacy, English skills "halt" at about a third-to fifth-grade level. Most congenitally deaf people can't be expected to understand the whimsical aspects of English wordplay, much less enjoy it. Consequently, much English humor, even if it's written, is "oral-based" and not accessible to them. It excludes them. So, no, they would not appreciate this kind of humor at all.

Real Deaf humor is visually based. It encompasses mime, gesture, cinematic effects (like zooming, close-ups, fast and slow motion), and a lot of spontaneous sign-play. Although hearing people without prior exposure to ASL can enjoy the beauty and cartoon-like wit of signing, much of it is as incomprehensible to them as "Hearing" humor is to those born deaf. You really need a strong background in ASL to begin to appreciate the nuances and whimsy of Deaf humor.

As for translating English puns and phonetic wordplay into sign or fingerspelling, it doesn't work very well. Humor is an "in-cultural" attribute, and it translates badly. As that proverb about analyzing humor goes, it's like dissecting a frog—you can take it apart to see how it works, but it dies in the process.

▲ ▲ ▲

A slight digression

In response to the original **DEAF LIFE** installment, David Anthony, a Deaf reader in Boulder, Colorado, wrote:

I take issue with the conclusions [here].

I also take issue with the implications in the title "For Hearing People Only." Let's stop referring to "hearing people" as though they be a superior group of human beings on a higher plane. (I don't mean British Airways or American

Airlines, ha ha! Geddit? Higher plane? Oh, well, I was only trying to be plain-ly punny.) Let's refer to hearing people, especially those who have inept hands in Deafness, for what most of them really are: non-Deaf. They have no inkling of what we Deaf people are, want, need, and can do. Their only concern is to un-Deaf us as much as possible.

They are the people responsible for the situation [you] describe so aptly: "Far too many Deaf children receive a strictly inferior education. . . . [And] English skills 'halt' at about a third- to fifth-grade level."

It is this "strictly inferior education" (applying to non-Deaf as well as Deaf children) which accounts for anyone (Deaf or non-Deaf) being unable to appreciate puns and other English word-play.

The first two examples of 'homonym' (phonetic) humor involve not just an awareness of sound but also of pronunciation and spelling. The second two examples have nothing at all to do with homonyms (or homographs, or, what [the reader asking the question] really means, homophones), or phonetics, for that matter. They have to do with a person's stock of words and common phrases, spelling skills, historical-cultural knowledge—and ability to read and write and play with and enjoy words, whether English or ASL.

Being Deaf, Percy (Oh, I know Percy's not your name; I was just punning *per se*) has nothing to do with understanding English or ASL or any language.

David Anthony
Boulder, Colorado
(True self born Deaf and mother father both true self self born Deaf; English tease tease like, and English teach teach like.)

Our reply:

Arguing about terminology is tricky. We titled the feature "For Hearing People Only" not out of deference to their "superiority," but because so many hearing people are pathetically under-informed, misinformed, or, on the brighter side, curious about Deaf people. We thought they warranted a special feature where they could share their questions and get straight answers elucidating different aspects of Deaf culture. (Of course, we're aware that Deaf people read it too!)

Hearing people do not think of themselves as "non-Deaf." While we agree that the term may be apt in many instances, if we titled the feature "For Non-Deaf People Only," hearing readers would undoubtedly bypass it. (To digress a bit: we're thinking of starting a parallel feature for our Deaf readers, which we may title or subtitle "For Deaf People Only." Not "For Aurally-Handicapped People Only." True, many hearing people feel that "aurally-handicapped" or "hearing-impaired" is a more apt term for us. But they're not *our* terms. We didn't title our magazine "**HEARING-IMPAIRED LIFE.**"

About homophonic humor: we chose the jokes as good examples of this basic genre of humor. This, too, can be argued over. Due to space limitations, we had to concentrate on Deaf children's educational deprivation. Of course, many hearing children suffer the same deprivations. It's futile to over-generalize about the Deaf community. But we can speak broadly. We don't say "everyone;" we say "many."

Thanks for sharing your views. The pun-ishment was a pleasure.*

* Letters to the Editor, **DEAF LIFE**, April 1990.

Fake and real ASL humor

There is a category of visual jokes that rely on signing—somewhat. E.g., the well-known pun on "pasteurized milk." The signer repeats the sign for "milk" while moving his fist steadily from before his right eye to beyond his left. The joke is that "pasteurized" looks like "past your eyes." A similar visual joke has the signer poking her thumbs in her ears, the fingers waggling, as though she's typing. What does this represent? "Stereotype."

Jokes like these are not considered examples of true ASL humor, although they are popular among Deaf people. Such puns, it should be noted, are amusing to Deaf people who understand English. Those with a mediocre or poor understanding of English won't get the joke.

True ASL humor can be caustic, witty, or simply silly. One popular schoolkids' joke (if it can be called a joke) is what we call "nining." The joker discreetly flashes a "9" at another person, who has to poke her forefinger through the 9, or risk getting a gentle karate chop on the neck by the joker if she isn't fast enough. The origin of this joke is obscure. Some schoolchildren keep "nining" long after they graduate and enter adult life.

A far more bitter example of ASL humor is the joke about the three men—a Cuban, a Russian, and a Deaf American—who meet on a train (or in a high-rise hotel—there are variants). The Cuban takes out a fine, fresh Havana cigar, lights it up, takes a few leisurely puffs, and tosses the unfinished cigar out the window. He explains, "We have so many cigars in Cuba, we can afford to waste them." The Russian then takes out a new bottle of fine native vodka, pours himself a shot, then casually tosses the nearly-full bottle out the window. "We have so much vodka in Russia, we can afford to waste it," he says. Then the Deaf man picks up his sign-language interpreter and tosses him out the window: "We have so many hearing people in America, we can afford to waste them."

Not all ASL humor is this nasty, however. ASL lends itself to extravagantly exaggerated mimicry, playful, imaginative signing, and stories more notable for the wizardry of the signer than any particular plot or subtext.

Chapter 10

Are there such things as accents among signers from different areas of the country or world?

ndeed there are! One fascinating aspect of sign language is that every signer signs differently, developing their own unique style. Some sign abruptly; some carelessly; some gracefully. Some sign small, some large and clear. Just as with spoken languages: everyone enunciates a bit differently, and there will be a great difference in quality between the voice of a trained performing artist and that of someone who slurs, mumbles, and has sloppy articulation. Alumni of deaf schools and Gallaudet, for example, have acquired distinctive modes of signing identifiable with their *alma maters*. Instead of vocal accents, signers have gestural/kinetic accents—differences in *visual* intonation.

Conversely, every sign-language system "works" differently. Thai Sign Language (from our observation) looks very formal; the face has a tighter, more deadpan look. As we've noted, British Sign Language (BSL) might, at first glance, be mistaken for American Sign Language, but it "moves" completely differently. A native user of BSL who learned ASL would undoubtedly retain a BSL intonation or "accent."

In the past, even within the boundaries of one European country, signers from one city might not understand signers from a different city. But in the United States, ASL has achieved a remarkable level of homogeneity. Native signers from one area can easily understand those from a distant area. However, as with spoken American English, there are many regional variations, with some signs peculiar to a specific area or community (such as Deaf Blacks in Georgia). There are several different "regional" signs for "Halloween,"

"Christmas," "birthday," and "outside," for example. (It's especially true with sexual signs.) You can't necessarily guess right off what part of the country a signer is from, but the variations can be (and have been) pinpointed, mapped, and studied. And, yes, there is such a thing as Sign dialect humor. A skilled storyteller can make effective use of comic "hillbilly" sign, pompous "Oxford English," or hip "jive talk."

There are differences between the ASL usage of a college graduate and a relatively uneducated grassroots-Deaf person. We have white-collar and blue-collar ASL. Steven L. Schrader, a veteran deaf firefighter and EMT with a strong ASL background, has noted that he encountered many uneducated "poor and underprivileged" deaf persons in North Carolina, and that their signing was extremely difficult to understand. "They spoke their own dialects, along with American Sign Language used in a 'street smart' way."[*]

As in any culture, such differences can be used as weapons of oppression. Linguistic snobbery certainly exists in the Deaf community. Those who are proud of the purity of their ASL, those who enjoy showing off their advanced "Englishy" vocabulary (with lots of big fingerspelled words), and those who have learned ASL relatively late in life—all have very different accents, and each may look down on the others. The choice of codes—ASL or a form of Signed English—has immense political and social implications. Until recently, Signed English was considered correct, educated, "high-class," and ASL "low-class."

Deaf people do tease each other lightheartedly about their accents. There are bilingual hearing people—primarily those with Deaf parents—whose ASL accent is "pure." Since relatively few hearing people become really fluent signers, a native signer can usually (though not invariably) recognize a hearing person by the slightly halting quality of their signing, expression, and movement, and the way they mouth words while signing. "Oh, you sign with a Hearing accent!"

---

[*] **Silent Alarm: On the Edge with a Deaf EMT** (Washington, D.C.: Gallaudet University Press, 1995), p. 113.

A few American regional Sign variations.
Top row: *birthday*; center row: *soon*; bottom row: *outside*.

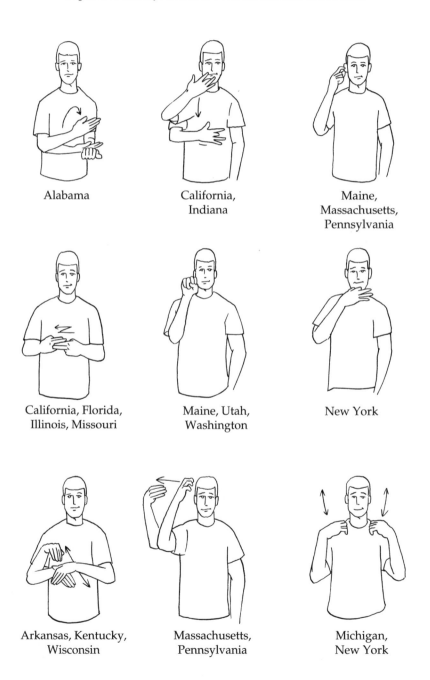

Alabama

California,
Indiana

Maine,
Massachusetts,
Pennsylvania

California, Florida,
Illinois, Missouri

Maine, Utah,
Washington

New York

Arkansas, Kentucky,
Wisconsin

Massachusetts,
Pennsylvania

Michigan,
New York

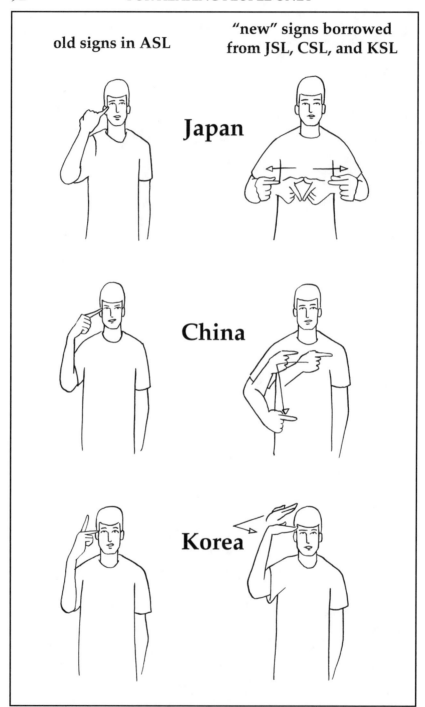

old signs in ASL

"new" signs borrowed
from JSL, CSL, and KSL

Japan

China

Korea

Chapter 11

I heard that there are new, nonracist signs for Korean, Chinese, and Japanese that don't involve reference to slanting eyes. Would you please describe these, and any other new signs regarding ethnicity or nationality that come to mind?

—Susan Gibson, Dallas, Texas

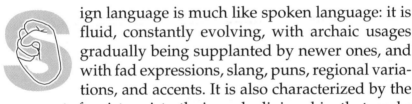 ign language is much like spoken language: it is fluid, constantly evolving, with archaic usages gradually being supplanted by newer ones, and with fad expressions, slang, puns, regional varia- tions, and accents. It is also characterized by the same sort of sexist, racist, ethnic, and religious bias that marks other languages. Prejudices of the times and social attitudes are faithfully reflected (and encapsulated) in ASL.

Case in point: "female" and "male" signs. Signs indicating feminine gender (*woman, girl, wife, mother, daughter, aunt, cousin, niece, grandmother, lady*) are made on the cheek near the chin and mouth; signs indicating masculine gender (*man, boy, husband, father, son, uncle, cousin, nephew, grandfather, gentleman*) are made at the brow. The traditional explanation is that the "female" signs reflect the old-fashioned, typically feminine gesture of tying bonnet-strings while "male" signs reflect the likewise old-fashioned, typically masculine gesture of tipping a cap. However, sign-critics have noted that signs for "gabby" and "gossipy" are also made in the "feminine zone," while signs like "think," "intelligent," "brilliant," and "genius" are made in the "masculine zone." And the common initialized sign for "gay man" isn't made near the brow (the "male" zone) but on the chin (the "female" zone), as is the sign for "lesbian."

Likewise, everyday ASL contains signs that could be construed as racist: the common signs for *Black* and *Africa* indicate a flat "Negroid" nose. Although other "ethnic" signs (e.g., *Greek* and *Roman*) are made on or in front of the nose (suggesting an aquiline "Roman profile"), they aren't used as slurs, while a variant of the "Black nose" sign corresponds to the epithet *nigger*. It can be, and is, used as an out-and-out insult. The graceful new sign for *Africa* represents the shape of the continent, and keeps facial profiles out of it.

But some African-American Deaf people prefer the *old* sign for *Black*.

As for the sign for *Polish*, with the thumb brushing the underside of the tip of the nose, it is not generally considered an "insulting" sign . . . but how do native Polish Deaf people feel about it?

The term "Oriental," denoting persons from the Asian-Pacific nations and cultures, has lately come under fire as being patronizing and inaccurate. The traditional signs for *Japanese*, *Chinese*, and *Korean* all indicate the stereotypical "Oriental slanted eyes." While "slant-eyes" is not acceptable spoken English (it's a slur), many people still use the "slant-eyed" signs, unaware that these are now considered offensive and that there are better signs in use.

Instead of emphasizing "slanted eyes," the new signs suggest something of the native culture of these peoples: the new sign for *Japanese* is the one used by Japanese people themselves, and symbolizes the curved island of Japan, which, according to ancient belief, was created by the gods. The new *Chinese* sign indicates a traditional side-fastened Chinese jacket. The new sign for *Korean* suggests a towering crown or martial helmet with side-flaps.

Not all "ethnic" signs are considered offensive—although

some members of the particular groups might well take offense. The sign for *Italian* connotes "Catholic;" *American Indian* connotes "feathers and warpaint."

There are old and new signs for *Jew/Jewish*. Some people find the old sign for "Jew" ("beard-on-chin") offensive—and not only Jewish women. They object to that sign's similarity to the sign for "grabby/greedy/miserly." Indeed, the sign "Jew" is used as an insult to mean a greedy, unscrupulous person, just as it has been in spoken English for centuries. Jews themselves have devised a new sign that symbolizes the unrolling of the Torah scrolls (the core Jewish scriptures) plus the agent marker ("Torah" + "person" = Jew). But many Jews continue to use the old sign anyway, sexist or not. It's simpler and quicker. It remains to be seen whether the new sign will achieve as wide a currency as the old one has. New Jewish signs (without a Christian bias) are still being developed.

Virtually all cultures have their own sign languages (and variations thereof), and it might be enlightening to "listen" to what they have to say.

Sign language is not impervious to change. It can grow; it can adapt to modern needs. All signers can participate in the process of re-creating a language that reflects modern sensibilities, cultural sensitivity, and respect for diversity. There is always room for improvement—and for creativity.

Chapter 12

"I want to learn bigger signs."

Just recently I went to cheerleading camp. There I met four deaf girls. They were the only thing that made me want to stay at camp longer. It was very interesting to my friend and I. Even though they couldn't hear, they were the funnest people to be with.

The reason I'm writing is because I'm really interested in how to talk sign language in bigger signs so if I see them I'll be able to talk to them. It's very important to me. I was watching a show the other day and a little deaf kid got lost and everybody was trying to talk to him in words; they had no idea he was deaf until someone came along who knows sign language. If I see someone like that who needs help, I want to be able to help them. Sign language is something I would never take for granted. I want to know if there's anything you can send me that will help me learn bigger signs.

—Tammy Kirk, Fairfax, Missouri

he best place to start is your local public library. Ask the main, reference, or language-department librarian (depending on how large the library is) where you can find materials relating to sign language, and resources and media on Deaf Studies. The library should have at least a few helpful books you can check out. And if you can't find anything, you can have the librarian contact another library to get it for you via interlibrary loan. The library may also be able to point you towards local resources, such as community sign-language classes, Deaf clubs, or organizations.

The Internet also contains some good resources. Animation has made its way into sign-language-oriented sites. There are also CD-ROMs, DVDs, and videotapes that can help you practice and improve your signing. You may be able to borrow some of these from the library. And if you don't have viewing equipment at home (a computer, TV, and VCR), the library probably does. Most public libraries offer free Internet access, although users may be limited to an hour or 90 minutes of daily access during library hours.

Community-college bookstores may have some sign-language textbooks, but since these are aimed at college students, they're accordingly more technical. Some commercial bookstores, especially chains, usually have a sampling of sign-language and Deaf Studies books in stock. This reflects the growing popularity of ASL and increasing "Deaf Awareness" among laypeople. These bookstores can special-order a book (or CD-ROM) they don't have in stock. And you might want to check your computer-software store. But before you decide to order or buy something, try to borrow it from the library first to see if you like it and can benefit from it. Sign-language videocourses and books that are bought but not used are a sorry waste of money and media.

As for making the signs bigger, all you need to remember is that the normal "signing space" extends from the top of the head to the waist, and from shoulder to shoulder. When communicating with another deaf person, make sure to give her enough space to sign freely *and* to get a clear view of your signs. Signers tend to stand a bit further away from each other than hearing people do while talking. A comfortable distance—at least an extended arm's length—ensures good readability. Ask those you're signing to. They'll show you.

The important thing is to get into practice, and, if possible, find someone who's skillful in signing to practice with. That makes it more fun.

Signing space: the upper torso and head

Chapter 13

I've noticed that when someone uses the ILY sign in public, some of my Deaf friends have dismayed expressions on their faces. Don't they like it?

he best-known Deaf sign isn't strictly ASL, but a combination of three letters of the standard American-European manual alphabet: I, L, and Y (i.e., **I Love You**). Bend your middle and ring fingers into your palm, extend pinkie, index, and thumb, turn your palm outwards, and you have it.

For all its new-found popularity, the ILY sign has supposedly been around for approximately a century. **Deaf Heritage** has traced it as far back as 1905. If so, the ILY fell into disuse after its creation, but was never entirely forgotten. However, many of those who attended schools for the deaf during the 1950s, 1960s, and 1970s don't recall seeing an ILY *anywhere*. It achieved "star exposure" in the mid-70s after Presidential candidate Jimmy Carter picked it up from a group of Deaf supporters in the Midwest. (His predecessor, Gerald Ford, had also learned it from Deaf people.) During his famous Inauguration Day walk down Pennsylvania Avenue (most other presidents rode grandly in limousines), Carter was photographed flashing the ILY to a group of Deaf people on the sidewalk. These photos, front-page-style, were published in the national media. Deaf people, who recognized the sign immediately, were delighted. Instant fame for the ILY.

That was in 1977. Since then, it seems, everyone's gotten into the act. We've seen ILYs all over the place, including the national news—video footage from Operation Desert Storm (1991) showed a U.S. soldier on a tank, triumphantly flashing it. Deaf people and their hearing friends have made the ILY arguably the best-known handsign in the world, competing in popularity with the classic "V-for-victory." It's even been used to summon help. Some years back, we read an account of a deaf couple whose car broke down on a highway. They stood by their disabled car, trying to flag down passing motorists, without luck. Then they thought of trying the ILY. It worked. A truck whizzed by them, then braked, backed up, and pulled over. It turned out that the folks who owned the truck had a young daughter who watched *Sesame Street*, and had picked up the ILY sign from series regular Linda Bove. When she saw the couple standing by their car bravely flashing the ILY, she cried, "Daddy, stop! Those people are deaf, and they need help!" And the girl's father did stop. Help came.

And so the ILY has become the best-known symbol of the Deaf community. In catalogues specializing in Deaf-oriented products, you can find ILY jewelry, charms, vases, mugs, keychains, stickers, magnets, sun-catchers, figurines, rubberstamps, stationery, and T-shirts. It has been incorporated into first-class original works of art, too. Some deaf (and hearing) people love the ILY so much that they avidly collect ILY paraphernalia—much as others collect Barbie dolls, Grateful Dead mementos, or knickknacks representing their sign of the zodiac.

In the process, an intimate, tender sign has lost most of its original force and virtually all significance. What was once a charming and concise way to say "I love you" now means "Hiya."

The ILY has become so popular and widespread, so ubiquitous, that it's become a visual cliché—the "Smiley Face" of Deaf Culture. What we have is a case of overkill. And with overexposure comes abuse. You can find hearing people who have no previous acquaintance with Deaf people or sign language (and no intention of learning more about either), giddily flashing the ILY at every deaf person (or every person they *think* is deaf) whom they run across. Sometimes these well-meaning folks aren't even making the handsign correctly. (Do it wrong and you usually end up with the sign for "bullshit"—not the sort of thing you'd want to wave at a stranger.)* It's as though these people think the "ILY" is the be-all and end-all of Deaf-Hearing communication, some kind of magic catchword, a talisman. Once they learn the ILY, they're okay with deaf people, they're safe. No wonder that some deaf people react with quizzical expressions. They're thinking, "What's up with this one?!"

Among Deaf people, it's acceptable to flash the ILY at another person from a distance, as it shows up well. It *is* considered gauche to flash the ILY at close range (unless both parties know each other well and like the sign). If an uninformed hearing person walks into a gathering of Deaf people and cheerily waves the ILY, s/he had better be prepared for some sour looks!

Some of us love the ILY; some tolerate it; some are sick of it. To some, it's not cute anymore, just corny. Some Deaf people hate the ILY, really loathe it. It makes them shudder to see it, and they have to repress a momentary urge to thwack ILY-flashers off their feet. That could account for those dismayed expressions you've seen. They're restraining themselves.

---

* This is what happened to the unfortunate Vice President Walter Mondale during that same Inauguration Day parade. **Deaf Heritage** describes how Mondale, "following [Carter] in an open car, unfamiliar with the symbol, but gamely trying to respond to the same group [of Deaf well-wishers], was seen innocently waving an obscene gesture!" (Chapter 15, p. 373.)

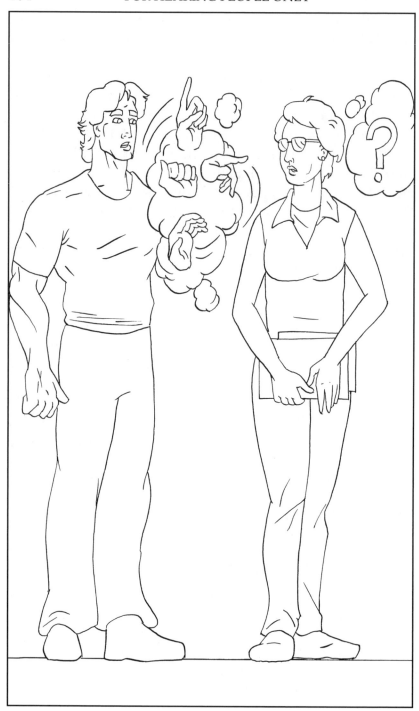

Chapter 14

"I know it takes a great deal of practice, but do you have any information on how to better accomplish fingerspelling?"

In the first [ASL] class I took, we learned fingerspelling. However, I am having trouble "reading" fingerspelling from another speller. My speed is also slow. I know it takes a great deal of practice, but do you have any information on how to better accomplish this?

—Roger Mindel, Wheaton, Maryland

ingerspelling is a vital kinetic-visual skill, an essential component of sign-language communication. A basic knowledge of fingerspelling will take you a long way, as you can fingerspell any word you don't yet know the correct sign for (or have forgotten, or just aren't sure about). As each handshape corresponds to a specific letter of the alphabet, it's not particularly difficult to learn. Some adult beginners master fingerspelling in a couple of hours or less; others never seem to get the hang of it. Having a friend or tutor to practice with can made a big difference.

Motivation is as important as dexterity. Clarity is more important than speed. It's important to know how to form your letters correctly and clearly, keep your fingers from kinking, avoid bouncing your arm and flopping your wrist, maintain a smooth flow, and stay in practice. This, of course, takes time and dedication. Jerkiness, bouncing, and staring at the spelling hand in self-conscious dismay are dead giveaways for the amateur klutz!

We assume you've learned the basics and know the difference between K and P. Setting aside a half-hour every day for
practice (if you're a punctilious sort) is ideal. But you can use
any duration of "captive time" (such as a bus or taxi ride, solo
waiting, watching a boring TV program or a string of commercials, a visit to the laundromat, or finding yourself at the
tail end of a long checkout line) to run through the alphabet
a few times. You can take a favorite poem or brief prose item
and see if you can fingerspell it clearly. (Try the Gettysburg
Address, a psalm or hymn, a Robert Frost or Emily Dickinson
poem, a brief article or letter, a list of names and addresses
from your address book, tongue-twisters, or even a recipe!
And then there's mirror-practice . . .

It's important to know how to form numbers clearly. Most
numbers, with the exception of the "thousand," "million,"
and up, are made on one hand. A few numbers (such as "25")
use "shorthand." Here's where it's ideal to drill and practice
with a skilled signer.

To fingerspell well, you need a certain degree of manual
dexterity, and this can be improved through exercise. E.g., the
classic routine of slowly squeezing a medium-hard rubber
ball a number of times each day, or using a spring-tension
gizmo specifically made for strengthening the hands. (These
are available in sporting-goods stores.) You can also try
stretching broad rubber bands (the kind used by the U.S.
Postal Service) to strengthen individual fingers. Or check the
physical-therapy books at your local public library for hand-
strengthening and dexterity-enhancing exercises.

The important thing is to get used to using your hands as
tools of verbal communication—a new voice. Mangled letters, self-conscious giggling while spelling, unrelated ges-
ticulations (such as "erasing" mistakes from the air), and a
general aura of embarrassment underscore one's awkward-
ness and lack of confidence—none of which help communication. It's okay to make mistakes, of course. Learn from
them, and grow beyond them. Get good feedback. Sign

confidently; your skills *will* improve with practice.

Most sign-language textbooks start with fingerspelling exercises. We found a promising oversize booklet in the Rochester Public Library: **Expressive and Receptive Fingerspelling for Adults** by LaVera M. Guillory (Baton Rouge: Claitor's Bookstore, Publishing Division, 1966). The Library of Congress number is 66-17803. The Dewey call number is (q or Oversize) 371.912 G961e (or similar). If you want to go whole hog, you can buy self-instructional videotapes or CD-ROMs (or may even be able to borrow them from your local public library, as we've already noted). DawnSignPress, for example, has a 2-hour videotape by Joyce Linden, *Fingerspelling: Expressive & Receptive Fluency*, which includes an instructional booklet with practice suggestions. This is especially useful for improving the fine points: maintaining the best orientation of your palm, and forming the letters to show the most "configuration." Clarity is the goal.

But you don't need to spend a lot of money on enhancing your fingerspelling skills, really. Once you know the alphabet and the numbers 1 through 999 (which, again, is really not difficult—children pick these up almost instantaneously), you're armed. You can practice on your own.

As always, the best advice is to get real-life practice—with others. If you have any friends who are native or veteran ASL users, and who are very patient, go for it! Ask them to drill you on expressive and receptive spelling. (And cherish them.) If they're willing audiences, tell them stories; translate favorite passages to them. Make this a part of your everyday conversations—real-life practice. They can give you the kind of feedback no mirror can.

Skilled ASL users fingerspell sparingly, but at a characteristically "lightning" pace. Yes, it's possible for an adult beginner to achieve great fluency in fingerspelling. You have to train your eyes to "see quickly," just as you have to train your hands to coordinate. It's a valuable skill that's well worth the time and effort invested.

Chapter 15

Should all hearing people be required to learn signing, and if so, what are the absolute essentials?

e believe that *all* children should learn how to fingerspell,* at the very least, while they're preschoolers or in first grade. There are several compelling reasons for this.

● Preschoolers are at the prime age for language acquisition. They take to fingerspelling "naturally," and master it quickly.

● It's good practice in the acquisition of hand-eye coordination and manual-dexterity skills. No fancy equipment is needed—just a chart or some cards, perhaps a videotape or some *Sesame Street* clips, a depiction of the English alphabet, a pointer, and, above all, a good teacher.

● Fingerspelling is a real godsend in emergency situations. Suppose you're choking, have a bad cold or respiratory ailment, or (for whatever reason) can't vocalize. A pencil and pad may not be handy or practical here; there may not be sufficient time to jot anything down. You *can* communicate by fingerspelling. Those who know the manual alphabet will be able to understand you readily.

● More broadly, it's a useful survival skill for *anyone*—deaf, hard-of-hearing, *and* hearing. Supposing you need to communicate with someone, but you're separated by a sound-proof window, or you're several stories away from each other (one person's on the sidewalk, the other at a third-story window). Shouting either won't carry or won't do. Fingerspelling will. (This, of course, depends on the angle of vision, eyesight, and distance. If you're both equipped with binoculars, you can read each other's fingerspelling across a considerable distance.)

● Underwater—as we've already mentioned—a basic knowledge of fingerspelling and signing can be a real life-saver.

● Supposing you're at a play, movie, assembly, or religious ceremony where whispering isn't convenient, as it will annoy others (and possibly get you into trouble). Fingerspelling provides a discreet way to communicate. (It's quieter than paper and pen—no telltale rustling and scraping.)

● And—conversely—supposing you're at a blasting-loud rock concert where shouting (no matter how hard you try) is futile. You *can* fingerspell. Other possible maximum-noise settings are: a roaring fire or waterfall, a hurricane, a thunder-storm, an airport, truck, any workplace where workers wear protective earplugs, a crowded athletic stadium, or (God forbid) a riot, disaster, or combat zone.

● Kids in classrooms can "pass notes" to each other behind Teacher's back with a minimum of risk if they know how to fingerspell. This expedient has been used by savvy hearing children for years. (Traditionally, CODAs—children of deaf parents—taught their friend this "secret code," and it at-tained popularity in certain public schools.) And, um, yes, they *have* used fingerspelling to cheat on tests. (One student relays the correct answers to another, using a desk or legs as a shield.) We're not advocating that fingerspelling be used for this purpose. But it *is*. Kids have, after all, been passing notes, cribbing, and cheating since schooldays began. To forestall this, we encourage teachers to stay alert and lively, not talk to the blackboard, and interact *with* the students. But if teachers are boring the students and punishing them for whispering or passing notes, fingerspelling offers a less risky way to survive the boredom. We speak from experience.

● A working knowledge of fingerspelling enables hearing people to communicate with Deaf people on a basic level. You never know when you're going to run into Deaf people—at a rally? A town meeting? A party? By the side of the highway when you (or they) need assistance? It's good to be prepared.

And what if you have a Deaf neighbor or mail carrier and just want to say "Hi?" Or if you find yourself behind a Deaf family in a long supermarket-checkout line and just want to offer a friendly greeting?

● You never know when someone in your family may become deaf. Or yourself, for that matter. What with the pandemic of noise pollution, it's certainly a possibility. We don't mean to denigrate the pain of adjusting to sudden (or gradual) hearing loss, but if you're in this situation, you'll find that possessing a working knowledge of fingerspelling obviates at least some of the anguish of being stuck "between languages."

● Need another reason? How about this?—Fingerspelling is fun, and kids enjoy learning and playing with it. There are so many creative uses! It can be employed as part of a reading-skills program—e.g., fingerspelling bees! It could even be introduced as part of a class project on alphabets, commonly-used codes, and signaling systems—nautical flags, Morse, Braille, railway lights, international symbols and signs, etc. In contrast with most other codes, fingerspelling is easily retained and "carried." The standard manual alphabet used in the United States, Canada, and much of Europe may not be universal, but it's certainly widely used. Another possible project would be to study and compare manual alphabets around the world—why the difference between the U.S. and British alphabets if spoken English is used in both countries?

● If you're beset by a "deaf peddler" trying to push a manual-alphabet card on you in exchange for your "suggested contribution of a dollar" or "pay any amount you wish," you can tell him/her what you think. Also, since you've already mastered the ABC, you don't need an ABC card. "S-O-R-R-Y, I A-L-R-E-A-D-Y K-N-O-W T-H-I-S"—or, more succinctly, "G-E-T L-O-S-T!"

● Although most sign-language courses begin with fingerspelling, it's not the *same* thing as sign language, although it can be a component. Fingerspelling has a different origin from sign language, having been invented by 16th-century Spanish Benedictine monks tutoring young deaf noblemen in speech and literacy skills (so they could retain the family fortunes). It's been used as an oralist *and* a manualist tool. Signing incorporates fingerspelling—a number of signs are initialized (e.g., "department" with the "d," "family" with "f," and "team" with "t"). Having mastered the basics of fingerspelling, children can move on to basic ASL signs — and all kids seem to love "zoo signs."

Not all fingerspelling is good fingerspelling. As with any skill, it has to be learned right, done properly, and kept sharp. Rusty and malformed fingerspelling is practically useless. Since manual communication requires practice, refresher sessions should be scheduled every semester. Seize every opportunity to stay in practice.

Fingerspelling is a most useful communication and survival skill that everyone can profit from knowing. There are no philosophical or methodological excuses.

---

* By "fingerspelling," we mean the 26 letters of the alphabet plus numbers (0-19, 20s through 90s, 100 ["C"]). With the exception of "thousand" and "million," and larger quantities, these can be formed with one hand, which is handy if you're using binoculars or carrying something. If you've ever played "fingerspelling bingo" with a skilled signer, you'll know that it presents a challenge to "read" as the pace quickens. Good receptivity practice!

Deaf Awareness 5-Minute Quiz

Chapters 1—15

Answers are on the bottom of the page, upside down.

True or False:

1. American Sign Language is quite similar to British Sign Language, just as spoken/written American English is very close to British English.

2. Although there is no single sign language used by Deaf people around the world, various forms of "international sign language" exist.

3. Most Deaf people know how to sign in Braille.

4. The Abbé de l'Epée was the first educator who recognized that sign language was the natural language of the deaf, but thought that it was a collection of signs without grammatical structure.

5. All sign languages have the same basic structure—the subject comes first.

6. Various writing systems have been developed for ASL, but outside of textbooks, none are in very wide use.

7. Deaf children usually learn sign language from each other.

8. ASL has no real regional variations or accents, since it isn't a spoken language.

9. Signers are changing the stereotypic and prejudicial quality of some racial/ethnic signs to reflect a more positive view of racial and ethnic diversity and cultural heritage.

10. The "ILY" sign has been in widespread use since World War II.

Answers:
1. False; 2. True; 3. False; 4. True; 5. False; 6. True; 7. True; 8. False; 9. True; 10. False.

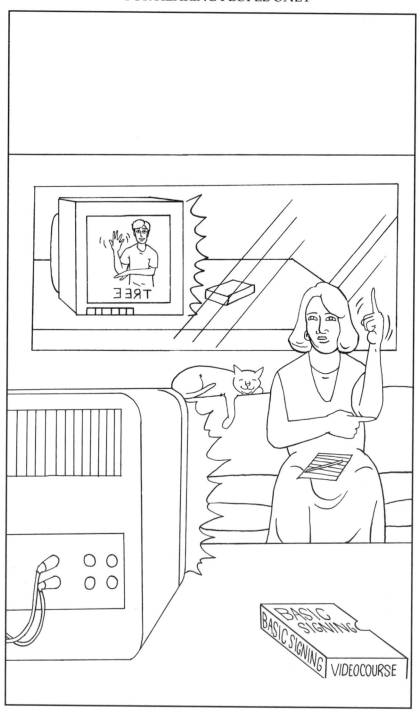

Chapter 16

"Are there any home correspondence courses in Basic Sign?"

Dear Sir, Madam:

Received your article for "hearing people only" and like to have more information about deaf people and their culture. Because of injury received in WW II I slowly lose my hearing (nerve damage). I take sign language at Bakersfield College but so far total confusion because of different teaching of same words and different signing of same words. I live rural area in California and it is hard to find deaf persons to talk or sign to. Are there any home correspondence course? because colleges are total concentrated on grades. All I want to learn simple signs if you meet a deaf person every day talk. What are Pidgin Sign English?? I am grateful for any information you can give me.

Thank you so much in advance.

—Theodora Scrivner, Lebec, California

SL is, of course, best learned in company with a fluent signer. So what to do if you're geographically isolated? We don't know of a "home correspondence course" in Basic Sign, but home videocourses in Basic Sign, ASL, and Sign literature are available from media companies such as DawnSignPress and Sign Media. Dr. Martin L. A. Sternberg's classic **Dictionary of American Sign Language** is available as a multimedia program—great news for those with computers and a bit of cash. One advantage of instructional videos and CD-ROMs is that you can go at your own pace in relaxed surroundings—your own living room or study. The major disadvantage is that videotapes and multimedia programs are costly and you can't browse around and sample them before you buy. You also need the appropriate platforms: a VCR and TV screen, or computer. What's good for one student may not be practical for another.

We've already mentioned public-library resources, which enable you to borrow some multimedia programs that you might otherwise not be able to afford. Still, the offerings may be limited. Or they may be plentiful. Thanks to interlibrary networking, material owned by one library can be made available to patrons who live in small towns or isolated regions of the same county or state. It's certainly worthwhile to ask about this. The great advantage of borrowing this material is that if you don't like the program, or don't find it suitable for your needs, you're none the poorer. And if you do like the program enough to make the financial commitment, you can order it from a mail-order or Internet source, secure in the knowledge that it will benefit you.

If you don't have access to a VCR or computer, there are some good and enjoyable books on the market. Still, you need face-to-face practice to make sure that you're forming the signs correctly. We've watched hearing children and adults teaching themselves signs from illustrations. They usually got it wrong.

Evidently, you've had considerable difficulty because you've picked up a number of different signs for the same word or concept. Many Deaf people use "regional" signs—their signs will vary according to where they're from and which school they attended. Different teachers favor different signs. For adults learning to sign for the first time, some confusion is unavoidable. Even common signs like "what" and "yesterday" may have several variants. They're equally acceptable, but one form (different from the ones you already learned) may be more prevalent in your signing community. What you can do is keep track of the variations you run into. You can make your own flashcards or a chart in your notebook with descriptions, diagrams, or coded sketches. (Or have a friend help you design them.)

As for community resources: Since you live in California, you can contact your local GLAD (Greater Los Angeles Council on Deafness) office, or DCARA (Deafness, Counseling, Advocacy, and Referral Agency) in San Leandro, and ask the folks there for more information or advice on just which materials would be best for you. The GLAD and DCARA bookstores should have a variety of texts and self-study materials like flashcards and videotapes.

Note, too, that several community colleges and agencies offer beginners' Sign classes in a noncompetitive atmosphere. Many people who take such classes are deafened adults or friends of deaf people. And ALDA (the Association of Late-Deafened Adults) can provide you with support and networking.

(See next chapter for a response to the question on Pidgin Sign English.)

"I am going to the store."

Signed Exact English

I AM GOING

TO T-H-E STORE

Pidgin Sign English

I AM GO

TO T-H-E STORE

American Sign Language

STORE THAT ONE I

GO NOW

Chapter 17

What is Pidgin Sign English?

ere we go again—another labeling problem! But first, a definition of what a "pidgin" is. The word *pidgin* (which has nothing to do with birds) evolved from the word *business*. *Pidgin English*, the full term, is a corruption of *business English*. **The American Heritage Dictionary** defines *pidgin* as: "A simplified form of speech, usually a mixture of two or more languages, that has a rudimentary grammar and vocabulary and is used for communication between groups speaking different languages."

Roughly speaking, PSE (which stands for Pidgin *Sign* English or Pidgin *Signed* English) is an impromptu blend of American Sign Language and American English signs. It's commonly used when ASL-Deaf people communicate with hearing (or deaf) people who are not fluent in ASL, but who do know some signs and fingerspelling. PSE enables native ASL signers and native English speakers to comfortably communicate with each other.

The syntax (grammatical structure) of ASL is *very* different from that of English. They are two distinct languages. English is primarily an oral/aural (spoken) language; ASL is visual/gestural/spatial. Since they "work" in completely opposite ways, you can see the difficulty of blending the two.

However, signers are an ingenious lot. Because so many hearing people—native English speakers, that is—are unfamiliar with ASL and have difficulty with its "foreign" syntax, signers have "bridged the gap" between English and ASL by employing a sign system that is neither pure ASL nor pure English, but which borrows and modifies elements from both languages. Pidgin Sign English, in other words, is a method of communication—not a distinct *language* as such—that uses signs borrowed from ASL in a basically English word order, but with some grammatical characteristics of ASL.

PSE denotes a naturally-developed or informal sign system, as distinct from invented or "artificial" systems of Manually Coded English. Keeping track of these labels is a tricky business. Other terms for PSE (more or less equivalent) are "Sign English," "Ameslish," or "Siglish," depending on whether you're describing non-English or non-ASL signing. Yet another term for PSE is "Contact Sign Language." And those who don't like any of these terms prefer to call it "American Signed English," "English signs," or even "English sign language." Confusing? In practice, it's fairly simple. Whatever works, works.

Professor William Newell has some enlightening comments about makes PSE PSE:

> Pidgin Signed English is a term coined in the 1970s to distinguish "naturally occurring" forms of English-like signing. Actually, it is a misnomer, because PSE is not truly a "pidgin" in the same sense that other pidgin languages exist in the world. Pidgin languages are very crude, rudimentary forms of "mixed languages." PSE would better be considered a form of ASL where the users mix ASL vocabulary with primarily English word order. But PSE (contact variety ASL) is really a more robust form of communication than is the typical "pidgin" language.

It should be noted, however, that PSE is *not* the same as Signed English. PSE omits some English grammar and words, and has more "pure ASL" signs in it. Particles such as *a* and *the* are commonly omitted, but forms of the verb *to be* are retained. PSE uses more fingerspelling than ASL, but less than Signed English.

Because PSE uses signs in an English word order, it's possible to speak and sign at the same time. It's an adaptable, flexible, and widely used approach. Chances are, when you see a sign-language interpreter in class or "covering" a public event, or see a deaf person chatting with a hearing friend who's not highly skilled in ASL, they're using PSE. Since ASL is an extraordinarily flexible language, ASL users readily understand signers who use Signed English or PSE—provided that the signing is clear.

When Deaf people communicate with people (hearing *or* deaf) who aren't fluent in ASL, they tend to "switch codes" to Signed English or PSE, which are more readily understandable by native English users, as they conform fairly closely to the grammatical structure of English. Hearing people rarely get to see "pure" ASL being used in their presence. What they take for ASL may actually be PSE.

How does one recognize PSE? Here's a very simple example. In PSE you would say, "My name is T-H-E-O-D-O-R-A." You would be using the standard ASL signs for "my" and "name," in an English word order. The sign for "is" would be the same as the sign for "true," not the initialized version (which is Signed English). In ASL you would say, "My name T-H-E-O-D-O-R-A."

Chapter 18

"How do I know if someone is using ASL or signed English?"

How do I know if someone is using ASL or signed English? I have some sign language skills which I have learned from family members who are deaf but just recently I learned that there is a difference. I always thought it was just one language, that is, sign language. So I am wondering if you would inform me a little bit more about ASL, maybe some rules or some examples if possible.

—Shelley MacLean, Sydney, Nova Scotia

When sign-language students talk about all the different kinds of sign systems, Manually Coded English systems, and variations thereof, they use the term "continuum." What's a sign-language continuum, anyway? It's a diagram representing the entire population of sign-language users—from the purest Signing-Exact-English approach to the purest ASL approach, and all possible blends or variations in between. Think of a broad arc. On the right are the "pure ASL" users; on the left, the "pure English" users. Pidgin Sign English, which borrows features from both ASL and English, would be situated in the middle of the arc, a bit towards the right. Signed English would be a bit more towards the left. But both are distinct from ASL.

As we've already noted, English and ASL are two *very* distinct languages. One is orally/aurally based; the other is visual/gestural/spatial. It's possible to transpose any English sentence into a visual/gestural/spatial equivalent—at the crudest level, it can be done with fingerspelling, which simply shows each letter as a different handshape—a manual code. It is considerably more difficult to render ASL into spoken or written English. Every time it gets translated, it loses something. When you say "signing," it can be a basic manual rendition of English, or it can be true ASL. There are many shades of possibilities—and many opportunities for confusion as well.

ASL, it should be emphasized, is not synonymous with "sign language." The term "sign language" can be loosely employed to mean *any* sort of sign-based communication, including manually coded systems. So taking a course in "Basic Sign," "Basic Sign Communication," or even "Basic Sign Language" won't necessarily introduce you to ASL, but to some or many of the components of communicating in ASL.

"Signed English" is not strictly the same as "Sign English," but for the sake of simplicity, that's the term we're using here. We define "Signed English" as English rendered into sign, essentially following the syntactical pattern (sentence structure) of English, not ASL. The signs may be borrowed liberally from ASL usage; the arrangement follows English word order. English markers such as *-ly* are denoted by special signs or are spelled out.

How do you tell ASL from Signed English on sight? Very roughly speaking, you have to catch the rhythm of the signing. ASL has a different flow, a different "look" from Signed English. The rhythm is entirely different because the syntax of ASL is so different from Signed English. In ASL you would sign "YOU BUY CAR MAYBE YOU?" or "CAR BUY YOU MAYBE?" or "YOU—CAR BUY MAYBE?" (depending on your emphasis and signing style), while using the facial-grammatical question marker, the eyebrow raise/brow crease, and a subtle tilting forward of the head. In Signed English or Pidgin Sign English you'd sign something like "WILL YOU BUY CAR, MAYBE?" with more mouthing of the English words.

To someone not familiar with the language, an ASL conversation looks like a lightning-quick, intense "pantomime" of sorts. ASL is very expressive, eruptive. Since the face is used as a grammatical marker, expressions are "exaggerated" and held momentarily. There is very little mouthing of *words*. Signs and phrases are often repeated for emphasis: "YOU-GO-FINISH, WHY?. . .WHY?" ("*Why* did you go?")

One way to "tune into" ASL is to try to catch the sentence subject. In ASL, the subject, the topic of the sentence, often comes first. Modifiers (such as adjectives) often come *after* the subject. Signed-English systems follow the syntax of spoken English, and thus place verbs and modifiers before the subject. This makes signed sentences a bit easier—or more difficult—to "read." It depends on your visual-communicative background.

As for the political ramifications, be aware that some ASL advocates look askance at Signed English (i.e., as an everyday medium of communication among deaf people). Signed English, in this view, "dilutes" and "distorts" pure ASL. It employs many initialized signs, a number of which have found their way into "permanent" ASL usage, and are certainly acceptable to most Deaf people. But woe betide the signer who inadvertently uses one of them while talking to a purist!

What many people, purists included, may not realize is that "pure" pre-Signed-English ASL absorbed a number of initialized French signs, such as "look at/see," with the distinct "V" handshape, which was borrowed directly from the LSF sign for *voir*. This sign is often described as iconic, with the extended index and middle fingers supposedly mimicking the two eyes as they look (rather like snail's eyes on stalks). But it's actually an old initialized French sign. Research has uncovered the "real meaning" of more of these signs.

So it cannot be said that initialized signs are automatically bad, intrusive, non-ASL usage. Which contemporary initialized signs are acceptable ASL and which are not is a matter of dispute. Don't let that stop you. Keep practicing, and have fun.

Chapter 19

What is Total Communication?

otal Communication ("TC") seems to have become one of the most misunderstood, misinterpreted, and misapplied terms in contemporary usage.

TC, as a term, was first used by educator Roy Kay Holcomb in 1968. As an alternative to the inflexible oral/aural approach, TC quickly caught on. Although certainly popular in the U.S. and abroad, notably the Scandinavian countries and Australia, TC has proven a bit tricky to define. The Conference of Educational Administrators Serving the Deaf (CEASD)[1] defines TC as "a philosophy incorporating the appropriate aural, manual, and oral modes of communication in order to ensure effective communication with and among hearing-impaired persons." It "refers to the right of the deaf individual to have easy access to a wide spectrum of useful forms of communication. However, most people who use the term mean the method of communication used by deaf students that combines both speech and sign (or fingerspelling)."[2]

Combining modes is actually quite an old practice. Several of the earliest oralist teachers employed fingerspelling and some form of sign language to teach speech and writing. This was true even at the famed Braidwood Academy, which held the monopoly on education of the deaf in the English-speaking world for three generations.

At U.S. schools for the deaf, ASL was freely used both inside and outside of the classroom during the first 60 or so years. (This is the period we refer to as the "Golden Age.") The ascendance of oralism in the late 19th century brought a much more narrow, rigid outlook: pure-oralism. All forms of manual communication (including fingerspelling) were banished from the classroom. Signing—any form of signing—was prohibited. This policy remained in effect at virtually all schools for the deaf for several decades.

Edward Miner Gallaudet, the founder and first president of Gallaudet University, advocated the "combined approach"— ASL used in the classroom, but with optional classes in oral articulation for those who might benefit from them. Recognizing that the educational tide was turning against Sign, he saw the combined approach as a sensible compromise. In those days, speech training was *optional*. Previous experiments with articulation classes in signing schools had shown that very few (if any) congenitally deaf children derived any significant benefit from them.

TC is thus a throwback to an earlier outlook, a broader view that held that the acquisition of speech is not the be-all and end-all of deaf education, just one aspect of it. As a philosophy, TC was something of a breakthrough—a belated recognition that deaf children had the right of access to any form of communication that they felt comfortable with and would benefit from. Obviously, this should include ASL, but in practice, ASL is still extremely rare in the classroom. "Signing" in the classroom almost always means some form of MCE such as SEE-2.

Although TC is, strictly speaking, a philosophy and not a method of communication, it is commonly but inaccurately used to mean "Simultaneous Communication" (a.k.a. "Sim-Com"), a method of signing while talking. (Sounds easy, but it isn't—it often ends up as a badly tossed salad of spoken English and broken and skipped signs.) TC is *also* used to describe oral schools. We recall seeing a newspaper item about an oral school in Israel. A teacher was quoted as saying (more or less), "We believe in total communication. We train the children not to rely on sign language alone." (We therefore infer that sign language is discouraged there.) TC has become, it seems, a fashionable euphemism for "oral." Oh, sure, maybe by their definition of TC, they toss in a little signing, but the emphasis is undoubtedly on speech.

The label "Total Communication Program" is therefore no guarantee of quality. There is no universal standard. Parents should check out any TC program before enrolling their child. One British family's experience is instructive. Lorraine Fletcher, seeking a rich BSL-affirmative nursery-school environment for her deaf son, Ben, with Deaf adults providing good language models, and other deaf children for him to interact with, investigated two schools for the deaf. One was oral; the other committed to TC. But Fletcher found remarkably little difference between the two schools in what went on in the nursery level. While the older children at the TC school did "indeed have the benefit of a signing environment . . . the wealth of language observable [there was] nowhere in evidence [on the nursery level]." The emphasis was on spoken English. There were no deaf teachers or facilitators (aides). And there were few deaf children; most were hearing.[3]

The newest trend in deaf education, the "Bilingual-Bicultural" approach, is a more radical departure from traditional practice; it uses ASL in the classroom to teach English. It is closer to the original ASL-in-the-classroom mode first used in Hartford in 1817. TC should not be confused with the "Bi-Bi" approach. The two have different approaches and aims. And, politically speaking, they're at loggerheads. Some advocates of TC are fervently anti-Bi-Bi; they adamantly oppose using ASL in the classroom.

According to the TC philosophy, attention must be paid to the individual needs of each deaf child. This calls for top-quality teaching and flexible programs. A child who has a fair amount of residual hearing may be happiest in an oral/aural program, while one who is profoundly deaf may be happiest in an ASL-affirmative environment. This is the ideal. The reality, as we all know, is another matter entirely!

[1] Formerly called The Conference of Executives of American Schools for the Deaf.

[2] "Total Communication," **Gallaudet Encyclopedia of Deaf People and Deafness**, 3:173-175.

[3] Lorraine Fletcher, **Ben's Story: A Deaf Child's Right to Sign** (Washington, D.C.: Gallaudet University Press, 1987), pp. 140-143.

Chapter 20

I heard that ASL is the 3rd most used language in the U.S. If this is true, why don't all universities accept ASL as a foreign language?

We asked Dr. Sherman Wilcox , Chair of the Department of Linguistics, University of New Mexico, Albuquerque, an authority on ASL as a second/foreign language. He has some pertinent comments:

irst, I'm not sure that the figure, "third-most-used language," is correct. But, really, if it is not the third it is pretty high up there and the point is still correct. Why don't most universities accept it? I think because of very deep-seated misunderstandings about what ASL is, also, probably, some not very nice prejudices. My experience is that the belief that ASL can't be a foreign language is based on lack of knowledge of the facts about the language. People have some preconceptions, assumptions about ASL, and then they use good logical thinking to come to conclusions about whether ASL is a foreign language, but because they had faulty preconceptions their conclusions are wrong. So even though people will often say they realize ASL is a language, they don't really fully understand the truth of that statement. They just sort of mouth the words! So, typically, a university professor will say, "Well, it's not a language." Of course, that's not true. Then they will say, "Well, it's not foreign; it's used in this country." But of course, many languages are used only in this country and still are accepted as foreign languages. Here at my university, Navajo is accepted as a foreign language.

It's a very good question and so interesting because it really goes to the heart of people's understanding of what ASL is. It really brings out strong feelings. You know, I can predict now pretty accurately what hearing people will say in reaction to a proposal to accept ASL as a foreign language. First is the "It's not a language" argument, then "Well, it's not foreign." I joke sometimes that "foreign" is in the eye of the beholder. After all, to my American Indian friends here in New Mexico, we Anglo-English speakers are the foreigners. Then people will say, "There is no culture." Well, we can prove them wrong on that one pretty easily. Then they will say, "There is no written literature in ASL." This is a little tougher and I prefer to spend some time going into detail on it. I prefer to first answer: Yes, you are correct. There is no written literature in ASL, but there *could* be. ASL can be written. Writing systems have been designed for ASL but the community of ASL users hasn't accepted them yet, and maybe never will. But in principle, it is possible and really is no different from, again, my pet example, Navajo. Fifty years ago, people could not write Navajo. A man created a writing system. Now some Navajo people can read and write Navajo. Many cannot. Some think it is good; many think it is silly. Just like the Deaf community. And of course many Navajos are bilingual— Navajo and English. Same as Deaf people. So when we talk about literature it is important to recognize that for a bilingual community the literature can be in two languages. Then, after that, I think, is the time to bring up videotape, etc., as ways of sharing ASL literature.

Which states officially recognize ASL as a foreign language? It isn't easy to find up-to-date information, even on the Internet. Gallaudet University's "Info to Go" listing of states recognizing ASL as a foreign language was, at press time, most recently updated in March 1998.

As of that date, there were 30 such states: Alaska, California, Connecticut, Florida, Georgia, Illinois, Indiana, Iowa, Kansas, Kentucky, Louisiana, Maine, Maryland, Massachusetts, Michigan, Montana, New Jersey,

New York, Ohio, Oklahoma, Pennsylvania, Rhode Island, South Carolina, South Dakota, Tennessee, Texas, Utah, Virginia, Washington, and West Virginia. Each state's law is different. Some states (like Georgia) accept ASL "in limited circumstances;" others (like Ohio) grant more comprehensive recognition. Even in states that haven't granted official legislative recognition (or have no current proposals under consideration), ASL is accepted for academic credit in a good number of postsecondary programs, a limited number of high schools, and a few elementary schools. As Dr. Wilcox has noted, "the list grows daily!"

As he notes in his Website, "the type of acceptance can vary from school to school. Some institutions have formal policies accepting ASL in fulfillment of the undergraduate foreign-language requirement. Others accept ASL only within certain colleges, divisions, or departments. Still others [excluded here] may accept ASL on an *ad hoc* basis for certain majors."

In addition to numerous community colleges, some of the colleges and universities that accept ASL in fulfillment of foreign or second-language requirements are U. Alaska-Fairbanks, U. Arizona, ASU, U. Arkansas at Little Rock, Cabrillo, CSU (Fresno, Hayward, Monterey Bay, Northridge, Sacramento, San Marcos), Mt. San Antonio, Scripps, Stanford, UC-Berkeley (entrance, not exit, requirements), UC-San Diego, UC-Davis, USC, U. Colorado-Boulder, Yale, American, Catholic, Georgetown, Howard, U. Central Florida, U. Florida, U. North Florida, U. South Florida, U. Georgia (Athens), U. Hawaii (Manoa), C. Southern Idaho, William Rainey Harper, John A. Logan, MacMurray, U. Chicago, Butler, Indiana U., Purdue, U. Iowa, U. Kansas, U. Louisville, U. Maine (Machias), U. Maryland, Boston, Elms C., Holy Cross, MIT, Northeastern, U. Mass., Madonna, Michigan State, U. Michigan, C. St. Catherine, U. Minn., William Woods, UNH (Durham, Manchester), UNM, C. St. Rose, C. Staten Island, Medgar Evers C., NYU (School of Education only), Keuka, NTID, Russell Sage (Albany), SUNY (Brockport, Buffalo, Geneseo, Oswego), U. Rochester, Vassar, Gardner-Webb, UNC (Charlotte, Greensboro, Wilmington), Antioch, Kent State, Miami U. (Ohio), OSU, U. Akron, U. Cincinnati, Wright State, Youngstown State, Xavier (Cincinnati), East Central/Oklahoma State, Oklahoma Baptist, U. Oklahoma, Western Oregon, U. Pennsylvania, U. Pittsburgh, Neumann, Brown, Clemson, Maryville, Tennessee Temple, Abilene Christian, Stephen F. Austin, Baylor, Dallas Baptist, Lamar, Lubbock Christian, Howard Payne, San Antonio C., Southwest Texas State, Texas A&M-Commerce, Texas Tech, Texas Wesleyan, Texas Woman's U., Trinity U., Mary Hardin-Baylor, UNT (Denton), U. Texas (Austin, Pan American, San Antonio), U. Utah, Utah Valley State C., Brigham Young, George Mason, U. Virginia, Central Washington, Centralia, Eastern Washington, Evergreen, Pacific Lutheran, U. Washington, Washington State, West Virginia U. (School of Journalism), U. Wyoming. (This listing, by state, doesn't purport to be comprehensive.)

Chapter 21

"How do deaf people feel when a hearing person approaches them in public using sign language?"

My question is: How do deaf people feel when a hearing person approaches them in public using their language? Example: I'm in line at the store and I notice two deaf people busy in conversation. I've never met them before but I'd love to say hello and find out more about them. Almost always I never do for fear I'll come across sounding paternalistic: "Hi, I can help you, I can interpret for you," or bragging: "Hi, I know what you're saying and these poor hearing people don't."

I believe my motives are pure. I'm fascinated with your language, culture and history but really I don't know what to say, or **shouldn't** say in these situations.

Thank you.

—Alis Coates, Granada Hills, California

It's perfectly okay to be fascinated by Deaf culture and the way Deaf people communicate, and quite understandable to be intrigued by seeing them signing in public. But when it comes to a hearing stranger joining in their conversation with an offer to "interpret" or to "help," some Deaf people are going to resent it, and may react with embarrassment and annoyance. If Deaf people need help with interpreting, *they* will ask for it. Offers of help, however well-intentioned, are seen as patronizing, perpetuating an offensive stereotype of Deaf people as helpless and vulnerable.

To approach or not to approach? This question is widely discussed among Deaf people. Some like the idea; some do not.

Most Deaf people appreciate a hearing stranger's interest, especially if it shows a positive attitude towards sign language. We have seen older children who mimic and mock the signing of Deaf people because they think it's funny. While this attitude may be forgivable in children, it's inexcusable in adults. It's okay to be fascinated by signing while admitting one's ignorance of it. Those who have learned the basics (whether they have a deaf friend, relative, employee, boss, or co-worker, an interest in visual communication, or simply because they find it fun) and want to continue to improve their signing skills should be encouraged. We all have to start from scratch at some point in our lives.

Needless to say, the more skillful your signing (receptive and expressive), the better your chance of establishing a friendly conversation. Deaf people find it particularly annoying when hearing strangers come over, acting chummy, mangled fingerspelling and butchered signs flying off their hands.

As for letting Deaf people know that you enjoy their language, it's all common sense. Whether or not to greet them depends on the setting. For example, if the Deaf people are in line at a bank or store, it's best not to say anything, as they're preoccupied, busy, or in a hurry. If, however, you see signers waiting in a long supermarket-checkout line, at a bus stop, or sitting near you in the bus, it's okay to say "Hello, how are you?" as there are fewer distractions and more "captive time." Just remember not to control the conversation. Let them control it.

If you get rebuffed, don't take it personally. Take it in stride, as a negative learning experience. It happens to all of us.

Chance encounters between hearing and deaf persons may have profound repercussions for both parties. Time and time again, we have seen how young hearing people have met deaf peers at camp or church, or had deaf neighbors or a deaf classmate. Learning sign was part of the process of striking up a friendship. Occasionally, the hearing person continues his or her interest in sign language, even to the point of choosing a career as an interpreter or in a milieu where they have frequent and direct contact with Deaf people. It happens. More frequently, such encounters changes their attitudes towards deaf people for the better. They gain a measure of understanding of differences and diversity, of communication modes. And the deaf people likewise benefit from the interchange. They gain friends and allies.

Back in the old days, when deaf people's communicative options and mobility were limited, they depended heavily on their hearing relatives and neighbors for help. Some very proud Deaf people would go out of their way to avoid "bothering" their neighbors, even if it entailed additional inconvenience for them, and the neighbors were willing to help.

Nowadays, Deaf people tend to be better educated and more self-confident. They're more sophisticated, more responsible for themselves, and more independent. In everyday situations, they don't need help. They can manage quite nicely by using simple signs that hearing people can understand, or writing notes.

But sometimes, if the situation is serious—if there's a bad communicative breakdown—you should offer to help: "Can I help you?" Such an offer may be eagerly accepted: "Yes, please!" It's comparable to situations involving hearing people. If a hearing person is in distress, if there's a bad communicative breakdown, another person's offer of help is welcome. Same with Deaf people.

Chapter 22

"I understand it is bad manners to watch people Signing without their knowing that you also Sign. But is it bad manners to interrupt people who are Signing and telling them that you are taking courses in ASL even if you sign in English?"

I understand it is bad manners to watch people signing without their knowing that you also Sign. But there's always that tendency for a student to see if you can understand anything. Is it bad manners to interrupt such people and tell them that you are taking courses in ASL even if you sign in English?

I'm writing this in response to an article our ASL teacher gave us, reprinted from **DEAF LIFE**, "ASL: What is it?" [See Chapter 1.] And as it says, ASL is a beautiful and expressive language and a pleasure to learn and observe.

Thanks for your time and help.

—Roger Mindel, Wheaton, Maryland

or all practical purposes, there is no such thing as a "private" ASL conversation in public—that is, within eyeshot of other people. What two Deaf people are discussing is out in the open for everyone else to see. Signs can be read straight across a crowded room, a campus quad, or from a balcony or window several stories up! Signing conversationalists in a "Voice" environment rely on the non-comprehension of the surrounding hearing crowd to safeguard the confidentiality of their talk—that is, they assume that since nobody else will understand what they're talking about, they're "protected." Anyone who wants to have a private talk in an ASL environment (such as the Gallaudet campus) has to duck behind the shrubbery, use a jacket as a "sign-shield" (holding the jacket out with one hand, signing with the other), or adopt a smaller, discreetly formed, disguised style of signing that snoopers will find harder to read—the visual equivalent of a whisper. In some public signing environments, like a college cafeteria, club, lobby, or bus, it's fair game to watch others signing, and to join in.

It's *not* bad manners to enter a conversation, but it should never be an intrusion. It all depends on the situation and whom you're with. You have to ascertain the mood of the interchange—if it's casual and relaxed, chit-chat style, and you're reasonably certain the Deaf people will accept your presence, you can draw near, wait for a suitable opening, gesture/wave for attention (or use the gentle shoulder-pat approach), and sign, "Oh, you're Deaf? Ah, good! I know some sign language," or "Hello, I saw you signing. I'm taking an ASL class now," or the like. Be prepared to introduce yourself, fingerspell your name, and give your namesign.* The more skillful your signing is, the easier it will be for you.

Deaf people meeting each other for the first time often converse for 5 or 10 minutes, then exchange their names—usually fingerspelling it first, then giving the namesign, and possibly an explanatory comment about why they have that particular namesign—before they part. Be prepared for this. It's a normal part of ASL-based interaction. You, of course, can ask about their namesigns—if they have one, and if so, what significance it may have. This makes a good icebreaker, and shows that you are savvy about namesigns.

There's no real way to predict how others will react. Some will undoubtedly be warm, bemused. Others may give you the "freeze-out" treatment. Use your intuition and play it by eye. Pay careful attention to their expressions. If you get a sour response (scowls, frowns, cold stares, shrugs, or "Well, I-don't-know" grimaces), you should politely but assertively and quickly excuse yourself and exit, or simply back out of the interchange. If you're lucky enough to get a welcoming response, make the best of it. This is the best practice you can get—real life.

Let the others control the conversation. Listen and watch. You can make a learning game of it—see how much you understand, if you can keep up with the lightning pace of ASL interchanges—*if* they continue using ASL near you. As we've mentioned, Deaf people often politely "code-switch" to PSE to make it easier for the hearing participant or onlooker, so it isn't at all easy for hearing persons to drop by and watch an ASL interchange at close range, and to participate. Still, it can be a challenge to keep up with a PSE conversation. Be confident, be alert, be sensitive, learn, and have fun.

* A namesign is a personalized, distinctive sign, often but not invariably based on the first initial of a person's first or last name, and which is used to refer specifically to that person in social or formal conversations. A namesign is always bestowed by another Deaf person, and can be a humorous or affectionate way of commemorating a salient detail of a person's appearance, ethnic identity, habits, passions, or quirks. It can even be a bit of sign-play or a visual pun.

Some namesigns have colorful histories. For example, the namesign given to Dr. William C. Stokoe, a clawed 5-finger handshape touched to the right forehead, represents the cockade on a Scottish bonnet. Stokoe celebrated his Scottish heritage with great enthusiasm, going so far as to practice playing the bagpipes on the Gallaudet campus, and dressing up in full kit (kilt, sporran, bonnet, *etcetera*) on occasion.

A similarly affectionate namesign was given to Dr. Elisabeth A. Zinser in the aftermath of DPN: "E-on-the-heart."

Laurent Clerc's namesign depicted the scar that disfigured his right cheek. (When he was a year old, he fell from his high chair into a kitchen fireplace). Thomas Hopkins Gallaudet's namesign symbolized the spectacles he wore, with an initialized "G." This sign is also used for "Gallaudet University."

Deaf people devise and use namesigns for teachers, administrators, public figures, leaders, and presidents. These can be "nice" or "nasty," depending on the signer's feelings about them!

Chapter 23

I'm always getting asked where I learned sign language. Do all deaf people do that?

eaf people, meeting a hearing person who signs, will often ask, "Where did you learn sign language?" They have a keen curiosity about it. Maybe not all deaf people do it, but we'd wager that most deaf people who meet hearing persons who know Sign want to know where and how they learned it, and why. Do you have deaf parents? Deaf sisters or brothers? Deaf friends? Learned it in school? A community college? By tutoring? Naturally, they'll want to know who taught you—a Deaf teacher? A hearing one? What are their names? Your responses are of tremendous interest.

If you're being asked questions like these, you might feel initially uncomfortable. Or you can take it as a subtle compliment. Being "grilled" like this is not necessarily a sign that you're being scrutinized by suspicious Deaf people and failing to satisfy their expectations—although it *can* be that.

Some Deaf people are a bit skeptical when they meet a hearing person who signs beautifully. ASL is the language of Deaf people. It belongs to them, and they feel protective of it. Our experiences have taught us to be wary of certain hearing people who are skillful signers. Some of them think they're above deaf folks; they use their skill to gain cachet° in the Deaf community, and manipulate deaf people to satisfy their own craving for power. Their skill in ASL is a tool used to enlist the trust and respect of deaf people. Not all hearing people who are "native ASL-quality" have our best interests at heart.

A hearing person who signs beautifully is still something of a rarity. If you have Deaf parents or a Deaf sister or brother, those are the usual ways a hearing person gains native fluency in ASL. You're recognizable, familiar. But *if* you've learned ASL by taking classes in, say, a community-college setting, and achieved a high level of skill, a Deaf person will be impressed. Often such a hearing person will be welcomed into the Deaf community—if s/he has respect for Deaf people and their culture. Such hearing people will be able to fit right into the Deaf social arena. And they will, of course, understand why they're being questioned. It comes with the territory.

The situation is parallel to that of an American woman who visits France—not as the stereotypical tourist fumbling with a phrasebook and blurting out mangled and *mal à propos* French ("Ou est le bistro? Ou est le toilet?"), but someone who speaks French beautifully, who understands French culture, who knows just what (and what not) to say and do, and who can blend right into the native population. Imagine, if you're a Parisian, meeting such an American. You'd be delighted, no doubt. You would accord her a warm welcome. And you'd say, "Let's party!"

Deaf people will want to know the name of your teacher for several good reasons. Curiosity is the obvious one. But they may also wish to help you. Local Deaf communities often maintain a lively grapevine, in which the merits and demerits of various sign-language and ITP teachers are enthusiastically discussed and compared. Members of the local Deaf community often know which teachers are considered good and which ones aren't.

So when you encounter a Deaf person and tell her that you're taking an Intermediate Sign Language class at Celestia Community College, and that Jan Jones is your instructor, you'll most likely get an immediate response: "Oh, *good!*" (with the appropriate facial grammar and sign registering pleasure and affirmation) or "Oooh, *bad!*" (with the expression registering dismay, a recoiling of the body, and the sign for "awful" or "I-don't-like that." Deaf people like to warn hearing students about bad teachers and to encourage them to take classes taught by good ones. (What constitutes a bad teacher? One whom they know possesses inferior qualifications, and/or has a bad attitude. Politics may also be involved. The Deaf person you're talking with may possibly have a personal grudge against the teacher—so be forewarned.)

Another important reason you'll be asked is to ascertain if the teacher is certified. The American Sign Language Teachers Association (ASLTA) is the national certifying body for ASL teachers in schools, colleges, and universities. ASLTA certification is considered to be a good criterion of a teacher's skill. Those who hold the highest level of certification are considered the best, the tops in their field. ASLTA requires all participating teachers to be periodically re-evaluated to maintain current certification. They are compelled to keep their signing skills sharp, or they lose certification.

Not all skilled ASL teachers are members of ASLTA (and this is a problem), nor is certification compulsory for all ASL teachers (another problem), but possession of ASLTA certification is a reasonably reliable indicator of a teacher's effectiveness. If your teacher holds certification from ASLTA, you know what you're getting.

You don't want to take a college-level sign-language class taught by a relatively unskilled, uncertified, scantily qualified teacher who has only recently finished a few sign-language classes; you want a seasoned veteran with native or near-native fluency and a good attitude. That's why Deaf people ask. In most cases, they're in a good position to know what's what and who's who. And they'll be happy to share their knowledge with you.

cachet: a mark of distinction, individuality, or authenticity.

Chapter 24

In my pamphlets and textbooks, Deaf people are portrayed as being delighted when "the Hearing" learn Signing. But I get the impression from other sources that Deaf people resent hearing people doing that. What's the real situation?

t depends on what your motivation is in learning how to sign, your attitude, the context, who's teaching you, who's learning with you, and whom you're mingling with. Some Deaf people consider themselves guardians of Deaf culture, an embattled way of life, and are fiercely protective of ASL. They seek to "preserve the purity" of the language, which has been becoming increasingly "polluted" by "foreign" intrusions such as MCE.[1]

ASL is a living language, and like any other living language, it is subject to change. It is constantly evolving. (Remember how incensed some conservative French citizens were by the incursion of Americanisms like *le weekend, le drugstore, le caddy, le hot dog,* and *les blue jeans*?) ASL, too, is constantly picking up and trying on "foreign loan words." Fad signs appear, blaze briefly, and die out. New signs are constantly being devised to keep pace with technology and the news. All go through a sifting process—the useful ones are retained, obsolete ones dropped.

There is, however, a difference between influences "naturally" picked up and shared among Deaf peers, and artificial constructions—*to be* forms, initialized signs like *doctor* with a *d*, and notorious suffixes like *-ness* and the participle *-ing*—

which are imposed from without, namely by hearing (and some deaf) educators. Many Deaf people (by no means extremists) feel that such intrusions degrade the beauty of ASL. Keep in mind that ASL is the one thing Deaf people here can truly call their own. It is the precious inheritance of the Deaf community, passed from parent to child, or more commonly, child to child. It has survived the efforts of "well-meaning" oralists to wipe it out. Its users have experienced the terrible humiliation of being robbed of their language. Many older Deaf people recall how they were forbidden to sign in class or public, punished for being caught signing, forced to sign on the sly. In some schools for the deaf, signing is still officially banned. At such schools, deaf children are, to some extent, compelled to keep their signing secret. But most of us can sign freely and openly, and creatively speaking, we've been making the most of it. Now that we are experiencing a great flowering of ASL artistry—theater, poetry, sign mime, storytelling, religious signing—there is an understandable fear that "the Hearing" are going to try to take it over and wrest it from its rightful possessors.

Deaf citizens rightfully resent hearing people's learning ASL so they can take over agencies serving Deaf people—in other words, take Deaf people's jobs away while increasing their own power in the Deaf community. We feel that there is no shortage of qualified Deaf candidates for such jobs, and that since hearing people have an unlimited choice of jobs elsewhere, our preference is for Deaf people themselves to coordinate the agencies that serve their own community. That's hardly a snobbish or chauvinistic attitude. Deaf people, after all, are still barred from many positions. Learning someone else's native language to enhance one's own personal power and make money from their community is a form of exploitation we're all familiar with.

There is nothing intrinsically immoral about a hearing person's learning ASL to fulfill a foreign-language requirement or so s/he can better communicate with Deaf friends, co-workers, etc. It can be a wonderful thing. But Deaf people rightfully resent the attitude 'I'm going to become fluent in Sign so I can *help* the Deaf, *interpret* for them, *save* them.' Some interpreters *are* good; some are *bad*. Some respect Deaf people; others enjoy having power over them. Look at it this way: to some Deaf people, an interpreter is a hearing person who earns money off Deaf people's language.[2] Who earns more— interpreters or the Deaf people who teach them ASL? (Clue: An interpreter can earn as much as $50 an hour; an ASL teacher, as little as $3 an hour. And who enjoys the proceeds of ASL books published by mainstream publishers? Hearing or Deaf?)

Many feel that ASL belongs to Deaf people, period. And you can't blame them for that. Do *not* be discouraged. Proceed wisely.

[1] According to Robert F. Panara, the distinguished deaf professor, scholar, and author, the "Combined Method" (classroom signing) has long included ASL and MCE. He told us, "Signed English was the mainstay method at Gallaudet and Schools for the Deaf all during the years 1880 to today in the attempt to combat and counteract Oralism." So Gallaudet College alumni had a distinctive "Englishy" style of signing. This style is lampooned in the Bragg-Bergman play **Tales from a Clubroom**. Gallaudet University alumni still have a distinctive style of signing nowadays—but it's *very* ASL.

[2] See Chapter 91 for a discussion of this issue.

Chapter 25

Why do so many Deaf people have trouble with English?

ecause English is primarily a spoken language. All hearing children of English-speaking parents absorb it unconsciously, starting from the moment they're born. They're surrounded with English; bombarded with it from all sides! They listen; they imitate. Effortlessly, it seems, they begin to put together grammatically correct sentences well before they learn to read. Children who are born deaf (or deafened in infancy) are excluded from this process. Since they cannot hear this "language bombardment," they cannot benefit from it. The lucky ones whose parents are fluent in ASL start school already knowing a language. Those whose parents cannot (and will not) sign are often forced to start school without any real language at all. This can have disastrous effects on their educational development. As Deaf educator Sam Supalla has pointed out, you can't learn a language in the classroom unless you already know a language.

Moreover, ASL is grammatically disparate from English. The two couldn't be more different. English is an eclectic Indo-European language, a rich hybrid of Anglo-Saxon syntax, Old French, Old German, a generous measure of Greek/ Latin vocabulary that retains a wealth of grammatical quirks and irregularities. ASL is not a simple string of word-pictures in the air, it's a visual/gestural language—a *very* different approach to communication from a spoken one. For example, ASL has plural forms, but *not* in a recognizably "English" sense. As Harlan Lane notes, "Body shift, sign reduplication, sign trajectory, using more fingers, and using more hands are all devices to indicate various kinds of plurals." ASL does not convey plurals with word endings, nor ongoing activities with participles, nor has it any use for other features that make good English *good English.*

The pathway of the history of deaf education is littered with discarded theories, approaches, methods, techniques, and language-development aids, most of them devised by oralist teachers. These include the Zenas F. Westervelt's "Rochester Method" (1878), which involved rapid-fire fingerspelling while speaking, George Wing's symbols (1883), and Katherine Barry's "Five Slate System" (1899). Edith Fitzgerald's "Fitzgerald Key" (1929) for teaching the rules governing written English by breaking down sentences into categories is still used is at least some schools. But how effective has it been? That's a question worth asking.

Various forms of MCE (SEE-1, SEE-2, etc.) are commonly used in the classroom to teach English. But they have not *really* succeeded in solving the Deaf-literacy problem. They presuppose a working knowledge of English grammar that many deaf children lack. A native ASL user often ends up writing English as though it conformed to the logic that governs ASL. The result: a barely literate pidgin.*

The writing of Deaf adults often reads as though it were written by a foreigner who came late to English. Experienced teachers can easily discern patterns: the persistent misuse of participles and infinitives, mis-pluralization, subject/verb, adjective/adverb, noun/adjective confusion, mix-up of active and passive voices, malapropisms, and so forth. We call this "Deaf English." It is not the writing of ignorant, unlanguaged persons, it's the writing of persons whose first language is ASL.

A few determined born-deaf persons acquire fluency not only in ASL but also written English. It takes years of agonizing work. It's possible. But rare. Most Deaf people have such a wretched experience with English that by the time they graduate from school with "minimal language skills," they're glad to have done with it. And that's the level of skill they maintain for the rest of their lives. It has nothing to do with intelligence. English is not their first language. ASL is. This is the crux of the ongoing English 50 controversy at Gallaudet University: should the English-proficiency requirements be eased, or should Deaf students be forced to struggle with a language that is not theirs?

Endless difficulty with English has certainly affected the quality of Deaf people's lives—not only their ability to enjoy reading, but their careers, their mobility, their access to information, and their relations with the hearing world. This is *not* a new predicament. It started several generations ago. It still starts with the family. The blame lies with parents who do too little to bring language to their deaf children at the earliest opportunity, a society that equates communication and language with speech, and an educational system that devotes far too much time to oral/aural training while prohibiting ASL in the classroom, while not devoting enough time to *really* teaching English to deaf students. And the Deaf community should share the blame for not having fought harder to prevent this from happening.

Instead of asking *only* why so many Deaf people can't read and write English, we should also be asking why so many hearing people, especially teachers and parents of deaf children, know nothing about ASL.

▲ ▲ ▲

Winning the invisible war

What can be done about the "Deaf literacy problem?" Plenty. One major cause is that many deaf children start school with language delays. They have been, in effect, excluded from environmental language bombardment that surrounds hearing children, who've been picking up English effortlessly. If their deafness goes undetected for a couple of years, this creates a debilitating language gap. This is the highly touted advantage of newborn-infant-hearing screening: if a newborn is deaf, and if the neonatal unit has a universal hearing-screening program, the parents are informed right away.

Supposing the baby is born hearing but becomes deaf as a toddler? Parents who suspect that their toddler has a significant hearing loss should take swift action: have the baby tested immediately. They shouldn't rationalize, postpone, or assuage their fears. What they do—or don't bother to do—can have lifelong repercussions for their child.

As far as preventing the "language gap" goes, the best remedy is action. Get language to the child immediately, provide a language-enriched environment at home, and foster early reading and writing skills *before* the child starts school. Gallaudet University's Outreach Program offers valuable materials for parents to teach them how to read to their deaf children.

Another big problem is that most schools (and that includes public schools just as much as schools for the deaf) simply don't devote enough time to teaching deaf kids reading and writing skills. The best way to acquire literacy is through exposure and practice. This means more reading and writing—in school and outside of it. More classroom time needs to be devoted to these skills than is presently done in many schools.

Parents need to get involved in their children's education. Monitor their progress, visit the school, talk with the teachers and administrators. Many parents, dissatisfied with the quality of schooling their children were getting, have pulled their children out and transferred them to another school or program. Some have even moved to another city—or state—to be near a school with a high reputation. Parents of deaf children should have high expectations and should demand the best possible education for them. This necessitates research, reading up, networking, and visiting and investigating schools, but it could mean the difference between a good education and an inadequate one.

Computers can be useful tools in promoting good literacy skills, but it's easy for deaf students to become computer-literate without being particularly English-literate. Teachers can utilize media such as journal-keeping, chatrooms, BBS, TTYs, videos (i.e., seeing them and then writing reviews), and E-mail to give students useful practice in written-English skills.

And, for deaf adults who want to improve their written-English skills, there is hope: Adult Basic Education/ESOL classes specifically for them, one-on-one literacy tutoring, distance learning, and instructional CD-ROMs.

One approach to enhancing reading skills that costs practically nothing is to utilize the public library: to start with good children's books (which are written simply and clearly, but present good English models, and are, above all, fun to read) and work up towards more complex writing. Many public libraries have an Adult Literacy/ESOL section containing grammar and style textbooks, workbooks (which can be photocopied by the borrower), vocabulary-building guides, and easy-access literary works such as short stories and simplified, illustrated summaries of classic novels. Reading for comprehension can be done with an enjoyable text such as **People Weekly**, jotting down unfamiliar words and idioms, and then looking them up. Everyone should have a good dictionary (whether secondhand or new), and keep it within easy reach. It's a worthwhile investment. The more it's used, the more valuable it becomes.

We believe that Deaf people who wish to improve their literacy skills can. Education shouldn't stop with the acquisition of a diploma; it should be a lifelong, ongoing process—an adventure.

* It *is* possible to teach English through ASL—the "Bilingual-Bicultural" approach. See Chapter 12.

Chapter 26

Why don't some
Deaf people like to read?

few reasons:

(1)—ASL is the native language of many Deaf citizens here, and has no traditional written form.

(2)—It was long considered more important for deaf children to acquire good speech articulation than good reading and writing skills. So speech was given prime emphasis above literacy. More time was spent on articulation than education. The results? A community with extensive oral training that they had little occasion to use, and a distressingly low level of literacy.

(3)—The attitude of the educational establishment: contempt for/ignorance of ASL, low expectations for deaf students, and a "brutalist" approach to beating the essentials of English grammar into their heads. In other words, teaching that doesn't teach.

(4)—Language deprivation during their earliest years, typical of hearing families that are already committed to oralism, or may simply be ignorant about the benefits of signing to their children. But even Deaf families who provide immediate access to language may not provide early exposure to books, if reading isn't important to them.

(5)—Not enough emphasis on reading and writing in school.

The two most common misperceptions about Deaf people and reading are actually two sides of the same coin:

(1) **The Silent Bookworm:** Some hearing people have the misconception that all deaf people instinctively adore books because the avenue of sound is closed to them. Deprived of music, the radio, conversation, don't they *love* to read? In their frequent isolation, don't books become their only friends?

(2) **The Illiterate Dork:** The other side of the stereotype is equally pernicious: some deaf people can't read because they're not as intelligent as hearing people, period. They lack mental stimulation; they can't think abstractly.

The facts: Both of these perceptions are romantic nonsense. Deaf people are social creatures who enjoy a variety of experiences—yes, even going to discos. If books play little or no part in Deaf people's lives, there must be a reason. It is *not* lack of intelligence or some deficiency in the ability to handle abstract concepts. There are a number of Deaf people who are fluent in ASL, yet enjoy reading. If English has been taught to them in a positive way (especially if they get hooked on books early), they can appreciate English literature as much as any native English-speaker. Literacy skills are not a true gauge of intelligence. Some very intelligent Deaf people complain that they seem to have a "language block" when it comes to reading and writing English.

A few emphatic points we'd like to make:

(1) Oralists commonly blame ASL for Deaf people's poor reading and writing skills. We believe that the blame lies elsewhere. True, the syntax of ASL is quite different from that of English, and ASL conveys no information about the pronunciation of words. But it is a language—a full-fledged, useful means of communication.

(2) This is an old complaint against various oral-based approaches. Our belief is that a deaf child needs a good basis in language—visual language—first, and once this is established, s/he can progress to written and spoken English.

(3) We believe that any teacher working with deaf students should have a thorough background in sign language, an understanding of how deaf children perceive the world, communicate, and interact. Teachers should understand their students' cognitive and communication skills, their minds and hearts, before attempting to educate them in English.

(4) It has been estimated that deaf students in residential schools spend perhaps 3% of their class-time on learning

English (grammar, style, vocabulary, and composition). That is far too little time for such a crucial subject!

Our quarrel is not with the English language as such, but the way it has been (and still is being) taught. No matter how beguiling or potentially enriching the subject, a bad teacher can turn the students permanently against it in no time at all. We all know this. Teachers whose underlying message is that deaf kids *can't* are the prime culprits. Boring, outmoded, and irrelevant material, hateful classroom experiences, and the suppression of the child's native language are not limited to deaf schools, but the consequences are just as destructive. The kids get lost very soon.

In the previous chapter, we noted that literacy (or illiteracy) training begins in the family, well before children start school. Many deaf children have started school without any functional language. They come from a "language-impoverished environment." The common-sense approach would be to give them an immediate grounding in a visual language, then use that language to teach English as a second language. English is *not* a visual language; it's primarily an aural one. But what if ASL is not used or recognized by the teachers? Suppose only a signed form of English—not ASL—is acceptable usage in class?

Deaf students cannot be expected to appreciate "the beauty of the English language" if it's been battered forcibly into their heads. The traditional deaf-ed approach was to drill them, drill them, drill them in English grammar. Parse sentences, list the parts of speech, make charts, construct diagrams. *Huh? What is this stuff about, anyway?* Could the kids appreciate something they've never understood—much less enjoyed? If they never get beyond "bad, mad, pad, and dad" or drills in sentence diagrams, they won't stick around to luxuriate in the delights of Jane Austen or Shakespeare. Why bother?

What about taking a few minutes to browse through the books in the library? Wouldn't that tempt them? For a bright hearing child, a library is a repository of knowledge, a treasure-house, a portal to the world of the imagination, a quiet place to read, to browse, to daydream, a pleasant interlude in a noisy, stressful day. For generations of deaf children, however, the library was where you got sent as a punishment for misbehaving. Small wonder that many Deaf adults have bad memories (if they remember at all!) of what went on inside their classrooms, and feel absolute indifference to anything that smacks of libraries and literature—tools of the oppression they were subjected to.

And then there's the ordeal of speech therapy and speech training. Is speech a gift? The birthright of all deaf children? Many deaf children who endured the endless hours of training would have been pleased to decline such a gift. Endless hours spent on auditory training, listening skills, and speech—and their articulation was still poor. Alas, they were still deaf. And what's more, they wanted to be deaf!

In earlier times (i.e., the ancient days of the Kennedy Administration), it was not that uncommon for therapists to strike young deaf children. Because they were misbehaving? No, because they mispronounced a word when they repeated it. A word they couldn't even hear.[1] This was a nasty throwback to the old oralists' methods of physically abusing deaf pupils to "aid their comprehension."

Let us not forget that it was the oralists who brought the obnoxious concept of "oral failures" into the deaf-ed vocabulary. After oralism had become firmly entrenched as the prime method of instruction in schools for the deaf, all new students were routinely started in oral classes. No signing was allowed. If they made progress, they were kept in the oral department. If they didn't thrive, they were finally transferred to the manual department. Oral and manual students were kept rigorously segregated at all times, lest the oral students' progress be compromised by interaction with signing students. Oral students were not supposed to "fall back on" signing. The schools didn't want their "oral successes" contaminated by their "oral failures." This repressive system had tremendously negative repercussions on the students' literacy skills—to say nothing of their self-esteem. Even in these supposedly enlightened times, the legacy of the oralists is still felt in many schools for the deaf. As we've mentioned, there are numerous approaches to teaching English to deaf students, but few of them embrace ASL.

One Deaf man who has difficulty reading and—even more so—expressing himself cogently in written English, and will undoubtedly have that problem for the rest of his life, attributes his distaste for reading and writing English to his classroom experiences:

> I hated what went on in my classes. There was too much oralism. The teachers were hearing. I felt they looked down on us. Always criticizing our writing—'wrong this, wrong that.'
>
> Imagine a class of 30 black kids with a white man teaching them. The kids normally use Black English. The teacher instructs them in correct standard English. Do they bother listening? Even if this white teacher is married to a black woman, it doesn't matter. It doesn't make him black. White teacher, white attitudes. Put a black teacher up there teaching those same kids correct English—that would be different.
>
> Same thing with deaf kids. If we had a deaf teacher who understood what it means to be Deaf, how a deaf person thinks, it would have been different. A deaf teacher would understand our heads. Such a teacher could use ASL to teach English—ask us to describe something or tell a story in sign, accept our signing, give us positive feedback, then explain the rules, teaching us how to improve our writing. Constant interchange. That'd be good.
>
> Having a black wife doesn't make a white man Black. Learning how to sign doesn't make a hearing person culturally Deaf. (That is, unless they are *very*, *very* convincing—e.g., if their parents were deaf.) My teachers looked down on the deaf. Even if they signed, they looked down on us; they had a Hearing attitude. No, it's not a matter of patience—the imaginary white teacher could be very patient with the black kids. Still wouldn't reach them. Patience isn't the factor. Attitude is.[2]

We'd like to emphasize that this view, although it represents one deaf man's opinion, is necessarily simplistic. Not all deaf teachers make good English teachers! We know of another deaf man who majored in English at CSUN, which has a good academic reputation, and taught briefly at Gallaudet University—and who proved to be a notably incompetent English teacher. Sure, he's Deaf—but he just didn't have the right quality. And vice versa. Quite a few hearing persons (who had deaf parents and shared the "Deaf experience") have been outstanding English teachers.

Perhaps attitudes are changing, but considerable damage has already been done. First deaf children have language withheld from them by parents who have been told not to sign. Then they're denied access to their own language in the classroom. They are often under the sway of teachers and administrators who don't know ASL and have contempt for it. English (oral, written, and signed) is used as a tool of oppression. The library is turned into a place of punishment. They are schooled in low expectations. And then they're criticized for doing badly in English and hating to read! Grown, they are penalized by Hearing society for being illiterate.

We'd like to re-emphasize another point: many alumni of oral schools and mainstreamed public schools share the same English-literacy problems and frustrations as alumni of schools for the deaf.

The average literacy skills of deaf adults, according to that oft-cited and endlessly repeated pseudo-statistic, generally remain at a third- to fifth-grade level. Small wonder that among many grassroots Deaf, English is relegated to a second-class, crudely utilitarian mode of everyday communication—TTY conversations, occasional notes and letters. Used, but not cherished.

Deaf people do like magazines, particularly those with lots of pictures. **People** and **Us** are very popular; they're heavily illustrated and the stories are brief. Newsmagazines may be scanned for the pictures, but not read. Too inaccessible. Some deaf people enjoy **National Geographic**, if only to browse through its glorious full-color photo-essays. Some read news-papers, for the sports coverage. Many deaf viewers watch but don't understand TV captioning—it's a barrage of incompre-hensible advanced (and occasional phonetically mangled) English whizzing by. Whether to offer simplified or verbatim captions is a touchy issue![3]

We personally know one deaf guy who bought a new set of **Encyclopaedia Britannica** that he proudly displayed in his living room—and never opened. That's equivalent to hearing people displaying attractively-bound foreign-language clas-sics on their bookshelves, to impress the visitors. This man also belonged to a sci-fi book club and read the selections, but didn't really understand what he was reading. And his written English was, well, typical. Most deaf people are more honest about their distaste for reading and writing English. And you really can't blame them for feeling that way. They've suffered plenty. Some of them don't care if they have been deprived of the enrichment and pleasure afforded by plays, poetry, short stories, memoirs, letters, classic fiction, or high-quality nonfiction; it's just something that's irrelevant to their adult lives.

But . . . if good English skills are an important communica-tion tool in the workplace, and if deaf adults are serious about wanting to improve their skills, this *is* a subject that can indeed be mastered. We don't believe in impossibilities. Even with English.

---

[1] On brutal speech therapists: The source for this statement is my own personal experience (MSM). In all fairness, it should be noted that modern speech therapists are a better-educated, savvier, more sensitive breed than the previous generations. They are trained to treat young deaf children with respect. Anyone caught punishing children by subjecting them to physical abuse would most likely lose her/his job in short order, and be prosecuted.

[2] A free adaptation of an informal interview in Sign.

[3] See next chapter.

Chapter 27

Doesn't closed-captioning help deaf people improve their English?

here's no denying that closed-captioning is wonderful. However, we need to ask just how much deaf people are getting from it—certainly a pertinent consideration.

Some deaf people prefer interpreters on TV. A few programs, notably Christian and Catholic-oriented ones, feature them in fairly unobtrusive oval "inserts" in the lower right-hand corner of the screen. There are definite advantages to this. Captioning is best appreciated by those with a reasonable degree of fluency in written English—a fluency many Deaf viewers simply do not have. They feel more comfortable with ASL than written English. In rendering audio to written text, captioning functions like a newspaper article being unscrolled—flat words, with no particular emphasis. In contrast, a TV interpreter's signs, facial inflections, and rhythm can convey a much clearer visual sense of what's being said.

There is a basic disagreement within the captioning industry itself: whether to display captions that are a *simplified* translation of the audio-script, or captions that are a *verbatim* (word-for-word) transcript. Advocates of verbatim captioning feel that it's unethical and insulting to alter the wording; deaf and hard-of-hearing viewers deserve to read exactly what's being spoken, no more, no less. Advocates of simplified captioning argue that many deaf viewers cannot comprehend some of the vocabulary on TV. By simplifying the text, they're making it accessible *and* keeping up with the rapid-fire pace of the dialogue. The argument isn't likely to be resolved, at least soon. (At this point, verbatim captioning seems to be more widespread.)

Closed-captioning has the potential to increase English skills among deaf viewers, but there's no hard-and-fast evidence that it's happening yet. From our own experience, we've seen Deaf viewers with typical reading skills watching ABC's captioned *World News Tonight*; when asked about what they've just seen, they say they don't fully understand what's going on. So it's safe to say that at least some of the captioning is simply incomprehensible to many deaf people. There is, moreover, the troublesome fact that some real-time captioning, about 10%-15% by our estimate, reads as a meaningless phonetic "garblemush"—"deny airings" for "teenagers," for example. (It happens every night.)

Glasnost, perestroika, "rapprochement," "trade embargo," "sanctions," "aggressiveness," "pessimistic," "impasse," "conservative," "liberal," "middle-of-the-road," "recession," "covert operation," "ethnic unrest," "money-laundering scheme," "qualitatively speaking," "clear the decks," "pre-emptive strike," "dispatched an emissary," "limited endorsement," "stealth candidate," "sting operation," "drug czar," "skullduggery," "miscarriage of justice." Such foreign loanwords, "ordinary" words, phrases, idioms, and occasional slang in common currency on the nightly news, are all outside the normal Deaf usage. To see is not *necessarily* to understand.

▲ ▲ ▲

A captioning mini-primer

The history of captioning audiovisual media (television, movies, live events, notetaking, videocassettes, CD-ROMs, DVDs, and Internet multimedia programs) is intermeshed with the boom in technology and the emergence of the Deaf community as a political force.

A detailed discussion of this history of captioning is beyond the scope of this book. It's a subject in itself. Here are a few highlights.

In 1972, the Caption Center at WGBH, Boston's PBS affiliate, began rebroadcasting Julia Child's much-loved series, *The French Chef*, with open captions several times weekly, implementing a socio-technological revolution. This was followed by the late-night *Captioned ABC News* in 1973. Deaf viewers were delighted, but TV executives were less enthusiastic. In fact, they were unwilling to allow their programs to be open-captioned, arguing that the captions would prove distracting and annoying to hearing viewers.

In 1974, the Federal Communications Commission agreed to reserve a previously unused broadcast bandwidth, Line 21 of the vertical blanking signal, for closed captions. While open captions are visible to all viewers, closed captions are visible only on televisions with a decoder box or microchip. In 1979, the National Captioning Institute was formed as a nonprofit organization to provide closed-captioning to the industry and to market TeleCaption decoders.

There are two kinds of captioning: real-time (live) and offline (pre-recorded). Real-time captioning has numerous applications, including computer-assisted notetaking (CART) and live presentations at conferences. It uses a combination of computer technology and skilled stenocaptioners. Offline captioning is used for movies and DVDs. Real-time captions are "roll-up;" offline captions are "pop-on."

Since October 1993, built-in decoder circuitry has been mandatory for virtually all new television sets. Meanwhile, the captioning industry has experienced phenomenal growth.

The Telecommunications Act of 1996 has profound implications for captioning consumers.

Nowadays, deaf consumers have an impressive array of choices. In some cities, deaf viewers can now enjoy a weekly open-captioned movie at a cinemaplex. Many DVDs are available with closed-captioning. We're concerned about captioning (or the lack of it) in multimedia computer programs and games, however. We've seen tremendous progress . . . but we still need to be vigilant.

Chapter 28

What do deaf people think of all this controversy about methodologies and literacy and all this criticism of deaf schools? If the old schools for the deaf were doing something right, what was it?

iteracy is the cornerstone of an education. As we've already noted, back in the old days, long before the terms "Manually Coded English" or "Sign-Supported Speech" or "Contact Sign Language" or "Pidgin Sign English" were coined, many people received their early education at home. This had certain advantages. Your teachers were your parents (usually Mother) or older siblings; you had a one-to-one relationship with them, got plenty of attention, and went at your own pace. Your library consisted of a couple of prized classics: the Bible and, possibly, Gibbon's **Decline and Fall of the Roman Empire**.

If you were a deaf child in a hearing family, that, of course, complicated matters. If your family could afford to hire a private tutor, you might make some progress in learning to read, write, and cipher (do basic arithmetic). Since there was no system of accreditation, your tutor might, or might not be, good.

When the Hartford Asylum opened in 1817, deaf children and adults finally had access to a real education. It is instructive to study how those early classes were conducted.

Since the Hartford Asylum was originally a Congregationalist institution, the school day began with a religious service. The students had breakfast at 7 and studied until 9. Thomas

Hopkins Gallaudet and Laurent Clerc, the original faculty, conducted all classes, and used sign language, fingerspelling, and written English. Lessons were written with chalk on large slateboards placed on easels. From noon to 2, the students cleaned up and had midday dinner (lunch). From 2 to 3, they had instruction in writing. Handwriting was considered an art (as it should be). The tools were simple but required skillful handling: quill pens that had to be trimmed just so, dipped frequently, and controlled carefully, else they created messy blotches; India ink in bottles; paper; and blotters. From 3 to 6, there were more classes, then a light snack, and a walk or visit until 9, when all assembled for the evening service, and after that, retired.

What *kind* of sign language was used in those classes? We know that Clerc used a form of French sign language (Signed French, French signs, or LSF with methodical signs added), but the students adapted it to their own preferences; they had their own form of signing, influenced by the Martha's Vineyard dialect. They took Clerc's signs, borrowed a good number of them, rejected some (especially the methodical prefixes and suffixes), and changed others. Clerc was dismayed, but the students insisted on using the signs that pleased them. Linguistically, they were an innovative group.

What is noteworthy about this routine is its simplicity and emphasis on the tough stuff—reading and writing. The students got lots of practice. The earliest admission rules required students to be already literate. A number of them undoubtedly weren't. They were, however, highly motivated. Some of them were adults—the Fowler sisters, Sophia (age 19) and Parnel (age 28), and the folk artist John Brewster (age 51). We assume that all of them, whatever their backgrounds, were hungry for an education. (Imagine an adult student sitting in the midst of a bunch of first-graders! Inconceivable now, but not then.)

Also noteworthy: there was no speech training. No audiologists, no speech therapy, no FM systems.

Consider what else these students didn't have: no audio-visual equipment, no filmstrips, no slideshows, no videos, no movies, no TV, no Channel One, no art or social-studies classes, no computers, no calculators, not even an electric pencil-sharpener. No intramural athletics, no team sports, no skateboards or Rollerblades. No clubs, no cliques. We tend to see that as a life of deprivation. It is, however, possible to see it as a life without distractions. Without the innumerable technological diversions we take for granted today, the students were free to focus on acquiring a solid education. A good number of them became teachers of the deaf them-selves—the most honorable career a deaf person could pur-sue. Clerc and his colleagues educated several generations of deaf students who became highly literate adults, until the oralist "takeover" began later in the century.

We feel that criticism that schools for the deaf are not giving students enough training in literacy has some validity. All of us know deaf adults who graduated from these schools and from NTID, CSUN, and Gallaudet, and who have substandard literacy skills. Is ASL to blame? We don't think so. Even alumni of rigorously oral and mainstreamed programs in which sign-ing is banned or simply ignored have literacy problems.

Is there a magic key? Not really. If you look at the early schools for the deaf, you'll see that they were demanding. Hours were long, breaks few. Were they tedious? We know that with good teachers, time flies. A good teacher engages the attention of the students, knows how to keep them lively, is alert for signs of fatigue. What we know about those early teachers of the American deaf is that they were pioneers. And they were unhampered by ideological quibbles, pedagogical debates, and linguistic hairsplitting. They didn't worry about manual codes. They *taught*, making themselves understand-able to their students, using the simplest, most basic equip-ment, and their knowledge, experience, empathy, and drive. Was this the original Bilingual-Bicultural approach? Maybe—but the label is ours, not theirs.

Is it possible to go back in time? No. There has been a revival of interest in home schooling, but most parents don't want to take on that responsibility. Nor is it possible to reinstate the ambiance of the earliest schools. We are, after all, creatures of our times. What schools can do is to emphasize literacy as a primary goal—and to act on it.

▲ ▲ ▲

The charter-school option

Schools for the deaf are no longer viewed, at least in a political sense, as the "least restrictive environment" for most deaf children. Mainstreaming has made tremendous incursions into the Deaf community. More and more deaf children are being mainstreamed in local public schools. How well has this served the educational and social needs of deaf children? The experience of deaf students in mainstreamed public schools has been decidedly mixed. Much depends on the individual school: whether it has a well-designed program, or simply shunts the deaf kids into regular classes with an interpreter, whether the teachers entrusted with the responsibility for the deaf students have any real training in deaf education (and most don't), whether the school has a real commitment to providing accessible, high-quality education to its deaf students or is simply fulfilling a political-legal mandate.

Mainstreaming and oral-aural day programs have hit the deaf schools hard. Since the first edition of this book was published in Fall 1992, several deaf schools have closed, and several more are threatened with closure. Critics of deaf schools condemn them for providing a substandard education to the students they supposedly serve, consider them obsolete, and write them off as "relics."*

A welcome alternative to the traditional deaf schools, mainstreaming, and oral day programs is the charter school. A charter school is a private school incorporated and owned by the parents and teachers. Such a school is directly answerable to the parents for the progress and well-being of its students. Parents who enroll their children in charter schools typically have an active commitment to their children's education, and strongly support an ASL-based learning environment. Parents and teachers work together to ensure that the students are getting the best possible education.

Charter schools combine the best features of deaf schools (a rich Bilingual-Bicultural environment and an ASL-based education) and mainstreaming (allowing deaf children to come home to their families every afternoon).

Several Bi-Bi charter schools have opened up within the past decade or so and are now operating in various states: Magnet School of the Deaf in Lakewood, Colorado; Metro School in St. Paul, Minnesota, and the Jean Massieu Academy in Arlington, Texas, to cite three. And several more are being planned in other cities such as Seattle, which has no residential-school tradition but does have a strong Deaf community.

We believe that the more educational options available to deaf students everywhere, the better. Charter schools are an exciting new development that augment students' and parents' choices.

* For more details on closing schools for the deaf, see the next chapter.

Chapter 29

Why is there a movement to close down residential schools for the deaf in this country?

esidential schools have managed to survive the onslaught of oralism, declining enrollment, and other major challenges, although many are experiencing troubled times, and a few have closed in recent years. One giant problem is money. Not all residential schools for the deaf are state-run; some operate with very little government funding. Even so, state budgetary cuts are threatening the quality of their programs.

Mainstreaming sounds like a great, inexpensive alternative to costly state-run schools. Save the taxpayers money, right? P.L. 94-142, the controversial "mainstreaming law," has proven a real headache in the way it has been applied.[1] It was not originally intended for deaf children. It was designed to ensure that handicapped/disabled children's individual needs were taken into consideration for the most appropriate placement. Instead, it became an easy excuse to shift deaf children wholesale from residential schools into local day programs or public schools. Dr. Frank R. Turk, the distinguished Deaf administrator, teacher, and youth advocate, identifies three major weaknesses in the law: placements are routinely made without adequate input from trained professionals; certification and accreditation standards are lacking; and there is no provision for centralized and early-intervention programs.

Understandably, many parents want their deaf kids to be "normal"—to talk like everybody else and to go to local schools as "normal" children do. As Dr. Peter Seiler argues, there shouldn't be any more stigma attached to attending a state school for the deaf than to a prep school.[2] But the prospect of sending little Susie or Tom to a state-run institution terrifies some parents. Especially if their fantasy of the state school for the deaf is a Dickensian mill churning out an endless parade of illiterate, unskilled dorks. Parents tend to recoil at the (inaccurate) term "special school," which isn't surprising, considering the negative connotations it has acquired.

One problem the residential schools have long been struggling with is lower expectations. Many residential schools are simply not as academically challenging as their hearing counterparts. They may have difficulty attracting the best teachers, setting up the most stimulating curricula, and offering the highest-quality programs. Traditionally, graduating deaf students as a whole have scored significantly lower in academic achievement levels than their hearing counterparts, particularly in English skills. The better schools narrow the gap considerably. We know of no residential-school programs for gifted deaf students, though. Because of the relatively small deaf population, gifted, average, and sub-average students have traditionally been placed together. But some schools offer advanced classes for gifted students.

Newspaper reports of revelations of physical and sexual abuse of students and sexual harassment of staffers in residential schools across the country (involving allegations, accusations, lawsuits, and occasional arrests) generate bad publicity for the schools and, understandably, frighten parents. And these reports are eagerly seized as ammunition by opponents of schools for the deaf. Our advice to parents is: Check into the schools. Visit them. Ask tough questions. Investigate. Do your homework. And know how to communicate with your deaf children before enrolling them *anywhere!*

Parents *like* to have their kids going to nearby schools and coming home every afternoon. But as far as deaf kids are concerned, many mainstream programs haven't been notably successful. True, *some* mainstreamed deaf children thrive.

But many feel isolated and cheated of an education. (Ask them.) They may be the only deaf student in their class or school. Staffers are not necessarily trained to serve their particular needs. Teachers often cannot communicate with them. Their participation in sports and extracurricular activities is usually curtailed. Even with an interpreter, they are at an automatic disadvantage.

There are, however, some outstanding day programs for deaf students operating from or in conjunction with public schools. E.g., the programs at Manhattan Beach Intermediate School and Mira Costa High School in Manhattan Beach, California. And, as we've just noted, there are a few new magnet/charter schools for deaf children, with more, we hope, on the way. These serve to increase the options. Competition, if it strengthens the schools, can be a good thing. It's good to have choices. Imagine having to decide between *two* good schools instead of settling for the less objectionable of two unappealing options!

Closing the state schools and rerouting all deaf students to local programs is false economy. Conscientious administrators (and not necessarily just the deaf ones!) are dedicated to strengthening residential schools as a viable alternative to mainstreaming. Good residential schools offer advantages no mainstream program can: an abundance of trained professional staff, individual attention, a 24-hour learning/social environment, everyday exposure to ASL, full and equal participation in *all* activities, and Deaf mentors. Any existing communication barriers between the children are swiftly leveled. Many alumni of these schools remain close friends with each other throughout their lives. They see themselves as a community, akin to family—they are all deaf together, sharing the same experiences, challenges, language, and values. They have generally positive feelings about their education. Many deaf parents of deaf children know that this is the learning environment they want for their own kids.

Parents who want to be the prime influences during their

children's early and most formative years—the primary teachers, guides, and mentors for their deaf children—have qualms about sending them off to a residential school and giving them over to the supervision of strangers. They believe that they can offer their children something that no dorm parent or teacher can. They want their children coming home to them every afternoon; they want to talk with them directly about their everyday concerns and monitor their homework; they want to tuck them into bed at night. And not just on weekends. Such parents may be happier enrolling their children in a local public-school or day program. These parents include Deaf adults with strong ASL skills.

Choosing the best placement for a deaf child is no easy decision. Numerous factors are involved. Parents have to weigh the pros and cons of residential-versus-mainstreaming-versus-day programs, for there are pluses and minuses to each.

Granted, schools for the deaf are a very mixed lot. Some have well-deserved reputations for academic excellence. Some just don't have terribly good track records at turning out literate, "quality" graduates. Some have gotten embroiled in sex-abuse or physical-abuse scandals. But the fact is that they fill a vital need, and without the deaf schools, Deaf identity and culture would be threatened with extinction. As the 19th-century oralists knew, strike at the deaf schools, and you strike at the very foundation of the Deaf community. Suppress the signing of deaf children (although they will find ways to sign secretly), and they will be more tractable. Keep them away from each other, under the control of hearing adults, and they cannot easily form a community.

Contrary to the commonly held view that the Deaf community supports the schools for the deaf because they are the recruitment and training ground for the next generation of the Deaf culture: we wish to clarify a point. The schools do not exist to produce members of a Deaf club. They exist to educate deaf children. The better ones do just that.

There may be a threat, but there is a backlash at work. The future of the schools depends heavily on the support of the Deaf community. It is important that Deaf constituents organize and make their views known to their legislators. On the other front, the Deaf community needs to *enlist* not only hearing parents of deaf children (who are often our staunchest allies), but *educate* the teachers, the whole deaf-educational establishment itself, and the professionals who make their living ostensibly serving the needs of deaf children—and *this* is the biggest challenge of all.

[1] Originally titled "Education of All Handicapped Children Act of 1975," P.L. 94-142 was reauthorized in 1990 as P.L. 101-476, "Individuals with Disabilities Education Act" (IDEA).

[2] "I believe that the proper name for residential schools for the deaf should be the 'state school for the deaf' or any other name similar to this. The school for the deaf has a dormitory only as a convenience to the parents because of the distance for most hearing-impaired children. There should be no stigma attached to attending a state school for the deaf which is no different from attending a private boarding school."—**DEAF LIFE**, September 1991. Dr. Seiler, then superintendent of the Illinois School for the Deaf, is deaf himself. He and Dr. Turk were quoted in this cover feature on 12 deaf superintendents/directors of schools for the deaf.

There are now somewhat less than a dozen of them in the States, down from a record high of 18 in 1995. Although the number of deaf superintendents has since dwindled, the ones currently on the job are working hard, struggling to improve their schools, get needed revenues, and confront the future.

▲ ▲ ▲

"'Hearing parent' is not a dirty word"

We originally published this chapter in the September 1991 issue of DEAF LIFE. The concluding sentence read: "On the other front, the Deaf community needs to educate hearing parents of deaf children—and this is the biggest challenge of all." Shortly afterwards, we received a poignant letter from Barb and John Boelter, parents of a deaf child, objecting to this statement. The Boelters were a bit unusual in their active commitment to giving their daughter, Shannon, as much exposure as possible to ASL. (Shannon, they told us, spent two days a week at a Deaf friend's house, and her language "is tested at 9-12 months above her age!") Their view makes an insightful counterpoint to ours. We published their letter in full in our "A Few More Words" department (August 1992), and are reprinting it here.

As the hearing parent of a deaf daughter, 18 months old, I must take exception to your response to the question regarding residential schools in "For Hearing People Only" in the September issue. Other parents I have spoken with share my views.

We have known that our daughter was deaf since she was 5 months old. Since that time we have learned more about deafness, deaf education and Deaf Culture than some parents learned in a lifetime. Your comment, ". . . the Deaf Community needs to educate hearing parents of deaf children—and this is the biggest challenge of all" is insulting to parents like us who have recognized from the beginning that our daughter needs the support and guidance of the Deaf community to grow and find her own identity. We have sought out and listened to the advice of deaf people in connection with every decision we have made.

We are trying to pave new ground in our local schools by pushing for bilingual/bicultural education. Our daughter spends 2 days a week with a deaf family to learn ASL in its natural environment and see successful deaf adult role models. We also participate in as many Deaf Community activities as possible.

I know that hearing parents years ago cannot be blamed for believing "experts" who told them not to sign with their kids. I think I understand why older deaf people feel such strong ties to their residential schools. But on the other hand, parents today who do recognize the social, educational and emotional needs of their deaf children should not be penalized for what parents didn't do in the past. "Hearing parent" is not a dirty word and deaf people as a group should be more sensitive to this type of stereotyping.

I do not want a residential school to be the only option for a quality education for my child. With a stimulating home environment and participation in the Deaf Community, she will be able to achieve her potential and learn about Deaf Culture while in the family setting. Any child should learn life's really important lessons at home, i.e., values, self-worth and unconditional love. A school should provide only part of a child's educational and social needs.

Perhaps if deaf parents were told over and over again that they were not able to provide an appropriate environment and identity for their hearing children, they would understand our frustration.

Give hearing parents a chance. Work with us, not against us, to get the best possible education in all settings. With the help of our deaf friends, we will raise happy, educated and proud deaf children who will be a credit to both cultures.

Respectfully submitted,

Barb and John Boelter
Eagan, Minnesota

[P.S.] I realize that this may be longer than most of your letters but please publish it as I feel it represents a viewpoint that may not be known to many deaf adults. They may feel their Culture is at stake, but my child is at stake and until someone faces that situation, you cannot understand. Thank you.

Chapter 30

What's the best clearinghouse for information about deafness?

he best place to start is your local public, school, or college library. Depending on size and location, they're likely to have at least a few basic books on deafness and sign language, and possibly some periodicals of interest. Ask the reference librarian to help get you started in the right direction. (See the bibliographic listings at the end of this book.)

Since most public libraries now offer Internet access for all library patrons, if you don't have your own Internet-capable computer, you can go online at the library. All you need is a valid library card—and that's free. Users may be limited to, say, an hour of Internet access per day. Certain sites may not be accessible, and certain applications unavailable. Still, it's a good way to log into the superhighway. If you are new to the Internet, you can sign up for a free orientation course, or ask a librarian to help you get started.

Perhaps your library has a copy of the 3-volume **Gallaudet Encyclopedia of Deaf People and Deafness**. If not, ask if you can borrow it through interlibrary loan.

The best overall resource center, and a good starting point if you have a fairly clear idea of which direction you want to go, is the **Laurent Clerc National Deaf Education Center** at Gallaudet University (formerly called the National Information Center on Deafness). Its address is 800 Florida Avenue N.E., Washington, D.C. 20002. ☎ 202-651-5051 (Voice); -5052 (TTY); -5054 (fax). The NDEC has a Website, of course, and you can do a keyword search there or through a search engine such as Google.

Gallaudet's Bison Bookstore has a mail-order catalogue featuring a wide variety of books (including Gallaudet University Press publications) and multimedia on Deaf issues.

The **National Association of the Deaf** (NAD), whose headquarters are at 814 Thayer Avenue, Silver Spring, MD 20910, also has a Website. ☎ 301-587-1788 (Voice); -1789 (TTY). For questions pertaining to law and deafness, contact the **NAD Law Center**.

Another possibility is the **GLAD Bookstore**, 2222 Laverna Avenue, Los Angeles, CA 90041. ☎ 323-478-8000 (Voice/ TTY). GLAD has its own Website.

Besides Gallaudet University Press, several publishers, notably T.J. Publishers, DawnSignPress, Harris Communications, and Sign Media, specialize in Deaf-Culture and ASL-related multimedia. ASL is particularly suited to the medium of videotape/CD. DawnSignPress, for example, produces ASL videotapes and CDs as well as books.

Addresses and TTY, voice, fax, E-mail, and URL listings for many local and national deaf organizations, institutions, agencies, clubs, interest groups, and businesses, all handily arranged by state and by category, with useful information on multimedia/telecommunications access and contact information for many deaf people, can be found in TDI's **Blue Book: National Directory & Resource Guide**. TDI (formerly called Telecommunications for the Deaf, Inc.) is located in Silver Spring, Maryland. ☎ 301-589-3786 (Voice); -3006 (TTY). Ask your library for a reference copy of the directory.

For medical aspects of deafness, try **The Encyclopedia of Deafness and Hearing Disorders** (Facts on File), or contact the Deafness Research Foundation.

And keep in mind that Gallaudet, NTID, CSUN, NAD, TDI, the Alexander Graham Bell Association for the Deaf, SHHH, and GLAD, to cite just a few, all publish magazines and other useful material, such as reprints and pamphlets.

Happy hunting!

Deaf Awareness 5-Minute Quiz

Chapters 16—30

Answers are on the bottom of the page, upside down.

True or False:

1. Synonyms for Pidgin Sign English include "Ameslish," "Siglish," "Contact Sign Language," and "American Signed English."

2. Signed English uses lots of signs borrowed from ASL in an "English" word order, but isn't the same as ASL.

3. Some programs that label themselves "Total Communication" may not even have fluent signers on the staff, nor offer access to sign language.

4. Under no circumstances should a hearing person offer to help a Deaf stranger.

5. A native American language (like ASL or Navajo) can nonetheless qualify as a "foreign" language.

6. Since all ASL teachers in schools and colleges hold ASLTA certification, it's not really necessary to ask an acquaintance who their sign-language teacher is, except out of curiosity.

7. Numerous Manually Coded English systems have been devised by hearing teachers and are no longer used.

8. The availability of closed-captioned media has made Deaf illiteracy obsolete.

9. Deaf people hate to read because they have difficulty thinking abstractly.

10. There are several noteworthy alternatives to mainstreaming and traditional schools for the deaf. These include charter schools.

10. True.
1. True; 2. True; 3. True; 4. False; 5. True; 6. False; 7. True; 8. False; 9. False;
Answers:

Chapter 31

"My wife teaches children with learning problems. Would there be any information to help her better recognize children with hearing problems or anything related?"

Through my [ASL] courses, my wife has been able to help hearing-impaired children (at least to recognize their problems) and a child who's hearing but his parents are deaf. The little boy speaks okay, but sometimes he reverts to an English version of the ASL sentence structure. Teachers were beginning to think something was wrong. He was merely translating into spoken language the language he was raised with. My wife is helping him learn the written English now. She teaches children with learning problems.

Would there be any information to help her better recognize children with hearing problems or anything related?

—Roger Mindel, Wheaton, Maryland

here's certainly no shortage of information—the prob-lem is deciding where to start exploring. A few books that may prove useful are listed in the bibliography in the back of this book. New ones are coming out all the time. It's boomtown.

Book titles and bibliographic data can be searched on the Internet. On Amazon.com's Website, several additional titles of related interest are automatically listed below each main title "profile," to encourage buying multiple titles. It's also an enjoyable way to browse topics and go off on tangents.

The libraries of NTID/RIT, CSUN, and Gallaudet are prime resources. RIT's Wallace Memorial Library's Website, for example, has a useful listing of links organized by subtopics. Books and multimedia packages with an early-intervention focus are listed in the sites for Gallaudet University Press and Butte Publications, for instance. Some of these are geared towards professionals, some for parents. Some, if not all, can be obtained via interlibrary loan.

As for organizations and agencies: Do a bit of riffling around in the current **TDI Blue Book**. Start with national organizations such as the American Society for Deaf Children, AGBAD, HEATH Resource Center, NAD, NARIC, and TRIPOD. Also try GLAD (California). Then zero in on the local, county, and state agencies.

Since this question was originally asked by a resident of Wheaton, Maryland, we referred him and his wife to the Maryland section of the **Blue Book**. We noted that Maryland, together with Washington D.C., has the nation's heaviest concentration of Deaf organizations and agencies, so there are plenty of listings!

We suggested Maryland's Office for Individuals with Disabilities, and Montgomery County Department of Family Resources, and encouraged these readers to contact Maryland School for the Deaf, which has campuses in Frederick and Columbia—all of which might be able to give them some useful leads. Ditto the state education agency: e.g., Maryland State Department of Education/Infants and Toddlers Program & Preschool Services Branch, and the National Information Center for Children and Youth with Disabilities (Washington, D.C.), and Beginnings for Parents of Children Who are Deaf or Hard of Hearing (Raleigh, NC).

And don't forget that trusty resource, the Laurent Clerc National Deaf Education Center at Gallaudet University (which provided some of the above leads). In fact, any readers with similar questions should check its Website **first**.

A few of the many available works on deaf children, early intervention, and education:

John W. Adams, **You and Your Deaf Child: A Self-Help Guide for Parents of Deaf and Hard of Hearing Children** , 1997

Beryl Lieff Benderly, **Dancing Without Music** (rpt.), 1990

Frank Bowe, **Approaching Equality: Education of the Deaf**, 1991

M. Diane Clark, Marc Marschark, and Michael Karchmer, eds., **Context, Cognition, and Deafness**, 2001

Carol J. Erting and Marc Marschark, eds., **The Deaf Child in the Family and at School: Essays in Honor of Kathryn P. Meadow-Orlans**, 1999

Virginia Frazier-Maiwald and Lenore M. Williams, **Keys to Raising a Deaf Child**, 1999

Robert E. Johnson, Scott K. Liddell, and Carol J. Erting, **Unlocking the Curriculum: Principles for Achieving Access in Deaf Education**, 1989

David Luterman and Mark Ross, **When Your Child is Deaf: A Guide for Parents**, 1991

Marc E. Marschark, **Psychological Development of Deaf Children**, 1997

—**Raising and Educating a Deaf Child**, 1998

Kathryn P. Meadow-Orlans, **Deafness and Child Development**, 1980

Eugene Mindel and McKay Vernon, **They Grow in Silence** (rev. ed.), 1987

Donald F. Moores, **Educating the Deaf: Psychology, Principles, and Practices** (5th ed.), 2001

Donald F. Moores and Kathryn P. Meadow-Orlans, eds., **Educational and Developmental Aspects of Deafness**, 1990

Paul Ogden, **The Silent Garden: Raising Your Deaf Child** (rev. ed.), 1996

Barbara R. Schirmer, **Language and Literacy Development in Children Who are Deaf** (2nd ed.), 2000

Sue Schwartz, ed., **Choices in Deafness: A Parents' Guide to Communication Options** (2nd ed.), 1996

Barbara Luetke Stahlman, **Language Across the Curriculum: When Students are Deaf or Hard of Hearing**, 1999

David A. Stewart and Thomas N. Kluwin, **Teaching Deaf and Hard of Hearing Students: Content, Strategies, and Curriculum**, 2000

McKay Vernon and Jean C. Andrews, **The Psychology of Deafness: Understanding Deaf and Hard of Hearing People**, 1990

Geraldine P. Wallach and Katharine G. Butler, **Learning Disabilities in School-Age Children and Adolescents: Some Principles and Applications**, 1994

Margaret Walworth, Donald F. Moores, and Terrence J. O'Rourke, eds., **A Free Hand: Enfranchansing the Education of Deaf Children**, 1992

Chapter 32

I've been working with a deaf man for 20 years. He's an excellent lip-reader. Recently I met his friend, who uses sign language. I tried to communicate with him and couldn't. I was shocked. Can't all Deaf people read lips?

ne of the most common "Hearing" misconceptions is that all deaf people have this magic ability to "read lips." All too often, the first question a hearing person asks a new deaf acquaintance is, "Can you read my lips?" (Note the irony here: This is the *one* question *all* deaf people can undoubtedly speechread!) Even if the answer is "yes," the hearing person will often exaggerate his or her mouth movements and talk abnormally slowly, which of course makes communication that much more difficult. If the answer is "no," the deaf person may be perceived as a poor sport and/ or a nitwit, and whatever potential there was for communication will be totally nullified. ("Huh? How can she say no? She answered my question correctly, didn't she? Is she playing games?")

Lipreading involves a high proportion of guesswork and "instant mental replay." Only some 30% of all spoken sounds are visible on the lips. Many sounds, like "b," "p," and "m," are virtually impossible to distinguish by watching the mouth. And what about homonyms (homophones)—"blue" and "blew?" They look *and* sound identical! Moreover, everyone makes sounds a bit differently; everybody's voice and articulation are different. A stranger, whose speech patterns are unfamiliar to the lipreader, presents a more formidable challenge than members of the household or close friends. All this means that even a skilled lipreader must rely to some extent on guesswork to understand what's being said, using the context to fill in the inevitable gaps.

Anyway, 'lip-reading' is a misnomer. A more accurate term is *speechreading*. Speechreaders don't just look at the mouth; they read the entire face: the eyes, the way the eyebrows tilt or the brows knot when certain words are emphasized. They note changes in expression, shoulder shrugs, posture, gestures. They also note any props the speaker is carrying; their surroundings. Picking up these *associational cues* is an art in itself. It requires a high degree of attention. It can be exhausting.

Everybody (hearing as well as deaf) makes use of some degree of speechreading at times. For deaf people, it's a survival skill. Even so, some consider speechreading skill an inborn ability, like dancing. Many deaf people never become very proficient at it. If all else fails, hearing people should forget the "rubberlipping" and try the old standby, pencil and paper.

▲ ▲ ▲

Speechreading protocol:
a few words of advice

Nothing creates so much anxiety in Deaf-Hearing relations, it seems, as the fateful first encounter. A few suggestions to make it a bit easier for all those involved:

1. Facial Topography: Many deaf people who are skilled speechreaders have difficulty "reading" men who have full or unkempt beards and/or thick, sweeping mustaches. Men and women who don't remove sunglasses or doff hats that overshadow their faces also create difficulty for deaf readers. People who nervously shield their mouths with their hands while talking or who take frequent furtive glances to the side, breaking eye contact, drive us crazy. It's best to remain relaxed, focused, and confident as possible.

2. Popping the Question: If you run into a deaf person (and we're assuming that you don't know sign language or fingerspelling, which is the case with the majority of hearing folks), ask politely, in as natural a way as possible, "Can you read my lips?" or "Can you speechread me?" Don't over-enunciate (exaggerate) your question. You don't *have* to point to your lips (but most hearing people do this instinctively); if you do, do it discreetly—don't ham it up, repeatedly jabbing at the air in front of your mouth. You're not auditioning for a third-rate sit-com; you're trying to communicate.

3. What Comes Next: If the deaf person shakes her/his head or says "No," be friendly. Don't shrug, throw up your hands in dismay, or mumble, "Sorry." And whatever you do, *don't* walk away. Try to establish some common ground. Get a pen and paper. Use a paper napkin. As a last resort, scratch letters on your vertically-upended palm. (Don't bother "writing" letters in the air, however—this *never* works well.) If you want to badly enough, you and your deaf fellow citizen will think of *something*. Human beings are a pretty ingenious species. Two persons who have a language or modal barrier and *really* want to communicate will usually find a way around it.

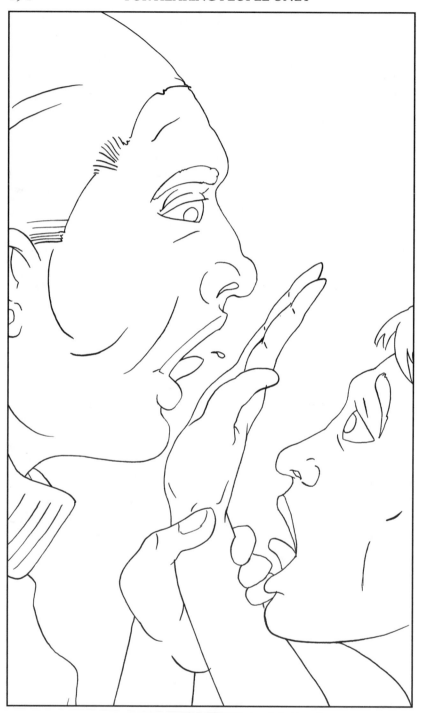

Chapter 33

Most speech pathologists I know are nice. Why don't deaf people like them?

—Susan Leventer (a speech pathologist and psychologist),
Rochester, New York

here is a long-standing love-hate relationship between audiologists and their deaf clients. So let's say that we have a problem with some of them. An attitude problem.

We have a similar problem with numerous members of the medical profession. These include physicians, ENT specialists, nurses, audiologists, speech pathologists, rehabilitation counselors, and clinicians.

Doctors and audiologists are usually the ones who deliver the news to the parents that their little Susie or Tommy is deaf. They sometimes counsel the parents and provide, depending on the doctor or audiologist in question, varying information: pamphlets, a guidebook for parents, a list of contacts and organizations. Or nothing at all. How the doctor or audiologist handles "breaking the news" can have profound repercussions to the parents and the children. And, sad to say, not all doctors and audiologists handle it in a way that's a credit to the profession.

Audiologists measure and chart the pattern of hearing loss—its range, its severity, the amount of residual hearing. They make recommendations to the parents that are usually not taken lightly. Their words carry weight—for better or worse. And in many cases, it *has* been for worse.

Speech pathologists take up where doctors and audiologists leave off. Theirs is the task of molding the speech of the deaf children entrusted to their care into a reasonable semblance of the "normal" speech of hearing people—to develop a pleasant speaking voice, a formidable challenge to those born deaf or early-deafened. They drill their clients in correct pronunciation, teach them how to form sounds correctly, differentiate their vowels, consonants, and diphthongs, put the accent on the correct syllable, gain awareness of their movements, control their breathing and voicing, develop polished articulation and intonation (this is the tough part) and, in general, acquire good speech skills—as good as possible. They do so with wildly varying degrees of success. Many of them are dedicated professionals and perfectionists. Some are appreciated by their clients, regarded with warm affection or quiet respect. Some are seen as demanding but fair. Some are simply resented because speech training is largely monotonous, grueling work. Others are seen as villains—brutal, insensitive, demeaning. Still others are simply annoying. Or bores.

Now, we need to emphasize that most ASL-Deaf people are not opposed to speech training. We recognize its utility. It has been part of the curricula of schools and programs for the deaf in the States for over a century. Even Deaf parents of Deaf children believe in giving them practice in speech. Some deaf children benefit from it, and some develop good speech skills that they find useful in their everyday lives or on occasion. But, we add, for too many children it is a frustrating waste of time—time that could be better employed on enhancing their literacy skills. Speech training is neither synonymous with "communication" nor with "education." It supplements them, but it should not supplant them.

What makes speech training a monotonous waste of time—or valuable practice in a vital communication skill? Much depends on the speech pathologist.

We have a problem with the way some speech pathologists see their deaf clients. To put it bluntly, they have contempt. Deaf equals defective. Deaf people possess pathological auditory equipment. They are broken and need to be fixed. They are categorized (and dehumanized) as "hearing-impaired individuals." They need help—from elite hearing professionals. Deaf culture is an illusion. ASL is okay for adult social situations, but deaf kids shouldn't learn it unless they fail with the oral/aural method. There's no point in exerting ourselves, since these deaf people aren't going to amount to much, anyway.

And, let's face it, some of the speech therapists we've known all too intimately weren't good or inspiring teachers, and did nothing to make their sessions enjoyable, or even rewarding. Too many of us have had experiences with therapists of the brutalist school: punish the kids when they mispronounce, and they'll get the message. Fine message.

A Deaf man who graduated from a Midwestern school for the deaf in 1981 shares an all-too-vivid recollection:

> My speech therapist gave me a vicious pinch on my arm every time I mispronounced something. Yes, it was painful. She stopped pinching deaf kids in 1975, and why? Because the state legislature passed a law in 1974 prohibiting teachers and staff from using physical punishment on students. It was now considered "abuse." She should have been shot.

To be fair, the figure of the sadistic speech therapist has gone the way of the ear trumpet and spinster teacher as an appurtenance of the past. From what we know, the contemporary generation of speech therapists are savvier, more sensitive, and take a more enlightened approach than some of their predecessors did. They enjoy their work, and find it rewarding. And it shows.

That said, we would like to re-emphasize the point that there are indeed some speech pathologists who respect deaf people, have a positive attitude towards the Deaf community, and even use sign language (to the delight of their clients). But, we emphasize, all too few do. Too many—too many of the ones we've known—adhere to a narrow pathological view. They don't recognize ASL, nor the important role it plays in our everyday lives. To them, it simply doesn't exist, or it's merely irrelevant. They don't know anything about it, and don't want to know.

A recollection (LL):

> Years ago, while I was in graduate school at the University of Kansas, I realized that my hearing was deteriorating badly, and so was my speech. I enrolled in one-on-one speech-therapy sessions with a succession of soon-to-graduate student therapists. It was grueling work, but I gave it my best. The therapists were all young women, dedicated and serious.
>
> One day, my speech therapist—I'll call her "Sandra"—and I went to the cafeteria in the Student Union for lunch. A group of deaf kids from the Kansas School for the Deaf happened to be there on a visit, and I watched with envy and joy at their rapid-fire signing. (My own sign skills were, at the time, pretty much nonexistent.) They were excited about visiting a college campus, and were very animated.
>
> But when I turned to Sandra, ready to make some remark about how happy and excited the kids looked, and how I wished I could talk with them, I noticed that she had a look of grim disapproval on her face. She was actually frowning!
>
> Sandra, obviously, did not appreciate the sight of a bunch of deaf kids signing away. To her, there was something distasteful about it. Her reaction troubled me. Naïve as I was, I couldn't understand *why*. All she could say was, "They should be using more speech."
>
> I did get up and go over to the kids, and tried to communicate with them, to say hello, that I was glad to see them, but my lack of both skill and vocabulary meant that I couldn't understand their signing or convey any sort of articulate message. I wonder what they thought of this strange character who came over and signed, fumblingly, "I love you!"
>
> It was my first direct encounter with Deaf children, and while I was delighted to glimpse them, I was frustrated that I couldn't understand them, and was troubled by my speech therapist's negative attitude. Why did she have to react that way? Later I learned, and understood.

Another recollection (MSM) emphasizes the need for honesty between therapist and client:

I recently had lunch with an oral-deaf woman I'll call "Becky." She could sign, yes, but she was essentially an oralist. She had graduated from a well-known oral school for the deaf, and was awfully proud of her speech. She used it all the time. Her teachers, her parents, her audiologists, and—most of all—her speech therapists had been telling her all along what *wonderful* speech she had. They lavished endless praise on her for her *wonderful* speech. She had kept in practice after graduating, and was confident that her speech was indeed outstandingly clear.

We went to a McDonald's together. Now, I'm a Deaf man who avoids using his voice as much as possible. I placed my order by pointing to this item and that item on the display menu at the counter. I received exactly what I wanted.

Becky insisted on using her voice to place her order. She declared: "*I want to talk!*" And when her order arrived, everything was wrong. She hadn't gotten *anything* she'd ordered! She tried to set the matter straight by talking to the staff at the counter, but I could see that they didn't understand her. So I ended up solving the problem myself. I asked Becky, "What do you want?" I speechread her responses and pointed to various items on the display menu, just as I'd done for myself. This time, they got the order right.

After Becky and I sat down at a table, she exploded with anger. She was absolutely furious. "My speech therapists told me I had *good* speech! And now these people here don't understand me! They *lied* to me! I don't think I will trust my voice anymore. I'm going to have a meeting with my speech therapist and tell her, 'You liar!'"

Her tirade erupted in audible speech, accompanied by her awkward signs. I sat there and listened empathetically.

We're all for a better relationship between speech pathologists and their deaf clients. We want them to be well-trained professionals who have a good understanding of Deaf/Hearing communication issues, Deaf history, and insight into the Deaf mindset and human psychology in general. We would like the therapist/client relationship to be one of mutual respect and honesty. Not one of antagonism or deception.

Chapter 34

"A deaf woman in my office does not speak. However, we do hear actual understandable words from her once in a while. Has someone has worked with her in speech? And is it wrong to want her to verbalize?"

I have recently taken a new job with a congenitally deaf woman in the office. As a manager, I felt it necessary to at least try to learn enough to communicate with this woman; enough Sign Language to be fully understood, and, as important, to learn about the deaf and their culture. Needless to say, it has been, so far (several months) a real eye-opener and extremely interesting. I find it hard to believe that this culture and language is so prevalent around us, but, as a hearing person, I knew absolutely nothing about it.

Anyway, I have taken here at work a very basic course in Sign Language. It really didn't get into ASL as such, mostly vocabulary to be put together into Signed English. The woman at my office can understand what little I know. I am presently enrolled at Gallaudet in their beginning ASL course.

The woman in my office does not speak. However, we do hear actual understandable words from her once in a while. Does this mean that at some time, someone has worked with her in speech? And is it wrong to want her to verbalize? I recently read a biography of Gallaudet and understood there are two schools of thought on this subject, but since this woman does work and live in a hearing English-speaking society, is it wrong to want her to be able to speak? Of course, I'm not trying to get her to do this or anything, just wondering.

—Roger Mindel
Wheaton, Maryland

t's not *wrong*—it's human nature. Most parents of children newly diagnosed as deaf are terrified at the prospect that little Susie or Tommy will never be able to speak. Traditionally, oral schools have emphasized speech training above literacy skills, although the graduates of oral schools don't necessarily end up with better articulation than those from signing/Total Communication schools. Oralists maintain that career opportunities are better for speaking deaf than for non-speaking (sign-dependent) deaf—an understandable but questionable conviction.

But if speech is the portal to success, is non-speech the automatic gateway to second-class citizenship?

Virtually all deaf adults have had a heavy dose of speech and auditory training. It's an inescapable fact of life for deaf schoolchildren, whether the school be residential, state, private, or public. Oral training is part of the TC curriculum. But as we have already noted, there is no consistent standard of quality. Not all speech training is equally effective, nor all speech therapists equally good. Many speech-therapy programs have been haphazardly (or downright badly) administered. There are skillful speech therapists—*and* a lot of brutal, ineffectual, plain bad ones—just ask around.

And, obviously, not all deaf children benefit from speech training. Good articulation is notoriously difficult both to achieve and maintain, especially for those born deaf or early-deafened. How well can you modulate your voice if you can't hear yourself speaking? If you have *never* heard yourself speaking? You can never really be sure how you sound—the only cues are the expressions on the faces of your listeners. Or comments such as "Sorry, I can't understand you" (the polite version), or "Gee, what planet are you from?" (the rude version). A scary thought? Many deaf people have endured plenty of humiliation and pain from the reactions of others to their "strange" voices. They *know* that their voices sound harsh and unpleasant; they're embarrassed about using them.

Some of our most distinguished Deaf leaders, past and

present, have never uttered intelligible words. Others (a relative few) are highly skilled speechreaders with good oral articulation. When dealing with hearing non-signers, some Deaf people who prefer not to vocalize, nonetheless try to accompany their PSE signing with speech. It's a matter of personal preference, what oral-deaf advocate Ken Levinson calls "comfort level."

As for your wanting your Deaf co-worker to verbalize, that really has to be her decision. If she feels comfortable with it, she will. You can, of course, ask her how she feels about talking with her voice, and what kind of experiences she's had with speech therapy and auditory training during her school years. But speech should never be forced on, or demanded of, deaf people. (Neither should signing be forced on hearing people!) It should be voluntary.

Chapter 35

"If you're deaf, how come you can talk?"

his question was asked by a high-school student whom one of us (LL) met at a local science-fiction convention, around 1985. We have been pondering it ever since.

The quick 'n' easy answer is "Well, some deaf people have good speech skills and others prefer not to use their voices at all. Deaf people are individuals. They shouldn't be stereotyped. Moreover, most deaf people have perfectly normal vocal apparatus." The more strictly accurate answer is impossibly long and complex. To give even the most rudimentary of answers, one would have to bring in labels. And labels are dangerous things.

Moreover, it's a touchy issue. To speak or not to speak—is that a choice? A political mandate? If we don't use our voices, do we give hearing people the wrong impression? If we do use our voices, are we oppressing other Deaf people? Whatever we do, are we encouraging labeling and stereotypes?

As we have already pointed out, virtually all deaf children receive speech and auditory training, no matter what kind of school they attend. The quality of this training, however, runs from excellent to execrable. And, as we have already pointed out, some children enjoy the training and find it rewarding. Others loathe it. Likewise, deaf people possess a wide range of speech skills, ranging from superb to passable to substandard to nonexistent: "You'd never know she was deaf, to hear her talk." "He has good speech for a deaf person." "She talks like a foreigner." "He talks badly." "She never talks." And consider the none-too-tactful criticisms of deaf speech made by parents, teachers, *et al*.: "You sound like an animal."

The Deaf community recognizes several distinct groups, as

far as identification-by-communication-mode goes. (The labels refer to specific categorical signs, made on the cheek or the throat.)

1.) Those who are born-deaf, including the hereditarily deaf, and who have a strong Deaf-cultural affiliation—especially those from Deaf families. A few ASL-Deaf people may have relatively clear speech. They usually disdain using their voices, but may use them to communicate with a hearing sister or brother, or other close relative they feel comfortable with, even if they otherwise "sign all the time." Some may use hearing aids. Labeled "Deaf."

2.) Those who are born-deaf or early-deafened and have developed good speech skills, but who become ASL-fluent as young adults. They may use their voices when dealing with hearing people, or may simply discontinue using them. Even if they prefer to use ASL for most situations, they occasionally use speech, e.g., to order from a restaurant menu. Labeled "deaf-speech" (the "Deaf" sign made on the throat).

3.) Those deafened in later childhood who have retained clear speech but who attended schools for the deaf after they become deaf, are ASL-fluent, and have joined the Deaf community. Labeled "HH-voice" (the "HH" sign made on the throat). Note: Deaf people who use their voices are sometimes labeled "hard-of-hearing" even if they're audiologically deaf, but this isn't a accurate label, since many of those who have clear speech can't use the telephone (our line of demarcation between "deaf" and "hard-of-hearing").

4.) Progressively-deafened or late-deafened adults. Labeled "ex-hearing." This is a pejorative label, and reflects the cultural disdain felt by some ASL "purists" for "arrivistes."

5.) Deaf persons from hearing families who have oral/mainstream backgrounds and have learned sign language as young adults, but who aren't fluent signers. Labeled "oral."

6.) Hard-of-hearing persons from Deaf families who have a 60 dB or so hearing loss. 60 dB is the usual cutoff point for admission to a school for the deaf and identification as "deaf." These people may be able to use a telephone with or without amplification. But they can also enroll in schools for the deaf and identify themselves as "Deaf." They may be ASL-fluent. Labeled "HH-voice."

7.) Strictly oral-deaf people who don't know how to sign, refuse to learn even the rudiments, and may have a political bias against the Deaf community. They don't identify themselves as "Deaf," but as "deaf" or "hearing-impaired." Labeled "hearing-in-the-head."

It should also be noted that there are some hearing persons who don't use their voices when in the company of Deaf friends, co-workers, relatives, or clients. The classic scenario is a sign-language interpreter who goes to a restaurant with several Deaf friends. When the time comes to order, she does not interpret for them, but signs instead. This puts everyone in the party on equal footing. The responsibility for understanding them and taking their orders is placed solely on the server, not the interpreter. But the server may think that *everyone* in the group is Deaf. (In this case, the question would be: "If you can hear, how come you're not talking?")

So much for the general categories. So much for identity-by-modality. Is there any hope for us? Well, labels can be discarded, or they can be transcended. People are not labels. We are more important than categories. Our prime concern is that there *be* communication. We place clear communication above linguistic purity and access above political bias. The spirit of communication is far more important than the dogma of mode. Speech is but one way to communicate. So is sign language. But even when neither way will bridge the gap, there are usually other ways.

We wonder if that high-school student, now an adult, has since met other Deaf people, and maybe picked up some sign language. And, we hope, found other, more probing, questions to ask.

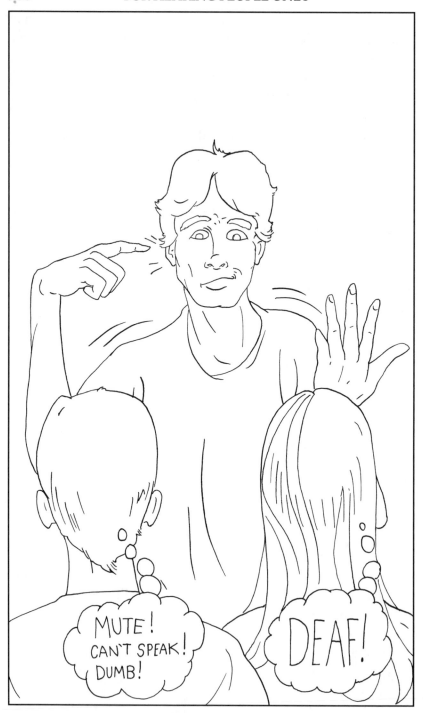

Chapter 36

What do you call a deaf person who doesn't speak?

—Helen Levitan, Haverhill, Massachusetts

ou call her or him a deaf person, that's what. Back in the not-so-good old days, hearing folks felt the need to make a distinction between deaf persons who "could talk like a normal person" and those who didn't. Those who didn't speak were branded "deaf-mutes" or "deaf-and-dumb."[1] Is it a question of the *inability* to speak? Hardly. We have yet to meet a deaf person who doesn't have the full complement of vocal equipment. And **all** deaf children, no matter what kind of school they attend, are subjected to an intensive regimen of speech therapy and auditory training. (Some, of course, refuse to continue. But many do because their parents insist on it.) This means that, technically, virtually all deaf children *can* speak.

It is estimated, however, that a congenitally, profoundly deaf child has, at most, a 5% chance of developing intelligible speech. We have to be realistic. Because they cannot hear themselves talk, profoundly deaf people cannot control the pitch, inflection, or loudness of their voices. Some have had humiliating experiences when they tried to "talk normally" in public and were greeted by screwed-up, disdainful faces that said, "Ugh, you sound like a freak!" From our own observations, the quality of a deaf person's intonation has little, if anything, to do with the kind of education they've received—oral or sign-based. We've met alumni of the Clarke School, the best-known oral school in the country, who have become full-time signers and whose voices are just as unintelligible as any other deaf voice.

Paradoxically, deaf children whose first language is Sign tend to develop better speech than those who are given intensive early oral training without exposure to signing. Why? Having a solid foundation in a visual language (i.e., ASL) makes it easier for the child to pick up another language—i.e., spoken English. Such children are more confident in their speech than those without the early exposure to Sign. All along, the oralists have been warning parents that if their deaf children learn to sign first, they'll never develop coherent speech! Or that signing interferes with speech development. Hogwash.

Developing "normal" intonation is, however, a long, arduous task for a deaf child. The value of these hundreds (thousands?) of hours of auditory/speech training is questionable in some cases, especially when the adult chooses not to speak. As we've noted, Deaf-rights advocates are not against speech training as such; they feel that the immense amount of time invested in this therapy could be more fruitfully employed in developing good English skills—reading and writing, that is.

A person who is hard-of-hearing (mildly to moderately deaf) or late-deafened will generally have much clearer speech than one who is born deaf or early-deafened. It is unfair to compare the speech skills of those who are born deaf or early-deafened with those who had the advantage of having been able to hear their own voices for years! Learning to speak presents far different challenges to those born profoundly deaf and those born with a moderate loss.

To speak or not to speak? It's strictly a matter of personal preference and comfort. Every deaf person is an individual. If s/he feels comfortable using his/her voice, we say fine. But a good number of deaf people do not, and we insist that their feelings be respected. Hence the complaints about Marlee Matlin's 1988 Oscars "speech." Matlin has always used her voice, enjoys doing so, feels confident enough to take speaking roles, and stays in training. But how typical is she? Most Deaf people don't have the luxury of a Hollywood articulation coach and feel oppressed when their bosses/friends/ parents ask them, "If Marlee can talk so nicely, why can't *you*?"

Matlin, of course, had no intention of oppressing other deaf people. As she publicly noted afterwards, she wished to acknowledge both major factions of the Deaf community: those who sign (without speaking), and those who speak (without signing). Since she doesn't speak and sign together (à la Sim-Com), she did one, and then the other.

Speech is a survival skill—useful in some situations, but optional. Many Deaf people lead full, productive, happy lives without it—and they deal with the Hearing world every day. Bernard Bragg (who, by the way, does *not* use his voice) has a touching anecdote in his autobiography, **Lessons in Laughter**, about entering Fanwood[2] knowing all the sounds except "k"—the one sound his Deaf mother had never learned to make and couldn't teach him. Having struggled to master this sound in his articulation class, he insisted on teaching his mother how to make it. He drilled her relentlessly until she could say "k." Now, he writes, she could go into a luncheonette and, without embarrassment, order a cup of coffee.

---

[1] Some British and Canadian people (including newspapers) still persist in using the obnoxious term "deaf-and-dumb" to refer to *any* deaf person, even those with good speech. Newspapers in the States still use the offensive term "deaf-mute" to refer to deaf persons who communicate primarily in sign language. We urge our readers **NOT** to use these terms. "Deaf" is simple, accurate, and dignified.

[2] Fanwood is the popular name for the New York School for the Deaf in White Plains, the second-oldest such school in the United States.

Chapter 37

Is it OK to use the term "deaf-mute" in reference to a deaf person who can't talk?

o, it's no longer an acceptable term. "Mute" refers to someone who *cannot* talk, that is, produce intelli-gible speech, or someone who has mal-functioning or missing vocal cords. "Mutism" is a medical or psychological condition—the *inability* or *refusal* to produce sounds. Virtually all deaf persons are physically *and* psychologically normal in this area. They have vocal cords and voices, just as the vast majority of hearing people do. This also applies to deaf people who prefer to communicate exclusively in sign language. Their vocal apparatus is perfectly normal. But, being deaf, they cannot hear themselves talk, and thus, cannot easily modulate their voices. Consider: If you were born deaf or became deaf as an infant and have never heard yourself talk, it's extremely difficult to talk clearly, with normal intonation. So signing is the natural mode of communication for many deaf people; speaking can never be. A few deaf people have good clear articulation—better than some hearing people—but most don't. It's a matter of personal preference, deciding what we feel most comfortable with.

Why isn't "deaf and dumb" an acceptable term?

Think about the last time you used the word "dumb." You used it to describe something stupid, clumsy, or foolish, right? A century ago, this term was in common use. Nobody thought twice about its propriety. It's outmoded now, and insultingly inaccurate. We're aware that this term is still used in England to describe someone who is deaf, but that doesn't say much for the discernment of those who persist in using it.

As for the correct term, why not simply say "deaf?"

A note on "politically correct" terms

Originally, the terms "deaf-mute" and "deaf-and-dumb" were not considered pejorative; they simply referred to a severely or profoundly deaf person who didn't speak. "Semi-mute" referred to a moderately deaf person or one who had become deaf after learning how to speak, both of whom could profit from articulation training.

Nobody thought twice about the political correctness of such terminology. The American School for the Deaf was first called "The Connecticut Asylum, at Hartford, for the Education and Instruction of Deaf and Dumb Persons," although, it should be noted, some of the deaf people involved disliked having "Asylum" in the title. The original name of Gallaudet University was "Columbia Institution for the Deaf, Dumb, and Blind," then, after it was chartered, "National Deaf-Mute

College." (It was renamed "Gallaudet College" in 1894.) The first publication in the "Little Paper Family" (1849) was **The Deaf Mute**. At its 1880 founding, the National Association of the Deaf called itself "National Convention of Deaf-Mutes." No disrespect was intended or inferred. These terms simply reflected the prevailing 19th-century belief that deafness caused muteness.

Ironically, it was the oralists who began trying to abolish the term "mute." They made grandiose claims that all deaf children could be taught how to speak. But the Deaf community (who knew better) refused to believe it. They did *not* want to speak, and did *not* want to be identified as speaking deaf. Because the oralists tried to suppress sign language in favor of speech, Deaf leaders preferred to continue calling themselves "deaf-mutes," as it made the oralists uncomfortable. Identifying oneself as a "deaf-mute" thus became a symbolic act of defiance to the oralists' explicit goal of "making the deaf speak." It was wielded as a cultural badge of pride. As the great Deaf leader George Veditz remarked, "If oral magicians who yank educational rabbits out of silk hats and pearls of speech out of the mouths of those who have never heard, choke over it, why, bless 'em!"

Nonetheless, the terms "deaf-and-dumb" and "deaf-mute" gradually faded from acceptable usage. Sensibilities have changed since Veditz made his whimsical comment. All deaf children now get a stiff dose of speech training (we have the oralists to thank for that), so there is little point in splitting the deaf population artificially into speaking and nonspeaking categories. "Deaf-and-dumb" and "deaf-mute" are now politically incorrect, period.

We dislike these terms because they now convey a negative attitude. "Deaf and dumb" does not connote pride or wholeness. It conjures a pitiful, pathetic, dull-witted image, with a hint of subnormal intelligence. "Deaf-mute" suggests that a deaf person is doomed to a life of silence, without speech, without hope. We've run into these terms repeatedly, and we find them annoying, inaccurate, and insulting.

How widespread are the terms "deaf-and-dumb" and "deaf-mute"? They seem to be more common in England and Canada than here, although that's not saying very much. We've seen several examples of headlines from the British press that made us cringe, but then, we've seen American headlines that were just as bad. In England, "deaf and dumb" is used to describe even deaf people who can speak clearly. The British Deaf Association, for one, has been waging a public-education campaign against this term. But entrenched attitudes, and the thoughtless terminology that reflects them, die hard.

Some U.S. newspaper and magazine reporters still use "deaf-mute." Possibly they think it adds "color" to the story. "Deaf-mute woman slain" makes the deaf victim sound more victim-like than "Deaf woman slain" or "Bronx woman slain." "Deaf-mute held in slaying" sounds more lurid and criminal-like than "Deaf man held in slaying."

We have found the term "deaf-mute" in contemporary books (e.g., **A Day in the Life of America**). This is bother-some, because a book's influence is more permanent and pervasive than that of a newspaper. Books are kept. They have influence. Staying power. Once they're published, they stick around. They go onto library shelves. They get bor-rowed and re-borrowed, read and reread by schoolchildren and adults. And you can't fire off a letter to the author that gets published in next Monday's morning edition.

We have also seen these terms on television, not from the anchors or reporters, but from hearing people being inter-viewed. Actual examples: "He's a deaf-mute." "My neighbor's a mute." "She's deaf and mute and went to the deaf-and-dumb school." A number of hearing people who really should know better are caught using phrases like these. If you're going to be quoted by the press or a TV reporter, please, think twice! (Or just *think!*)

We'd like to note that **DEAF LIFE** has an occasional feature, "Oh, No! Not Again!", which "showcases" examples of these offensive terms as used in contemporary media. Readers have sent in examples, and we've run across a number of them ourselves. We find them all over the place.

So what *are* the correct terms? Understandably, some hearing people find the simple, blunt, four-letter word "deaf" a bit hard to swallow. "Deaf" can mean not only "unable to hear," but "heedless" or "unwilling to listen." Common expressions such as "deaf to their pleas," "their appeal fell on deaf ears," "turned a deaf ear," and "the silence was deafening," have a decidedly negative connotation. To some people, "deaf" still connotes something shameful. Recent euphemisms include "hearing-impaired," "hearing-handicapped," "hearing-disabled," "auditorily handicapped," and "non-hearing." Most deaf people dislike these terms, as they promote a negative image of deaf people as broken ears or malfunctioning machinery. "Deaf" refers to the medical fact of hearing loss, but can also designate pride and cultural affiliation (i.e., "**D**eaf"). Fussy terms like "auditorily-handicapped" don't.

Some members of our community honestly prefer "hearing-impaired" to the more archaic "hard-of-hearing"—and vice versa. "Hearing-impaired" may be useful as a way of designating all those with various degrees of deafness, including mild, moderate, severe, and profound hearing loss. But those who insist on using this term should best employ it in combination, i.e., "deaf/hearing-impaired/hard-of-hearing." That way, nobody gets left out. The majority of deaf people prefer the simple term "deaf."

We'd like to note that the International Federation of the Hard of Hearing, the World Federation of the Deaf, NAD, and the Pennsylvania Society for the Advancement of the Deaf, have all agreed that the term "hearing-impaired" is no longer acceptable, and that "deaf/hard-of-hearing" should be used in all future references.

"Silent" overkill

Another bothersome word is the cliché "silent." This adjective is sometimes used, albeit inaccurately, to describe the Deaf community and its favorite mode of communication. "Silent" isn't necessarily a negative word, but if it's used as a euphemism for "deaf," it *can* be.

We are aware that there are "Silent" Clubs, "Silent" athletic teams, and "Silent" publications. "Silent" is a quaint way of indicating that we don't communicate in speech, i.e., that we're deaf. However, some Deaf people find it a bit tiresome, as when the Deaf reality is described as "a silent world" or "a world of total silence." Some of us feel that the concept of silence simply doesn't apply to our reality. True, a gathering of Deaf people may be quieter in terms of vocal noise, but Deaf people are *not* soundless creatures. We do *not* exist in a soundless vacuum.

Deaf people sometimes accompany their signed conversation or reactions (e.g., to television) with a variety of grunts, clicks, snorts, whoops, or chuckles. We laugh and cry; we utter sounds to express incredulity or surprise, just as hearing people do. Since we can't hear ourselves well (or can't hear ourselves at all), we often have no idea of just how loud we *are*. In a Deaf-culture context (e.g., a Deaf hangout, or an NTID/RIT dorm lobby), this is not a problem. When we're "in public," that is, among hearing people, this can sometimes get us into trouble.

Deaf people sitting at tables, especially if they're eating or holding a cup or glass in one hand, use the table as a signing base, thumping it as part of their signed conversation, to express a spontaneous reaction, or to get someone's attention. The sign for "right/correct" is one "pointing" handshape (active hand) struck down onto another "pointing" handshape (passive or base hand). But Deaf people eating and talking together often dispense with the passive hand and simply strike the sign onto the table. What hearing people in the vicinity hear is a sharp thwack.

To get someone's attention, we stomp on the floor. That can be noisy. What is a normal and acceptable aspect of Deaf culture may be unthinkably rude or gross (i.e., noisy) in Hearing culture. If you're a jittery hearing person living in an apartment just below a bunch of Deaf people, we don't have to educate you about noise. (You have our sympathy.)

"Silent" suggests sensory deprivation, mutism, and isolation, none of which accurately describes the Deaf experience. (When we think of a "silent world," we envision a scuba diver's paradise, complete with coral reefs and exotic varieties of brilliantly colored, intricately patterned fish and crustaceans. Not quite our everyday reality.)

If you think of the Deaf world as a silent one, how do you account for the fact that Deaf people like noisy discos, percussion music, loud jukeboxes, and stomp-dancing? We enjoy fireworks just as much as hearing people do. We love the explosions of color, the booming and the crackling.

As applied to the Deaf experience, "silent" *can* be apt, poetic, even amusing. But we think it's misused and overused. "Silence" is like a hot spice—it should be used sparingly. Too much sears the palate, numbs the senses, and spoils the feast.

▲ ▲ ▲

What do others call us?
And what do we call ourselves?

What's in a name? That which we call a rose
By any other word would smell as sweet . . .
—William Shakespeare, **Romeo and Juliet**

"Sticks and stones may break my bones, but names can never hurt me," goes the old children's rhyme. Many a mother has taught that rhyme to a daughter or son who came home crying after being taunted. Parents have tried hard to convince their children that names aren't important, that they're harmless and can't *really* hurt anyone, and that to respond with tears and fury is to overreact. But life is not that simple. There's no denying that names *are* important, and labels—names applied to a group—can have a profound effect on the members of that group. Labels can build self-esteem. Or they can be used as weapons to degrade and insult. A label influences what we think of ourselves. It creates expectations that are fulfilled.[1] To name something is to have power over it.

As deaf people, we have a vital interest in the labels applied to us by the hearing majority. Labels help us understand the mindsets of those who do the labeling; we can recognize the image others have of us, true or false, and identify stereotypical thinking. We can measure what progress we've made, and gauge how far we have yet to go.

Progress comes slowly. All of us have different opinions—some of us prefer the term "hearing-impaired" to "deaf" or "hard-of-hearing." Some deaf people still insist on using the term "deaf and mute." We need to examine these labels and see why they're used, and by whom, and what image we *really* want to promote. We need to understand them, monitor them, and confront them. When we find these terms still being used by those who should know better, we need to remind the users. We have a right to express our opinions forcefully, to object to the way we're labeled, and to insist on change. And we have the right to choose what we wish to be called.

DEAF AND DUMB/DUMMY
Real-life examples:
*"Look at the **dummies**, talking with their hands!"*—woman in a restaurant, early 1980s

*"Admirers of the **deaf and dumb** actress Elizabeth Quinn will warm to her biography, written in association with Michael Owens, called **Listen to Me**."*— **Inside London** (a free cultural-events magazine for tourists), August/September 1985

*"By using signs like those used by **deaf-and-dumb** people, scientists have been able to teach several gorillas to express feelings and ideas."*—Michael Fitzpatrick, **A Closer Look at Apes** (New York: Gloucester Press), 1987

*"Ex-**Dynasty** star Emma Samms has dumped another man—this time breaking the heart of a handsome **deaf-and-dumb** actor to whom she had publicly confessed in sign language: 'I love you.'"*— **The Globe** (a supermarket tabloid), October 3, 1989

*"You'd have to be **deaf, dumb and blind** not to want to grow up to be a dynamic, exciting person."*—Frances Cohen, quoted by Roxanne Roberts in a feature on a gossip columnist, **Washington Post**, July 28, 1990

*"You've proven that love can be not only blind but **deaf and dumb** as well."*—Ann Landers, in her December 5, 1990 column

Dictionary definition:

deaf-and-dumb, *adj. Often Offensive.* deaf-mute (def. 1). [1150-1200; ME *def and doumb*]—**Random House Dictionary of the English Language**, 2nd Edition, Unabridged (1987)[2]

Quotes:

Terminology has a long and sordid history in the world of deaf people. "Deaf and dumb" was the status quo *for many years. People who use it still (yes, some still do) may claim that they only mean "dumb" to indicate that deaf people can't talk, but the word carries with it the definite implication that deaf people are stupid.—* Richard Nowell[3]

I asked my father the next day, "Why do you let them call you Dummy?"

He shrugged, his nostrils still full of cotton from the [upholstery] shop. "I tell them my name is Ben. I tell everyone my name is Ben, but they call me Dummy. It is easier for them. They remember me."

I was enraged. "You are not a dummy. You are my father and a smart man. Tell them over and over that your name is Benjamin."

He smiled wanly, tired with the long day's work. "It is all right. I know I am not dummy, that is enough."—Ruth Sidransky[4]

Our view:

The great-granddaddy of all negative labels. Surprisingly, this was originally a reasonably neutral term.[5] It was based on an ancient misconception that deafness caused the inability to speak—if you were deaf, there was also something amiss with your capacity for speech (and, it followed, if you couldn't speak, you couldn't reason).

Although the vast majority of hearing people now know that deaf people have perfectly normal vocal apparatus, the usage still persists. We've found recent examples in England, Canada, and the States. The British Deaf Association, for example, has been conducting an ongoing campaign to educate the media and public (and to convince them once and for all to stop using the term), and publishes a pamphlet, "DEAF PEOPLE ARE NOT DUMB: A BDA Guide for Sub Editors on the correct terminology associated with deafness," which provides a concise explanation of why the term "dumb" is offensive, inaccurate, and just plain wrong.[6] In the States, the battle is fought on a newspaper-by-newspaper basis by readers who write personal letters to editors to try and set matters straight. It's slow going. Despite all the urgings, British newspapers (especially the more lurid ones) seem quite unconcerned about the propriety of the term. And American newspapers will quote interviewees who use these terms, without comment. So "deaf-and-dumb" manages to stay in usage.

The vulgar form of this term, "dummy," is a crude insult. An old nickname for deaf people—athletes, co-workers, neighbors—it's now used by hearing people to mean "stupid." Ernest Tidyman deliberately used it for the title of his book about Donald Lang, the languageless deaf man accused of murdering two prostitutes. He took the most shocking and offensive term he could—the same term used by other hearing people to describe Lang—to make readers uncomfortable, to make them think about the ways Lang had been labeled all his life.[7] Even so, some readers and TV-viewers have complained about the title, fearing that it promoted the use of an insulting term as though it were acceptable.

People who don't consider themselves prejudiced will utter the most extraordinary things in unguarded moments. In the first example quoted above (told us by a friend), two hearing women sat down at a table in a restaurant and ordered. At the next table sat three friends—two Deaf women and a sign-language interpreter (who was, of course, hearing). They were having an animated conversation in ASL. One of the two hearing women stared at them, nudged her companion and said out loud, "Look at the dummies, talking with their hands!" They snickered. The interpreter overheard this and relayed the information to her friends. They decided on a plan of action. They sat quietly for a few more minutes, then stood up together, turned towards the two women, made identical "Who, me?" gestures (exaggerated shrugs, palms-up), and said aloud, in unison: *"WHAT DUMMIES???"* The two women turned scarlet. They were *so* embarrassed that they got up and charged out of the restaurant right then and there—they didn't even wait for their lunch to arrive. We hope that they learned a lesson.

DEAF-MUTE

Real-life examples:

*"When police arrived, the couple's 5-year-old **deaf-mute** daughter was mopping up her mother's blood."*—from a story in the Gary, Indiana **Post-Tribune**, March 6, 1990, "Battered wife used the system, was still murdered by husband," AP byline

3 deaf-mutes murdered in Clifton; baby spared—headline in the **North Jersey Herald & News**, March 26, 1990

*"In December, authorities in Taipei uncovered a gambling ring composed entirely of scores of **deaf-mutes** operating via fax machines."*—Chuck Shepherd, "News of the Weird" (syndicated feature), **City Paper** (Washington, D.C.), July 1990

*"My father knew a **deaf-mute**. His name was Putt and he was homeless. He lived in a rowboat. Putt had been gassed in World War II and was a strange and mixed-up guy."*—Congressman Joseph P. Kennedy II, interview in the **Boston Globe**, August 9, 1990

Dictionary definitions:

deaf-mute, *adj.* **1.** unable to hear and speak.—*n.* **2.** a person who is unable to hear and speak, esp. one in whom inability to speak is due to congenital or early deafness. [1830-40; trans. of F *sourd-muet*]—**Random House Dictionary**, 1987

deaf-mute also deaf mute. *Offensive.—n.* A person who can neither hear nor speak.—*adj.* Unable to speak or hear.— **American Heritage Dictionary of the English Language,** Third Edition, 1992

Quotes:

A person who is deaf cannot hear; a person who is mute cannot make any sounds. Rarely do these two conditions appear in the same person. Most deaf people have fully functional vocal apparatus. They may not speak intelligibly but this has to do with the type of deafness, age of onset, and the type and amount of speech training received in the course of an individual's education. Speech proficiency has nothing to do with a person's intelligence or linguistic capabilities. Most deaf people who do not speak well are fluent in American Sign Language and literate in written English. To hearing people the term "deaf-mute" is loaded with negative connotations. The Deaf community doesn't need someone of your stature and influence perpetuating the use of this outmoded label.

(. . .) Your description of Putt made deaf people appear childish, helpless and dependent. Sure, Putt was only one deaf person but stories like this form the basis of people's stereotypes.—Kim Schive, Arlington, Massachusetts, letter to Congressman Kennedy[8]

The more recent term, "deaf-mute," may not be quite as bad [as "deaf-and-dumb"], but it is still pretty terrible. Besides being inaccurate, since deafness and an inability to produce voice are not connected, it also leads the general public into many misconceptions. And some people shorten it to just "mute," seemingly losing the whole point about the characteristic of the individual. (I recently heard someone say, "I've got two cousins who are 'mutes'.")— Richard Nowell[9]

Our view:

A hundred years ago, "deaf-mute" was an acceptable term. (Gallaudet University was formerly called "National Deaf-Mute College," and nobody seems to have objected.) At one time, Deaf people were proud to call themselves "deaf-mutes." Oralists disliked the term "deaf-mute;" their goal was to assimilate all deaf people into Hearing society by making them learn how to speak. When the oral method began gaining popularity among hearing teachers, administrators, and wealthy do-gooders, Deaf people resented the grandiose claims that *all* deaf people could be made to speak, and clung to the old term (which the oralists wanted to abolish), to emphasize their political stance: 'We are deaf, and we refuse to be forced to speak.' "Deaf-mute" was thus a term of pride. How times change! The term gradually faded from "acceptable" usage, ironically enough, as the oralist movement gained power over the education of deaf children. By the 1920s, all deaf schools in the States had made the switch (or been forced to switch) to the oral method, so—supposedly—all deaf children *could* be made to speak. No more "deaf-mutes." Gradually, the term became obsolete—but it has never completely disappeared.

Today, even in schools where sign language is used freely, virtually all deaf children receive speech therapy and auditory training, so the old distinction between speaking and non-speaking deaf has become moot. We all know (don't we?) that it is extremely difficult, if not impossible, to modulate your voice if you can't hear it. If deaf people prefer not to speak, it's not because they *can't* speak but because, being deaf, they can't properly modulate their voices. Whether or not a deaf person speaks intelligibly is largely a matter of choice—an individual decision based on how comfortable they feel about vocalizing.

What was once a "reasonable" term has become degrading. "Deaf-mute" no longer means "proud non-speaking Deaf signer." It now carries a negative connotation, suggesting the pathetic, subhuman, mentally backward, helpless. That's why the vast majority of deaf people dislike it.

It's a fact of life that labels help to sell newspapers, especially tabloids.[10] "DEAF-MUTE WOMAN FOUND SLAIN" is more lurid, more shocking, than "BRONX WOMAN FOUND SLAIN." It makes her more of a victim. The general reader reacts more strongly to "DEAF-MUTE MAN JAILED" than to "CHICAGO MAN JAILED." A "deaf-mute man" seems more threatening, more sinister, than "Chicago man." It's a cheap trick, but an old one. We hasten to add that not all journalists are irresponsible and insensitive. According to the standards of the Associated Press (AP), "deaf-mute" is NOT acceptable, and thousands of newspapers in the States comply with these standards. Media coverage, when done in a sensitive, thoughtful way, has done much to increase "Deaf awareness" throughout the world, and we applaud it.

Nonetheless, a distressing number of newspapers, radio talk-show hosts, police departments, etc., still think "deaf-mute" is an acceptable term. Or they don't think at all.

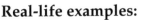

DEAF AND MUTE

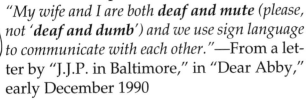

Real-life examples:
*"My wife and I are both **deaf and mute** (please, not '**deaf and dumb**') and we use sign language to communicate with each other."*—From a letter by "J.J.P. in Baltimore," in "Dear Abby," early December 1990

*"Rachelle has had quite a hard life because of her disability. She's **deaf and mute** and went to the **deaf-and-dumb** school. Rachelle's extremely hard-of-hearing, so anyone who gives her an ounce of love, she'll pay back in tenfolds."*—Leo Tessier of Canada, talking about his daughter, on **Unsolved Mysteries**, February 19, 1992

Our view:
As the first example shows, even intelligent, sensitive people (deaf as well as hearing) fall into the trap of thinking that "deaf and mute" is an acceptable term. (**TIME** Magazine still uses it.[11]) Ironically, "J.J.P. in Baltimore" was sharing a "old

but true" story about a sophisticated deaf gentleman who meets an ignorant hearing man on a train and gets the better of him in a positive and good-humored way, and obviously wanted to show readers of this extraordinarily popular column that deaf people were intelligent and sophisticated!

As for the second example, it's sad to see ignorance so nakedly displayed, on prime-time TV, yet.

MUTE

Real-life example:

"My neighbor's a mute and there's a man in her house."—Odessa Ray of Chattanooga, Tennessee, re-enacting the 911 call she made on behalf of her deaf neighbor, Annette Armour, in *Rescue 911*, March 27, 1990[12]

Dictionary definition:

mute—*n. Offensive.* One who is incapable of speech.—**American Heritage Dictionary**, 1992 (one of several meanings)

Our view:

A term used by uneducated people. On *Rescue 911* in 1990, we saw a re-enactment of how a deaf couple with no TTY coped with a housebreaker at night. The mother (fluent in ASL) grabbed her hearing son (also fluent in ASL) and ran next door. The boy told the neighbor what was wrong. This neighbor immediately phoned 911 and said by way of explanation, "My neighbor's a mute." Question: why couldn't she have said, "My neighbor's deaf," and saved a bit of time? Exactly how does "mute" equal "deaf"? "Mute" means refusing or unable to speak. This suggests that some hearing people still see deaf people solely in terms of their supposed inability to utter articulate sounds.

We now leave traditional terms and move onto modern ones. "Deaf-and-dumb," "deaf-mute," "deaf and mute,"

"mute"—these terms are part of our past, symbolizing the way society viewed us.[13] We're not advocating that they be expunged from dictionaries, nor do we advocate bowdlerization of historic accounts. All we ask is that these terms be recognized as obsolete. They are inaccurate and, therefore, offensive. We've moved beyond them, and we need to move beyond the others as well.[14]

HEARING-IMPAIRED

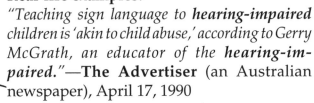

Real-life examples:
"Teaching sign language to hearing-impaired children is 'akin to child abuse,' according to Gerry McGrath, an educator of the hearing-impaired."—**The Advertiser** (an Australian newspaper), April 17, 1990

"Janice Wuertz, a sign-language interpreter for the hearing impaired, started daily finding herself at age 32 fighting off 'sleep attacks' during the day."—John G. Hubbell, "New Help for Troubled Sleepers," **Reader's Digest**, September 1992

"There is a clear need in the United States for improved methods and models for early identification of hearing impairments in infants and young children. Approximately 1 of every 1,000 infants is born deaf. Many more children develop some degree of hearing impairment by the age of 3. Reduced hearing acuity during infancy and early childhood interferes with the development of speech and language skills. Moreover, delayed identification and intervention may impede the hearing-impaired child's ability to adapt to life in a hearing world or prepare for life in the hearing-impaired community."—William H. Hall, Director of Communications, Office of Medical Applications of Research, Public Health Service, February 5, 1993[15]

Dictionary definitions:
hearing-impaired, *adj.* **1.** having reduced or deficient hearing

ability; hard-of-hearing: *special programs for hearing-impaired persons.—n.* **2.** (*used with a plural v.*) hearing-impaired persons collectively (usually prec. by *the*).—**Random House Dictionary**, 1987

hearing-impaired *adj.* **1.** Having a diminished or defective sense of hearing, but not deaf; hard of hearing. **2.** Completely incapable of hearing; deaf.—**hearing-impaired** *n. (used with a pl. verb).* Persons who are deficient in hearing or are deaf: *the speech was interpreted in sign language for the hearing-impaired.*— **American Heritage Dictionary**, 1992

Quote:
*At recent meetings of the International Federation of the Hard of Hearing, World Federation of the Deaf, National Association of the Deaf, and Pennsylvania Society for the Advancement of the Deaf, it was agreed the term "**hearing-impaired**" was no longer an acceptable term, instead future references would be to deaf/hard of hearing.*—Lillian Hoshauer, Manager, Deaf-Hearing Communication Centre, Inc., Springfield, Pennsylvania[16]

Our view:
A modern euphemism[17] for "deaf." Now quite common, but much resented. Note that the dictionary definitions are contradictory (reflecting confusion in usage). As the first three definitions suggest, it's not really equivalent to "deaf"— it means "hard-of-hearing," more or less. Deaf and hard-of-hearing people are two distinct groups with different aims, although they do share a common need for accessible communication (e.g., captioning, telephone access). "Deaf" and "hard-of-hearing" are not synonymous, but those who use "hearing-impaired" seem to think so.

The phrases "sign-language interpreter for the hearing-impaired" and "interpreted in sign language for the hearing-impaired" are fairly common usage. It doesn't make sense to us. "Hearing-impaired" people do not use sign-language interpreters. Deaf people do. (And since sign language is the basis of Deaf culture, you might as well capitalize that "D.")

As noted above, the World Federation of the Deaf and other organizations agreed in 1991 that the term "hearing-impaired" was no longer acceptable usage, and that references should be to "deaf/hard-of-hearing." Unfortunately, a lot of people haven't yet gotten the message.

At any rate, "hearing-impaired," *not* "deaf/hard-of-hearing," seems to be the preferred term in the medical field. "Deaf" has a decidedly negative connotation[18] among the rehabilitationists. They may not give a reason, but they clearly prefer to avoid using it.

"Hearing-impaired" defines deaf people solely in terms of broken or defective ears. The same hearing people who prefer "hearing-impaired" to "deaf" tend to be professionals in the audiological-rehabilitation field who take a narrow medical view of deaf people: that deafness is a deficiency that needs to remedied with auditory devices, therapy, and implants. Hearing loss is something to be "aided" or "corrected." Deaf ears are malfunctioning mechanisms to be fixed. Deaf persons are consumers of expensive devices to make them more "normal."

Can you imagine a "National Theatre of the Hearing-Impaired"? We can't. "Hearing-impaired" ignores all positive aspects of deafness: the Deaf community, language, and culture. Rehabilitationists don't want to recognize these, anyway.

We dislike "hearing-impaired" (and its "aurally-handicapped" variants) because it categorizes deaf people as broken machines. This label makes us seem less independent, less capable, less human. The emphasis should be on the person, not the impairment; on what we *are*, not what we lack.

Not all habitual users of the term are in the medical field, of course. We've gotten many press releases from "mainstream" companies that have done commendable things like setting up TTY lines, training personnel in the fine points of deaf-hearing communication, and hiring and promoting deaf people. However, a number of these companies (or at least their press-release-copywriters) persist in using the term "hearing-impaired," carefully avoiding the word "deaf." When **DEAF LIFE** published these press releases, we generally edited out the term, unless there was a good reason for keeping it. Three examples of unedited press releases:

*According to UL Vice President Jim Beyris: "With the new UL Standard and the first UL Listing of smoke detectors designed specifically for them, the **hearing-impaired** community can now increase their safety through the use of these detectors." (fall 1992)*

    *__Hearing-impaired__ consumers will be able to reach Royal Caribbean to request brochures and have questions answered. **Hearing-impaired** consumers wishing to book a Royal Caribbean cruise will be asked to contact the local travel agent of their choice.*
    *"We recognize the need for booking and information systems which are readily accessible to the **hearing-impaired**," said Rod McLeod, Royal Caribbean's executive vice president of sales, marketing and passenger services." (mid-November 1992)*

*Said John Story, Executive Vice President for British Airways USA: "This enhancement enables British Airways to reach a growing part of the traveling population. As a customer-responsive and caring airline, it recognizes the need to provide the necessary communications link to all **hearing-impaired** individuals, who now have an easier time arranging their travels in order to experience British Airways' high-quality products and customer service." (winter 1992)[19]*

What would these corporate executives think if they realized that the term they use so freely is offensive to the majority of the very people whose patronage they're trying to attract?

Some folks seem to think "hearing-impaired" is a more polite term than "deaf." But there is nothing unpleasant or undignified about the term "deaf," so no polite substitute is needed.

True, "hearing-impaired" doesn't pack the offensive wallop of "deaf-and-dumb" or "deaf-mute." It *is* negative and annoying. We don't run into the old negative terms all that often, but we run across "hearing-impaired" every day. Trying to set matters straight on an offender-by-offender basis can be exhausting—an endless task. However, we, as Deaf people, possess a sense of humor. We can turn the tables on those who label us. An ad for Flying Words Project, an ASL-poetry-performance series, read "Voice-interpreted for the sign-language-impaired."

HEARING-HANDICAPPED
Real-life examples:
*"Making technology accessible to the **hearing handicapped"***—HEAR NOW's old motto, circa 1989. It now reads: "Making technology accessible to the hearing impaired."

*"Gallaudet students have **hearing handicapping** conditions."*— From a United Methodist News Service press release, September 4, 1991

Quote:
*On February 1, 1993 we changed our name from the Association for the **Hearing Handicapped** to CONNECT SOCIETY. We also changed our slogan to* Deafness, Education, Advocacy, Families . . . *which forms the acronym, DEAF.*

Why the change? Because our stakeholders didn't feel that our old name said enough about what we do and what we stand for.— announcement from CONNECT SOCIETY, a community-based agency in Edmonton, Alberta, Canada

Over a decade of promoting Deaf Awareness

Our view:

A cute way of saying "deaf" while avoiding the word "deaf." Excuse the pun, but this sounds like doublespeak.[20]

Again, we don't like being categorized as a group solely on the basis of our hearing deficit. We are not *that* handicapped—most deaf people don't have a physical disability that interferes with their mobility. It's society that *makes* us handicapped by keeping so many opportunities inaccessible and refusing to learn how to communicate with us. The majority of our deaf readers don't even consider themselves handicapped.[21] We don't think in terms of deficit but wholeness.

AUDIOLOGICALLY HANDICAPPED

Real-life example:

*"A coalition of business and community leaders, chaired by Nevada First Lady Sandy Miller, herself a teacher of the **aurally handicapped,** will spearhead the fundraising drive."*—From a November 1989 press release about a caption-decoder campaign in Nevada[22]

Our view:

More doublespeak. This label includes variations like "aurally handicapped," "auditorily handicapped," and "auditorially handicapped"—fancy medical-sounding replacements for "deaf." Again, Deaf people resent this emphasis on broken auditory equipment. Why the need for such fancy, space-gobbling terms?

One of the government-funded National Institutes of Health is called "National Institute on Deafness and Other Communication Disorders." This is profoundly ironic in light of the fact that Deaf people, who use a sophisticated visual-spatial language, have contributed greatly to our understanding of communication and cognition.

HEARING-DISABLED

Example:

*The **hearing-disabled** community will benefit from the ADA.*—(We've seen something like this around somewhere)

Our view:

Modernization of "hearing-handicapped." We still come across occasional references to "hearing-disabled individuals" or "the hearing-disabled community." Since "disabled" has become a popular replacement word for "handicapped," euphemisms for "deaf" take a parallel course, logically enough. How far can you take it? Current replacement terms for "handicapped" are "physically challenged" and "differently abled." We haven't seen "audiologically challenged" or "differently-hearing-abled" yet, but at the rate things have been going, it's just a matter of time, isn't it?

Richard Nowell proposes the term "persons with hearing loss" to include both deaf and hard-of-hearing. He says, "Alternatives like 'hearing-challenged' seem very stilted to me."

HEARING-DEFECTIVE

Examples:

*Improved technology brings new hope to **hearing-defective** individuals.*—(See comment on previous example)

*"Children of **defectives** often feel guilt."*—Psychiatrist at a large oral deaf school, to Lou Ann Walker, daughter of Deaf parents, circa 1976[23]

Our view:

Disabled people were known as "defectives" in the old Soviet Union. We don't know what terms they use now, but we hope they're less chilling than this.

Likewise, we hope that the psychiatric/psychological profession in the United States has cleaned up *its* act.

NON-HEARING

Real-life example:

"The National Theatre of the Deaf combines the spoken word with sign language to create a visual language theatre that is enjoyed by both hearing and non-hearing audiences."—Southern Bell pamphlet

Quote:

*In referring to Deaf people as "**non-hearing**," Southern Bell reduced Deaf to a sterile, sub-average population. Better that they should say "**hearing-impaired**"—even that cringe-inducing term is less debasing than "non-hearing." Perhaps they should use the terms "**Deaf**" and "**non-Deaf**." Wouldn't that be something?—*Stacey Bradford, Flagler College, St. Augustine, Florida, in a letter to Southern Bell[24]

Our view:

A colloquial replacement term for "deaf." It tries to avoid the negative connotations of "hearing-handicapped" and "hearing-impaired." Unfortunately, it's still a negative term—it describes deaf people in terms of what they're not—rather like saying "nonwhites" to describe Blacks.

CAN'T HEAR

Real-life example:

"Goldie can't hear!"—written by a Kansas City orthodontist's nurse on a deaf woman's medical-history form, 1984

Our view:

Not so bad, but not so good, either. Nowhere near as

offensive as "hearing-impaired" or "hearing-disabled," this term still carries a slight whiff of the negative. The word "can't" has long been employed as a deadly weapon against the dreams of deaf children. ("You can't do that, you're deaf.") We prefer to accentuate the positive. Also, the label "can't hear" is misleading, as it implies that it's simply a matter of loudness, that shouting will remedy the problem. It doesn't.

DEAF

Real-life example:
*"Beginning in January 1993, all of the classic episodes of the long-running CBS series M*A*S*H are accessible to **deaf and hard-of-hearing** television viewers."*—The Caption Center, from a press release, February 16, 1993

Dictionary definitions:
deaf, *adj*. **1.** partially or wholly lacking or deprived of the sense of hearing; unable to hear, **2.** refusing to listen, heed, or be persuaded; unreasonable or unyielding: *deaf to all advice.*—*n*. **3.** *(used with a plural v.)* deaf persons collectively (usually prec. by *the*). [bef. 900; ME *deef*, OE *de[e]af*; c. MLG *d[o]of* ; D *doof*, OHG *toub*]—**Random House Dictionary**, 1987

deaf *adj.* **1.** Partially or completely lacking in the sense of hearing. **2. Deaf.** Of or relating to the Deaf or their culture. **3.** Unwilling or refusing to listen; heedless: *was deaf to our objections.*—**deaf** *n. (used with a pl. verb).* **1.** Deaf people considered as a group. **2. Deaf.** The community of deaf people who use American Sign Language as a primary means of communication. [Middle English *def*, *deaf*, from Old English *de[e]af*]. USAGE NOTE: Some critics have lately introduced a distinction between the lowercase noun *deaf*, which is used to refer simply to people with extreme hearing disorders, and the capitalized noun *Deaf*, which refers to the culture and community that has grown up around the use of American Sign Language as a primary means of communication.—**American Heritage Dictionary**, 1992

Quotes:
*"**Deaf** people can do anything . . . except hear."*—Dr. I King Jordan, first deaf president of Gallaudet University, 1988, quoting Fred Schreiber (1972)

*For the sake of clarification in identifying people, why don't we use one word—DEAF—for those of us who are deaf, hard-of-hearing, and deafened, with no measurement of our hearing loss? Let's look at ourselves as one People with our sub-cultures. . . . Let's use the word—DEAF—which is a simple word that everyone understands universally. (Please don't use '**Hearing-Impaired**' on us as it is a classically negative and medical term.)*

*If you, the readers, don't like the simple word—DEAF—why don't you make a survey and ask deaf people to come up with a better word? I tried a new word—"Seeing"—once before, but it did not work out at the time. . . .My point was that we could get together and pool our thoughts to come up with a better word. **WE** can change words. . . It is time to develop a better and more simple word to define us: deaf, hard-of-hearing, and deafened people.*—Julianna Fjeld, response to Stacey Bradford[25]

*There are three words I'd love to see eradicated from the English language: "handicapped," "disabled," and "**hearing-impaired**." Those three words make it look like there's something wrong with me and I am not normal. I resent that very much! Who gives the hearing people the right to decide who's normal or who's not? I like the term '**deaf**' because it is non-judgmental.*—Michele Westfall[26]

Our view:
Our readers have told us that they overwhelmingly prefer "deaf" because it's a simple, non-judgmental term. In a "Faxview" opinion poll, 90% of our respondents said they

preferred the term "Deaf," 1% "Hearing-Impaired," and 8% identified themselves as "Hard-of-Hearing."[27]

Terms like "hearing-impaired" and "non-hearing," in their narrowness, exclude the possibility of a language and culture; "deaf" is inclusive. So why doesn't everybody use the term? If we have a solution, why is there still a problem?

Some hearing people are squeamish about using the word "deaf." It makes them shudder inwardly. (Could it be because it sounds like "death?" One of us once got a letter from an uneducated hearing friend saying, "I thought you were death.") Or they avoid the term because they feel it's not dignified. After all, one of its meanings is decidedly negative: "refusing to listen." Or they feel it's crude—*deaf* **is** a 4-letter word. They prefer fancy-sounding terms like "hearing-impaired," which sound more polite, softer—deodorizing an "unpleasant" reality.

Do we need to have this reality deodorized, however? What's wrong with saying "deaf" to mean "deaf"? *Why* is "deaf" considered a dirty word? *Why* do so many companies advertise services and TTY numbers for "the hearing-impaired" when they could save 12 characters of precious ad space by saying "deaf"?

Traditionally, deaf people have been regarded with fear and hostility. There was something strange, even scary, about deaf people. They were considered cursed, devoid of a soul, creatures to be pitied. Even today, there is something taboo about deafness in American culture. A common response to a fearful topic is denial. This carries over into our language and, of course, advertising, which tells consumers what they want to hear (excuse the pun). Who wants to admit that they're going deaf? So they say, "I have difficulty hearing," or "I have a slight hearing loss," or "I have a moderate hearing impairment." Nobody out there in mainstream-advertising-land, it seems, is willing to use the 4-letter word.[28] An ongoing advertisement in **Reader's Digest** for a popular in-the-ear hearing aid reads, "I'm *not* deaf!" Righto.

What Deaf people have been doing, in a variety of ways and mediums, is to stand up boldly and tell the world, "We're deaf, and it's all right to be deaf. We have a history, a language that is the source of our culture, a heritage, an ethnic identity. We have a folklore and a sense of humor. We are human and whole. Many of us communicate differently from hearing people, but we are just as normal as hearing people consider themselves to be."

Deaf can be a positive identity. Deaf is another way of being human. And "Deaf" is what *we* prefer to be called.

WHAT NEXT?
Quote:
"The [British] media views deaf people as defective, pathetic, people who need help. Obviously, the press thinks deaf people are second-class citizens. . . .

"We all know the media is important because of awareness, publicity, but it goes far beyond that; it involves a question of public attitude. Attitude is looked on as one of the biggest barriers to true integration, and also helps influence the individual's personality. If the media portray deaf people in a negative, labeling way, that is passed on to the hearing society, who will then pass it on to deaf individuals.

"If we don't change people's attitudes towards deaf people, we will never be equal, never. Before we do that, we've got to sort it out, make it clear about who we are, how we define ourselves. Then we can move together with courage, strength, and conviction, and take on the media."—Doug Alker, Director of Community Services for the Royal National Institute for the Deaf, London, England, "Misconceptions of Deaf Culture in Media and the Arts," presentation, The DEAF WAY Conference, July 1989[29]

DEAF LIFE now uses "deaf" and "hard-of-hearing." (Actually, that's been our practice for some time.) We leave quotations containing terms like "hearing-impaired" when we feel they're absolutely necessary; otherwise, we edit them out.

You can help spread the word by telling your friends and colleagues that "deaf" and "hard-of-hearing" are the preferred terms.

Whenever you come across an offensive label in a newspaper, magazine, TV or radio talk-show interview, advertisement, or everyday conversation, confront the users. Write a letter to the reporter, editor, newspaper, magazine, station, company, or ad agency explaining why the term shouldn't be used, and what the proper terms are. Use your own words, and be polite. Your local public library can help you track down the addresses and the names of the "top brass." (In "Oh, No! Not Again!" and "Letters to the Editor," we've published several letters of complaint that can serve as models.) Remember, labels *can* become obsolete. Dictionaries and editorial style sheets *can* be updated. People's attitudes *can* change. We *can* do something about negative labels by taking a positive approach.

NOTES

[1] We now know that labels (*slow-track*, *backwards*, *gifted*) can directly affect a child's sense of self-worth and performance. We recall one experiment in which a group of "below-average" schoolchildren were re-labeled "academically gifted." As if by magic, their performances improved. They responded as though they *were* indeed gifted.

[2] The **American Heritage Dictionary** contains no listing for "deaf-and-dumb."

[3] "I'm Training You to Teach Students Whose Ears Don't Work Right," eighth installment of "The Way I Hear It," **DEAF LIFE**, December 1991.

[4] **In Silence: Growing Up Hearing in a Deaf World** (New York: St. Martin's Press, 1990), pp. 192-193. This incident took place in 1940.

[5] See, for example, Mark Twain's **Huckleberry Finn** (1884). There are two "genuine" deaf characters in the book—Jim's hapless daughter Lizabeth and the English gentleman William Wilks—and one character who fakes deafness (the duke).

[6] "Letters to the Editor," **DEAF LIFE**, August 1992.

[7] Ernest Tidyman, **Dummy** (New York: Bantam, 1975), "Author's note." A TV-movie adaptation, also titled *Dummy*, premiered in 1979, and got excellent reviews.

[8] "Oh, No! Not Again!" **DEAF LIFE Plus**, January 1991. Congressman

Kennedy is the son of Robert F. Kennedy, assassinated in 1968.

[9] "I'm Training You to Teach Students Whose Ears Don't Work Right."

[10] **tabloids**: smaller-size newspapers with emphasis on brief, sensationalistic stories focusing on crime, violence, and sexual scandal, instead of "serious" but less colorful news. Headlines and reportage tend to be feisty and opinionated. E.g., the **New York Post** and the **Daily News**, as opposed to **The New York Times**. However, the **Post** and **Daily News** have on occasion given fair coverage to Deaf issues, and prestigious papers like the **Times** have used unacceptable terminology. Supermarket tabloids such as the **National Enquirer**, **Sun**, **Globe**, **Star**, and **Weekly World News**, which focus almost exclusively on scandals and lurid, gossipy stories, have carried some of the most offensive coverage we've seen.

[11] **TIME's** cover story, "Death by Gun" (July 17, 1989), included a brief account of Patrick Kappus and his daughter Emma, of Brunswick, Georgia, both shot to death on May 1, 1989. Mr. Kappus and his wife were described thus: "a deaf-mute . . . she is also a deaf-mute." One of our readers wrote a letter of protest to **TIME** and got a response. **TIME** told her that the briefs had been taken directly from police reports. So the police evidently described the victims as "deaf-mutes," and **TIME's** writer copied it. **TIME** apologized to the reader. (See "Letters to the Editor," **DEAF LIFE**, March 1990.) However, **TIME** was soon at it again. An article on Max Ernst by the famed art critic-historian Robert Hughes in the April 22, 1991 issue contains a reference to "a school for deaf and mute children."

[12] "Captionwatch," **DEAF LIFE Plus**, May 1990.

[13] "Deaf-and-dumb" and "deaf-mute" don't have visual counterparts; there is no corresponding phrase, "blind-and-dense." This reflects the fact that blind people have traditionally commanded more respect from society. There *are* parallel euphemisms: "visually-impaired," "visually handicapped," "non-sighted," "can't see," etc. Most blind people prefer the term "blind."

[14] A few deaf people dislike the old term "stone-deaf," used to refer to someone who's profoundly deaf. See Mary J. Thornley's objection to "stone-deaf" in "Oh, No! Not Again!", **DEAF LIFE Plus**, December 1991. Most deaf people don't seem to consider this offensive, though.

[15] News Briefs, **DEAF LIFE Plus**, April 1993.

[16] "Letters," **DEAF LIFE**, November 1991.

[17] A **euphemism** is a "good" or "polite" word used as a substitute for a "bad" one—to soften or mask an unpleasant truth, or make something sound better: *passed away* instead of *died*, *pre-owned* for *secondhand* or *used*, *sanitation engineer* for *garbage collector*; *comfort station* for *public toilet*. Contemporary English language is full of euphemisms. They can be

annoying or unintentionally amusing.

[18] **connotation**: the underlying meaning or implication of a word beyond its literal sense. Consider these different words for *fat*: *overweight, corpulent, fatso*, and *buxom*—all have different connotations, ranging from rude to polite, humorous, even affectionate. (See note to Chapter 111.)

[19] These examples were published (all in edited form) in our December 1992 and January 1993 News Briefs (UL—12/92, p. 20; Royal Caribbean—12/92, p. 15; British Airways—1/93, p. 22).

[20] **doublespeak**: language that is deliberately vague, misleading, or inflated, especially that used in official corporate and government statements. Examples: *air support* instead of *bombing; precipitation activity* for *rain; covert operation* for *burglary; revenue enhancement* for *tax increase*.

[21] See "Faxview: Readers' Responses," in **DEAF LIFE**, February 1993: "Do you consider yourself handicapped?" 87% of our respondents said no; 13% yes.

[22] News Briefs, **DEAF LIFE Plus**, January 1990.

[23] Lou Ann Walker, **A Loss for Words** (New York, Harper & Row, 1986), pp. 150-151.

[24] "Oh, No! Not Again!" **DEAF LIFE Plus**, August 1991. Q.v. Julianna Fjeld's response, "Letters," **DEAF LIFE**, December 1991: "We at the National Theatre of the Deaf are very respectful and appreciative of Southern Bell for sponsoring our performances. The unfortunate choice of words in their promotion in no way lessens the fantastic work they do on the artistic and cultural levels. Southern Bell has long been recognized for its involvement with and support of the deaf community." The term "non-hearing" was probably the work of a copywriter working from NTD/Southern Bell press kits who thought "non-hearing" sounded more "genteel" than "deaf."

Deaf people aren't the only ones with an "image" problem. What should we call older people as a group? What's a dignified but honest term that *everybody* can accept? *Elderly, aged, old-timers, retirees, over-60s, Golden Agers, senior citizens*? Many people hate being called "senior citizens." Not all older people are retired. And so forth.

[25] "Letters," **DEAF LIFE**, December 1991.

[26] "Faxview: Readers' Responses," **DEAF LIFE**, February 1993.

[27] "Faxview: Readers' Responses," **DEAF LIFE**, December 1991.

[28] Well, not exactly. Companies like The Caption Center and Merrill Lynch, which specialize in or have departments catering to deaf consumers, correctly use the word "deaf" in their ads. But "deaf" is notably absent from other companies' ads aimed at the mainstream market.

[29] **DEAF LIFE**, October 1989, p. 29.

Authors' note: This chapter addendum is an adaptation of **DEAF LIFE's** May 1993 cover story.

Chapter 38

"Can 'Deaf' be used as a noun (as in 'the Deaf') or should it be used only as an adjective?"

As a librarian actively pursuing increasing both library service to the deaf community and deaf awareness, I find myself walking a tightrope. There is an inconsistency in what people who are deaf expect of hearing people and in regard to vocabulary.

When I first became involved with the deaf community I was told NOT to use deaf as a NOUN. It is an adjective so, of course, we should always say or write "deaf people" or "deaf community." I find that logical and correct, and yet organizations use deaf as a NOUN and actually use hearing as a NOUN too when referring to deaf and hearing people.

Recently I've become aware that a number of individuals don't want to be designated as "deaf artist" or "deaf writer." Rather they are "writers who happen to be deaf." While I can understand this also it's a little difficult to say the above phrase or write it consistently.

I guess physical characteristics are different from ethnic, racial, or religious affiliations but at the same time, we use those both as NOUNS and ADJECTIVES; i.e., "Jews" and "Jewish People."

Anyway, can you help me with my dilemma?

—Shushano Long, Cleveland Heights, Ohio

mong members of a group (e.g., ethnic or religious), certain permissible ("in-group") expressions take on a negative connotation when used by outsiders. Some Deaf people will actually use the word "Deaf" to mean *a Deaf person*: "A group of Deafs traveled to Hawaii." This would be unacceptable usage from a hearing person; it would undoubtedly be construed as an insult. And not all deaf people like that usage. Likewise, some deaf persons use the word "Deafie" as a term of affection; other deaf persons dislike it.

Some deaf people object to the phrase "the deaf." They feel that it devalues the humanity of deaf people. They prefer to be seen as *people* first. The preferred term is "deaf persons," "deaf people," or even "deaf community" instead of "the deaf." (Capitalization of the "D" is optional. It depends on whether you're referring to culturally Deaf persons specifically, an inclusive group or subgroup of deaf persons, or the entire deaf population of a city, county, state, or nation.)

Using "the Deaf" without "people" or "community" is certainly acceptable usage in the Deaf community, especially if it's part of a title. Witness: National Theatre of the Deaf; National Association of the Deaf; National Fraternal Society of the Deaf; National Technical Institute for the Deaf, Registry of Interpreters for the Deaf; Dogs for the Deaf, Inc.; *etcetera*. The meaning here is unambiguous: nonprofit organizations representing a deaf constituency or institutions, agencies, and other entities serving the needs of the deaf population, or, in the case of NTD, showcasing its creativity. In some cases (as with NFSD/FRAT), the usage reflects the fact that these entities were founded by deaf people.

Similar adjectives are often used without their referent word "persons" or "people"; e.g., *The Young and Restless*, "the gifted," "the blind," "the handicapped." Deaf people use "the Hearing"—or even "Hearings"—in the same way. One gets used to it.

It's impossible to formulate hard-and-fast rules about common informal usage. Much depends on the sensibilities of the deaf persons in question, how strongly they identify with the cultural-Deaf community, how important (or marginal) their deafness is in relation to their work, and how they feel about hearing people using the term "the Deaf." For example, *Deaf writer* versus *writer who happens to be deaf.* Consider the differences in connotation. Of course, it helps to have some familiarity with the corpus of their work. When in doubt, proceed cautiously.

In conclusion, we'd like to share an anecdote from Richard Nowell, a veteran interpreter, teacher, researcher, administrator, audiologist, and parent counselor who has worked extensively with Deaf performers, and who is currently Associate Professor in "Education of Persons with Hearing Loss" at Indiana University of Pennsylvania. His view is worth noting:

> Many years ago when I was still a new professional in the field of education of persons with hearing loss, I attended a meeting at Gallaudet. I presented a talk in which I made several references to "the deaf." After my presentation was finished, a deaf man (I have no recollection who it was) came up to me and gently signed to me something like this:
>
> "When you use the term 'the deaf,' you seem to be talking about us as if we were all the same. That offends many deaf people. It's better to say something like 'deaf persons' instead of 'the deaf.'"
>
> He didn't act angry with me. He didn't embarrass me in front of other people. He didn't make me feel bad. He simply taught me an important lesson in a very constructive way.
>
> Although I won't say that I have never slipped and used the term "the deaf" since then, I have done my best to avoid it. And after our conversation, I felt even more strongly that I liked being part of the Deaf World. There is a right way and a wrong way to teach dumb hearing people like me this kind of lesson.*

* "I'm Training You to Teach Students Whose Ears Don't Work Right," the ninth installment of his series "The Way I Hear It. . .," **DEAF LIFE**, December, 1991.

Chapter 39

When I use the word "handicapped," my deaf friends get angry. Why is that?

here are two basic ways to see deafness: as a physical disability or an ethnic difference. The "disability" outlook includes describing deafness as a "communication disorder," a physical defect, or a disease; the "ethnic" outlook sees deaf persons as whole, possessing a distinct language and culture. Needless to say, if *we* believed that being deaf amounted to no more than living under a disability, we wouldn't have started **DEAF LIFE**. Or written this book.

The word "handicap" has an interesting origin: gaming. According to the **American Heritage Dictionary**, it derives from *hand in cap*, "originally a lottery game in which players held forfeits in a cap." It now carries a variety of meanings, primarily the one associated with horse-racing: "a race or contest in which advantages or compensations are given different contestants according to their varied abilities or experience, to equalize the chances of winning." It also means (a) "a deficiency, especially an anatomical, physiological, or mental deficiency, that prevents or restricts normal achievement;" (b) "any disadvantage or disability," and this is the definition we're concerned with. The term "handicapped" is likewise defined as (1) "disabled or crippled;" (2) "mentally deficient;" (3) "having or being under a handicap. Said of a contestant."

Of course, if you consider deafness in purely medical terms, it's a disability, it's a disorder, it's a deficiency, it's a handicap. But suppose that deaf people overwhelmingly rejected this view because they found it too limiting? The majority of deaf people do *not* see themselves as handicapped. As in the statement originated by Frederick C. Schreiber and popularized by Dr. I. King Jordan: "Deaf people can do anything . . . except hear." We can't hear? Isn't *that* a disability? By this definition, *everybody* has a disability. Some hearing people can't dance; some have no artistic skill whatsoever; some have lousy coordination; some have no sense of humor; some have poor memories. Yet these same folks would not be eager to let themselves be labeled as "handicapped." Deaf people who dislike being similarly labeled don't like being lumped into one misleading category and dehumanized: "Handicapped? What do you mean? I live a full life. I work; I pay taxes."

The "ethnic" view sees deaf people as different from hearing folks, but just as whole—not merely as possessors of a set of defective auditory paraphernalia. This is a sensible and humane view, although it is not one held by the majority of doctors, specialists, and audiologists—those whose business it is to "fix" what's "wrong" with deaf people's "hearing disorders."

The Federal view of deaf people is that all deaf people are handicapped/disabled. One faction in the Deaf community endorses this view. They feel that since society is based on sound and they're excluded from full participation in a sound-based society, they're entitled to receive compensation in the form of Social Security Disability (SSD) and Supplemental Security Income (SSI) benefits. They believe that society owes them compensation for the hardships they endure.

Another faction argues, "No! We have a culture. We have a community. We're fine. We need to get the Federals to understand that we're a culture. We don't have a handicap. Our hardship is more of a communication barrier than a physical disability."

Unfortunately, "handicapped" has acquired a negative connotation. It suggests social inferiority, poverty, hopelessness; it solicits pity, not respect. It makes us shudder. Some deaf people consider it an insult, equivalent to calling a Black person "nigger" or a Hispanic-American "wetback." Not all deaf people object to being called "handicapped." But it's not a bad idea to avoid using the term. Why not simply say "deaf"? If you want to know how *they* feel about the "H-word," ask them directly.

Every person, deaf, hearing, or whatever, is an individual. Let this not be forgotten. We need to get beyond the limitations imposed by labels. Seeing—*really* seeing—people in terms of something more than a "physical deficiency" isn't just socially courteous, it's politically smart as well.

Chapter 40

I'm a student in a sign-language class. I've noticed that my deaf teacher uses the term "hearing" to describe me. I find it very strange that deaf people do that. Why do deaf people use the terms "hearing" and "hearings"?

et's engage in some wild generalization and divide humanity into two factions: deaf and non-deaf. The non-deaf people constitute the majority; the deaf people, the minority. Any majority group uses terms to describe themselves (insiders) and the minority (outsiders). Conversely, the minority, which sees *themselves* as insiders, uses its own terms to describe the majority (outsiders). Deaf people commonly use the term *hearing* (singular noun) or *hearings* (plural noun) to describe the non-deaf majority. As used by deaf people, it means "people who can hear," i.e., non-deaf. The word "hearing" is, of course, found in the dictionary, meaning "the capacity to hear" or "the range of audibility." But this particular usage is not. It's a specifically Deaf usage. As such, it may come as a shock to some non-deaf folks.

As we pointed out in the introduction, non-deaf people—that is, people with completely functional audiological organs and normal hearing—don't think of themselves as being "hearing." They take their normal hearing for granted, as they do their other faculties. *Hearing* is a term employed by the deaf outsiders, applied to the non-deaf insiders. This kind of label can make the "labelee" uncomfortable.

How important are labels? Our long and bitter experience as an oppressed minority group has shown that labels can be powerful weapons. (We have already noted this in Chapter 37.) Labels have caused us an immeasurable amount of damage—in terms of self-esteem, pride, and squelched potential, as well as the more tangible economic sense. The labels that have been applied to deaf people throughout the millennia have called attention to our supposed deficits—"deaf-and-dumb," "deaf-mute," "deaf and mute," "mute," etc.—never our strengths. These labels emphasize our apparent freakishness, not our normality. No member of the majority culture would endure labels like these, calling into question their very ability to *think*.

So here we have a case of the tables being turned. Deaf people, seeing their own deafness as a normal characteristic, much like an ethnic identity, see the non-deaf majority as the outsiders, the different ones, the people who lack a Deaf identity. They use the indispensable term *hearing*. It's not necessarily a pejorative term (after all, once upon a time "deaf-and-dumb" was a placidly neutral expression), but it can be employed as a weapon, a put-down. It can be equivalent to an ethnic slur. It depends on the context.

The sign for *hearing* is an extended index finger making a quick repeated horizontal rolling motion in front of the mouth, symbolizing speaking-with-the-voice. Communicating with hearing people, deaf people occasionally use the term *hearie*. The sign is made like *hearing*. *Hearie* can be used as a term of insult applied to one hearing person, or can refer to a group of hearing people, or society (the "Hearing" culture) in its most general sense. *Hearing* can describe attitudes, mindsets, lifestyles, values, even culinary preferences. (As in the original playscript for **Children of a Lesser God**, when Orin calls veal piccata and sushi "*'hearing'* food.") Familiar Deaf expressions of exasperation are "They're just a bunch of hearings" or "What do you expect from hearings?" Then there's the ultimate expression of prejudice: "I don't like hearings."

A new term, *hearo* (or *hear-o*), describes a deaf person who apes hearing people.* The sign for *hear-o* is literally "hearing-in-the-head"—shifting the *hearing/hearie* sign from the mouth to the forehead. The sign itself has been in currency for some time. (It's analogous to a Black person calling another Black person an "Oreo"—Black on the outside, white inside.) *Hear-o* is an equally pejorative term. Whether or not you find it amusing depends on your point of view.

Aren't these labels insulting? Not necessarily—they reflect a normal human trait of expressing belonging to a group and distinguishing ourselves from those who are different. The terms used by deaf people to insult or poke fun at the hearing majority cannot compare with the nastiness of the terms the hearing majority has long used against us.

* And remember, folks, you read it here first!

Chapter 41

Do all deaf people benefit from hearing aids?

—Michal Davidowitz, Rochester, New York

o. A hearing aid is not a miracle machine. It's a tiny amplifier. It makes sounds louder, and that's all it can do. It amplifies everything it picks up, without distinction—all sounds that happen to pop up in the immediate area as well as distracting background noises like traffic. A hearing aid (the familiar analog type, at least) cannot "zero in" on the voice or voices you most want to pick up; it doesn't work selectively, as our hearing does. And it cannot make other people's speech clearer, merely a bit louder. So if a speaker's articulation is not particularly good—for example, if he's a mumbler—or if his face is not clearly visible, a hearing aid is of very little help.

Because even severely deaf persons have some degree of recognition of certain sounds, many do wear powerful hearing aids to pick up whatever sounds they can; they feel that an aid helps make them more aware of what's going on. Others do not feel comfortable with an aid and don't like to wear them. Many Deaf people function quite well without any electronic doojizmos.

There *are* sophisticated digital aids that can be programmed to pick up the frequencies of speech, or even whispers, and are promoted as having the ability to "focus" on the speakers the user most wants to hear, to the exclusion of background noise. They are designed for users with moderate deafness. Severely and profoundly deaf people, we've been told on good authority, do not benefit from digital aids. Never having had the opportunity to try out any of these models, we can't say for ourselves how effective they are.

How does a deaf person decide whether or not to wear an aid? As part of "early intervention," even newborns can be fitted with aids. Traditionally, young deaf children, even profoundly deaf ones, have been fitted with aids, especially in mainstreamed schools. This decision is made by the parents, educators, and audiologists who want the child to be "as normal as possible." It may even be official school or state policy. The child's own feelings have seldom, if ever, been taken into account. The implication is that a hearing aid gives a deaf child a semblance of normality—makes him or her more like a hearing child, more part of "the hearing world." Often, the actual benefits of wearing an aid (if there are any) are far outweighed by the sheer discomfort. Not surprisingly, some of these children grow up with bitter memories of being forced to wear bulky body-pack aids, enduring the discomfort, even pain, of being plugged into a machine that amplified gibberish. (Ironically, repeated exposure to loud amplification can damage or destroy the child's residual hearing— the very residual hearing that those audiologists are striving to protect!) Children with this kind of background are understandably unenthusiastic about wearing aids.

Most deaf children in residential schools are encouraged to wear aids, but some enlightened professionals recognize that even heavy amplification isn't really going to benefit some kids. Some parents let the children decide for themselves. Some kids who fight the aid when they're young choose to wear one when they're older. By the time a child is old enough to leave home and set off for college, work, or whatever, s/he can decide whether to continue wearing an aid. No deaf child or adult should ever be forced to wear one. It should be a matter of personal choice.

Some Deaf people, we've noticed, wear aids all the time— even when they're with other Deaf people who sign fluently! Others wear them when they want to listen to a concert or something of special interest on TV, or to use a telephone or an audio loop in a theater. Others never wear them.

Adults who feel that an aid might help them can get tested by an audiologist, and try some of the many aids on the market before choosing the one that's best for their needs. Expense is, of course, a consideration. Hearing aids, particularly the digital models, are exorbitantly costly. For those of modest means, they are simply unaffordable. Analog models are somewhat cheaper, but still represent a considerable investment. We're talking several hundreds, or even thousands, of dollars here. And that doesn't include the batteries.

Although cochlear and auditory-brainstem implants are looked on as potential destroyers of Deaf culture, hearing aids have long been an accepted part of our culture. Why? They're removable, and don't involve invasive surgery. The attitudes of those in the hearing-aid industry, however, have not shown much warmth towards the concept of Deaf culture, since it's antithetical to their interests. A group of proud Deaf people (who refuse to feel ashamed of their inability to hear or to participate in hearing social interactions) aren't going to be enthusiastic consumers of audiometrics, since they don't feel an overwhelming need to "get hearing help." Deaf pride doesn't sell hearing aids.

The hearing-aid industry prefers to see deaf people in terms of audiological deficit and social debility, as potential consumers of their expensive circuitry, not as members of a cultural-linguistic minority. In some of their PR releases and ads, they scrupulously avoid using the word "deaf," favoring vaguer, less threatening terms like "hearing loss" and "hearing impairment." The emphasis is on overcoming one's "social difficulties," not on confronting or embracing one's differentness. To them, "Deaf" is invisible.

This helps to explain the ambivalent attitude some Deaf people feel towards hearing aids, and why some with moderate loss, who putatively might benefit from amplification, refuse to wear them. Sure, hearing aids can help boost one's sound perception . . . but what have the makers, executives, and PR folks really done for our community?

The cochlear-implant controversy

A cochlear implant is a "bionic ear" device. A small receiver is implanted in the mastoid bone behind the ear; an array of electrodes (24 for the 24-channel device) is inserted surgically into the cochlea (the snail-shaped organ of the inner ear). This operation involves drilling a hole in the skull. After one month of healing, the implantee is fitted with an ear-level microphone and a transmitting coil attached by a cord to a speech processor, a sort of mini-computer. The microphone picks up sounds, relays them to the speech processor, which transmits them to the receiver behind the ear, which sends the signals to the internal device, which stimulates the auditory nerve, which sends these signals to the brain, which interprets them as sounds.

Older models, like the familiar 22-channel implant, had a noticeable magnetic disk clamped onto the scalp and cords poking out of the wearer's head. The less obtrusive 24-channel implant looks remarkably like a behind-the-ear hearing aid, with fewer external components than the 22-channel device, but still requires head surgery to install.

Candidates for implants are those who have little or no usable hearing in one or both ears. A cochlear implant does *not* completely restore hearing to the implanted ear, nor is the quality of sound completely "natural." An implantee, ideally, will be able to hear a wider variety of sounds and, with intensive therapy, develop better speech patterns. They may or may not be able to use the telephone.

The long-range effects of such a device are unknown. What sort of effect the constant electronic stimulation may have on the tissue and nerves of the inner ear is likewise unknown. Many deaf people feel that this is a drastic expedient. Hearing aids, vibrotactile devices, auditory trainers, and FM systems are at least removable. A cochlear implant is there to stay.

Results have been mixed. While some children and adults certainly benefit from an implant, others have benefited very little. In a few cases, the results have been horrible—e.g., the body painfully rejects the implant. It's impossible to predict how much benefit a deaf person will derive from an implant. The implantee may enjoy considerable improvement in the quality of sound, or moderate, or practically none.

Needless to say, cochlear implants are fantastically expensive, so the companies who manufacture them tout their "cost-effective" benefits. They claim that a child with an implant will have more options and better social, educational, and job opportunities. It's estimated that no more than 1% of the deaf population are good candidates for implants, yet implant advocates are enthusiastic about the possibility of wiping out deafness—making it "obsolete."

The Deaf community is certainly not against children, teenagers, or adults voluntarily receiving implants. Late-deafened adults often make excellent candidates. A number of ALDAns (members of the Association of Late-Deafened Adults) have received implants, and enjoy them. A few have gotten mediocre results, and a very few have had bad results.

Unlike hearing aids, cochlear implants have continued to generate considerable controversy, although things have lately quieted down a bit. One problem we have is sorting the propaganda from the facts. The cochlear-implant industry targets not only adults but parents of deaf babies and children, and its slick, glossy promotional literature, touting the benefits of implants, should not be taken as plain truth. And since implantees have had such a wide range of experiences with their implants, their stories range from Gothic horror tales to ecstastic testimonials. An unknown number of implantees no longer use their implants; a few have gotten them surgically removed. In some cases, they felt they weren't benefiting from the device; in others, they simply didn't want it in their heads anymore.

Chapter 42

Isn't it possible to have the best of both worlds— ASL *and* a cochlear implant?

n the summer of 1990, the U.S. Food and Drug Administration approved cochlear implants for children aged 2-17. Previously, only adults had been able to get implants. Now the green light was given to implanting children without their consent. With the emergence of the smaller 24-channel implant in the late 1990s, the age of implantation was subsequently lowered to infancy.

Deaf-rights advocates tried, but were unable, to prevent the FDA from approving implants for children. Many of us were disturbed by the FDA's decision. Why?

For one thing, Deaf people themselves—deaf children grown up—have had no say in the matter. Their views, and their real concern for other deaf children, formed by long and hard firsthand experience, are typically dismissed as irrelevant by those who have the power—the hearing oralists, scientists, executives, audiologists, and governmental officials.

We believe that deaf children should be exposed to sign language as well as speech, as part of a Total Communication or Bilingual-Bicultural curriculum. They can choose whatever mode they feel most comfortable with. They can elect to wear a hearing aid, and when they're old enough, voluntarily receive an implant. Or not. The issue is choice.

In the Deaf-cultural view, an implant is the ultimate invasion of the ear, the ultimate denial of deafness. Those who make the decision to implant children choose to risk the children's health so that they can hear more sounds and develop clearer speech. Children attending oral schools and mainstream programs are the most likely to be implanted.

Their parents, the ones who choose to have their children implanted, are in effect saying, "I don't respect the Deaf community, and I certainly don't want my child to be part of it. I want him/her to be part of the hearing world, not the Deaf world."

But the situation is actually a bit more complicated than that, since an increasing number of children in residential schools or TC programs are getting implants, too, and their parents may have an affirmative attitude towards ASL.

For over a century, medical professionals have been advising parents of deaf children that they must never, *ever* use sign language. If they do, their children will never learn to speak properly. Parents of children who receive cochlear implants are (in most cases) required to commit them (and themselves) to a grueling oral/auditory program. There is absolutely *no* room for sign language there. Exposure to ASL, goes the argument, only impedes an implanted child's progress. The doctors make this clear when they counsel parents of prospective implantees: do *not* sign. Should the parents persist in signing to their child (and, in some cases, children choose signing for themselves), the clinic may drop them.

What is the clinics' rationale? Sign language interferes with the acquisition of speech. Well, here we are in the technological age of enlightenment, but in terms of attitude, it's back to the Dark Age. Some things never change.

The aim of an oral/auditory program is to teach a deaf child to speak, speechread, and use her/his residual hearing. Adding a cochlear implant intensifies the "rehabilitation" process and puts an added burden on the child. S/he spends several long months learning to interpret the electronically processed sounds as meaningful speech. The outcome is totally unpredictable. Some children thrive; others fail. How many fail for each one who succeeds? Half? Most? We don't yet know.

Isn't it possible to have the benefit of both the oral/aural and sign-language packages? Ideally, yes, but in practice, it often doesn't work out that way. Parents of children who receive implants have, by and large, already committed themselves to the oral/aural approach. Most of them have not learned even the rudiments of signing, and, moreover, have absolutely no intention of doing so. They believe that they are making *the best* decision for their child. And in this, they are reinforced by the doctors, audiologists, and speech pathologists. So the child starts out without exposure to spoken *or* visual language. As a result, some of these children may already have a sizable "language gap" when they receive their implants.

Some of these doctors and clinicians (and the parents themselves) perpetrate the stereotypical notion that parents who choose the oral/aural regimen have higher expectations for their children than do those who choose an ASL-based mode. *Sure, the oral/aural approach is tough, but so rewarding! We know what is best for our kids.* Who doesn't want the best for their children?

But if parents choose to deny their child exposure to and practice in sign language, they're choosing the hard way. Which is not necessarily the *best* way.

We're not speaking from the standpoint of rigorous double-blind scientific studies, but from long, bitter, and painful experience. Let's put it this way: we personally know many deaf people. And of the many whom we know, many of those have complained bitterly about the oral/aural regimen they were subjected to as children. We know *none* who complained about being subjected to a rigorous sign-language regimen! Indeed, they almost always picked up sign-language skills from other deaf children—not from a teacher, pathologist, clinical manual, or a member of the medical profession. From their peers. That says something, doesn't it? If they complain about the quality of their education and upbringing, they're apt to say things like: their schooling wasn't academically demanding enough; the doctors told their parents not to sign; their parents couldn't communicate with them; speech therapy was a boring and hateful ordeal, their teachers had low expectations for them. *Etcetera.*

Some medical/audiological professionals would undoubtedly claim that they respect sign language and present it as a legitimate option to parents. But some of them have nonetheless encouraged low expectations, whether or not they counsel shocked and bereaved parents to learn sign. The implant industry, on the other hand, takes an aggressively "positive" approach: *See how much your child can accomplish with our product! For a deaf child with an implant who can talk and listen, the sky's the limit! Implanted deaf kids can do ANYTHING! The implant lets them be NORMAL! They can be part of the mainstream of life and participate FULLY!*

We *know* that early exposure to sign language benefits deaf children. We *know* that complete reliance on a strict oral/aural regimen can create a debilitating language gap. We *know* that doctors are dead wrong when they play the absolutist game: *either take the strict oral/aural approach, or get the heck out of my clinic and put your kid in a signing program. Total Communication? Sorry. We don't practice that. Either commit wholeheartedly to our way or go elsewhere.* We *know* that parents are often hoodwinked into choosing implants. We *know* that implants are aggressively marketed to parents, as ASL is not.

As noted in the previous chapter, some deaf people who have received cochlear implants had such bad experiences with them, or have flourished in a newly-acquired ASL milieu, or simply wish to affirm their Deaf identity, that they stopped using them, and a few have gone through the trouble of having them surgically removed. We're curious to know if the implant industry takes any note of this. Some young implantees—relatively few, so far as we can see—may manage to develop good bilingual skills in an ASL environment while benefiting from their implants. But what about the hazing they endure from their non-implanted peers? In a school for the deaf, an implant can hardly be a status symbol.

And what does the implant do to promote good language skills? Literacy? The picture is still inconclusive. We'd like to see more objective research here.

The implant industry, nonetheless, is doing booming business. More and more deaf children (and babies) are undergoing surgery, the whole oral/aural *shtick*, and mainstreaming. Deaf people have ASL and the perspective of experience. The implant/medical industry has the money, the clout, the networking, the referral system, and the market.

Do doctors care what deaf people think? Do they listen? From what we've seen, no. There are exceptions, but the exceptions are few. Deaf people are largely seen as patients, clients, involuntary consumers, and subjects. Expressing our views is one thing. Making ourselves heard is another matter entirely.

I (MSM) met an interesting and energetic woman during one of my "conference stops," the 1997 ITHI conference in Chicago. She is deaf (not late-deafened), and had recently received a cochlear implant. She signs fluently (not ASL, more of a PSE orientation), and is very supportive of Deaf culture. She is adamantly opposed to the idea of giving deaf children cochlear implants. She said (and I'm quoting her from memory), "I'm against cochlear implants for kids. It's not right. It's just not *appropriate*. Implants are not something that should be forced on kids. They're something that should be a matter of choice—by the wearers themselves. Deaf children should wait until they're adults, then they can choose this for themselves—if they want. My implant doesn't help me tremendously, it helps a little. Implants for kids are a *bad* idea."

On the bright side, we predict that many of these implanted children will choose to join the Deaf community when they reach adolescence or early adulthood. It is our challenge to be there for them, to welcome and support them, and to encourage them to bring their unique perspective to enrich our collective experience.

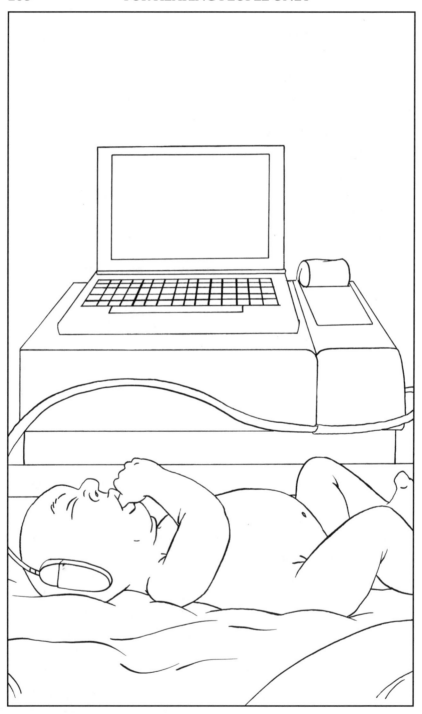

Chapter 43

Why are deaf people against universal infant hearing screening? Isn't it a good idea to detect hearing loss as soon as possible?

any deaf people feel jittery about the prospect of statewide hearing-screening tests adminis-tered to all newborns in hospitals. Screening is enthusiastically endorsed by the Alexander Graham Bell Association for the Deaf—i.e., oral/ aural advocates. Signing-Deaf people are split on the issue. So our feelings are decidedly mixed.

Screening uses headphones (with disposable earplugs) hooked up to a machine that measures brain response to sounds.[1] It has three advantages: it's non-invasive, quick, and said to be extremely accurate. The baby sleeps through the whole business. In a few minutes, a diagnosis can be made. This is a much more efficient approach than the old haphazard methods—clapping the hands behind the child's back, slamming doors, banging pot-lids together, dropping heavy objects, stomping, yelling—any of which can yield "false readings."

The problem is not the screening test as such, but what happens immediately afterwards. Our major qualm is that these tests are administered by audiological personnel—essentially the same folks who have traditionally broken the news to parents that their child is deaf, and who have encour-aged them to have low expectations and/or place the child in an oral/auditory or mainstream program.

So our big question is: who gets first crack at the parents? Representatives of the oral/aural or the signing sectors? Do the parents get a fair presentation of the options—or are they automatically routed onto the oralist path? Do they truly understand that the options include residential or day sign-language-based programs? Are they referred to other parents of deaf children? To Deaf adults who can provide a wealth of experience, wisdom, and reassurance?

There are many advantages to having a baby's hearing loss identified and confirmed immediately after birth. Traditionally, many deaf children have gone unidentified until they're 3 years old (or even older), by which time their their hearing counterparts are already putting complex sentences together. Some of these children never catch up, language-wise. We agree that it's infinitely better for parents to know that their baby is deaf right away than not to know—to start out with this knowledge instead of losing out on communication and language development for 3 years, then trying frantically to "make up for lost time." There is always the hope that they will become educated, supportive, and involved. But in reality, we know that not enough parents do. Even though they "want the best" for their child, too many are easily convinced that the road to "normality" must be a strictly oral/auditory one, and that all they have to do is speak up a bit, or mouth words into the child's face. Or subject the child to an expensive dose of head surgery.

What do parents do *after* they realize their child is deaf? We question the negative attitudes that many parents and audiological/medical personnel have towards the Deaf community and sign language. Consider, for example, this passage from a **Reader's Digest** writeup about Curtis Pride:

> With an irreversible 95-percent hearing loss, Curt attended special classes in his Washington, D.C., suburb. But the studious boy never learned signed language. Instead, Sallie and John chose a program to help their son read lips. They were aware that some children who used sign language would never learn to speak because they could fall back on the signing when they were misunderstood.
>
> —Michael Bowker, "The Loudest Cheer," **Reader's Digest**, May 1994

Reader's Digest is extraordinarily popular. Its cover proclaims: "World's Most Widely Read Magazine . . . Over 28 million copies in 17 languages bought monthly." Now, we ask, if Sallie and John Pride, educated and intelligent professionals living in Silver Spring, Maryland, one of the world's great centers of Deaf population, could have this "sign-language-is-a-crutch" attitude, and if **Reader's Digest** could publicize this misconception as if it were a fact, what does this bode for us?[2]

Here's a similar passage from a glowing "medical miracle" story in a popular supermarket magazine about a mother whose born-deaf son received a cochlear implant when he was a toddler. (The article details Kim's grief and frustration but says nothing about any early attempts to get language to Zak, or any contact with Deaf people, before Zak received his implant. Evidently, she never tried signing.)

> As time passed . . . Kim's heartache grew. He'll have to go to a special school, she knew, where he'd learn to speak with his hands, read lips.
> And that wonderful giggle Zak had—the doctor said that would fade away too. "Without the feedback of hearing himself, he'll stop making sounds."
> My silent son in a silent world, Kim's heart ached.
> "It's time," the audiologist finally said. "Zak's past a year old. He should start learning sign language."
> Kim nodded. "But I can't bear to think of all he'll miss," she wept.
> The audiologist paused. "You know," she said, "doctors can do something called a cochlear implant . . . "
> —Janna Graber, "It's a whole new world!"
> **Woman's World**, January 16, 2001

The cochlear-implant industry has mounted a successful marketing campaign, playing on the hopes and fears of parents: *Do you want your child to be normal? To be a full participant in the mainstream? Do you want her to be part of the action? Do you want him to excel academically?* Implants are actively promoted in oral programs for young children. We suspect that parents of newly-diagnosed deaf children are a prime "sucker market" for implants. When the screeners arrive, can the Nucleus 24 salespeople be far behind? That's what worries us.

It's important for parents to understand that they have to get language to the child immediately. For many of us, that means visual communication. For others, speech and speechreading. For some, a multi-modal mixture (Total Communication). But the evidence shows that even hearing babies recognize and respond to gestures long before they are able to communicate in speech, and that they can learn to use a number of simple signs before they can articulate spoken words, so we encourage parents to learn and use signs, gestures, pantomime, and pictures. But will they?

The first thing that many parents do, at the urging of audiologists, is to purchase hearing aids. Some children may benefit from them, as we've noted, but for others, the annoyances outweigh whatever benefits they may derive. We wonder why parents are so enthusiastic about choosing costly "solutions" like aids (several hundred dollars each; a couple thousand for the fancy digital models) or cochlear implants ($40,000-$50,000 a pop), while they disdain learning sign language ("too much trouble"), when they can sometimes get *that* for free! Yes, free. Some schools for the deaf and community agencies offer early-intervention programs in which trained teachers or Deaf volunteers visit the baby and parents, play with them, and teach communication skills. Even if the parents buy videotapes, CD-ROMs, and books, hire a sign-language tutor, or enroll in a community-college Basic Sign course, it's still cheaper than buying an implant or aids and the endless succession of earmolds and batteries. Establishing a parents' network and making friends in the Deaf community costs practically nothing.

After purchasing audiometrics, the next thing that many parents do is endeavor to teach their deaf child to speak. What the child needs is immediate access to *language*. This is *not* synonymous with speech. Exposure to speech doesn't make a languageless child "languaged" overnight.

Some children who were virtually languageless during their first years nonetheless catch up and excel. But most parents want to give their children every possible intellectual and communicative advantage. And the more involved they get, the better their odds become.

We believe that reading and writing skills, not speech skills, are of prime importance, and should be acquired first. Literacy, not speech, should be the cornerstone of a deaf child's education. Deaf children should learn to read early. Once they have a solid foundation in visual communication and basic literacy skills, then they can focus on developing and polishing speech skills. But speech should not take precedence. Clear communication is of the utmost importance. Sign language is an excellent tool for communicating to deaf children. Deaf adults, whatever their preferred mode, can provide tremendous support to the family.

If *these* things are taught to parents, we have no objection to screening.

---

[1] The most popular tests used in newborn-hearing screening are *auditory-brainstem response* (ABR) and *evoked otoacoustic emissions* (EOAE). ABR measures the brain's response to sound input to determine whether the ear is functioning properly. EOAE monitors the sounds produced in the inner ear in response to electronic stimulation.

[2] Curtis Pride, an expert speechreader, has never learned sign language, a fact noted in several published articles. Pat Jordan's **Sporting News** cover story (May 2, 1994) explains that "even as a child, Pride refused to learn sign language. He saw that as a sign of defeat." Robert F. Panara met John Pride several years ago, and told us that his attitude towards sign language had changed considerably—he felt more positively about it. As for Curtis, his public statements about his non-use of sign language have evolved from the flirtly negative ("I don't plan to [learn it and] I am not curious about it") to something a bit more diplomatic— "Maybe I'll learn it someday."

Chapter 44

When deaf people meet deaf parents of a new baby, they always ask if the baby's deaf or hearing. Why?

—In response to a dare by Phil Jacob,
West Orange, New Jersey

As we've already noted, the vast majority of deaf couples have hearing children. And the vast majority of deaf children have hearing parents. Some 10% of deaf parents have deaf children. Thus, Deaf families (deaf parents with deaf children) are a rarity. At large get-togethers of Deaf people where whole families turn out, you'll find that most of the children there are hearing. And most of them are (to a greater or lesser extent) bilingual. Deaf adults, seeing them, will invariably ask the parents, "Deaf or hearing?" And most (no matter the answer) will try to initiate a friendly conversation with the kids: "Hi! How are you? Having fun? What's your namesign?"

When seeing a new baby for the first time, virtually all hearing folks ask, "Boy or girl?" and/or "How old?" and/or "Is the baby healthy?" But virtually all Deaf folks ask: "Deaf or hearing?" They want to get a "fix" on the baby's cultural identity, so to speak—to see if the baby's "one of them" or not. Deaf identity is of prime importance in their lives. Being Deaf is seemingly more important than being "healthy"—more important than just about anything else.

We've compared being Deaf to sharing an ethnic identity. Since most deaf people are born into hearing families, membership in the Deaf community is usually not inherited (the way ethnic identity usually is) but acquired. Traditionally, it's been transmitted from child to child; it's an elective cultural affiliation. And it's a bit like being part of an extended family or tribe whose members are widely scattered.

As Arden Neisser points out in **The Other Side of Silence**, "[T]he deaf adult community continues to show a strong, sensitive, altruistic commitment to all deaf children—most of whom are other people's children."[1] As we have already pointed out, this commitment is very much a part of our lives. Deaf adults feel an immediate bond, a deep empathy, with all deaf children. Some hearing parents resent this bond. They feel that they're expected to give their deaf children up to the Deaf community, instead of keeping them in their own families (and, by extension, the Hearing community), where they "rightfully belong." And some parents go to extraordinary lengths to keep them there. Others accept their deaf child's need to meet and interact with other deaf people. They make positive efforts to establish their own link to the Deaf community. Instead of "surrendering" their children to this community, they become part of it. The connection enriches their lives.

Deaf people unrelated by blood often become extraordinarily close—witness the many deep and enduring friendships formed at residential schools. (And consider the large number of Deaf-Deaf marriages.) It's not far-fetched to say that deaf children often feel closer to other deaf people than to their own hearing families. This can be heart-rendingly sad for parents of these children who feel that, in sending them off to residential school, they're losing them to the Deaf community—an alien world. But it is also heart-rendingly sad that so many parents can't even communicate with their own children. And every child has a right to free access to communication and community.

We don't mean to imply that all hearing parents are insensitive to their deaf children's needs, nor that deaf parents necessarily do a better job of parenting deaf (or hearing) children. It takes great courage to accept differences—especially when it's *your* child who's "different."[2]

When deaf people ask other deaf people if their children are deaf or hearing, it's not necessarily an indication of snobbery—although some Deaf people consider *any* members of the hearing human race as unworthy of their respect. (If you see them snubbing the hearing children while lavishing attention on the deaf ones, you'll know that you're dealing with this type of character.) More often, it's an affirmation of their empathy with other deaf people. To them, being Deaf is something positive, something to be cherished—and celebrated.

[1] Arden Neisser, **The Other Side of Silence** (New York: Knopf, 1983; rpt. 1990, Gallaudet University Press), p. 282.

[2] Q.v. Mark Medoff's *Children of a Lesser God*. At the very end of the play, Sarah (who previously told James she wanted deaf children) says, "I don't want deaf children. . . . I just don't have the right to demand that anyone be created in my image."

Chapter 45

Why do most deaf parents raise a hearing child better than hearing parents a deaf child?
(If you cannot answer or agree, may a tribe of your researchers increase!)

—"Avid Reader," Jackson, Mississippi

s with so many other aspects of the Deaf reality, it all depends on the individuals—in this case, the parents and the child.

Hearing children of hearing parents begin communicating by babbling, then putting sounds together, playfully, then making recognizable words, then forming complete sentences, expanding their vocabularies daily. By listening, they absorb spoken language effortlessly, unconsciously. And they learn by imitating others—in this case, their parents, who give them constant feedback, correcting mispronunciations and grammatical errors. Hearing children of deaf parents often lack this vital auditory/oral feedback process. Since so many deaf adults don't use their voices (unable to hear themselves speak, they can't modulate them properly), or have unnatural-sounding voices even if they *do* speak, their children often don't pick up good speech patterns—clear articulation, intonation, modulation of volume, and expression. They tend to develop poor early speech patterns. A number of them require speech therapy once they start school.

Much depends on the home environment—how intellectual it is, and whether or not a hearing child of deaf parents has access to other hearing children, relatives, and family friends, who can act as good "speech models." Consider a hearing child of deaf parents who live on a farm. Their nearest neighbors may be miles away. These children would have little or no early exposure to spoken language, and, conversely, far less opportunity to develop good oral skills. (Having a radio or TV helps, but they're no substitute for real face-to-face interaction.) A hearing child of deaf parents in a friendly, well-populated town or urban neighborhood would undoubtedly have an easier time of it.

Some deaf parents are simply indifferent to their children's communication needs. They need exposure to speech? Too bad. Let them get it somewhere else. (Their situation roughly parallels, but doesn't equal, that of a number of DOHAs who are, effectively, stuck in a language-deprived environment.)

Preschoolers are routinely tested for language skills. Unfortunately, this puts many hearing children of deaf parents at an immediate disadvantage. They are often labeled "language-deficient" because ASL, not English, is their first language. They're in roughly the same pickle as Spanish-speaking children who get similarly labeled. They may be absolutely fluent in their native language, but that skill doesn't count in an English-speaking environment.

Needless to say, most deaf parents (by our estimate, a good 90%) are aware of the problem, concerned about their children's well-being, and do something about it. They want to know where to go, what they can do, where to get help. They ask questions, call the schools, and try to find preschool programs that can benefit their children. They ask hearing neighbors or relatives to spend time with their children, to talk with and read to them, to give them practice in listening and articulation skills.

Hearing children of Deaf parents, of course, do have a native language, which puts them ahead of deaf children of hearing parents who can't communicate effectively with them. However, they tend to lag behind hearing children of hearing parents, who already have an advantage in spoken-language skills and socialization. Nonetheless, with proper speech training and classroom support, hearing children of deaf parents will do fine. They'll catch up, and sometimes surpass their classmates.

All deaf Americans are, to a lesser or greater extent, bilingual. They are surrounded by Hearing-American-English-language culture. They cannot help absorbing it. (In the case of English, sometimes forcibly.) Consequently, they tend to understand the demands of the Hearing world far better than the Hearing world understands their needs as Deaf people. Involved in a "mixed" conversation, they will go to great lengths to make sure the hearing person understands them. (They will "switch codes" from ASL to PSE, fingerspell, speak, write, use body language, or a combination of modes.) They are sensitized to the need for accessible communication. Their experience as members of a Deaf community and a Hearing society gives them a dual perspective. Ideally, they *can* do a fine job of raising their children, deaf or hearing, as bilingual citizens.

It's foolish to make sweeping generalizations about hearing children of deaf parents (CODAs), but for some, the bilingual-bicultural orientation obviously influences them in their choice of careers. Their childhood experience, judging by the accounts we've read and have been told, gives them a unique and valuable perspective. Many become interpreters. Others become teachers (ASL being a popular specialty), administrators, linguists, researchers, social workers, service providers, performers, or writers. Most enjoy their affiliation with the Deaf community, and remain fluent signers. They maintain a lifelong connection to the community and an abiding interest in Deaf affairs.

No doubt, a tribe of researchers is undertaking studies right now to determine just how hearing children of Deaf parents learn, and what effect the early exposure to ASL may have on their English-language development. May the treasury of knowledge increase!

Over a decade of promoting Deaf Awareness

Chapter 46

Parents of deaf children have been telling us what they think is best for their children when they really don't know them. How come?

—Howard Palmer, Jackson, Mississippi

ost parents, it seems, have this profound conviction that they know what is best for their children, simply because their children are theirs.

For many hearing parents who have just learned their child is deaf, s/he is the first deaf person they've ever met. That's a perilous position from which to start.

Hearing parents of deaf children *think* they know their children. But they do *not* know what effect deafness will have on their children's lives. Few parents are clairvoyant. They have to make decisions based on their knowledge (which may be scanty or nonexistent), their desire to learn, their own prejudices, expectations, concepts of "normality," and instincts. These qualities vary from parent to parent. Some are eager to learn all they can about deafness, the Deaf community, and communication. They have an open attitude towards sign language, a willingness to venture into new territory. Others have an innate oralist bias, a rejectionist attitude towards sign language ("it's alien to us"/"we don't need it"/"what use is it?"), and use the information they acquire to bolster their unshakable conviction that their way is the right way. Others, although initially open to the idea of sign language, are unwilling to make a commitment to learn a new way of communicating, and so choose the opposite approach: a cochlear implant, oralism, and mainstreaming.

Still others, who opt for the oralist/implant approach, change *their* minds, enroll their child in a signing program, learn to sign themselves, and connect with the Deaf community. And still others don't much care one way or another.

There's really no way of predicting what any parents will ultimately choose. Parents, like all other members of the human family, are a cussedly unpredictable lot.

One major problem is that what is "best" for one child—or family—may not be "best" for another. Some parents can agree to sending their child to a residential school. Others cannot. They feel that they alone can provide the best environment, that their influence during their child's crucial formative years is irreplaceable, that they can give their child something no other person can. They want to be the ones to personally teach them, guide them, transmit ethical values, religious faith, and family traditions, monitor their progress every day, and tuck them into bed each night. They are right, of course. Parents who send their child to a residential school acknowledge the importance of growing up in a Deaf environment, with no communication barriers. They, too, are correct. Parents who send their child to a high-quality day or magnet-school program for deaf students are enthusiastic about their choice—but these options are available in only a few cities. There are always options, and options mean hard choices. Most choices involve a trade-off. Some parents cannot find *any* satisfactory option.

What makes matters especially sticky is the bitter division between the oralist and sign-language factions. Emotions run high. Oralists and ASL advocates can be equally extreme, dogmatic, and unyielding. And parents who find themselves bombarded with this well-meaning but high-pressure advice, solicited or not, may resent it, even fight back. Some resent what they interpret as the Deaf community's attempt to tell them what to do with their children. Conversely, Deaf advocates (some of whom have deaf children themselves) resent the parents' stubborn refusal to listen to what they have to say. They are, after all, speaking from their own experience as grown-up deaf children. They're the ones who have paid the price.

Unfortunately, the media spotlight seems to focus on parents who decide to give their children cochlear implants and enroll them strict oral regimens, and not the ones who choose an ASL-affirmative approach. Popular media portrays ASL advocates as dangerous fanatics, or just blanks them out. Parents of implanted children make glib public statements about giving them the best possible start, letting them participate fully in the real world, being normal, *etcetera*. Some of these parents become regular PA systems for the implant lobby, recruiting other parents, parading their children around to the media and Congresspeople, making them testify before legislative committees. This doesn't prove who's right, just who has the most aggressive PR campaign.

There is, of course, no one "right way." What works splendidly for one family may be a disastrous mistake for another. Some deaf children thrive in residential schools. Others do best in day programs, or even mainstreaming. Some children, i.e., those who became deaf after acquiring spoken language, do well with implants. Others don't. Some never connect with the Deaf community. Others are happiest when they make the connection. Both oralist and sign-affirmative parents point to their successes. So what does that prove?

That deaf children thrive and succeed under wildly divergent circumstances may not be due so much to the rightness of the parents' choices as to the resilience of the human spirit. Children can and do succeed against the odds. They can learn to communicate in the parent's chosen mode, even though they take the hard road instead of the easy path. They can become multi-lingual and multi-modal. Or pass as hearing.

However, we need to be realistic. Too many parents never learn to communicate with their deaf children. This is definitely *not* the right way. If parents want to spare their children the agony and frustration of being cut off from communication, they should learn to sign. If they refuse to do so out of some methodological bias, they are not acting in their children's best interests. We know of plenty of deaf adults who are products of oralist upbringings and are bitter and angry about it. Their #1 complaint seems to be that their hearing parents couldn't and wouldn't learn how to communicate with them. We have, however, never encountered a single deaf person who complained about their hearing parents' learning how to sign. In fact, they were proud of it—and all the happier for it. ("My parents learned to sign so they could communicate with me. I love them for that!")

We have faith in the intelligence and flexibility of many parents. They want what's best for their children. But they are open-minded enough to ask, "What *is* best for my child?" And "What's best for me? What's best for my family?" They recognize that all children are individuals; what works for one may not work for another. They seek a better understanding of their child—and themselves.

But even parents who love their children and make carefully-considered decisions make mistakes. With the benefit of hindsight, some of them later look back and admit that they were misled, that they blundered. Some, even if their grown children explain how and why it was wrong, remain convinced of the rightness of their choice.

We have to live with the consequences of our parents' choices, good and bad. Who knows best? If the parents do, so do the children.

Deaf Awareness 5-Minute Quiz

Chapters 31—46

Answers are on the bottom of the page, upside down.

True or False:

1. All deaf people develop a remarkable talent for lipreading.

2. Some speech pathologists give deaf children an inaccurate notion of their speech skills, praising them for good articulation that they don't really possess.

3. Vocalizing should be a deaf person's choice, and not something imposed from above.

4. At one time, the terms "deaf-and-dumb" and "deaf-mute" were not insulting. Most people believed that deafness caused muteness, so these terms simply reflected prevailing belief.

5. The adjective "silent" is especially descriptive of the Deaf reality, since deaf people communicate quietly and never make noise.

6. Some people dislike using the word "deaf," even when they're describing culturally-Deaf people, because they feel it's impolite.

7. The vast majority of members of the Deaf community enthusiastically agree that they're handicapped.

8. Doctors have long told parents of deaf children not to learn or use sign language because it interferes with the acquisition of speech skills. But native signers find it easier to acquire good speech skills.

9. A good number of hearing children of Deaf parents choose careers as interpreters, sign-language teachers, or service providers.

10. That deaf children thrive under a rigorous oral-aural regimen only proves that the oralists are right.

10. False.

1. False; 2. True; 3. True; 4. True; 5. False; 6. True; 7. False; 8. True; 9. True;

Answers:

Chapter 47

Do deaf parents breed deaf children?

his may not sound like a civilized question, but it's certainly one that has been asked many times in many cultures, by supposedly civilized people. And it's still being asked.

There is a philosophy (or pseudo-science) called *eugenics*, which deals with inherited characteristics and the possibility of improving those of succeeding generations by choosing "suitable" parents. Suitable parents would be encouraged to breed, while unsuitable parents would be discouraged, even prevented, from having "inferior-quality" children. Eugenics was an exceedingly popular topic in the 19th century, when many hearing educators and philosophers decided that it was better for the "future of the race" if deaf people could be prevented from reproducing more deaf people. Even Alexander Graham Bell, whose own mother and wife were deaf and who invented the telephone while seeking an "assistive-listening" device for hard-of-hearing people, subscribed to this absurd notion. In his **Memoir Upon the Formation of a Deaf Variety of the Human Race**, he discussed various measures for preventing deaf people—whom he called "undesirables"—from breeding. He proposed legislation to prohibit deaf people from marrying each other, although admitting that this was an impractical expedient.

However, as a result of the wide publicity given to Bell's theories, an unknown number of American deaf children were sterilized. During the early years of the German Third Reich, the Nazis carried this practice even further, forcibly sterilizing many deaf Jewish and Christian schoolchildren, teenagers, and young adults to ensure that they would never be able to breed "defectives."

Over a decade of promoting Deaf Awareness

Ultimately, the desire to "cleanse" society of its "defective" and "undesirable" members led to an organized campaign of "hygienic" euthanasia. Chronically ill, diseased, incapacitated, mentally and physically handicapped, and emotionally traumatized patients were rounded up in institutions and hospitals, herded into ambulances, and asphyxiated by having carbon monoxide pumped in from the fuel lines after the engines were started. It was an agonizing way to die. Thus the Reich began to purge itself of its "defectives." Some 1,600 deaf persons were murdered during this purge.

What are the facts? Simply this: An estimated 90% of all deaf people have hearing parents. And 90% of all deaf parents have hearing children. The facts speak for themselves. Anyone who wants to prevent deaf babies from being born should prevent *hearing* people from breeding.

In earlier generations, some tyrannical parents tried to prevent their deaf children from marrying or from having children, unwilling to have them transmit deafness.* This was not only cruel but futile. Most "deaf genes" are carried and transmitted by, and inherited from, hearing parents. Furthermore, the genetic tendency towards deafness is a tad unpredictable. It often pops up at random. Hypothetically, the same hearing mother and father may have several hearing children and several deaf, or all deaf, or all hearing, or all hearing but one, or all deaf but one.

More than 60 kinds of hereditary deafness and hearing loss have already been identified. There is much we don't yet know, but we do know something about the relationship between a few specific genes and deafness, and are constantly learning more about the way these genes alter the regular biochemical function of the sensory cells.

Hereditary deafness can be *autosomal-dominant* or *autosomal-recessive*. For autosomal-dominant genetic traits (e.g., Waardenburg's syndrome), only one parent needs to be a carrier of the gene. In autosomal-recessive genetic traits (e.g., Usher's syndrome), both parents must be carriers of the gene.

According to **Dr. Koop's Medical Encyclopedia**, "For an autosomal dominant disorder: If one parent is a carrier and the other normal there is a 50% chance a child will inherit the trait. (...) For an autosomal recessive disorder: When both parents are carriers of an autosomal recessive trait there is a 25% chance of a child inheriting both abnormal genes (developing the disease). There is a 50% chance of a child inheriting one abnormal gene (being a carrier)."

Deafness runs congenitally in only a small percentage of families. The genes causing hereditary deafness (several of which have been identified and chromosomally mapped) may be transmitted through hearing persons for generations before they "express" themselves. Even babies who are born deaf may not have inherited their deafness genetically; they may have been prenatally deafened as a result of exposure to the rubella virus, for example. Early-deafened children may have gotten their deafness from a bacterial or viral infection (e.g., spinal meningitis), high fever, or accident. Those deafened by exposure to a virus, illness, or accident would not necessarily be carrying any deaf gene whatsoever—even if one or both parents *are* deaf.

The odds are therefore against a deaf parent having a deaf child. But, despite what the tabloids say, for a deaf child to be born into a deaf family is no tragedy. Indeed, it can be a blessing. What Bell and many others never recognized, much less appreciated, was the quality of life in Deaf surroundings. Far from being "defectives," many Deaf families have enjoyed rich, fulfilling lives. Most deaf parents who have deaf children immediately accept them as normal, something a good number of hearing parents must struggle to accomplish. To Deaf parents, deafness *is* normal. There's nothing wrong, bad, inferior, shameful, or defective about it. They don't see themselves as "afflicted." They don't feel repulsed or guilty if their offspring are deaf. Since so many Deaf parents are fluent signers, deaf children born into such families begin life with complete immersion in the language of the parents. The communication barrier, so common in hearing families with deaf children, simply doesn't exist. So deaf children of Deaf parents often start school with a considerable advantage over deaf children from nonsigning hearing families.

Deaf children of Deaf parents have traditionally been the transmitters of sign language and Deaf culture to their schoolmates; the leaders, the boat-rockers. They tend to grow up with a sense of independence, self-confidence, and pride that many deaf children of hearing parents initially lack. Paternalistic hearing people do not take kindly to the idea of dynasties of uppity Deaf folks. Few of our oppressors have ever sought the truth beneath the invidious stereotype.

We could also add (as we've already noted) that hearing children of Deaf parents often choose careers that are related to communication, language, or community—interpreting, teaching ASL, law, the arts, or social services—capitalizing on their native exposure to sign language and maintaining a close connection with the Deaf community. Their experience as hearing children of deaf adults (CODAs) enriches their lives.

The quality of parenting, not the health of the auditory nerves, is what's important. To make a general statement: since many Deaf parents have positive feelings about their own deafness, they are correspondingly more accepting of others' deafness, and transmit those feelings to their own deaf children, who grow up with a positive self-image, a more comfortable sense of identity, than do many deaf children of hearing parents. As noted above, that's a definite advantage.

Deaf parents can offer what any good parent does: acceptance, love, patience, wisdom, warmth, morality, and guidance towards eventual independence. And sometimes, their influence on their children extends beyond the immediate circle of family and friends, like ripples widening across a pond, and benefits society at large.

* See, for example, Lou Ann Walker's **A Loss for Words: The Story of Deafness in a Family**. Walker's Uncle Garnel, her father Gale's eldest brother, had gotten married, but had been ordered by his domineering father not to have children—so the family story went. But Gale Walker, who was, like Garnel, early-deafened, had not been ordered to do likewise.

In her memoir, **In Silence: Growing Up Hearing in a Deaf World**, Ruth Sidransky, who writes lovingly about her Deaf parents Mary and Ben (as Walker writes about her parents Gale and Doris Jean), recounts a painful incident involving her first love and fiancé, Sammy.

> Marriage. I was stunned. I decided to tell Sammy that my parents were deaf. This time he flinched. It was imperceptible, but flinch he did.
>
> Courageously, I disregarded his body message and continued, "You'll have to meet them. They are wonderful."
>
> I saw his dimples as he smiled with his full rich being. "I'll be glad to meet them." There was not a quaver in his voice and I was reassured. Sammy would be different.
>
> He met my parents with the usual awkwardness that confronts the stranger to human handicap. (…)

Having met them, Sammy reached a decision:

> He swallowed his breath and in even tones said, "I have something to tell you."
>
> I waited for him to continue.
>
> "I don't know how to say this."
>
> I waited.
>
> "Ruthie, my Star Eyes, I cannot marry you. I do not want to have deaf children."
>
> I sat still, wordless.

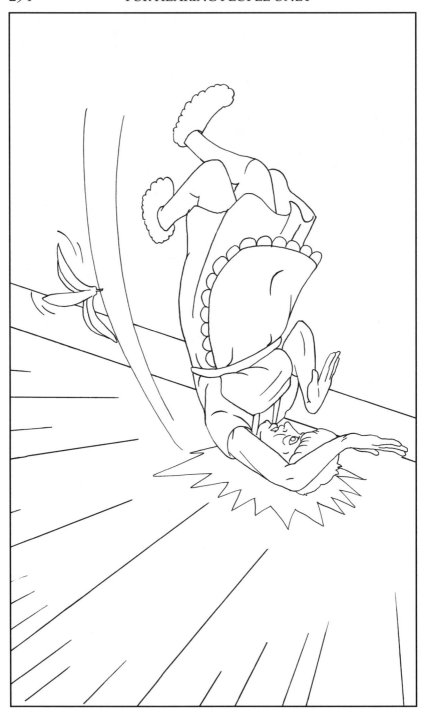

Chapter 48

"Is hearing loss common in my family because of heredity, or because my grandmother fell down during her pregnancies?"

I have been reading some articles of "For Hearing People Only" and noticed if someone has questions, to write for information.

I have an uncle and aunt who are brother and sister; they are both deaf. Their mother, my grandmother, is deaf in one ear. My aunt has a daughter who is deaf in one ear and my uncle has a daughter who has some hearing loss in both ears. I have been diagnosed with Meniere's Disease.[1] I am curious to know if it is possible for all this hearing loss to be hereditary in my family as it is quite ironic. My uncle and aunt were both born deaf, and the doctor told my grandparents that the reason why they are deaf is because my grandmother fell down during both pregnancies. Is this just an explanation due to lack of knowledge or is this possible?

If you can't answer [this question,] I understand; I thought I would inquire anyway.

—Shelley MacLean, Sydney, Nova Scotia

It looks as though your family carries a genetic tendency towards hearing loss, deafness, and hearing disorders. Assuming one gene is responsible (and there may be a number of them), it *expresses* itself (shows up) to different degrees among different members of your family; more females than males seem to be affected. It is not *that* uncommon for deafness and hearing disorders (possibly including Ménière's disease) to run in families. One of our staffers is congenitally and genetically deaf. Although his mother is hearing, she was a carrier of the gene for deafness, as (hereditary) deafness ran in her family. One of her two sons was born deaf, the other hearing. It's like the genetic tendencies toward nearsightedness (myopia), color-blindness, diabetes, or obesity. Some 10% of deaf people have deaf parents. So "deafness" genes are mostly carried throughout the hearing population.

There is much we don't yet understand about genetics. But we'd wager that babies are *not* born deaf because their mothers fell down during their pregnancies! Your grandmother's doctor was absolutely mistaken. We're sure of it. Why? A simple medical fact: the fetus floats weightlessly, completely surrounded by fluid, in the amniotic sac— a great shock absorber—further protected by the mother's body *and* the layers of clothing she will undoubtedly be wearing—unless she slips in the bathtub!

We consulted a veteran nurse-midwife, and she assured us that if a woman suffers a fall during pregnancy, *she* may hurt, but the fetus will, in all likelihood, be absolutely safe. If a pregnant woman suffers a bad fall, she *may* have a miscarriage. But in most cases, she will carry the pregnancy safely to term; the baby will be born healthy. (In many instances miscarriages are spontaneous, unconnected with a fall or injury; there is a chemical imbalance or something physiologically amiss with the embryo, and the body expels it.)

And *if* the mother's fall *were* to injure the fetus, why would it affect only the baby's inner ears? It would seem more logical for a baby injured before birth to be born with dislocated limbs, not defective hearing. It also seems quite improbable that falls during two different pregnancies would result in the exact same thing: deafness. Now, assuming that your grandmother *did* fall during both pregnancies, it's possible that her falls were the result of a balance problem that was itself hereditary. In other words, the same hereditary inner-ear problem could have caused your grandmother to feel dizzy, lose her balance, and fall, *and then* showed up in her children as well. There's no sense blaming the poor woman for falls that may or may not have happened. It's pretty obviously a genetic problem, and there is a simple genetic explanation.

In the days when very few people understood much, if anything, about heredity, folklore ascribed all manner of birth defects and disabilities to the mother's misdeeds or mishaps: children born with cleft palates, for example, were thought to result from a hare's running across the mother's path while she was pregnant.[2] Such beliefs caused the unfortunate mothers (as well as the children) tremendous guilt, pain, and shame. It's easy to say that the doctor should have known better; this was only a couple of generations ago. But genetic research of deafness is a relatively new field, and old presumptions die hard.

If you or your relatives are curious or concerned about the possibility of transmitting deafness to your children, we recommend you see a genetic counselor, who can test you, give you a more informed idea of the odds, and provide reassurance.

---

[1] Ménière's disease is "an inner-ear disorder of unknown origin that causes hearing loss, dizziness or vertigo and tinnitus (noises within the head). [It] affects more than one million Americans and can be extremely incapacitating."—Carol Turkington and Allen E. Sussman, Ph.D., eds., **The Encyclopedia of Deafness and Hearing Disorders**, pp. 121-122.

[2] Even more dire is the old English folk belief that it was the *devil* in the form of a hare. So both mother and child were in league with the devil— accursed. (See Chapter 50.)

Chapter 49

How do people become deaf?

e're either born deaf or become deaf. A person born deaf is said to be *congenitally deaf*; one who becomes deaf after birth is *adventitiously deaf*. Adventitious deafness can be either *prelingual* (occurring during the first 3 years of life), or *postlingual* (occurring after age 3). And the area of postlingual deafness is further subdivided into *childhood deafness*, *pre-vocational deafness* (becoming deaf while still a teenager), or *post-vocational deafness* (becoming deaf while an adult). A "deafened adult" is one who became deaf after age 19. One can also be described as *early-deafened* or *late-deafened*; one's deafness as *early-onset* or *late-onset*.

Interestingly, more males than females are born-deaf and early-deafened, but since women tend to outlive men, there are more late-deafened elderly women than men.

Many Deaf people (i.e., those with a strong cultural affiliation to the ASL-Deaf community) are congenitally deaf or early-deafened. Deafness that runs in families (*genetically transmitted*, *hereditary*, or *inherited deafness*) is a relatively rare cause.

More common is prenatal exposure to a virus. The rubella (German measles) epidemic of 1963-65 affected many pregnant women whose children were subsequently born deaf. Cytomegalovirus (CMV), the Rh factor, and prematurity are three other causes of congenital deafness. When no specific cause can be determined, one's deafness is described as "of unknown etiology." This handy phrase crops up in the medical histories of a large number of deaf people. It accounts for roughly half of all known cases.

It should be noted that *congenital* and *hereditary* deafness are *not* synonymous. Not all congenitally deaf people have hereditary deafness. Children born deaf because of prenatal exposure to the rubella virus may not be carrying any "deaf gene" whatsoever. Conversely, a hereditarily deaf person may be born with normal hearing that progressively deteriorates.

Although rare in terms of overall incidence (3 cases per million births), *Usher's syndrome* (US) accounts for some 10% of all cases of hereditary deafness. It's named after Charles Usher, M.D., a Scottish-born ophthalmologist who studied families in Southern England with a high incidence of deafness and progressive blindness, and initially reported his findings in 1913. US, an autosomal-recessive trait, is a blanket term for several hereditary disorders in which profound sensorineural deafness is accompanied by progressively deteriorating vision (*retinopathy* or *retinal dystrophy*), similar to or identical with *retinitis pigmentosa* (RP), a progressive form of blindness caused by abnormal buildup of pigment in the retina, the inner "image-recording" area of the eye. Some doctors consider US a form of RP. But not all deaf-blind persons have US. Only a fraction of those with RP have US.

Waardenburg's syndrome (named after the eye doctor, P. J. Waardenburg of Holland, who first reported it) is an autosomal-dominant trait. Congenital deafness of varying degrees is accompanied by partial albinism, such as a white forelock in a head of dark hair, and extremely pale blue or different-colored eyes, and facial anomalies such as wide separation of the inner corners of the eye, and a broad nasal bridge. Not all people with WS have hearing loss, though.

There are two basic types of deafness: *sensorineural* (also called "nerve" deafness), and *conductive*. Some people have both.

Conductive deafness affects the "hardware" of the middle ear: the eardrum (*tympanum*), the tiny bones (*auditory ossicles*)—*malleus* ("hammer"), *incus* ("anvil"), and *stapes* ("stirrup")—behind the eardrum, or the mastoid bone surrounding the inner ear. It may be caused by a buildup of earwax that blocks the canal, fluid in the middle ear, inflammation, a perforated eardrum, or ossification or fusing of the bones. Sensorineural deafness affects the "software"—the delicate microscopic sensory cells ("hair cells") of the cochlea, the coiled snail-shell-shaped center of hearing and balance in the inner ear, or the auditory nerves. While conductive deafness can often be treated, sensorineural deafness is usually irreversible. It may be imperceptibly gradual or bizarrely sudden. And it may be accompanied by *tinnitus* (abnormal ringing, buzzing, or whooshing sounds in the head) and/or dizziness.

Adventitious deafness can be caused by accidents (as when I. King Jordan was hurled off his motorcycle), bomb or shotgun blasts, injuries, extreme chill, high fever, bacterial or viral meningitis, other viral infections such as mumps, measles, chicken pox, or encephalitis, genetic diseases such as neurofibromatosis-2 (with acoustic neuromas—tumors that attack the auditory nerves), *cholesteatoma* (abnormal growths that displace the eardrum and conductive bones of the middle ear), and reactions to certain (ototoxic) drugs, such as aminoglycoside antibiotics.

Gradual hearing loss can result from repeated exposure to very loud noise—e.g., heavily amplified rock-music concerts, commuting on the subway, constant exposure to industrial hazards such as operating a pneumatic drill, or even living too near an airport. *Otosclerosis*—hardening of the bones of the middle ear—is common among older people. Age-related hearing loss is also known as *presbycusis*.

There are numerous causes of deafness (only a few have been mentioned here), and you're likely to meet deaf persons from a wide variety of "backgrounds."

Often a Deaf person will greet a stranger by asking "Are you Deaf? Were you born deaf?" That's their way of "sounding out" the new person—getting a quick idea of their ethnic identity, so to speak—their background, outlook, and place in the Deaf community.

Chapter 50

Is deafness "bad karma"?

oughly speaking, *karma* (or *karman*) means effects, fate, or destiny. Hinduism and Buddhism, for example, teach that a soul is born and reborn many times, in different forms. **The American Heritage Dictionary** defines karma as "the sum and consequences of a person's actions during the successive phases of his existence, regarded as determining his destiny." The **Longman Dictionary of Contemporary English** defines it a bit more simply as "the force produced by a person's actions in one life on earth which will influence his [or her] next life on earth." In other words, what you do in this life will have an effect on your next life. This has led to the tragic belief that a deaf or disabled person must have done something bad in a previous life to deserve the punishment of being born "defective."

The idea of being "cursed" is by no means limited to Hindus or Buddhists. In ancient Greece, fathers had the right to abandon "defective" babies, who were taken in baskets to the mountains and left there to die of exposure and starvation.[1]

The ancient Egyptians, however, took a more compassionate view of physical disabilities. Their tomb art portrays actual persons with deformed limbs and what we call "physical anomalies," and there are numerous depictions of blind musicians.

While the Torah carries an explicit prohibition against cursing the deaf,[2] the New Testament has a decidedly negative view. The few deaf persons mentioned in the gospels are described as possessed by an evil spirit.[3]

According to the Jewish Scriptures (a.k.a. "Old Testament"), God created deaf people as part of a divine plan. In Jewish society, deaf persons, while at a disadvantage, had certain rights. But the New Testament view—that deaf people were accursed—stuck. For thousands of years in Christian Europe, deaf people were considered not fully human, incapable of learning, and unworthy of salvation. They were excluded from the sacraments; they could not receive communion or confess their sins, and were not allowed to marry. They were, at least in the legal sense, outcasts. This attitude survives today, for example, in certain Latin American countries. Even in the United States, there is a widespread belief that God punishes parents through their children. Some people honestly believe that children are born disabled because their parents did something evil.[4]

Let it be said that the Roman Catholic Church, among others, has made tremendous strides in eradicating negative views and in combating prejudice against deaf persons. The Church produced the abbé de l'Epée, who devoted the latter half of his life to the education of deaf people—without seeking any glory or wealth for himself. His concern for deaf people was entirely disinterested. His original motive was spiritual—he wanted deaf people to have the chance to attain salvation through education. In stark contrast to the profit-motivated oralists of his time, such as Samuel Heinicke and the Braidwoods, he publicly demonstrated his techniques and freely shared his ideas with others. The National Institute was the world's first public school for the deaf. If the Deaf community could elect saints, the abbé de l'Epée would undoubtedly be its first choice.

The belief in reincarnation (or "transmigration of souls") is not limited to Hinduism or Buddhism, either. Plato accepted it (the Greek term is *metempsychosis*). Judaism certainly accepts it—the Hebrew term is *gilgul nefesh*, the "rolling" or "recycling" of a soul.

If you wish to take a mystical approach, you can look at karma (or reincarnation) either negatively or positively. In the negative interpretation, a soul is born as a deaf person as a punishment—i.e., bad karma. But according to the positive interpretation, a soul chooses to be born as a deaf person as a challenge or learning experience. The Deaf soul experiences the restrictions, prejudices, and hostilities of the hearing world so that it may progress to a higher level of spiritual understanding.[5] This in no way contradicts the doctrine of free will—that whatever our station in life, we have the freedom to choose how we respond to it. The ultimate challenge is to choose wisely.[6]

[1] As in Sophocles' classic Greek tragedy, *Oedipus*. Laius, king of Thebes, husband of Queen Jocasta, is warned by an oracle that his newborn son will ultimately slay him. He tries to forestall this by abandoning the baby to certain death on Mount Cithaeron—pinning the baby's heels together and stringing him up on a tree-branch. The baby is rescued by a compassionate shepherd, and Oedipus (whose name means *swollen foot* or *wounded heel*) survives, and ultimately fulfills the prophecy, killing his father, becoming king of Thebes, and unwittingly marrying his own mother, Jocasta.

[2] Leviticus 19:14: "You shall not curse the deaf, nor put a stumbling-block before the blind." However, in Jewish law (the Talmudic or Rabbinic tradition), deaf persons were considered "legally incompetent," whether or not they could communicate via writing. If you could not speak—i.e., were a *kheresh* ("deaf-mute")—you were not legally competent. Deaf-mutes (along with idiots, minors, slaves, and women) were considered legally incompetent by the majority of rabbinic authorities, capable by some. For a man, "legally incompetent" meant, for example, being disqualified from serving as a witness in a rabbinical court or being counted in a *minyan* (prayer quorum). All women, hearing or deaf, were automatically barred from these privileges. But the social reality was more complex than absolute. Deaf Jews could earn a living, study Torah, and (in some cases) marry. They could be part of the community.

[3] In the Gospel of St. Mark, for example, a father brings his deaf-mute son to Jesus, after the disciples are unable to cure him. The "dumb spirit" frequently throws the boy into violent convulsions; he foams at the mouth, grinds his teeth, and "pines away." Jesus exorcises the "dumb and deaf spirit":

> And when Jesus saw that a crowd came running together, he rebuked the unclean spirit, saying to it, "You dumb and deaf spirit, I command you, come out of him, and never enter him again."
> [Afterwards,] his disciples asked him privately, "Why could we not cast it out?" And he said to them, "This kind cannot be driven out by anything but prayer."
> (Mark 9:14-29)

—The New Oxford Annotated Bible, Revised Standard Version, 1973

As Paulette R. Caswell has pointed out, the boy seems to be an epileptic. For a long time, epileptics were considered "idiots" and "incompetents" in the eyes of the law. This attitude probably developed from the early Christian belief that they were possessed by "evil spirits." In the New Testament, deaf-mutes have not only a physical disability, but mental and spiritual ones as well. See "In the Eyes of the Law, Are We (Really) Equal?", **DEAF LIFE**, March 1992.

Also see John Vickrey Van Cleve and Barry A. Crouch, **A Place of Their Own: Creating the Deaf Community in America**, first chapter.

What about the Islamic view? There are several fundamentalist Websites (containing Koranic translations, etc.) that include pejorative references to unbelievers as being "deaf, dumb and blind." On the brighter side, Deaf Muslims are making some degree of progress—e.g., in getting sign-interpreted Friday-morning worship at a mosque in Cairo. Deaf Muslims have their own sign language, known as KSL. But the traditional Koranic view of deaf people is decidedly negative.

[4] This attitude is still found among tragically uneducated people. One eyewitness account:

When employed by Cherokee County EMS, after leaving Grady and before I started Tri-Comm EMS for the Deaf, I discovered a unique population of deaf people—mountain folks from the remote areas of the north Georgia mountains. In many cases these people had grown up with no knowledge of sign language. Their parents had improvised by inventing hand signals. . . . The most education that anyone, deaf or hearing, obtained would be the sixth grade. One eighteen-year-old girl that I met was the fourteenth child of parents who were in their sixties. She had never attended school. Her parents thought she was a punishment from God.

—Steven L. Schrader, **Silent Alarm: On the Edge with a Deaf EMT** (Washington, D.C.: Gallaudet University Press, 1995), p. 118.

[5] Incidentally, deaf people cannot participate in hypnosis or past-life regression, or any other practice that depends on listening to instructions or suggestions with one's eyes closed.

[6] As originally published in **DEAF LIFE**, this chapter was one of two that provoked strong complaints from readers. Two readers objected to the statement in Chapter 24 about interpreters being seen as people who "earn money off Deaf people's language." One of these two, an Episcopalian minister, also argued that the New Testament was simply reflecting the prevalent social attitudes of its time, and that Jesus, in approaching and healing the sick and disabled, who were considered outcasts, was working against these prejudices. Our response was that although both Jewish and Christian traditions have many admirable and positive elements, neither is free of negative attitudes towards deaf people.

Chapter 51

I know that the Deaf community includes both "deaf" and "hard-of-hearing." What other categories are there?

he term "Deaf community" can be broadly applied to include all those in the "hearing-impaired" end of the spectrum. This includes those deaf from birth ("congenitally deaf"), those who become deaf very early in life ("prelingually deaf"), those deafened later in life ("adventitiously deaf"), late-deafened adults, and hard-of-hearing persons of all ages. People who suffer from tinnitus, a disorder causing unnatural noises—buzzing, ringing, clicking, roaring—in the ears, should also be included, as tinnitus is a form of hearing impairment. The same for those with Ménière's disease, a more severe progressive inner-ear disorder that includes attacks of tinnitus and vertigo (extreme dizziness).

The Deaf community ideally includes those who are culturally Deaf—native and longtime ASL users—and those who are deaf but are oriented towards oral means of communication—auditory aids, cochlear implants, speechreading, and cued speech. Many culturally Deaf people wear hearing aids; some don't.

Moreover, the Deaf community includes a number of hearing people: parents and relatives of deaf children; friends, families, and spouses of deaf adults; supporters and advocates; teachers, administrators, professionals, and service providers. They respect Deaf people and have earned the respect of the Deaf community.

Since the decibel/megahertz audiogram chart is complicated, deaf and hearing people have devised informal ways to categorize themselves and others. Here are some useful (or confusing) terms. (Note that several overlap.)

Oral-deaf community: the segment of the deaf/HoH population that prefers to communicate by speech, speechreading, and uses audiometrics such as hearing aids or cochlear implants. A number of them also use sign language, but nonetheless advocate the "superiority" of oralism.

Culturally-Deaf community: the segment of the deaf/HoH population that uses sign language as an everyday means of communication and identify themselves as members of the Deaf culture. They may use hearing aids, but most eschew cochlear implants. (A few have them.)

Born-deaf: A person who has always been deaf; congenitally deaf.

Prelingually deaf: A person who was born deaf or became deaf before acquiring language/speech.

Postlingually deaf: A person who became deaf after learning how to speak.

Early-deafened: A person who became deaf during early childhood, whether by illness, accident, genetic tendency, or unknown cause.

Adventitiously deaf: A person who wasn't born deaf, but became deaf early or later in life.

Progressively deafened: A person who wasn't born deaf but became deaf gradually.

Late-deafened: A person who became deaf, whether suddenly or slowly, as a teenager or adult ("adult-onset deafness"). Since they've been hearing most of their lives, their perspectives and challenges are markedly different from those who have been deaf most or all of their lives.[1]

CODA: Hearing child of deaf adult(s).

DODA: Deaf child of deaf adult(s).

DOHA: Deaf child of hearing adult(s).

HOHA: hearing child of hearing adult(s).

Categorizing *can* easily become an exercise in absurdity. But the basic needs of the Deaf community as a whole, whatever "category" each member can be placed in, are clear enough: unrestricted communication and unrestricted access to everything hearing people benefit from and take for granted—TV programming (and commercials), education, government offices, public-service agencies, public announcements, hospitals, business networks—*right down to the totals on supermarket cash registers.* That means visual (or audio-visual) aids, sensitive architectural design, captioning, interpreters (whether sign-language or oral), better telephone relay services, more public TTYs,[2] and, equally important, more public awareness. There's still far too little.

The Americans with Disabilities Act was signed into law by President George Bush on July 26, 1990. It went into effect on January 26, 1992. It prohibits discrimination on the basis of disability in public accommodations, transportation, etc. The ADA includes deaf and hard-of-hearing persons. It is too soon to tell what sort of long-range impact it is having on the Deaf community. But things are astir. A flurry of ADA lawsuits on behalf of Deaf plaintiffs have already been filed, the cases making their way through the court system, precedents established.

As long as deaf people are discriminated against in schooling, employment, social and civil rights, as long as they are seen as "strange" and "different" and "second-class," they will protest, make themselves seen—and heard. All members of the Deaf community, as U.S. citizens, have specific needs, and our democratic society is obligated to ensure that those needs are met.

[1] See Chapter 54.

[2] A TTY (teletypewriter or, in its original incarnation, Teletype machine) is also known as a TDD (*telecommunication device for the deaf*). The newest terms, adding still more confusion to the alphabetic soup, are TT, TTP, or TexTel (all standing for *text telephone*). Since these devices aren't used only by deaf people, "TDD" isn't an accurate term. The preferred term is "TTY."

Chapter 52

What's the difference between "hard-of-hearing" and "deaf"?

here's fairly general consensus that "deaf" means "unable to hear normally." But "hard-of-hearing" is a much more nebulous term. There is considerable disagreement, if not downright confusion, surrounding this term and its "proper" usage. Strictly speaking, it means *having a mild to moderate degree of hearing loss*. But a number of people who are audiologically deaf identify themselves as "hard-of-hearing" or "hearing-impaired." Conversely, some audiologically hard-of-hearing people identify themselves as "deaf." Likewise, some audiologically late-deafened people variously identify themselves as "late-deafened" or "late-deaf" (which suggests that they accept their new identity as "deaf" and—possibly—a new affiliation with the Deaf community) *or* "hard-of-hearing" (which suggests that they're caught between both Hearing and Deaf communities—wanting to remain in the Hearing community, but having difficulty coping with hearing loss).

At one extreme, this term can be a form of denial—as when a newly- or progressively-deafened adult says "I'm hard-of-hearing" instead of "I'm deaf."

As we all know, some deaf people have good speech skills. Those that do variously identify themselves as "oral-deaf," "oral hearing-impaired," or even "hard-of-hearing." "Oral-deaf" is not the same thing as "hard-of-hearing," but some oral-deaf people refuse to call themselves "deaf." They'll proudly say, "I'm *not* deaf, I'm *hard-of-hearing*."

"Hard-of-hearing," therefore, isn't necessarily an audiological category; it's also a state of mind. As the late Loy Golladay, poet and former NTID professor, wryly noted, according to the Alexander Graham Bell Association for the

Deaf, if you lose your hearing after the age of 8, you're "hard-of-hearing," no matter how deaf you are!

A state of mind also leads to an attitude, and attitudes, as we well know, can easily engender snobbery. There is a fine distinction between an attitude of pride and dignity *and* an attitude of contempt for all who are "different." Some people who identify themselves as "hard-of-hearing" consider themselves the elite—possessing superior status in the Deaf community—and look down on those who identify themselves as "deaf." Likewise, some native-ASL users look down on signed-English users or anyone who thinks and acts too "hearing." Everyone, we suppose, needs to have something to brag about. And so with the Deaf community. Each faction looks down on every other one.

In the Deaf community, some hard-of-hearing people have looked down on deaf people, because they may feel rejected or torn between the Deaf and Hearing communities. They possess some degree of hearing, but not enough to function comfortably in all aspects of "Hearing" life. They're deaf to some degree, but may not be considered "true-Deaf" by other Deaf people.

Putatively, hard-of-hearing people are supposed to be able to function nicely in a Hearing context with the help of hearing aids or assistive-listening devices. In real life, this doesn't always work out so neatly.

The psychological boundaries of "hard-of-hearing" are somewhat fluid, ambiguous. In a sense, hard-of-hearing people have the leeway to define what they are and want to be called. But it is accordingly more difficult for them to choose a distinct cultural identity, since they're not completely deaf and not completely hearing. Audiologically, they straddle the fence between deaf and hearing. Some are quite happy as they are, whether they participate in either the Hearing or Deaf communities, or in both. Others, much as late-deafened adults do, grapple with a troubling sense of "in-betweenness."

Being hard-of-hearing can be damn tough. Depending on their background, schooling, and self-image, they may throw themselves enthusiastically into an ASL environment at the earliest possible opportunity, or remain determinedly mainstreamed. They may decide to identify as Deaf, to struggle to establish a comfortable identity as a Deaf person who can hear somewhat. Or they may choose to identify as a hearing person with a hearing loss. They may even try their durndest to pass as hearing.

A number of young HoH people enroll at NTID and Gallaudet. For some, this may be their first real excursion into the Deaf community. Some thrive in an ASL context; others find that they can't handle it, and leave. In some cases, they'll continue their education at a "hearing" college that offers support services, or find another tangent.

How do deaf people distinguish "hard-of-hearing" from "deaf"? The traditional criterion is the ability to use a voice telephone. If you have a hearing loss and can still use the telephone (even with amplification), you're hard-of-hearing. If you can't, you're deaf. Simple as that.

As journalist, author, and aviation buff Henry Kisor has noted, "Clyde Smith [President of the Deaf Pilots Association] told me that as far as he's concerned everybody with a hearing loss is deaf—there are only degrees of deafness. That's a workable philosophy. (My own is that if you can use the phone with a hearing aid you're HOH and if you can't you're deaf—I know that's a gross oversimplification, but it works for me.)" It works for us too.

Chapter 53

Are hard-of-hearing people part of the Deaf community?

his question leads to others: Do they want to be? Should ASL-Deaf people make better efforts to welcome them? How do hard-of-hearing people identify themselves?

There are not many valid generalizations we can make about the issue, because the hard-of-hearing population is determinedly diverse and stubbornly individual. Hard-of-hearing persons are part of the global community. They can be part of the Deaf community if they want to be. But does the Deaf community want them?

The situation is complex and sticky. "Hard-of-hearing" can denote a person with a mild-to-moderate hearing loss. Or it can denote a deaf person who doesn't have/want any cultural affiliation with the Deaf community. Or both.

As noted in the previous chapter, "hard-of-hearing" is not just an audiological situation, it's a state of mind, an attitude, and, in some cases, a psychological defense. ("I'm *not* deaf, I'm hard-of-hearing!") The HOH dilemma is a fence-straddling situation: in some ways hearing, in some ways deaf, in others, neither.

Where do HOH people fit into the scheme of things? There is deplorable prejudice in our community. But it's not simply a case of ASL-Deaf people snubbing HOH. We have seen plenty of HOH snobbery, too. It's not at all unusual for HOH children attending schools for the deaf to feel that they're "better" than profoundly deaf children. If "hearing" confers social status, then having perfect hearing is "best," having some hearing is "good," and having little or no hearing is "bad." So if "hard-of-hearings" are in the middle of the audiological hierarchy, they're below "hearings" but above "deafs." Does this seem ridiculous? Yes, but social interactions are guided by such distinctions. And our self-identity and social perceptions (who we are, whom we choose to interact with, etc.) may be profoundly influenced by our early exposure to these distinctions.

That's one reason why deaf and HOH people have taken to the Internet with such enthusiasm. Social distinctions don't apply in cyberspace . . . except when it comes to sound effects and telephonics. In general, the Internet doesn't care whether you're deaf or HOH . . . as long as you're participating.

"Hard-of-hearing" can be used as a self-descriptive label to avoid any identification with signing-Deaf. It thus includes persons who are profoundly deaf, which adds to the semantic confusion. We're startled when we see news releases or articles about "hard-of-hearing" people getting cochlear implants. We were under the impression that implants were prescribed only for profoundly deaf persons. Can one be profoundly deaf and hard-of-hearing? Apparently so. Can one be hard-of-hearing and ASL-Deaf? That's possible, too. Can one be hard-of-hearing and function as hearing? Of course. What about being hard-of-hearing and functioning as a member of both the hearing and Deaf communities? That's a delicate tightrope-balancing act, but it too is possible.

As for the political dimension: Hard-of-hearing people can be allies of the Deaf community . . . or enemies. They can choose to join or to ignore it. They can participate in the social, cultural, political, and legal life of the community along with culturally Deaf . . . or live their lives completely within the parameters of the "Hearing world." In a sense, they have more choice, and more leeway, than do audiologically deaf people. But they may (or may not) have a more difficult time establishing a satisfying cultural/social identity.

The term "Deaf and hard-of-hearing community" explicitly includes them. What about the term "Deaf Community"? Does it include hard-of-hearing people too? We feel that it should . . . that is, if the HOH people *want* to be included.

The National Association of the Deaf is technically for deaf *and* hard-of-hearing persons, but has long been identified with advocacy for culturally Deaf people. Howard E. "Rocky" Stone, an audiologically-deaf (late-deafened) ex-CIA agent who preferred to identify as "hard-of-hearing," founded Self Help for Hard of Hearing People, Inc., to focus on the needs and concerns of hard-of-hearing people, as distinct from "deaf" or "Deaf." SHHH's emphasis is not on cultural affiliation but in coping and getting social support and technological assistance. There is, of course, some overlap. Some SHHH members also hold membership in the NAD or other Deaf-oriented groups like ALDA—or the oralism-oriented Alexander Graham Bell Association for the Deaf, for that matter. These organizations have their own particular agenda, and while these agenda don't always mesh (e.g., the official positions on cochlear implants for children), there are many shared areas of concern: captioning of TV programming and movies, real-time captioning in classrooms and courtrooms, telecommunication/Internet access, public facilities (payphone TTYs, visual-signaling devices in hotel rooms, etc.), employment, and the implementation of the ADA.

One major point of contention between HOH and Deaf is the attitude towards sign language and ASL. If you don't sign or don't sign well, you're likely to be branded "hard-of-hearing." Does "hard-of-hearing" mean "shunning sign"? Not necessarily. Shortly after he retired as Executive Director of SHHH, Rocky Stone addressed a Commencement Day audience at Gallaudet University in sign language, and the gesture (no pun intended) was much appreciated. Should hard-of-hearing people be compelled to learn sign language, then? No. It should be a voluntary commitment. Should ASL-oriented events include oral interpreters for the benefit of hard-of-hearing nonsigners? That depends on the people involved. Do HOH people *want* to attend Deaf Culture events? If so, they should make their needs known to the organizers and planners—and get involved.

Chapter 54

What are some of the biggest problems faced by late-deafened people?

late-deafened adult is generally defined as someone who became deaf—whether progressively,
suddenly, or even genetically—after age 18. As a
rule, the later the age at the onset of deafness,
the more difficult the adjustment. Those who
become deaf as teenagers will have a relatively easier time
than those in their 20s, 30s, or 40s—which is not to say that
adjustment is easy for *anyone*; it's not. But a younger person
will usually find it easier to cope than someone with an
established career, marriage, children, and a stable pattern of
life. Teens have a certain amount of fluidity and instability in
their lives, and this can be an advantage. The more established the patterns, the more painful the unraveling.

Late-deafened people, as hearing persons who have recently lost or are progressively losing their hearing, have a
more complicated time of it than those born deaf or early-
deafened. To some extent, they can choose how deeply they
want to remain involved in the Hearing world and enter the
Deaf world—but they cannot function as "normal" hearing
people anymore. They grapple with the realization that they
can no longer enjoy certain "ordinary" things hearing people
take for granted—picking up a telephone and making a
whispered call, music, conversations, family dinners, interacting with children and grandchildren, chit-chat and jokes,
on-the-job communication, the everyday heard and spoken
details of life—"aural wallpaper." Virtually everything familiar and comfortable in their lives, the foundation of their
very sanity, is shaken. A late-deafened person sees his or her

identity coming undone, dissolving without any "resolving" in sight. It's not something that's solved by simply buying a TTY or enrolling in a Basic Sign Communication class. It can be devastating.

Late-deafness strikes at the very heart of relationships: the ability to communicate freely and openly with each other, to understand and to be understood. One tragic consequence is the breakup not just of friendships, but of families. A number of "rock-solid" marriages have fallen apart when one partner becomes deaf. Late-deafened workers sometimes lose their jobs. Isolation, depression, and suicidal impulses are the most dangerous result of this process. You're not hearing any more, and you're not culturally Deaf, so where do you fit in? What sort of future can there be?

One of the worst aspects of being late-deafened is the incomprehension of "well-meaning" relatives and friends, and the horrendous things that are said in the guise of consolation. A prime example: the obnoxious sentence, "You have to learn to accept your deafness." "Deafness" here has a decidedly negative connotation: Accept the fact that you're an auditory cripple. Accept the fact that you have to settle for an inferior form of existence. Accept the fact that your social life is kaput. Accept isolation. Accept *what*? Losing one's hearing is not necessarily the end of the world, but "advice" like this, intended to assuage grief, makes things worse. Hearing people say things like this to cover their own feelings of embarrassment. Or, perhaps, their utter inadequacy. Are they going to have to shoulder an additional burden of responsibility for communication? An unsettling prospect indeed!

The Deaf community has many things that are good about it, and many things that are bad—such as a kind of quasi-clannish, insular snobbishness in some of its members. (Not all, we emphatically add. Some.) Some late-deafened people, eager to reach out to and be accepted by the Deaf community, bravely venture into new territory—a Deaf gathering—only to find themselves getting the frozen-shoulder treatment. They're viewed as "hearings-in-the-head," and accorded the coldest imaginable welcome, which is no welcome at all. To be fair, not all Deaf people greet "newcomers" with hostile rejection, but some do, and it's enough to scare anyone off. Thus, the people in greatest need of understanding and support from this community are often treated with cruelty. And this is a terrible injustice.

Late-deafened people find their greatest support from each other—those who have experienced the forcible severance from the hearing world, and survived. That's why the Association of Late-Deafened Adults (ALDA) was founded, and that's the key to its considerable success. Networking. It's important for late-deafened people to know that they're *not* alone, and that their problems are real, not figments of their tormented minds.

Sharing one's painful feelings and frustrations with another person who has been in the same predicament and who can offer empathy and true understanding is often the first step towards rebuilding one's life. And many of these problems *do* have solutions.

Using a liberal dose of humor, sound advice, imagination, and technology, late-deafened people have done a splendid job of assisting other late-deafened people in coping with what they call "life after deaf." They have shown that even those who have been through the worst can indeed have a rewarding social life, fun, romance, and, above all, hope—everything that makes life worth living.

Chapter 55

"What is Deaf culture? Has anyone studied it from a sociological perspective?"

A question from the executive director of a Canadian agency serving Deaf and hard-of-hearing people:
Although we have many books and articles by deaf authors, I have not found a thorough description of Deaf Culture in one book or article. Many people ask our Deaf staff and Board members but it is too big a topic to get an easy answer to "what is Deaf culture?" We are a young and growing agency and we have several staff who are not familiar with Deaf Culture. Do you know of or have a good book, or brochure, that we could order and have available for those who are interested? Has anyone studied Deaf culture from a sociological perspective?

—Linda Evans, Victoria, British Columbia

One possible definition of U.S. Deaf culture (and there must be many!) is: a social, communal, and creative force of, by, and for Deaf people based on American Sign Language (ASL). It encompasses communication, social protocol, art, entertainment, recreation (e.g., sports, travel, and Deaf clubs), and (to a point) worship. It's also an attitude, and, as such, can be a weapon of prejudice—"You're not one of us; you don't *belong.*"

Despite the mighty efforts of generations of oralists, deaf people still prefer to communicate and mingle with their own kind. That is the psychosocial basis of Deaf culture. Deaf people in the United States have staunchly resisted the unstinting attempts of oralists to eradicate the use of sign language and assimilate them into the hearing mainstream. The simple fact is that deaf people who attend the common residential schools for the deaf—no matter what mode of communication is forced on them in the classrooms—tend to seek out other deaf people and communicate in sign language. This is true, to some extent, in other countries, but the U.S. arguably has the most sophisticated and creative—and public—Deaf culture of any. As such, it has been quite influential. Think of the internationally acclaimed National Theatre of the Deaf, which is an indirect offshoot of "community" institutions such as the Gallaudet Dramatics Club and Deaf-club productions.

Very broadly speaking, the people who adhere to the Deaf-culture view have attended schools for the deaf, where they picked up ASL from each other and developed a distinctly "Deaf" attitude, encompassing such things as outlook (there is, unfortunately, a certain anti-intellectual bias, a clannish snobbery promulgated in certain schools' cliques); sharing information through gossip; teasing and joke-playing; visual humor; and a passion for sports. Certain team sports, notably volleyball, bowling, softball, and basketball, are "Deaf tribal sports." In Deaf tribal sports, *everyone* gets a chance to participate. To Deaf people, sports are a social experience, a kinetic way of expressing "belonging."

Not all Deaf people are fond of the old cultural institution, the Deaf club. These establishments used to perform a vital social function. Deaf people, excluded from the inaccessible media of the radio and cinema, could get together there to share news, information, entertainment (subtitled foreign films and live ASL performances), or simply relax after work, gossip, and enjoy each others' company. (Which is not to say that these clubs were democratic. For many years, some clubs barred women or excluded them from holding office. In keeping with social and educational "norms," some were racially segregated as well—whites and blacks having separate clubs.) With the advent of captioned TV and home videos, the Deaf club has, in some instances, dwindled into a quasi-tavern where Deaf people go to watch captioned videos, drink, and gossip. Some clubs, though, have managed to survive, maintaining a high level of sophistication; some don't even have bars.

Some Deaf people do not believe that we have a full-fledged culture in the sense that Blacks, Jews, Italians, American Indians, or Hispanics have. Ethnic culture is generally transmitted from parent to child, with grandparents and other elders playing important roles. Most Deaf people, however, are born into hearing families; many hearing parents cannot even communicate with their own deaf children. In families where deafness runs congenitally, there tends to be a much stronger identification with Deaf culture—a powerful feeling of Deaf pride. As we've noted, Deaf children of Deaf parents tend to become the leaders in their schools—they are the ones who teach the other kids ASL. They question the rules; they think for themselves; they are often more "troublesome" than compliant.

Deaf people are not immediately recognizable as belonging to the Deaf culture in the same way that, say, an Amish woman or man is immediately recognizable as Amish. In contrast to most other full-fledged cultures, there is no distinct mode of dress, no special cuisine, and no uniquely "Deaf religion," although there are Deaf congregations and Deaf churches. These employ ASL (and some Deaf priests or ministers) in their services, but are largely offshoots of established ministries—Catholic, Episcopalian, Lutheran, or Southern Baptist. Deaf Americans look, act, eat, and worship as other Americans do. The only truly distinctive aspect, the core component that provides the framework and the cohesion, is our "Deaf language"—ASL in the U.S.A. and Canada. (And Canada has other sign-language traditions, too, notably LSF (*langue de signes français*) and LSQ (*langue des signes québéçois*). Deaf social customs are based not on any ancient religious, national, or ethnic traditions but on our practical communicative needs. Therefore, some folks prefer to classify "Deaf culture" as a subculture.

A major problem with trying to "track down" a definition of Deaf culture is that it's a relatively new concept. Broadly speaking, the idea of a separate and distinct ASL-based culture as a source of public pride arose during the Civil Rights-activism era of the 1960s. Previously, Deaf folks may have been proud of their language, clubs, and dramatic productions, but they were very shy about being seen signing in public. They were, to some extent, made to feel ashamed and inferior. It was a hearing linguist, the late William Stokoe, who finally recognized that ASL was, indeed, a full-fledged language. He was not enthusiastically received at first, not even by the Deaf community. But he succeeded in setting into motion a revolution—a radically new way of perceiving deaf people and the way they preferred to communicate.

"Deaf culture" as a conscious force is still in its early stages, creatively ever-changing, ever-evolving. Deaf people have long been involved in visual arts (painting, sculpture, design, etc.). A new "visual literature" live and on videotape/DVD is being produced—ASL poetry, plays, storytelling, humor, folklore, songs, sign mime—and it's exciting to watch it unfold. We call this the "Deaf Renaissance."

Several of the books listed in our bibliography illuminate and define, to some extent, Deaf culture. A prime resource is Carol Padden and Tom Humphries' **Deaf in America: Voices from a Culture** (1988). The authors are themselves Deaf—a notable exception to the old saw (no longer accurate) that all books about Deaf culture are written by hearing people.

Deaf culture has indeed been studied from a sociological perspective, but the old theories are in need of revision.[1] There are some useful published works—Paul C. Higgins' book **Outsiders in a Hearing World** (1980) comes to mind. There is undoubtedly a "boom" in this area—and more Deaf people writing books and theses, certainly an encouraging sign.[2]

As for Canadian Deaf culture, Dr. Clifton F. Carbin has published **Deaf Heritage in Canada**, a monumental history of the Deaf communities of Canada. It provides a Canadian counterpart to Jack R. Gannon's **Deaf Heritage**.

You may wonder if hearing people can be part of Deaf culture. Indeed, they can. Parents and families of deaf children, friends, supporters, and advocates, can all be part of the Deaf community. Deaf culture is by no means restricted to deaf "members only."

Consider such educational giants of the past as Thomas Hopkins Gallaudet, Edward Miner Gallaudet, and Harvey P. Peet. All of them devoted their energies and considerable gifts to furthering the cause of Deaf education. Without them, our history (and the state of our culture) would have been immeasurably poorer.[3]

Hearing children of deaf parents (like E. M. Gallaudet) often grow up with a strong affiliation to the Deaf community. Many of these CODAs are native ASL users and bilingually proficient in ASL and English; they sign so fluently as to be indistinguishable from Deaf people. (E. M. Gallaudet has been, so far, the only president of Gallaudet University who was a native signer.) As we've noted, some choose careers as professional interpreters; others, another deafness-oriented profession such as teaching, social work, or advocacy. They straddle both Deaf and Hearing cultures.

One such notable example was the late NTD performer, author, and ASL teacher, Lou Fant. Certain hearing educators, researchers, advocates, politicians, and "good neighbors" (like Senator Tom Harkin of Iowa or Professors Harlan Lane, William Stokoe, and Ursula Bellugi) can become honorary members of the Deaf community, part of Deaf culture, even heroes. Lou Ann Walker and Leah Hager Cohen, for example, have written movingly about their firsthand involvement with Deaf culture; their works have been published by mainstream presses.

1 Dr. Allen E. Sussman, Co-Director of the Mental Health Counseling Program at Gallaudet University, made some timely remarks at a 1991 conference:

> For too long the field of deafness, including education, rehabilitation, psychology and mental health, has been preoccupied with what is wrong with deaf people rather than what is right with them. Authorities and experts in the field are experts in what's wrong with them, but their experience in what's right with them appears to be lacking. This pathological view is perpetuated by the same experts and authorities, many of whom are not able to communicate meaningfully with deaf children and adults.
>
> Moreover, the psychopathological perspective is rampantly manifest in the literature on deafness, especially in psychosocial aspects of deafness. There are several books, book chapters, and professional journal articles and almost all are pathologically oriented, dwelling on the problems and liabilities from language deficiency to behavior disorders. The focus is on the capital D's such as: Disability, Dysfunction, Deficiency and Deviance. Most "Psychology of Deafness" and related courses in graduate training programs are also pathologically oriented, depicting deaf children and adults in largely unfavorable light, further contributing to this distortion and imbalance. The emphasis, again, is on what they *cannot do* rather than on what they can do; the emphasis is on *liability* rather than *assets* which many deaf people possess in overwhelming abundance.

—Allen E. Sussman, Ph.D., "Characteristics of a well-adjusted Deaf Person, or: The Art of Being a Deaf Person," paper presented at the first National Conference on Childhood Deafness, Sioux Falls, South Dakota, April 1991, and reprinted in **DEAF LIFE**, July 1991.

2 Carol Padden and Tom Humphries, **Deaf in America: Voices from a Culture**. Cambridge, Massachusetts: Harvard University Press, 1988.

Paul C. Higgins, **Outsiders in a Hearing World: A Sociology of Deafness**. Beverly Hills: Sage Publications, 1980.

See also:

Jerome D. Schein, **At Home Among Strangers**. Washington, D.C.: Gallaudet University Press, 1989.

Sherman Wilcox, **American Deaf Culture: An Anthology**. Silver Spring, Md.: Linstok Press, 1989.

Harlan Lane, Robert Hoffmeister, and Ben Bahan, **A Journey into the Deaf-World**. San Diego: DawnSignPress, 1996.

3 Peet headed the New York School for the Deaf (Fanwood) from 1831 to 1866, transforming it into a first-rate institution. One of the great early leaders in Deaf education, he began his career in 1822 at the American School for the Deaf (Hartford).

Chapter 56

Should a hearing person write about Deaf Culture?

ood question. If only insiders wrote about their own culture, the fields of sociology, anthropology, ethnology, and linguistics wouldn't exist! White scholars have written about Black culture, men about women's lives and literature, and non-Jews about Jewish history. Are their works without value because they were not "insiders"? Of course not. It may be brilliant, insightful, and eminently worthwhile. A researcher's objectivity and lack of preconceptions can be definite advantages. Yet an insider's view *is* important. To get a full picture, we want to balance the outsiders' views with what the insiders have to say.

Until fairly recently, everything that was written and published about Deaf culture was the work of "the Hearing." Should this analyzing of and "opinionating" about Deaf culture continue? It's not likely to stop. Is it good for us? Yes and no. Alexander Graham Bell used his meticulous research on the Deaf community *against* it. He and other oralists almost succeeded in wiping out Deaf culture. So powerful and influential was Bell that his notorious pamphlet, **Memoir Upon the Formation of a Deaf Variety of the Human Race** (1883), is still being discussed! And ASL still has not made a complete comeback. It has not yet been fully restored to the classroom. (To a large extent, neither have Deaf teachers. There are still too few.)

Earlier textbooks often adhered to the pathological model— emphasizing deaf people as less capable, abnormal, marginalized specimens of humanity, roughly the same view that our most ignorant contemporary journalists take, with scholarly trappings added.

Helmer R. Myklebust was a noted psychologist who once ran Northwestern University's Children's Hearing Clinic. Henry Kisor, who was acquainted with Myklebust, at least on a clinical level, describes him as "a renowned authority in the field of deaf education."[1] In the early 1950s, Myklebust published **Your Deaf Child: A Guide for Parents**, which makes absolutely no allusion to sign language. Not a *single* mention of it. Of Myklebust's textbook, **The Psychology of Deafness** (1957), Jane Maher, William C. Stokoe's biographer, notes: "For years this book was the standard training text at schools of education for teachers of deaf students. (...) In 1958 the administrators and board members of Gallaudet [College] saw fit to grant [him] an honorary degree [even though his] textbook . . . had contributed so greatly to the perception among educators that deaf students were deficient."[2]

Experts and scholars who adhered to the oralist view that speech was normal, therefore, sign language was abnormal, would naturally see deaf people in terms of deviance—even if they had personally worked with deaf people. Now, however, the majority of hearing researchers are equipped with a far better attitude towards deaf people and a better understanding of Deaf issues.

Recent and contemporary hearing scholars such as Harry Best,[3] Stokoe, Ursula Bellugi, Laura-Ann Petitto, and Harlan Lane have certainly benefitted the Deaf community and gained international respect for ASL and its culture. Hearing sociologists and linguists are paying more attention to the Deaf community and the dynamics of sign languages. Those who don't know ASL do field work with an interpreter.

The field of Deaf Studies (encompassing sociology, history, psychology, linguistics, neurolinguistics, and more) is, of course, no longer the exclusive preserve of hearing scholars. More and more Deaf people have been entering this field, starting with the pioneering students who worked with Stokoe at Gallaudet's Linguistics Research Laboratory in the 1970s. We now have several Deaf scholars who have done extensive research and published their findings in linguistics, sociology, and Deaf history. They have written new text-books and produced videocourses. They have been studying and documenting American Indian sign languages and the beginnings of new native sign languages in countries such as Nicaragua. They have enhanced our understanding of how deaf people lived and communicated in earlier times and other cultures, and how people use and process language. It's a vast, booming field, and there's room for both deaf and hearing scholars.

Some Deaf people feel suspicious of being made the subject of hearing scholars' studies, and understandably so. Sign language is the one thing that genuinely belongs to Deaf people, and it is the core of our identity. We have been robbed and cheated for over a century, and we don't want to lose it again. We do have the choice to cooperate or not in other people's research. We have the right to question the uses such research is put to.

But the best solution is for more Deaf people to master the complexities of written English, get advanced degrees, do scholarly studies on their own culture and community, publish them, and teach. This is happening. Much yet remains to be done. As the saying goes, the truth shall make us free.

1 **What's That Pig Outdoors? A Memoir of Deafness** (New York: Hill and Wang, 1990), p. 58.

2 **Seeing Language in Sign: The Work of William C. Stokoe** (Washington, D.C.: Gallaudet University Press, 1996), pp. 19, 27-28.

3 "Dr. Harry Best was a noted sociologist at the University of Kentucky. His **Deafness and the Deaf in the United States** (New York: Macmillan, 1943) was long considered *the definitive work* on the subject." —Robert F. Panara

▲ ▲ ▲

Yours and ours
(a few words to
prospective researchers)

Traditionally, deaf people have been the subjects, the clients, the patients, the figures in statistics, the inferior class. Those who had the power—the theorists, scientists, researchers, educators, bureaucrats—were hearing. That, assuredly, has been changing. More Deaf people are choosing to do scholarly studies of their own community. We consider this a healthy trend. But meanwhile, what about the majority— the Hearing majority? You will, of course, continue to be intrigued by the Deaf community, to study it, document it, compile statistics, and do field work and follow-up studies. That in itself is not bad. It can be admirable. If it contributes to the sum of universal knowledge, we're all for it.

The root of prejudice is the inability to accept human differences. Our major problems with the Hearing community can be traced to its refusal to accept our differences as valid. If they don't recognize our language, for example, they won't have much respect for our need for accessible communication.

We ask that anyone who seeks to write about our history, our community, our language, make a genuine effort to understand why we feel the way we do, why we communicate as we do, why we have the problems we are currently entangled with, and where they came from.

If you look upon deafness merely as a lamentable condition—"one of the most desperate of human calamities," as Dr. Samuel Johnson described it—you may be moved to pity at the thought that we cannot, as you do, enjoy the pitter-patter of rain on the roof at night, the song of the lark, or the whispered words of love. With all due respect to these goodly things, to dwell on the lack or loss of them is to miss the whole

point. We don't see ourselves as suffering sensory deprivation—that is, unless we sustain a sudden or progressive loss
of hearing, in which case we have a whole life to set back in
order. Many Deaf people do not mourn their lack of hearing;
they see themselves as whole persons, not wounded ears. It
may surprise you that a good number of Deaf people, when
asked if they would choose to become hearing if they could,
say no; they cannot imagine themselves any other way. They
cherish their identities, their wholeness, as Deaf persons.
"Deaf" is a part of our rich and complex total identity as
individuals. To us, being deaf is simply another way of being
human. To someone who adheres to the medical-pathologi-
cal view, deafness is a disability, a disorder, something
negative. It's a malfunction that needs to be fixed. To us, it is
an integral part of our personalities. Among ourselves, we
don't make a big *shpiel* out of it; it becomes subsumed in our
everyday reality. It becomes invisible.

Deaf people enjoy being different in the same sense that any
ethnic minority enjoys being different from the majority. We
cherish ASL; we feel close kinship with our schoolmates; we
have our jokes and fun, our poetry, our songs, our arts, our
pride. We have our disagreements, our squabbles, our ongoing philosophical feuds. As we have mentioned, some of it is
very in-group stuff, not easily shared with outsiders. But
that's true of any group.

We have much to teach society-at-large about things like
cognition, language acquisition, neurolinguistics, thought
patterns, and communication. And about oppression, prejudice, and the harvest that is reaped from years of low expectations.

Our concern here is attitude. If you *really* want to study the
Deaf community and gain valuable insight, it's a good idea to
learn Sign and become part of our community in some way.
Come as a student with an open mind, not as a judge who
already knows the answers and seeks only to validate pre-
conceived notions. We welcome advocates and supporters,
students and friends.

Over a decade of promoting Deaf Awareness

Chapter 57

"How did Alexander Graham Bell almost succeed in wiping out Deaf Culture?"

I have received the article titled "Should a hearing person write about Deaf Culture?" [See Chapter 56.] I have read several articles by your company & have learned a great deal about the Deaf Culture.

My question is this: in this particular article it mentioned Alexander Graham Bell almost succeeded in wiping out Deaf Culture. I would like to know how! I have obtained the article referred to & still can't see how that has set back the Deaf Culture. Perhaps you can point out to me what I am missing in that interpretation.

—Cissy Andes, Tucson, Arizona

ith the founding of the American School for the Deaf in Hartford in 1817, deaf education in America began in earnest, and so did the Deaf community. ASL (more accurately, a blend of methodical signs and what we now call LSF and ASL) was used to teach English in the classroom. Some of the best students stayed on after graduation and became teachers, and Hartford-trained teachers and administrators helped set up other schools for the deaf across the country. Educated deaf people entered a variety of professions. The "silent press" began publishing. Deaf clubs were founded. There was considerable interest in founding a college for deaf people.

After a brief "golden age" (1830s-1860s), ASL-based Deaf education came under attack from Alexander Graham Bell and other wealthy and powerful oralists. The oral movement in the States had emerged during the 1860s, and the Milan Congress of 1880 gave it added impetus. Bell, who founded the American Association to Promote the Teaching of Speech to the Deaf (now called the Alexander Graham Bell Association for the Deaf) was the leading oral advocate.

Bell was a phonetics teacher, brilliant inventor, and indefatigable social theorist—famous, wealthy, and enormously influential. Although he became a skillful signer and acknowledged the beauty of sign language, he believed that speech was of supreme importance, and that deaf people should assimilate into hearing society. According to Gallaudet University historians John Van Cleve and Barry Crouch, "Bell believed that deafness was a terrible curse . . . a pathological aberration [that] perpetuated negative genetic traits . . . that deaf persons weakened the society in which they lived."* After studying records of several schools for the deaf, he compiled his notorious paper, **Memoir Upon the Formation of a Deaf Variety of the Human Race** (1883). He desired to put a stop to the "alarming" growth of Deaf culture and prevent deaf children from being born. Accordingly, he proposed legislation against "the intermarriage of congenital deaf-mutes." Since he doubted this would work, he suggested three "preventive measures": eliminating residential schools, forbidding the use of sign language in the education of deaf pupils, and prohibiting deaf adults from being teachers of deaf children. His proposals almost succeeded.

The oralists wielded considerable political and educational influence. Inexorably, the tide turned against signing residential schools, and the Deaf community found itself outnumbered, outmaneuvered, and out-moneyed. The efforts of Bell and his colleagues led to the proliferation of oral day schools. And by the turn of the century, the majority of residential schools in the United States had switched to the oral method—sometimes forcibly. By 1919, the peak of the oralist "wave," 80% of residential schools had "gone oral." The remaining 20% used the "combined method," which means that while they still permitted signing in the classes, all students received speech and auditory training. Deaf teachers had been forced out of the profession. Signing and oral students were segregated. If oral students were caught signing, they were punished. Of course, they continued to sign among themselves, but had to do it covertly—in the dorms at night, or in the toilets. (Lou Ann Walker calls signing the Deaf community's longtime "guilty secret.") This had profoundly negative effects on their self-esteem as deaf people.

The real tragedy is that the oralists tried to force deaf children to speak, while denying them access to sign language—which meant that many of them had no effective access to *any* language at all, unless they signed to each other in secret.

Bell wasn't directly responsible for all of this oppression, but as an advocate, he paved the way. He helped empower the oral movement, funded it, and gave it credibility. His ideas, though, have not stood the test of time. Although residential schools are yet again under attack, oralism is in decline, ASL alive and well. We wonder what Bell would have said about the numbers of hearing high-school and college students who choose to study ASL as a foreign language! ASL-based artistry is thriving. The National Theatre of the Deaf celebrated its 35th anniversary in 2002. Deaf pride and awareness are growing, and we are beginning to emerge from the "Dark Age" of the past century—but slowly.

Even Clarke School, that bastion of oralism, finally recognized the futility of its old policy of penalizing students who were caught signing. Although signing is still not allowed in class, students can sign freely outside of class without fear of punishment. In signing residential schools and alternative programs, there is a definite trend towards the Bilingual-Bicultural model, which is in many ways a throwback to the Hartford model: using ASL to teach English.

* John Vickrey Van Cleve and Barry A. Crouch, **A Place of their Own: Creating the Deaf Community in America**, p. 145. See also Richard Winefield, **Never the Twain Shall Meet: The Communications Debate**.

Chapter 58

Isn't deafness a disability? If it is, why do deaf people consider it a culture?

rom a purely physical viewpoint, deafness is a disability. A handicap. Something designed to function well (the sense of hearing) doesn't function properly. So if you want to talk about "sensory impairments," "sensory handicaps," or "sensory pathology," fine. There's no denying that deaf people possess broken or imperfect auditory machinery. If being hearing is "normal," from a medical viewpoint, deafness is "abnormal." Damaged, defective, or nonfunctional auditory equipment—what makes deaf people deaf—makes us audiologically different from those with normal hearing. Go right ahead and wave those audiograms at us. We won't deny what we are.

However, we find this an unnecessarily restrictive view. It doesn't take into account what we do with our remaining senses, how creatively we cope, how we communicate, and, most significantly, the richness and color of our lives—*as deaf people*. And many of us do not see ourselves as pathological specimens but as members of a community. And please do not call it the "hearing-impaired community." We call it the "deaf community" or, to emphasize the cultural aspect, "Deaf community." Or, to be properly inclusive, "deaf and hard-of-hearing community." This emphasizes the fact that all persons with a significant degree of hearing loss share common concerns and have common needs, although our philosophies and preferred modes of communication may vary. And vary they do.

When you are discussing something that is strictly defined as a "physical handicap," how can that be considered a culture? As we have already pointed out, ethnic and religious groups have full-fledged cultures. Do deaf people? We're still arguing about that, of course. Signs of a full-fledged culture include language, literature, art, folklore, religion, distinctive cuisines, modes of dress, and social customs. ASL-Deaf people certainly do have a distinct language, folklore, literature, art, and social customs. In all other respects, though, we resemble our hearing neighbors. As we've already noted, we don't have a distinctive religion, cuisine, or costume. Since most deaf people are born into hearing families, we acquire our language and folklore, *etcetera*, from each other, not from our parents. Nor do we have a "Deaf ghetto" or "Deaf barrio," although deaf people often cluster in cities where there are schools for the deaf, because of the greater number of jobs open to us, opportunities to participate fully in community life, accessibility and acceptance, and ASL-oriented social and cultural events. There are, however, apartment buildings designed for deaf people (e.g., Pilgrim Towers in Los Angeles), and "retirement communities" like Columbus Colony in Ohio.

Those who advocate for Deaf rights cite the importance of ASL to our community. Of course. Deaf people created, refined, and use ASL as a living, breathing, continuously evolving language. ASL is the basis of what we call "Deaf culture." Some advocates go so far as to claim that deaf people are not disabled; we are a linguistic minority just like those whose primary language is Spanish or Chinese. Just as those who rely on foreign languages need the services of interpreters, so do ASL-Deaf people. We're not handicapped, just different. Well, then, according to this logic, if we don't have a disability, how can we take recourse in the Americans with Disabilities Act? Aren't deaf people included in its coverage? Doesn't it apply to us, too? Shouldn't we be honest about our needs as disabled persons?

Well, but . . . the disability lobby and the ASL-Deaf lobby have overlapping but not completely shared agenda. Persons with physical disabilities want to be mainstreamed into all aspects of community life. No more segregation. No more separate schools for the handicapped, with their oppression and low expectations. They want inclusion. Bring down the barriers. ASL-Deaf people, however, want to preserve residential schools for the deaf as a viable educational option for deaf children. For us, mandatory mainstreaming would only increase, not lessen, isolation. Our definition of "separate" is not the same as the one used by the disability advocates. Our aims are very different here.

We share certain concerns with the disability community: access to public facilities, quality education, fair opportunities, good jobs, stereotypical images and invisibility in the media, for example. While those with physical disabilities are concerned about mobility, for example, our concerns focus more on communication. We can be able-bodied but still claim protection under the ADA. We have lobbied for better telecommunications access and captioning—two concerns shared by oral-deaf and ASL-Deaf people. Some things we definitely have in common with the disability community, however: our experiences with discrimination and prejudice, and the necessity of getting our society to improve its *damned* attitudes.

Is deafness a disability or is it a culture? Does it have to be one or the other? Can it be both? If you want to give the most accurate answer, taking into account the complexities of being medically deaf and culturally Deaf, you'll have to be annoyingly vague. You'll have to say, "In some way, yes; in some ways, no."

Chapter 59

The Deaf community has been compared to a "ghetto that is disintegrating." Do you agree?

he September 1993 **Atlantic Monthly** contained a provocative cover essay by Edward Dolnick, "Deaf-ness as Culture." In response, **The Atlantic** received numerous letters to the editor, many written by hearing persons, and a few self-described oral-deaf readers. Several of them expressed tremendous contempt for the concept of "Deaf Culture." Here are excerpts from three such responses. The first is written by a hearing reader; the second by a reader who describes herself as "profoundly hearing-impaired."

> How dare deaf culturalists play their games with unwitting children? How dare they decide that theirs is a state which cannot be improved? How dare they, through vanity and pride, deny the blessings and wonders of sound?
>
> I posit this test, to gauge their true sympathies, whether humane or self-centered: What do deaf culturalist children of deaf culturalist children do when their baby is born hearing? Do they ignore its faculty? Do they deny the use of its ability? Do they poke its ear-drums out with ice picks?

> I ask, "Why inflict your silent world on future generations of deaf and hard-of-hearing children who can be helped to enjoy the whole world, and not just one little corner?"

A Canadian cochlear-implant surgeon responded thus:

> The cochlear prosthesis, on which I have worked for years with many other scientists, engineers and clinicians, will lead inevitably to the extinction of the alternative culture of the Deaf, probably within a decade. There will still be deaf people, some by

choice and some because the technology cannot address (yet) some forms of deafness, but they will be so thinly scattered that the Deaf culture will be unsustainable. (...)

Deaf culture shares many characteristics of the Yiddish culture of pre-war Europe (including uncertain status as a proper noun). Both reflect a triumphant expression of will and ingenuity to cope with criminally unfair ghettoization. Both are unsustainable in the absence of tragic circumstances from which they sprang. People who have devoted their lives to creating these alternative cultures deserve our highest respect and deepest sympathy even when they reject both as patronizing. Those who cannot be removed from a ghetto that is disintegrating will need all the support that our society can provide.

These remarks are indicative of the hostility with which some hearing and oral-deaf people view "Deaf Culture."

You can look at deafness as a pathological condition to be eliminated or remedied. Or you can look at it as a cultural attribute, a way of being human, even a way of life. To culturally-Deaf people, deafness is a part of their personalities that they cherish, that they consider special. Something that they consider worthy of passing on to their children. In accordance with this view, cochlear implants are not welcomed as the latest technological advance in the conquest of deafness, but as an unnecessary and undesirable invasion of a deaf person's body. It can be very difficult to persuade antagonistic (or simply ignorant) hearing and oral-deaf persons of the validity of this view. "Why inflict your silent world on future generations?" they retort. "How can you *deny* hope to deaf children?"

A ghetto is imposed on a population as a means of oppressing it, keeping it under control—powerless, demoralized, terrified. The modern-day image of "ghetto" is of a deteriorating neighborhood consisting of poor, disempowered, crime-ridden victims. The usual accoutrements include violence, illegal drugs, gangs, unemployment, schools that don't teach, and a pervasive feeling of hopelessness.

A neighborhood, a community, consists of persons who

live near, and/or associate with, each other because they want to. They derive a feeling of safety, security, and shared concerns. They enjoy the best possible quality of life from that affinity. A neighborhood is a desirable place to live. A community is a positive and powerful institution.

To focus on the Canadian doctor's negative and coldly hostile view: The Jews have traditionally chosen to dwell together, not only for safety and security, but to share their faith, languages, values, and traditions. True, Jews were *forced* to live in ghettos, in overcrowded, undesirable conditions. They were compelled to wear distinctive, sometimes peculiar-looking hats, cloaks, or badges; they were forbidden to dress certain ways, wear certain colors or styles, carry weapons, engage in most trades, own land, travel freely, *etcetera*. All of these were means of oppression, disenfranchisement, humiliation, and control.

The first ghetto was established by Catholic rulers in Italy to segregate the Jews—to prevent them from mixing with the Catholic populace, to forcibly hold them down. In Eastern Europe, having originally been invited to settle there by the rulers who wanted to boost their kingdoms' prosperity, they were gradually restricted to certain cities or areas of cities.

But the Jews made the best of the situation, creating vibrant, self-sufficient communities. At the heart were the synagogues—the houses of prayer and study—the schools and *yeshivot*, the marketplace (for commerce and socialization), and a rich home life. When they fled persecution, forced conscription, pogroms, massacres, and finally, systematic annihilation, they established a flourishing community on the Lower East Side in Manhattan. Was it a ghetto?

Within a generation or two, many of the inhabitants had migrated north to South Bronx (which was then a desirable, attractive, even tony middle-class neighborhood), to Brooklyn, or the suburbs. As they became progressively assimilated into American culture, they gradually lost their Jewish identity, to the point where their children's children or grandchildren were no longer recognizably Jewish. Was this, then, a good thing? If you feel that Jewish faith, identity, and traditions are worth preserving, no.

The Canadian cochlear-implant surgeon evidently never visited Boro Park or Crown Heights in Brooklyn, or Monsey, New York—three major Yiddish-speaking Orthodox Jewish communities. They are not ghettoes, but they *are* flourishing, densely populated Jewish neighborhoods. Their inhabitants choose to live there, as they can only live a full Jewish life surrounded by other Jews, with shops and institutions that cater to their needs as Jews—e.g., kosher butcher shops, Jewish bookstores, businesses owned and staffed by religious Jews, clothing stores that supply the particular styles that are deemed suitable. They have their own clubs, schools, books, and newspapers. *Etcetera.* Their languages are Yiddish, Hebrew, and English—and there's a flourishing Yiddish press. Yiddish, like it or not, is alive and well there.

A ghetto is imposed from without. In the case of deaf people, we have been encouraged (and sometimes compelled) to assimilate into the hearing community, to be "hearing, speaking" approximations, to forsake that "Deaf" aspect of ourselves, to be un-deaf.

But Deaf people *like* to associate with each other, to be in situations where they can communicate freely. The hearing community has not always permitted them freedom to do so. Alexander Graham Bell, who wished to cleanse the human race of its deaf subspecies, wanted to ban schools for the deaf, the deaf press, and deaf clubs for that purpose: they impeded the deaf person's assimilation into the hearing culture. Deaf schools and clubs not only fostered a sense of cultural identity and social cohesion, they also promulgated ASL. To us, it's a beautiful language created and refined by Deaf people. To Bell, it was another obstacle to be dismantled. Schools for the deaf were, on the whole, "pure-oralized" by World War I, but ASL was taught and transmitted among the students as a clandestine activity. It was preserved in the Deaf churches, clubs, and the dormitory toilets. ASL survived all attempts to wipe it out. Now, *that* says something.

We believe that there will always be deaf people. Geneticists may identify the genes that cause Usher's Syndrome and other forms of congenital deafness, but there will always be deaf and deaf-blind children born to untested parents. Those who have sufficient money may have their children undergo cochlear-implant surgery—but poorer families will not. That means that we will end up with a "class" of un-deafed deaf people who are financially comfortable, and a class of poor folks with strong Deaf identities (and, as it looks, substandard educations).

Despite some doctors' blithely clinical predictions, we don't think that implants will become as commonplace and inevitable as smallpox vaccinations. A number of conscientious hearing parents will refuse to have their children implanted. And we harbor dark suspicions that childhood implants are a medical fad that will run its course, and that there will be a vigorous anti-implant backlash—spearheaded by deaf adults who were implanted as children, and who have long since stopped using their implants.

In one sense, the Deaf community *is* like a ghetto: it is hard for us to establish free, open, and comfortable communication with the hearing community. There is, after all, a limited pool of persons with whom we can communicate openly. There are not enough interpreters to go around, and even hospitals and other major facilities may not provide them when they're needed. Prejudice and ignorance are still widespread. The boom in cochlear implants hasn't altered that a bit, as far as we can see. Current media images of deaf people and coverage of controversial issues are as superficial and uninformed as ever—with a few noteworthy exceptions (such as Dolnick's thought-provoking article).

That's not a ghetto of silence or unrepaired cochleas as much as it is a ghetto of attitude. And that's a ghetto we would like to demolish—right now.

Chapter 60

Is the Internet going to destroy Deaf culture?

espite our concerns about audio effects—most video clips on the Web aren't captioned—the Internet is a relatively Deaf-accessible medium. It has the potential to be a disruptive and isolating force in the Deaf community. But is it?

Consider the decline of the time-honored institution of the local Deaf club. Cut off from sources of information and entertainment taken for granted by hearing people (the radio, phonograph, telephone, television, and cinema—except for subtitled foreign films), Deaf people congregated at the club, watched a captioned or subtitled movie (or even one in ASL), socialized, discussed politics, swapped information, chatted, gossiped, and networked. These clubs were utilized by a geographically-limited pool of regulars, who would see (more or less) the same faces every time. Nor were the clubs known for their friendliness to outsiders—e.g., hearing persons, newly-deafened adults, and curious ITP students. And not all Deaf people enjoyed that kind of ambiance; many stayed away from the clubs. So one could say that the clubs had definite limitations and drawbacks.

After closed-captioned TV removed the main barriers to the nation's favorite information and entertainment medium, and after captioned home videos began making their way onto the market, more Deaf people became less inclined to go to the clubs, preferring to stay home and get their news and entertainment there. Of course, Deaf people have continued to travel and socialize. If anything, their enthusiasm for traveling to foreign and exotic locations—together—is keener than ever. But the upsurge in accessible mass media has led to the downfall of the club.

Television has served as a prime medium of disruption. Viewers would sit passively, taking in the onscreen action, for hours at a time. Aside from their flipping the channels or brandishing the remote control, no interaction was called for. TV has a well-known de-socializing effect: conversation comes to a halt when the action picks up.

The Internet has already taken a bite out of the TV market. During a 1996 lecture at NTID, Dr. Vinton G. Cerf, co-founder of the Internet (who is borderline-deaf himself), cited a survey that indicated that people were spending less time watching TV and more time surfing the Net.

To be sure, some Deaf people want nothing to do with the Internet or E-mail. Indeed, some of these folks don't even want to install a fax machine. They see the Internet as an intrusion, a distraction, a waste of time. They prefer keeping things simple. And there is something to be said for this view. But there is also something to be said for becoming computer-literate, just as there is for learning to use a TTY and fax-modem.

The Internet, as a mass medium, has had its share of controversy. And there is an immeasurable abundance of junk, rubbish, and poison to be found there. But even its detractors acknowledge that there are some excellent, valuable, worthwhile sites. We prefer to focus on the positive aspects.

The Internet is a more interactive, even social, medium than TV. Exploring Websites is more interactive than channel-surfing via remote control. Chatrooms, offering a highly interactive real-time experience, have become a popular feature. They are easier to use than relay services, and more fun. As many as 25 visitors at a time can carry on conversations in a single chatroom. Instead of having a one-on-one TTY conversation, chatroom visitors can participate in real-time conversations with a couple dozen other visitors at once—or have a private business talk. It's the most social text-communication media we can imagine.

MSM Productions, Ltd. launched DeafChat in late February 1998. Almost immediately, DeafChat began getting visitors from across the nation and abroad—including parents of deaf children, some of them distraught, who were seeking information, advice, encouragement, and support. DeafChat also got visits from curious hearing teens and adults (not just parents). We had a glimpse of the immense potential of the Internet to educate hearing people in general and to reach out to parents of deaf children—while providing a means for Deaf visitors to network and to share the positive (and negative) aspects of the Deaf experience: discussing their schooling, jobs, lives, families, issues, controversies, frustrations, and dreams.

Much of the conversation is, admittedly, trivial—fun yakking. Occasionally, it's serious. Regular chatroom users develop an online network of friends—and the relationships sometimes grow into real friendships, occasionally romance. Given a choice, Deaf people overwhelmingly prefer E-mail and chatrooms to TRS. Chatrooms can also be used for direct, and private, business conversations—or conferences. The ICQ and AIM real-time-message/chat programs are particularly useful personal/business applications. Wireless text pagers increase the flexibility of E-mail.

Videophone technology offers the promise of being able to carry on real-time conversations in ASL or any other sign language across the globe. Who wouldn't be excited about that prospect? Those who recall earlier generations of picturephones (such as NTID's much-missed Vistaphones) know how much gets lost in a text conversation, and how exciting and informative a video-conversation can be. We're looking forward to the day when videophones become affordable and technically sophisticated enough to be commonplace. Imagine having videoconferences with two or more global friends, their faces and hands showing up simultaneously as individual vignettes on one screen!

In a way, the Internet benefits Deaf Culture because it spreads information quickly. Deaf people are posting personal pages on the Web; more ASL resources are available.

Just as hearing people are doing, more deaf people are staying home to explore the Net. Some enthusiasts spend virtually all their free time surfing the Net, browsing favorite World Wide Websites and trying out new ones, by direction or at random. (This is an informal observation, of course.) Deaf people who would otherwise never have physically ventured into a public library or museum have this enormous wealth of resources at their fingertips. This is good, because many deaf people, as we have already pointed out, dislike libraries. They've been isolated too long, and are hungry for information and access. The Internet provides an unlimited helping of news, travel information, shopping, resources, directories, instruction, networking, medical and financial advice . . . the offerings are staggeringly endless.

The Deaf community is several years behind the hearing community in terms of technological savvy. But, given a few years of experience, they'll be catching up. And when they do, we can expect a new virtual Deaf community of savvy Net users.

Doesn't the Internet have negative aspects? Certainly. While it can be an excursion into an inexhaustible treasury of information, it can be the most contemptible sort of boob-tube escape from reality. There's a virtual anti-Deaf Culture community online. Some "Deaf" sites are trashy. The Internet's influence can be pernicious as much as positive. But it cannot be said to "destroy" Deaf culture. TV and home video may have helped push traditional Deaf clubs to extinction, but a new global Deaf cyber-club may be in the making. The Internet has the potential to bring down barriers between Deaf and non-Deaf, to provide a truly democratic and fully accessible meeting-place, to promote global understanding. This is an exciting prospect. And we can be the shapers of that future.

Deaf Awareness 5-Minute Quiz

Chapters 47—60

Answers are on the bottom of the page, upside down.

True or False:

1. Deaf persons were prohibited from marrying, or even forcibly sterilized, to prevent transmitting deafness. But since some 90% of deaf babies are born to hearing parents, anyone who wishes to prevent deaf babies from being born should prevent *hearing* people from having children.

2. Many babies are born deaf because their mothers fell down while pregnant.

3. Tragically, in some U.S. communities and foreign cultures, parents still believe that deaf children are a punishment from God.

4. Some hard-of-hearing people consider themselves Deaf; others identify with the Hearing community.

5. Late-deafened people have traditionally been eagerly accepted into the Deaf community and accorded a warm welcome.

6. Captioned TV and home videos have hastened the demise of the Deaf club as a community institution.

7. The only worthwhile studies of Deaf culture and community have been done by hearing scholars.

8. A.G. Bell, a skillful signer, considered sign language a major impediment to deaf people's full assimilation into hearing society.

9. The disability lobby shares many concerns with the Deaf community, but one major difference is their stance on separate schooling.

10. The Internet has had little, if any, effect on Deaf culture.

10. False.
1. True; 2. False; 3. True; 4. True; 5. False; 6. True; 7. False; 8. True; 9. True;
Answers:

Chapter 61

Are deaf people still stereotyped? If so, how? What kind of stereotypes are still popular?

stereotype is an image cut from a pattern instead of reality. It reflects more preconception than truth. Here are some of the most common (Hearing) stereotypes of deaf people, including some prevalent Hollywood stereotypes. (We have already discussed "The Silent Bookworm" and "The Illiterate Dork.")

The Silent Sufferer: Deaf people are seen as solitary social outcasts, terribly alone, more alienated than hearing characters. A particularly poignant embodiment of this view is the character of John Singer in Carson McCullers' classic novel, **The Heart is a Lonely Hunter**. This has been made into a movie (with a hearing actor, Alan Arkin, playing the character), and, more recently, a Broadway play (with the brilliant ASL-Deaf actor Bruce Hlibok in the role). Although tragically isolated, Singer is such an attractive, sympathetic character and a good "listener" that hearing people pour out their troubles to him. He finds happiness and fluent communication (in ASL) only when he's with his friend/lover Antonopoulos, who's loutish and mentally unstable but also Deaf. After Antonopoulos dies in a mental institution, Singer commits suicide.

In reality, ASL-Deaf people are social creatures. We suspect that they are somewhat less susceptible to depression and suicide than oral-deaf and late-deafened people. We have active social lives—visiting Deaf friends and inviting them over, participating in Deaf clubs and events. Hearing people often shun or patronize us because of the communications barrier, but rarely do they adopt us as spiritual mascots. John Singer is actually a symbol of alienated humanity. Deaf people are . . . people.

The Pathetic Waif/Emotional Basket Case: Popularized by *Johnny Belinda* (one movie version and two TV versions so far), and the more recent *Breaking Through.* Belinda and Laura, young, vulnerable, abused, languageless deaf women, are both victimized. Notably, both characters have been played by hearing actresses. In fairness, *Johnny Belinda* was the first major Hollywood movie (1948) to portray a deaf character and sign language in a positive light. Belinda's and Laura's stories are supposedly about empowerment. Both women are helpless and in trouble. Their being deaf and languageless adds tearjerker appeal to their plights.

Ironically, *Breaking Through* was based on a real-life situation: the experience of a young, languageless Hispanic-American woman who escaped her abusive family in Los Angeles, where she had been treated essentially as a slave. But the TV-movie version erased her ethnic identity, making her Caucasian, and nominally shifted the action to Florida. By the time the story reached the screen, much of the truth had been squeezed out of it.

Phyllis Frelich portrayed a more true-to-life character, Janice Ryder, in *Love is Never Silent* (based on the first part of Joanne Greenberg's **In This Sign**): an exploited textile worker who is angry and embittered—but understandably so. It was a brilliant portrayal, and Frelich has played other strong, multi-dimensional Deaf women. The role of Sarah Norman in *Children of a Lesser God* was written for her by Mark Medoff. One cannot imagine Frelich playing a Belinda. We will always wonder what a Deaf actress could have brought to the portrayal of Laura.

Super-Sleuth Who Can Read Lips Through Walls: Tess Kaufman, the character played by Marlee Matlin in *Reason-*

able Doubts, has something of this heightened capability. Communication is never a problem for her on the job. She has a signing partner. She interviews all kinds of unsavory characters, never has to "fake it," and holds her own splendidly in court. Ironically, in real life, Matlin wanted to pursue a career in law enforcement, but was told that because she was deaf, she'd be confined to a desk job. She ended up switching careers.

Super-Deafie with Novelty Value: Deaf guest stars on prime-time TV programs (e.g., Terrylene Sacchetti on *Doogie Howser, M.D.*) help the hearing regulars solve problems by using their ingenuity, imagination, and signing skills, while teaching them a valuable lesson or two, then exit. This is a problem with sitcoms. Each installment brings in a new character whose involvement with the regulars lasts for exactly one or one-half hour. Terrylene's appearance (as a member of a Deaf gang) in several sequential episodes of *Beauty and the Beast* was an exception. Matlin's role as a mayor on *Picket Fences* was a breakthrough in that she made return appearances. (More, please.)

In real life, hearing people who make friends with deaf people put aside time and energy to cultivate their friendship and learn to communicate. Of course, this doesn't jibe with the quick-bite sit-com style. Life is not served up in 10-minute segments between commercials, and problems aren't neatly resolved before the final credits.

Sleazy Card Peddlers: These characters prey on hearing people's stereotypical perceptions of the deaf. ("Oh, those poor deaf people. I'm glad to help out those who are less fortunate than me.") The hearing victim shells out a few bucks for a manual-alphabet card that s/he won't use, or some trinket worth a few cents. Most deaf people are hardworking, honest taxpayers. They buy cars and houses, rent apartments, travel, and go to supermarkets and shopping malls just like everybody else. We don't know of any deaf people who financed their college educations by peddling (i.e., begging). They got scholarships or worked their way through. Most of us bitterly resent the negative stereotype perpetrated by card-peddlers.

A sidenote: As for the deaf Mexican immigrants liberated from the "bondage ring": many Deaf people in Mexico believe that peddling trinkets on the streets is preferable to doing nothing, since educational and career opportunities for deaf people there are severely limited. (Perhaps we should say "nonexistent.") Those who came illegally to the U.S. were lured by promises of easy work, a good income, and better living conditions than they could hope for in Mexico. The way they were treated by their "customers" (who often gave them extra dollars for their trinkets), shopkeepers (who gave them free sandwiches and coffee before they started their comfortless days on the subways), and the city and government officials who provided for them after the ringleaders were arrested, tried, and convicted, says much for common sense and compassion. Most chose to stay in New York. What they wanted more than anything else was an opportunity to earn a decent living. None wanted to peddle anymore.

The Incompetent Dum-Dum: Some intelligent (?) hearing folks still believe that deaf people can't think, and treat them accordingly. Question: How many of us have been treated as though we were mentally retarded? Answer: a lot!

Exotic Alien: Deaf people are seen as exotic, weird, strange, alien, etc., not because of their personalities or characters, but simply because they're deaf. Particularly ASL-Deaf.

Life's Loser: Deaf people are seen as pathetic, victimized, weak characters. There is a prevalent notion in Hearing culture that you're "nothing if you can't speak." According to this notion, to succeed, you *must* be able to speak well. Those who prefer not to use their voices and rely on ASL for everyday communication are labeled with all sorts of negative terms—"deaf-mute," *etcetera.*

Evil Deafie: To some hearing people, there is something sinister about deafness . . . a holdover from the not-so-good old days when deaf people were considered accursed of God and were treated as outcasts (and still are, in some cultures). Newspaper coverage of crimes committed by deaf people sometimes emphasizes the deaf aspect. Lou Ann Walker's intimate portrayal of a Deaf gang, the Nasty Homicides, in **People Weekly** was a stereotype-buster.

God's Victim: Conversely, some hearing people see us as "touched by God" or "special to God" in some way, by virtue of our "affliction." This can be as insidious and patronizing view as the view that deaf people are cursed.

Tabloid Tragedies: Tabloid newspapers are awfully fond of labeling deafness a "tragedy," and calling us "deaf-mutes." E.g., "Tragically, her son was born deaf." "Sadly, she was born with the same affliction." It's difficult to develop a positive self-image if everybody tells you you're "afflicted" and that your being deaf is a "tragedy." The real tragedy is that we are prevented from achieving our full potential because of prejudice.

In our struggle to gain rights, empowerment, and better education for all deaf people, the last thing we need is to be branded as walking tragedies!

Stereotypes are a problem for us when they are used to keep us "in place," to restrict our freedom, to curtail our ambitions, to reinforce low expectations, and to legitimize prejudice and negative misconceptions. Stereotypical thinking is a symptom of ignorance. Ignorance is the most devastating of all disabilities, but the most easily cured.

Chapter 62

Is there a Deaf literature?

es, there is. By "literature," we mean fiction, nonfic-tion, essays, journalism, memoirs, stories, poetry, plays, and all manner of hybrids, with the emphasis on creativity. It might be useful to first make a distinction between "literature created by people who happen to be deaf" and "literature expressing a Deaf viewpoint." The two are not necessarily exclusive, but neither should they be confused.

Anyone familiar with the history of literature knows that there have been all manner of successful authors—male, female, young, old, of various races, religions, nationalities, ethnic/cultural backgrounds, and representing every physical and social possibility: blind, deformed, chronically ill, disabled, social outcasts, and, of course, deaf—born-deaf, early-deafened, progressively-deafened, late-deafened, and hard-of-hearing. A number of these have made contributions to the "mainstream" literary tradition. Some have also dealt with deaf themes. The great French poet Pierre de Ronsard (1524-1585) was partially deafened at age 16. There are no "Deaf themes" in his work. His contemporary Joachim du Bellay (1522-1560), famed for his sonnets, was progressively deafened. Pierre Desloges (1742-?), who was early-deafened, was the first known deaf person to write and publish a prose book—**Observations d'un sourd et muet sur cours élémentaire d'éducation des sourds et muèts** ("Observations of a Deaf-Mute on an Elementary Course of Education for Deaf-Mutes"), 1779. It contained a defense of sign language and noted the existence of a Deaf community in Paris.

In the United States, since the 1820s, there have been a number of professional deaf writers from various backgrounds. Deaf people have participated in all genres of literature: poetry, essays, biography, fiction, even battlefield dispatches. Early notables—to cite three—include journalist-advocate Edmund Booth, journalist-poet Laura Redden Searing, and bohemian Albert Ballin. Deaf people have made literary history by breaking into new genres—e.g., history (Jack R. Gannon's **Deaf Heritage** [1981] was a landmark) and playwriting (Douglas Burke's **The Good Peddler**, which debuted in 1961, was perhaps the first original play by a deaf writer). Connie Briscoe's novel **Sisters and Lovers** even made it onto the mainstream best-seller lists in 1995.

And that's just written/printed literature. Deaf creativity has another dimension entirely—based on sign language. Some of us feel that ASL literature is the only truly "Deaf" genre. As a genre, it is certainly original. It is a uniquely Deaf creation—there's no written counterpart. It could be said that the heart and soul of Deaf literature cannot be found in written books, but in the burgeoning library of ASL performances—stories, poems, song, plays. The videocam is the Deaf community's printing press, recording the works of newly-created Deaf literature.

If it's ASL, can it be literature? A common and insulting question is to ask, "Why hasn't the Deaf community produced a Shakespeare?" This is equivalent to asking, "Why hasn't there been a female Shakespeare?" As Virginia Woolf pointed out in **A Room of One's Own**, if Shakespeare had had a twin sister who shared his passion for words and hunger to create, she would not have been allowed to fulfill her gift; she would have been crushed. The society that produced a Shakespeare barred women from literary *and* theater careers. There were women of genius in the Elizabethan age. But the society they lived in had no use for the expression of that genius.

All of us are products of our times and cultures, and subject to the various restrictions of our lots—our genders, sexual identities, religions, beliefs, ages, racial-ethnic-socio-economic identities, wars, geographic locations, mobility, personalities, ambitions, what have you.

To have a literature, you have to have favorable conditions for it. Even though the London theater scene was relatively new, Shakespeare drew on the Greek-Roman tradition, early English plays in verse (a primitive genre), French and Italian romances, and so forth. Nor did he work in a vacuum—other English playwrights, friends and rivals, were also busy. One thing's for certain: The Elizabethans, lacking the hindsight of generations of Shakespeare scholars, didn't see his works as immortal masterpieces of drama, but as entertainment. They went to the theater for enjoyment—for fun. That was their TV. They were a hungry, enthusiastic audience, and a demanding one. They wanted lively dialogue, wit, humor, bawdy jokes, dazzling swordplay, and action. (We might well ask: If Shakespeare were living in contemporary U.S. culture, would he be writing scripts for TV sitcoms?)

In contrast to the well-established world traditions, ASL literature is in its infancy. It's a very new genre, so we don't yet have the advantage of hindsight. We have a new genre of scholarship, too. Research is being done on the criteria for ASL literature and ASL poetics.

Thus, instead of comparing contemporary ASL artists with Shakespeare (a futile proposition), it might be more instructive to try and understand how ASL literature uses visual-kinetic instead of written and spoken language, how it reflects Deaf perceptions, and if it represents a fresh cultural view. We could ask: What is its relationship to the European-U.S. tradition of mime and pantomime? To street theater? Folk art? To our traditions of the Gallaudet Dramatics Club and Deaf-club performances? To Deaf-theater traditions of other nations? What's being done on videotape/DVD? What's happening in the various local and regional Deaf theaters? Are they creating a new audience for original plays? Should ASL adaptations of mainstream plays be considered a new genre, or a hybrid? What are Deaf artists doing now? What do they have to say? How do they experiment with language and concept? How are they expanding the definition of "literature"? Where and how do Deaf people learn it? How do they teach it? Is there a market and an audience for it? Is it commercially viable? What are the criteria for quality? How can we recognize brilliance? What will ultimately endure?

Raymond Luczak, author, poet, critic, playwright, and filmmaker, has some provocative comments on the topic:

In the anthology **A Mighty Change: An Anthology of Deaf American Writing, 1816-1864**, the editor Christopher Krentz notes something that hasn't always been pointed out enough. Many of these deaf writers, because the concept of deaf pride had not yet been established, envisioned heaven as a place where they would regain their hearing; they were also influenced by the idea of religion redeeming their "handicap," that God would save them from themselves. To me, I've always envisioned such writers as "deaf-negative" writers: They look down on other deaf people simply because they wish to be hearing or at least regarded on a par with their hearing peers. Their role models are exclusively hearing, and because these hearing role models have succeeded so well in the world out there, they cannot seem to think it possible that they *could* succeed as deaf people themselves as opposed to being people with hearing problems.

David Wright, a British deaf poet who had the audacity to call his best-selling autobiography **Deafness** in the 1960s, described his first experience with deaf students who were signers as barbarians. Yet, for all his preference to keep his distance from the signing deaf community, he managed to have a translation or two published in the **New Yorker**. His most famous work was **Monologue of a Deaf Man**. My book **St. Michael's Fall: Poems** is the other side of David Wright's coin, in which the poet discovers liberation in the self-acceptance of himself as a deaf person.

More recently, Henry Kisor, a deaf book reviewer based in Chicago, sparked a great deal of controversy with his autobiography **What's That Pig Outdoors?** when he espoused the virtues of oralism over signing. He writes, "Riding the tiger of deafness today seems just a vainglorious notion, the striking of a noble but doomed pose, like those pigeon-splattered statues of Confederate cavalrymen in the courthouse squares of so many Southern towns." This is appallingly negative, especially because Kisor claims the reason he wrote the autobiography was that there wasn't enough literature about the deaf by the deaf. If he doesn't wish to ride "the tiger of deafness," he surely shouldn't have felt the need to write the book at all. His pride over his speech success is blatantly self-aggrandizing throughout the book: "[My parents and I] were all happy with Mrs. Swart, who thought my progress satisfactory in every way. She thought my potential such that she asked Mother and Dad whether they wanted me to speak with a New Jersey accent or cosmopolitan one."

It is most unfortunate that most deaf-theater companies don't take the initiative to support deaf playwrights by mounting their plays and allowing them to find their voices; as it is, they are more concerned with providing ASL translations of successful hearing plays rather than gamble on untried plays by talented deaf writers. If deaf theater wants to connect more strongly with their own communities, they need to start supporting their own playwrights and their work. Even the National Theatre of the Deaf (NTD) has produced only two (or three???) plays written by deaf playwrights in their 30-year history, which is shocking in that they are supposed to represent a very unique constituency.

Some deaf independent filmmakers believe that with the advent of digital video and affordable editing software that enable them to make movies very cheaply, they will finally be seen and heard in ways that Hollywood has previously refused to see and listen. These filmmakers, by scripting their own stories and telling them on their own terms, stand a much bigger chance of being seen and heard beyond the limited market of ASL-poetry videotapes, and influencing perceptions about deaf people by hearing viewers who see their work on the big—and small—screen. Because these deaf filmmakers have so few films made by other deaf filmmakers, they will no doubt have to use classic hearing films as a springboard to find their own "voices" as storytellers who see ASL as a language rather than as a symbol of communication perpetuated by many hearing screenwriters and filmmakers, thus contributing a new appendix to deaf literature in the process.

ASL-literary creators don't see themselves as imitators of a "Hearing" tradition, but as practitioners of a new, authentic mode of expression that's adventurous, lively, colorful, and politically potent. The most popular Deaf literary genre is ASL poetry (in which the distinction between "writer" and "performer" is happily blurred, and the barriers between performer and audience are broken down). Three of the most eminent ASL poets are Peter Cook, Ella Mae Lentz, and Clayton Valli. As time goes on, we're becoming more sophisticated, demanding better-quality expressions of Deaf artistry. It's an exciting medium. There is a unique chemistry between a good ASL performer and the audience.

Were Shakespeare around today, he might well admire it.

Chapter 63

I'm a hearing person who really enjoys movies—a cinema buff. I have two deaf friends who come with me to theatrical film showings. I've noticed that they're often bored, but sometimes excited. Can you help me determine which films have guaranteed appeal for deaf viewers?

f course, everyone's an individual, with distinct tastes. But since deaf people have been so long restricted by the lack of accessible movies, we can cite some very general guidelines.

As you undoubtedly know, motion pictures with real sound tracks—"talkies"—debuted in 1927, shortly before the Great Depression started. No popular medium ever became passé as swiftly and relentlessly as did silent movies.

During the reign of the "silents," deaf and hearing moviegoers enjoyed equality, although movie theaters had live accompaniment—a Wurlitzer organ or piano, or even a full orchestra—to provide the auditory color that was considered absolutely essential. When it came to following the plot and dialogue, though, deaf people were at no disadvantage. You may possibly be aware that Deaf people worked in the thriving silent-film industry as technical crew and performers—e.g., Granville Redmond, Albert Ballin, and Emerson Romero, to name three notables.

After the "talkies" took over, Deaf professionals left Hollywood, and Deaf moviegoers were left stranded. Deaf clubs

continued to borrow "silents" for their weekly film-screen-
ings until they were removed from circulation. Independent
Deaf filmmakers like Charles Krauel and Ernest Marshall
produced newsreels and shoestring-budgeted ASL features
of remarkable charm and style, which were enthusiastically
received. But Deaf people wanted to see mainstream feature
films, too—the blockbusters and B-movies that were making
Hollywood a billion-dollar industry, and which were part of
everyone else's experiences. Around 1947, Romero, a film
buff, tinker, and inventor, bought film reels and painstak-
ingly spliced in captions, but he was a solitary aberration.
Captioned films didn't become a practical reality until 1958,
when Congress established the Captioned Films for the Deaf
program in the Department of Education's Office of Special
Education.

Luckily, France, Germany, Italy, Sweden, and Japan, to
name five, developed their own film industries and exported
some of their best work. Foreign films shown here were often
subtitled in English, and thus accessible to deaf audiences.
(The essential difference between subtitles and captions is
that while *subtitles* simply translate dialogue into another
language, *captions* also describe all pertinent sound effects,
and specify who is talking.) Those who didn't live near a
cinema showing foreign films had to make do with those
shown on TV. (And some of the foreign films were dubbed—
a practice loathed by both deaf *and* hearing viewers.)

Then there are English-language movies with snippets of
foreign-language dialogue that is shown with subtitles (e.g.,
Elizabeth). In **Dances With Wolves**, only the American Indian dialogue was subtitled. When captions were added to
the prints distributed by TRIPOD, no distinction was made
between languages; everything was open-captioned in white
letters. Deaf viewers who saw these prints couldn't easily
distinguish Indian dialogue from English. One Deaf viewer
told us that he would have liked yellow captions for Indian
dialogue, and white for Anglo. But the closed-captioned

version shown on TV did make this distinction, so it was easier for Deaf viewers to understand.

Deaf people have, of course, continued to see English-language feature films (U.S.A., Canada, England, Australia, etc.), but have had very mixed experiences. Essentially, we've had to choose from these alternatives:

1. Action movies. We still miss the dialogue, but enjoy the big-screen action. Relatively talky movies (in which dialogue figures prominently) have an excessively high "incomprehension quotient" and should be avoided.

2. Read the book first (*Dune, Henry V, The Age of Innocence, Last of the Mohicans, Pride and Prejudice, Interview with the Vampire, Lord of the Rings* [a trilogy], *Harry Potter and the Sorcerer's Stone* [first of a series]). Since so many contemporary best-selling novels (Crichton, King, Rice, Steel, etc.) are automatically made into movies, and literary classics are constantly being filmed and remade, this sometimes works out OK.

3. Subtitled foreign films. Traditionally, Deaf people's top choice, as noted above.

4. Wait until the captioned home-video or digital-videodisc (DVD) version is released. This applies to "talky" films—where's there's a lot of dialogue (as opposed to visuals and action). This can take a good 6 months. And it's still iffy. (See comment below.) Some people don't want to wait. *And* there's a mammoth difference between seeing a feature film in all its first-run hoopla and glory on the big screen (e.g., *Titanic*), and buying, renting, or borrowing a videotape to be watched on your 30" TV. Much of the epic effect is lost.

5. If you live in a city such as Philadelphia or Los Angeles, you can see open-captioned screenings of megahits, by arrangement with TRIPOD. Because of the costs involved, only a tiny percentage of recent first-run feature films have been made accessible to deaf audiences this way.*

6. Silent films are constantly being rediscovered and resur-

rected. If you're very lucky, you may be able to catch a full-fledged international silent-film festival, or at least cinematic screenings of perennially popular Chaplin and Keaton classics. (If there's a revival cinema or museum nearby, you can ask—and make suggestions.) And if you're very, *very* lucky, you'll be able to see decent prints, shown the way they were intended to be.

At this point, those are the most feasible alternatives. Only a few theaters have participated in testing new devices such as closed-captioning goggles. (Captions are encoded on the bottom of the screen, but only viewers wearing decoder goggles can read them.)

Media Services and Captioned Films for the Deaf is another possibility. Again, the selection of captioned "mainstream" films is relatively limited. Still, this is a good source for documentaries and instructional videos.

As noted above, sometimes it's possible to "cram" for a screening—although this diminishes the element of surprise (especially if it's an all-new movie). Again, this depends on your friends' tastes. Many (if not all) major feature films have promotional tie-ins—e.g., hastily-written paperback novelizations (if the screenplay wasn't adapted from an existing work) or children's picture books profusely illustrated with photos or animation stills from the movie and useful plot summaries. If your friends don't mind spending extra money, they can buy some of the tie-ins, and decrease the amount of "lost" dialogue and plot—somewhat.

Jane Austen, Charlotte Brontë, Emily Brontë, Charles Dickens, George Eliot, E.M. Forster, Thomas Hardy, Nathaniel Hawthorne, Ernest Hemingway, Henry James, John Steinbeck, Edith Wharton, Victor Hugo, Alexandre Dumas, Gustave Flaubert, Leo Tolstoy, Shakespeare, George Bernard Shaw, Anton Chekhov, and occasional nonfiction classics have been regularly adapted into feature films, with varying degrees of fidelity to the originals. Your friends can borrow the novels, plays, or biographies from the library. Translations of foreign classics abound, and simplified versions of some English-language classics can be found in the Adult Basic Literacy section. There may also be useful information on the Internet.

They can also "prep" by reading reviews, advance-promotion writeups in cinema-buffs' magazines, **Entertainment**, **Variety**, etc. Also "pump" friends who have already seen the movie.

For most of us, the *only* alternative to cinematic screenings—if all else fails—is to wait until the movie is released on videocassette or DVD with closed captions. Don't bank on it, though. Many movie studios still have atrocious track records; some have reneged on their initial captioning commitment; still others, especially smaller and independent studios, refuse to caption their product because it's "too costly." That's why it's so difficult to find captioned PBS goodies.

In case you're wondering if movie theaters and the home-video industry are covered by the ADA, the answer is no. Thanks to the efforts of the powerful Motion Picture Association of America, they are not required to make their cinemas or video product accessible to deaf viewers. It's strictly voluntary.

If cinema managers/owners recognize a market and believe that there's a chance to recoup expenses and turn a reasonable profit by offering open-captioned screenings or other accessible attractions, they'll be more motivated to take the risk. Deaf moviegoers have worked with cinemas in several cities to make open-captioned screenings (whether on a one-shot, occasional, or regular basis) a reality. The surface has barely been scratched, though!

---

* In Rochester, New York, the Regal Henrietta, in the Regal Cinema multiplex chain, always has a current first-run open-captioned film, shown daily at regular times. Movies are changed regularly, so caption-viewers can catch a new one every week if they want. The choice is limited, but the viewing is good.

Chapter 64

At my daughter's wedding, I saw my nephew dance for the first time, and I was surprised to see him dancing so beautifully. How could he do that if he's deaf? My sister tried to explain how that could work. I still don't understand. Can all deaf people dance like him?

e personally enjoy seeing people doing what others imagine unthinkable—wrecking stereotypical notions of what's normal "handicapped" behavior. But the fact is that deaf people are very much individuals, and exactly like hearing people in that respect. And while some hearing people are terrific dancers and some are incredible klutzes, the same applies to deaf people. Some are just so beautifully coordinated, so creative with movement, so physically *free*, they've made professional or quasi-professional careers out of dance, while others equally deaf are stiff and awkward—hippopotami on skateboards. Since deafness can affect the sense of balance whose center is in the inner ear, many deaf people must struggle especially hard to achieve coordination and grace—and sometimes this makes them better, more motivated dancers!

We can learn to dance very well without being able to hear the music. What's required is a sharp eye, alertness, sensitivity to rhythm, and coordination—the same skills any good dancer develops. Dance classes set up for deaf students use visual cues, amplified music (with a vigorous bass section), and a lot of percussion—like tambour drums—that sends strong vibrations through the air and can be felt in one's bones (particularly the breastbone). On stage, without the help of the drum, they can keep mental count.

That deaf dancers "feel the vibrations through the floor" is something of a misconception. Since their feet are not in contact with the floor at all times, it's more accurate to say deaf dancers feel vibrations of the music through their bodies. They learn to keep a sharp eye-corner on what's happening, as well as developing and refining their intuitive, "internalized" sense of rhythm. Your nephew was keenly alert to what was going on and used his own everyday skills to keep perfect pace with the others.

He has some distinguished company. As an example of what a deaf dancer can achieve, consider the remarkable career of Frances Woods (real name: Esther Thomas). She was born totally deaf in 1907, yet became a professional dancer in 1926. She and her hearing husband, Billy Bray (real name: Anthony Caliguire), formed a team, dancing in hotels and taverns during the Depression, then in vaudeville (live routines) at the R.K.O. chain of theaters. Their routines included acrobatics, mime, and a variety of elements from popular dances of the day (such as the "Apache"). Both of them developed tremendous strength and endurance. One of Woods' celebrated routines concluded with her pretending to shoot Bray with a tiny pistol, then lifting him off the floor and carrying him offstage, slung over her shoulder. Woods designed and made all her own costumes. Robert L. Ripley (of "Believe It Or Not!" fame) called them the Wonder Dancers.*

Woods and Bray performed throughout the 1930s, 1940s, and 1950s, in many famous nightclubs and hotels, accompanied by some of the great bands, in the States and Europe. They even performed in London's famed Palladium. Long after retirement, they were still dancing together.

What about dance troupes? Gallaudet University has the well-known Gallaudet Dancers, who have performed publicly on and off campus. Yacov Sharir (hearing) founded the American Deaf Dance Company in 1976. Featuring a "mixed troupe" of deaf and hearing dancers, the ADDC enjoyed a promising but brief career. Musign, a Deaf comedy-dance-sign-music troupe, began touring in 1982. The American Dance Theatre of the Deaf was founded in 1986 by Adrienne Ehrlich (also hearing). Unlike the ADDC, this was an all-deaf troupe. ADTD's choreographer, Michael Thomas, was a progressively-deafened professional dancer who had once been the *premier danseur* (leading male dancer) of the San Francisco Ballet Company and suffered from attacks of vertigo and a progressive loss of balance. Thomas taught dance to deaf and hearing students and directed the RIT Dance Company from 1988 until his untimely death from AIDS in 1997. All of these Deaf-dance companies have disbanded, but the Gallaudet Dancers are still going strong, and dance continues at NTID/RIT.

Elsewhere, opportunities for deaf students are limited. The Joffrey Ballet once offered a class for Deaf students (in Manhattan, naturally). This was immortalized in **Silent Dancer** (1981), written by Bruce Hlibok and photographed by Liz Glasgow. The dancer was Bruce's sister Nancy.

A good number of deaf people love going to bars with well-amplified disco music. They love to dance to the loud, *very* loud bass section and the booming percussion. Many Deaf festivals and gatherings feature a disco-dance party, and these are typically well-attended. Even those who can't dance well have a great time.

Anyone who says that deaf people can't dance is a dolt. And anyone who says that *all* deaf people *are* good dancers is a bigger dolt.

* See Robert F. Panara's entries on Woods and "Dance" (Performing Arts) in the **Gallaudet Encyclopedia of Deaf People and Deafness**, and the chapter on Woods in **Great Deaf Americans: The Second Edition** (Deaf Life Press, 1996).

Chapter 65

Can Deaf people appreciate music at all?

here are many possible responses to this question, since deaf people show a tremendous variety of reactions. Poll a hundred deaf people about their feelings towards music, and you will likely get a hundred different responses. Some care nothing about music in any form. Others enjoy the booming rhythms of percussion. Some are good at carrying rhythms; others aren't. Some can dance to amplified percussion; others have no aptitude whatever. Some, who use and benefit from hearing aids, enjoy listening to radios. Some have CD players. Some have high-quality stereo systems (with lots of amplification) in their homes; others have no acquaintance with records, music CDs, tape cassettes, or radios in any form.

Deaf get-togethers often feature a "Deaf Disco," with a D.J. and CDs. The music is loud—very. Some attendees will be able to perceive the lyrics or the melodies; others will feel the booming bass and percussive track vibrating through their chests. This can be fun. As noted in the previous chapter, those who are good dancers (or not so good) enjoy themselves immensely at these affairs.

Deaf people, even those who don't use hearing aids or the audio capability of their TVs, often enjoy watching MTV for the visual rhythms and body language of the performers. Many music videos are now closed-captioned, so Deaf viewers can join in the fun. Even if they can't hear the music, the vocals, or the harmonies, they get something out of it.

Some Deaf people prefer to develop their own "sign-songs," rather like ASL poems but with added emphasis on rhythm. Others translate popular "Hearing" songs into sign; some Deaf and hearing children and adults participate in organized signsong choirs that give public performances. Some Deaf people object to the practice of translating "Hearing" songs into signs—especially by hearing performers. They see this as a forced hybrid of two very different cultures.*

The traditional view is, of course, that music is not part of Deaf culture. Deaf people have developed a rich visual-kinetic mode of communication and artistic expression. It owes nothing to the world's great musical traditions. However, there's no denying that we are influenced by popular American/Western/Hearing culture. Music is a pervasive influence in American life—and a controversial one.

Those who are hard-of-hearing (and remain so) are able to retain enjoyment of music. Even those who have difficulty with conversations can enjoy music, especially instrumental, to a varying extent. Late-deafened persons have the worst time of it, as they can no longer enjoy something that may have been an integral part of their lives, providing entertainment, comfort, intellectual pleasure, inspiration, relaxation, and artistic expression. Beethoven, as we know, continued to compose symphonies long after he became profoundly deaf, even though he could no longer hear the notes. From his letters, we can comprehend something of the anguish he experienced, being cut off from what was, after all, his life and sustenance. Ironically, he enriched the Hearing culture he no longer had access to. The remarkable career of Scottish-born percussionist Evelyn Glennie shows that one can indeed be deaf and a successful musician.

Schools for the deaf used to drill students in rhythm and music. In the heyday of military-style schools for deaf boys (Fanwood was the first), there were full brass marching bands. Some of the students were undoubtedly quite proficient, and, we imagine, had happy memories of their experience. They sounded good, too.

Some schools still have music programs. The credo is to participate voluntarily and get out of it as much as you can. But we imagine that such programs would be the first casualty in a budget-cutting campaign—and it's a rare school for the deaf that isn't feeling a severe budgetary pinch.

NTID, in particular, has a well-known music program, offering students an opportunity to play a variety of instruments (from violin to vibraphone) and to get individualized instruction. Amplification is liberally employed. There are public recitals at the end of each quarter, although the audience is sparse—the few friends and scattered relatives who show up are vastly outnumbered by the roster of students performing brief pieces with various degrees of skill. The students who participate are mostly those from oral backgrounds, continuing old interests. Those from a strong ASL background remain largely indifferent.

It all comes down to a question of aptitude, upbringing, and taste. Talented deaf musicians *can* succeed. But most Deaf people don't enjoy music, as they don't understand it; music appreciation is a foreign concept. If they're not exposed to it when they're young, if the language of music isn't presented to them in an accessible way, they're not going to seek it out when they're older. Such persons might well ask, "How in the world can I appreciate something I can't hear?" Yet others who are equally deaf could just as well say, "Well, as far as I'm concerned, I can't *imagine* living a life without music!"

* See next chapter.

Chapter 66

Do signsongs make sense?

1. It seems that many hearing children (and adults) are learning signs from their (hearing) teachers in order to sign and sing songs for (hearing) audiences. I am bothered by this. Do Deaf children and Deaf adults enjoy seeing hearing [people] sign and singing songs?

2. If Deaf children learn to voice songs for Deaf audiences, would this make sense?

3. Anyway, signing songs word-for-word is just a string of vocabulary words, not a translation. Where's the meaning?

—Holly P. Roth, Columbia, Maryland

ignsongs are an artistic hybrid, borrowing the concept of choral singing from Hearing culture and the signs (more or less) from Deaf culture. The idea is to present a visual harmony and counterpoint that complements the purely auditory dimension of a voice choir. It's a new twist on a traditional musical genre. Signsongs can also be performed by trios, duets, or soloists.

We're not sure who developed signsong, or when, but it has become a staple of Deaf-culture festivals. It plays a part in church services (signed hymns and psalms), public gatherings, and concerts. Deaf/hard-of-hearing sign choirs that perform publicly come and go. There's an annual Sign Choir Festival in Texas (sponsored by the Sign Music Foundation, based in Denton) that emphasizes imaginative approaches. Deaf artists participate, and not just those who perform signsongs either. It's a popular event.

So . . . are signsongs okay? Those who perform and enjoy watching them don't see any problem.

So why do some Deaf people have negative feelings about

signsongs? Several reasons. They're not a traditional part of ASL culture, not the way ASL sign-mime performances are. Sign mime, albeit a relatively new genre, utilizes elements of ASL poetry, storytelling, and drama, along with classical mime, borrowed from the Hearing tradition. In the hands of a skilled performer, sign-mime can be a tremendously exciting experience. The audience is invited to participate in the performance, using their eyes, emotions, and imaginations. It is very hard to draw lines of demarcation between sign-mime, ASL poetry, storytelling, and drama, because each may contain elements of the other genres. ASL is a powerful artistic medium—even for audiences who may not understand ASL. Such forms of performance art are seen as organic outgrowths of ASL.

Signsongs, then, are more of a Hearing form of expression than a Deaf one. So is it okay for hearing choirs to perform signsongs to hearing audiences? As Ms. Roth's questions suggest, some Deaf people (by no means extremists or linguistic fanatics) are bothered by this. Because signed songs utilize elements of sign language transposed to a musical genre, there's a political dimension. Deaf people who dislike the idea of signing songs simply avoid attending such events. Some have gone further. In the late '70s, Audree Norton, Gregg Brooks, and Julianna Fjeld publicly protested the use of a group of hearing students signing a song at an Academy Awards event. For one thing, they felt that it would have been more appropriate to let Deaf students sign the song. Give *them* the opportunity to show the beauty of sign language— *their* language. For another, they were concerned about the inauthenticity, distortion, and misrepresentation involved.

But . . . are signsongs really sign language? "Where's the meaning?" asks Ms. Roth. Meaning isn't the most important consideration here. Signsongs look pretty, which is, we suppose, why uninformed hearing audiences like them and why they have endured. Certainly, it can look nice if it's done well. But is it a legitimate means of artistic expression? Is there a taint of cultural piracy about it?

Most signsongs are performed in straight signed English—sung lyrics with signs pasted onto them, word for word. It's a dry approach, and tends to leave Deaf audiences bewildered. They don't understand this approach at all. Hearing audiences (especially those unfamiliar with real ASL) applaud, cheer, and think it's absolutely beautiful.

We suspect that some hearing teachers have their hearing students rehearse and perform signsongs to give them something to do with their hands while they're singing . . . i.e., to prevent fidgeting. Instead of having the choir stand immobile with only their mouths moving, they sign in synchrony with what they're singing.

Ms. Roth uses the analogy of Deaf students voicing songs to a Deaf audience. Another analogy is a choir that contains no Black or Hispanic members, singing African-American or phonetic Spanish songs, to a white audience. Does the prospect of seeing an all-white choir singing Black spirituals, faking Black pronunciation and musical mannerisms, make you uncomfortable? Travesty or tribute? Is there something artistically (and ethically) bogus about "borrowing" another culture's songs and appropriating them? Many of us would say no. Music is a universal language, and songs treasured by a culture become part of our global heritage. Unless it's copyrighted, it's free for the taking. But should this apply to signs taken from ASL, by the hearing, for the hearing?

Lest you think that we're "against" blending signs and song as a matter of principle, we hasten to add that we're not. There is a well-known signsinger named Sherry Hicks who performs ASL songs beautifully. She's a hearing woman—a CODA. And she performs for Deaf audiences, who are delighted, even enraptured, by the beauty of her songs. Since she has a strong native-ASL background, she understands what she's doing, and what Deaf people want. Her songs aren't cross-cultural pastiches; they bear the stamp of her artistry. That's an example we wish could be more widely emulated.

Chapter 67

"Do deaf people show a slight difference in their facial anatomy?"

I have often noticed a slight (but in no way unattractive) anatomical difference on many deaf, Deaf, and hard-of-hearing people. The upper lip is thinner or slightly turned up, and there are sometimes slight variations of the nostrils.

In my narrow "heary" range of experience, it seems to be more common among the hard-of-hearing than the Deaf. Is this caused by the medical problems that cause hearing loss or is it caused by the way the face is strained while trying to vocalize or hear other people? My daughter, who experienced severe trauma in one ear as a 5-year-old, has developed this trait. Again, I do not find this to be unattractive. In my totally unbiased opinion, I have a very beautiful daughter.

—a reader in Albuquerque, New Mexico

his is a fascinating question (actually, there are several psycho-socio-anthropological questions here), because it touches on a most subtle aspect of hearing loss: the possible differences between the way deaf and hearing people *look*.

Deafness has been called "the invisible handicap," and not without reason. It has long been argued that deaf people are not immediately recognizable as "deaf"—*unless* they wear hearing aids or other visible devices, clothing proclaiming their status as students of deaf institutions, "ILY" or "Deaf Culture" pins, or other identifiers. And, of course, unless they're seen signing in public.

This reader asks about the upper lip and the nostrils. From our experience (and we've met and interacted with hundreds upon hundreds of other Deaf, deaf, and hard-of-hearing people), we've found no evidence that they have thinner or more upturned upper lips than hearing people do. Or that their nostrils are unequal. A deaf or deafened person can certainly have a medical condition that affects the facial muscles, but we don't know any instances of deafness *itself* causing this kind of facial change. We'd call it deafness *in combination with* some other condition. "Medical problems that cause hearing loss" usually leave no telltale signs on the face. Otherwise, why do so many deaf children get misdiagnosed? It's just not visible.

We do note, however, that deaf people (on the whole) use their facial muscles differently from hearing people. In ASL, the entire face is used as a grammatical marker. The eyebrows, for example, are used to indicate questions, and the way the eyebrows are raised or knit and the head tilted specifies what kind of question it is. All this is subtle and momentary. Native ASL users employ a fleeting nostril-cheek-twitch to indicate "Yes, I agree with you" or "That's right!" Like the eyebrows, the nose is used as a unit of communication, so the nostrils may be momentarily dilated and "up-twitched," singly, during the conversational give-and-take. In contrast, when hearing people talk to each other, the nostrils are *supposed* to be relaxed. Twitchy nostrils are a seen as a symptom of stress or facial tic.

Facial expressions depend on the mode of communication as well as the mood of the communicator. Hard-of-hearing people, who have a hearing loss but struggle to function normally within hearing parameters, might well strain to attend, listen, and enunciate clearly; the tension would certainly be perceptible in their faces. ASL users have particularly intense-looking facial expressions because, as we've just noted, the face is employed grammatically. Uneducated hearing onlookers who happen to observe a real ASL conversation will sometimes say that the conversationalists "look angry at each other," even when it's a perfectly friendly chat.

Our facial muscles are extraordinarily flexible. We've all seen (or read about) actors who so literally identify with their characters that they assume the habitual expressions of those characters—even "between takes." We also recall reading an article in a popular magazine some years ago, focusing on the sometimes-astonishing resemblance between wives and husbands. After associating intimately with each other for years, their facial expressions tend to reflect each other's; certain expressive "configurations" become habitual.

The same goes for deaf and hard-of-hearing people: the demands of communication impose their visible signs on the expressions of the face. But if a deaf or hard-of-hearing person's face is in repose (i.e., idly waiting for a bus, reading, watching TV, or gazing into a computer screen), we don't think there are *any* distinguishing characteristics between a deaf face and a hearing one.

Chapter 68

Don't Deaf people have to wear dark colors?

rofessional interpreters, most of whom are hearing, do have a dress code for their job. To ensure that their signing remains as visible as possible, they usually wear solid colors. These don't have to be dark, just as long as they provide an appropriate background to their signing. Interpreters try to avoid wearing anything that could render their signing less distinct, or, heaven forbid, cause visual annoyance to the Deaf "signee."

Some college interpreters actually don a baggy black smock while on duty. We consider this practice distasteful, as it promotes an unattractive image of interpreters. We prefer to see interpreters wearing nice professional-looking outfits, or even casual shirts, sweaters, jerseys, jumpers, or dresses. They *don't* have to be black; they can be dark blue, navy, deep purple, dusty violet or teal, hunter green, cranberry, wine, gray—any relatively quiet, unobtrusive color that makes a good underpinning to the play of the hands and face.

Certain pastels and neutrals may work very well. Red and white are (usually) out. Flesh colors—peach, blush, some shades of tan and brown—are definitely out. So are hot (neon) colors, bold stripes, and loud, splashy patterns, which can give the Deaf signee a headache. Ornamentation such as rhinestones, glitter, shiny appliqués, or sequins, which competes with the wearer's signing for the viewer's attention, would be another unlucky choice. Novelty fabrics such as lamé, metallics, and anything with a shimmery, sparkly, or holographic effect should be saved for parties. Some male interpreters wear ties; many don't, to avoid too much "busyness" in the signing space of the upper torso. Many female (and some male) interpreters wear gold jewelry, including rings; jewelry isn't necessarily a distraction. Bracelets may be okay, if they're simple and plain. Wristwatches are okay. Clunky necklaces, especially obtrusively glittery ones, aren't.

Theatrical and artistic interpreters, whose signing has to be visible across the distance of a theater hall or auditorium, often wear dark solids. Black is perennially popular, especially for "shadow" interpreters, who are onstage right there with the costumed performers—clearly visible to Deaf viewers, but unobtrusive. Deaf performers (i.e., ASL poets) often choose similar dark solids. But there are no real hard-and-fast rules here, just the requisite of visibility. Colorful attire is by no means off-limits for theatrical signers. We've seen very colorfully costumed National Theatre of the Deaf productions.

NTD is exceedingly careful about the design of its costumes. All costumes for Deaf theater must take into account the readability of the signing (hands and face), and the lighting. Costumes have to provide a good background for the signing—not detract from or interfere with it. Proper lighting eliminates dark shadows across the upper torso, which would also impede the clarity of the signing. Clarity and visibility are the guiding principles of all Deaf-oriented theater and TV productions.

A sidenote: for TV productions, different rules apply for different audiences. In a normal "Hearing" TV production, you can have a tightly-cropped close-up of the face. But with a signed/ASL production, you can't. The shot has to encompass not only the face but the signing space as well—which includes the whole upper half of the body.* This limits the artistic flexibility of the camera. Close-up shots, so dear to filmmakers and TV, must be scrupulously avoided.

For Deaf people in everyday, off-the-job life, there are no rules and no restrictions. They wear what they like. (The same, of course, goes for interpreters.) If brightly-striped rugby jerseys and Hawaiian-print shirts are popular with young hearing people, they're popular with young Deaf people too. On a normal conversational basis, neons, glitter, polka dots, jungle, camouflage, and Pucci prints, picture T-shirts, even garish tie-dyes, don't present a real problem. Deaf people are just as fond of wearing sweatshirts inscribed with school names, political slogans, or cartoons as their hearing counterparts. And colorful sweaters in all imaginable patterns and colors. Some especially strident shirt-patterns or colors do make it difficult to see someone's signing across a distance. But ski masks, sunglasses, and hats that obscure the eyes, and thick, unruly beards and sweeping mustaches, may very well interfere with close-range communication. Sunglasses, hats, and masks, at least, are easily slipped off!

By the way, skilled signers can carry on conversations while wearing mittens . . . but that's another story.

* See Chapter 12 for an explanation of the signing space.

Over a decade of promoting Deaf Awareness

Chapter 69

Is it true that most Deaf adults from a residential-school background cannot sleep with lights on?

ne "quirk" about growing up Deaf (that is, attending a residential school and living in a dorm) is that we develop sensitivity to light. Deaf people associate light with the need to be awake and alert. We're not disturbed by auditory stimuli as much as tactile or, more so, visual ones—changes in light. Repetitively blinking lights are our sirens; stray washes of light are like random noises. We can only sleep in darkness—when there is a complete absence of visual stimuli.

Deaf people aren't born with a predilection for darkness. Children, deaf as well as hearing, are often frightened of the dark. For young children (and a number of adults), darkness often holds terror. That's why we have nightlights. We are reassured by their gentle glow. A good number of deaf children arrive at residential schools from homes where nightlights are used. But, once arrived, they're forced to spend their first night—and all their subsequent nights—in complete darkness. For some new arrivals, this is a traumatic experience. They spend a terrifying, sleepless night; they get up; they scream. Deaf children don't *choose* to sleep in complete darkness; they're *forced* to. And they gradually become accustomed to it. Thus habituated, they develop a preference for complete darkness—no nightlights, thank you. Light, when it comes during the time to sleep, is an intrusion, not a reassurance.

After they leave school or college and are on their own, the habit persists. It can cause bickering between couples, especially where one mate is not from a residential-school background—e.g., wife wants to stay up late in bed, reading, but husband argues, "I can't sleep with a light on!" Partners who want to stay together need to find a solution. Separate bedrooms might be one (space permitting)—or the mate who insists on staying up later needs to move to a different room until s/he goes to bed. Blindfolds are *not* a viable option—no deaf person we know of wants to bother wearing one.

Many deaf adults are so used to sleeping in complete (or near-complete) darkness, that if *any* light strays into their territory, they wake up. Or can't fall asleep. Some stuff rolled-up towels beneath their bedroom doors to block the strip of light that strays underneath the door when an outside light is switched on. A streetlight, a driveway lantern, the lightbulb-glare from a neighbor's window, a bathroom or closet light snapped on in another wing, a blinking all-night-café sign, the headlights of a passing car, lightning—are all bothersome. Heavy drapes, opaque curtains, blinds, or chinkless shades are a must. Even so, it is very hard to prevent "leaks."

Not *all* light is equally disturbing, though. White headlights are more annoying than red taillights. Red and blue lights are more easily "ignored" by deaf sleepers. Some deaf people install red or blue bulbs in hallway fixtures near bedrooms, so that when they retire for the night and someone else switches on the hall light, the colored light won't be as bothersome as regular white light, should it stray beneath the door.

A digression: The common conception of "nightclub" is a murky, even dim, place. There are jokes about Deaf nightspots (which do exist at NTID and Gallaudet, for example), where the lights are bright—so Deaf people can easily see each other's signs and faces—but the canned music is *very* loud—so hearing people can't possibly hear each other and are compelled to rely on, and thus improve, their signing skills!

The "darkness quirk"—universal?

After we originally published this chapter as an "HPO" column in the February 1995 issue of DEAF LIFE, we received this letter from a counselor at the Northeastern Gallaudet University Regional Center.

In response to your column, "For Hearing People Only," in the February issue of **DEAF LIFE**, Deaf adults from a residential school background are not the only ones who cannot sleep with lights on.

I am a Deaf adult from a "mainstreamed" background (the use of quote marks around the word *mainstream* means there were no support services of any kind given to me when I attended local public schools as a child), and I find that I cannot sleep with the lights on either. There are several other Deaf people I know with backgrounds similar to mine who have this same "quirk."

Perhaps you should conduct a survey to see whether or not this is a "quirk" that is universal amongst those of us born deaf or deafened at an early age.

Your magazine is wonderful. I keep current issues in my office all the time and find myself frequently asked where one can subscribe to your publication. Of course I keep copies of subscription forms on hand just in case!

Sidney G. Pietzsch
Counselor, Special Services for Deaf and HH People
Northern Essex Community College
Haverhill, Massachusetts

Chapter 70

Are deaf people visually sharper than hearing people?

he #1 favorite misconception about disabled people seems to be that when you've lost use of one sense, the other senses magically become sharper. There's no real magic here, just practicality. A blind person develops acute skill in using the remaining senses—touch, smell, hearing, a sensitivity to changes in the air—to live a full life. They don't really develop some kind of preternatural sonar. They use the capabilities everyone has. Likewise, deaf people learn to rely on visual cues. This doesn't make them visually smarter or eagle-eyed. They simply become more alert about taking in and processing visual messages. Paying close attention and noticing easily overlooked details is a survival skill. And not all deaf people are good at it, either.

If all deaf people were visually gifted, they'd all be artists and terrific drivers. Of course, this isn't so. While it's true that a number of deaf students choose design-oriented careers, many have no aptitude whatsoever. Although statistically, deaf people tend to be better drivers than hearing ones, some deaf drivers can be just as sloppy and careless as any hearing counterpart. We know color-blind and artistically untalented deaf people; we know bad drivers and careless ones.

Nor do you have to be deaf to acquire skill in ASL, which is a visually based language (as English is an aurally based one). Hearing children of Deaf parents who grow up using ASL every day naturally develop a high degree of skill, while deaf people who learn to sign later in life often lack that facility. It's not a question of innate genius but exposure and practice.

Deaf people use their eyes as hearing people use their ears. While hearing people tend to rely more on their hearing than vision, deaf people rely exclusively on their eyes. Alert Deaf signers tend to take better notice of the persons they're communicating with—the nuances of expression, the momentary glances, the subtle changes in posture that indicate a change in mood or a dwindling of attention.

The only thing that can accurately be said of *all* deaf people as a whole is that since they can't hear, they rely on sight, lights, vibration, and other tactile means to function normally.

▲ ▲ ▲

Living with Usher's Syndrome

Usher's Syndrome (also known as "Usher Syndrome") is a fairly common form of genetically linked deafness and progressive blindness. Persons with US are born deaf and typically start experiencing vision loss in their teens or as young adults. An abnormal buildup of pigmentation in the retina (*retinitis pigmentosa*, RP for short) causes gradual, irreversible deterioration of eyesight, starting with a darkening of peripheral vision ("tunnel vision") and night blindness. The progress of US is slow but inexorable. As yet, there is no cure or effective treatment.

Just about everyone in the Deaf community knows someone, or several persons, with US. The ones we personally know are talented, strong, high-spirited people who insist on living life to the fullest. They aren't saintly or superhuman—just normal, gifted, intelligent folks who happen to be deaf-blind (or Deafblind, as some prefer to write it).

Even though a diagnosis can often be made during childhood, during the primary-school years, doctors, counselors, and teachers have traditionally withheld the information from the child in the mistaken belief that it's better for them not to know. People with US emphatically disagree with that approach. The earlier deaf children know they have US, the sooner they can integrate that knowledge into their lives: learn to adjust, acquire coping skills and communication techniques, and choose a suitable career goal (i.e., one that doesn't have to be jettisoned later on because of encroaching blindness).

Since vision loss doesn't manifest itself until adolescence or early adulthood (sometimes even later), a person with US typically acquires a solid ASL/Deaf Culture background. Sign language is their first and preferred mode of communication. Some people with US are primarily oralists and have received cochlear implants.

Once their vision begins to deteriorate, people with US become sensitive to bright, glaring lights, and may wear protective glasses and use magnifying screens. Yellow text on a black background (as on US-accessible Internet sites) increases reading comfort.

▲ All incoming NTID students receive mandatory vision testing. It's not uncommon for previously undetected and undiagnosed conditions, including US, to turn up.

▲ In 2000, A.J. Granda, who has US, became the first Deafblind actress to portray the young Helen Keller, in Cleveland SignStage's production of William Gibson's perennially popular *The Miracle Worker*. Although Granda was an adult, she brought her own passion and truth to the role, which had almost always been played by sighted, hearing actresses.

▲ Other notable persons with US include actress/TV-show hostess Kim Powers (of San Antonio's Kaleidoscope TV), restaurateur Danny Delcambre (of Seattle's Ragin' Cajun), and scientist/lecturer Jelica Breuer Nuccio (also of Seattle). In their own ways, they have done much to educate the Deaf and Hearing communities about US.

Chapter 71

What difficulties do deaf people have when driving an automobile? Why is their insurance higher than a hearing person's? And do deaf people take the same test as hearing people?

eaf people have been driving automobiles since the first ones rolled out at the turn of the 20th century. According to **Deaf Heritage**, during the 1920s (a time of steadily increasing automobile accidents and fatalities), at least four states refused to license deaf drivers, and other states considered doing likewise. Deaf drivers ultimately won the right to drive in all states. As their good driving records became more widely known, hostility against them decreased.

Charging deaf people more for insurance is an old injustice. The National Fraternal Society of the Deaf (popularly known as "the Frat" or FRAT) was founded in 1898 as a response to discriminatory life-insurance practices. Deaf drivers aren't *necessarily* charged more nowadays because they're deaf. We suggest you check with hearing friends who share your insurance company, compare their rates, and see if there really is a difference. There are many factors involved in the tabulation of these rates, such as whether the car is new, old, a plebeian Chevy, or a patrician Rolls-Royce.

Currently, the major problem seems to be the discrimination deaf drivers face when trying to purchase a new car. Some dealers still refuse to allow them to test-drive a new car, supposedly because they're "risky." The Americans with Disabilities Act, which went into effect January 26, 1992, prohibits discrimination on the basis of disability. New-car dealers are required to eliminate architectural and communication barriers, provide auxiliary aids as needed, and ensure equal access to any transportation service provided to other customers. But it remains to be seen exactly what sort of impact the ADA will have here. Some new-car dealers are aware of the law; others aren't, but don't anticipate any particular problems, as they welcome all customers. We anticipate a number of lawsuits by deaf and disabled consumers against auto dealers who are not complying with the law.

Are the fears of jittery dealers founded? Statistics show that deaf drivers are just as good as hearing drivers, and, on the whole, a better safety risk. (*Now* can we have the keys?)

Although some hearing folks are surprised to learn that deaf people can drive, the fact is, driving is an almost completely visual activity for anyone. (How many drivers watch the road with their ears, anyway?) Hearing drivers routinely close their windows when the air-conditioning is on, effectively masking out auditory clues. CD players, cassette decks, radios, and cellular phones also mask outside noises. Trucks are much noisier than cars, and some truck drivers wear protective earplugs.

Under such circumstances, a hearing driver is in much the same situation as a deaf driver. But a deaf driver may have an advantage. Deaf persons "are already highly skilled in compensating for their hearing loss at all times by increased visual alertness."* Lacking auditory distractions, they tend to concentrate better. Studies have corroborated this. A 1968 study of every deaf driver in the Washington, D.C. area over a 3-year period "produced evidence that the deaf drivers had less than one-third as many accidents and only one-half as many traffic tickets as non-deaf drivers."

Deaf drivers can carry on animated conversations in Sign with other passengers. Although this involves momentarily glancing away from the road, it's quite safe. Most Deaf passengers share the responsibility of keeping watch with the driver and are quick to alert him or her; everybody looks after each other. When approaching dangerous stretches, such as highway curves, or if driving conditions are bad, or even if they're in a no-passing zone, drivers will temporarily halt their conversation so they can focus completely on the road. Or they will simply tell the others to hold off until they all arrive at their destination. Or, if the conversation is important and the emotional tenor is starting to mount, they'll pull over and stop.

Licensing tests vary from state to state, but we've never heard of any deaf person being turned down for a license solely because they're deaf. They take the same tests a hearing driver does. New York State driver's licenses, for example, list one or more pertinent restrictions: if a driver wears a hearing aid while driving, that will be noted, and all deaf drivers are required to have three full-view mirrors.

---

*   Particular thanks to the Laurent Clerc National Deaf Education Center at Gallaudet University and FRAT for the information utilized here. Quotes are taken from various articles excerpted by FRAT.

Chapter 72

Can deaf people be pilots?

ertainly. While deaf pilots may not yet be as commonplace as deaf bowling champions, they aren't exactly novelties. There may not be too many of them, but the numbers are slowly and steadily increasing.

Deaf people have participated in, and made their marks on, the history of flight, from the earliest days. Indeed, the first pilot to make a transcontinental flight may have been severely deaf. In 1910, newspaper mogul William Randolph Hearst offered a $50,000 prize to the first pilot to make a coast-to-coast flight in 30 days. Cal Rodgers (1879-1912), a well-to-do sportsman deafened by scarlet fever at age 6, had recently learned to fly and won the endurance prize at Chicago's International Aviation Meet. Chicago's meat-packing magnate J. Ogden Armour agreed to sponsor Rodgers' flight in return for his promoting Armour's new grape soft drink, Vin Fiz. A Wright EX Flyer, a canvas-and-wood biplane, was built for Rodgers, and named the *Vin Fiz*. He took off from the East Coast on September 17, 1911, and completed his flight at Long Beach, California, on December 11. Crashes, wrecks, mechanical problems, and injuries caused numerous delays. His elaborate support crew traveled by train in specially marked cars; he followed their route. Even though the 30-day deadline expired while he was halfway across the country—and the prize was withdrawn—Rodgers refused to stop. He became the first person to make a transcontinental solo flight.

Not long after his triumphant feat, he was killed in a crash. The restored *Vin Fiz* is proudly displayed in the Smithsonian's National Air and Space Museum. Everyone who knows about the history of aviation has read about the *Vin Fiz*. Many have seen it. But relatively few people remember who Cal Rodgers was, and what he accomplished.

One problem with attributing this pioneering feat to a "deaf pilot" is that we know very little about Rodgers' deafness. He was not a man of letters, nor much of a talker, and documentation on his childhood is exceedingly scanty. Therefore, we are forced to conjecture about the severity of his deafness and what effect it had on his personal relationships, and on his performance as a pilot. Henry Kisor suspects that some of the crashes he experienced just after takeoff were due to his not understanding his mechanics' spoken advice or warnings, and bluffing it instead of asking them to repeat or write it down. Or he simply may have been headstrong, a common trait among pilots!

The first known Deaf pilot to earn a license was Nellie Zabel Willhite of South Dakota (1892-1991). Deafened at age 2 by measles, she attended South Dakota School for the Deaf, and became a stenographer. Like many others of her generation, she was inspired by the exploits of Charles Lindbergh. With financial help from her father, Charley "Pard" Zabel, she began taking lessons in late 1927, first soloing in January 1928, and bought an open-cockpit Alexander Eagle Rock biplane, which she named *Pard*. When she received her private pilot's license in 1930, she became South Dakota's first licensed woman pilot. In 1934, working for an airmail-service company, she received a transport (commercial) pilot's license. Between 1928 and 1932, she barnstormed—participated in county fairs and air shows, doing stunts and taking passengers up for their first flights. She didn't earn much of anything, but she had a "good time." A charter member of the prestigious 99 Club, the pioneering organization of women pilots, Willhite remained actively involved in aviation for years. This high-spirited, colorful character died in 1991 at the age of 98.

Rhulin A. Thomas (1910-1999), a graduate of Missouri School for the Deaf and a Linotypist at the now-defunct **Washington Evening Star**, was the first known Deaf pilot to make a solo coast-to-coast flight. He accomplished this in

1947, in a 65-horsepower, single-engine J-4 Piper Cub—and, unlike Rodgers, who had the advantage of an elaborate support team, he was entirely on his own.

Those are our pioneers. Other deaf pilots of past and fairly recent years are cited in **Deaf Heritage**.

So who was the first deaf transcontinental pilot? Kisor puts it this way: "Cal Rodgers was the first pilot, hearing or deaf, to cross the United States by air. . . . He was the first *hard-of-hearing* pilot (or pilot of any kind) to make the trip, and Rhulin Thomas the first *deaf* pilot to make the trip. Thomas was the first deaf person to fly solo across the country without ground assistance, while Rodgers required a huge ground crew and a following train with a hangar car full of spare parts. . . . Clyde Smith [DPA President] told me he thinks both of them were in their own ways the first. Works for me, too."*

Nowadays, it's unlikely that most deaf pilots could earn and make use of a commercial license because of the stringent regulations regarding radio communications. Says Kisor: "Actually, several members of DPA do have commercial certificates [which enables them to fly cropdusters]. . . . It is definite that deaf pilots cannot earn Air Transport Pilot certificates (which airline pilots hold)." Deaf people in the United States are free to obtain private pilots' licenses, however—and they've been doing that in increasing numbers. Ultralight aircraft are especially popular.

The Deaf Pilots Association (DPA) was founded in 1994, and now numbers around 50 members in the United States. (The French have their own organization.) That's approximately one-fourth to one-half of the total number of deaf pilots in the States. DPA has both ASL-Deaf and oral-deaf members. Their shared passion is flying; they find ways to communicate with each other.

The main restriction on deaf pilots, of course, is the inability to receive radio communications. Many deaf pilots can use a microphone to announce their location to air-traffic-control towers, adding the phrase "deaf pilot, cannot receive." But most airports in the U.S.—especially the smaller ones—don't have control towers, and thus aren't radio-controlled. As Kisor, who proudly holds a "Private Pilot, Single Engine Land" rating, notes in his book, **Flight of the *Gin Fizz*** (1997), "in fact, many small airplanes carry no radio at all." So deaf pilots operate primarily in and out of "uncontrolled" airports (as opposed to "controlled" airports, which have towers), under Visual Flight Rules. In VFR, "all pilots rely on their eyes as well as established landing-pattern procedures." (Kisor's book, by the way, retraces Cal Rodgers' transcontinental *Vin Fiz* flight.)

The first obstacle to a deaf person's becoming a private pilot is expense. Taking flight lessons, buying the necessary manuals, etc., and renting or acquiring an aircraft, are all notably costly propositions.

The next obstacle is finding a flight school willing to take on a deaf student. Schools often discriminate against deaf would-be students by telling them "We're all booked up." Although a deaf person can sue a flight school for discrimination under the ADA, this is not conducive to developing a good relationship. It's better to shop around, network, even travel some distance to locate the "right" school.

The biggest hurdle is communication. Clear communication is a must—whether the student can speechread the instructor easily, or if the instructor knows sign language.

In the early days of aviation, deaf pilots could easily fly by sight. Nowadays, as noted above, radio communications have largely supplanted visual procedures, so it's a bit tougher for deaf pilots who have unclear speech.

What happens if all these obstacles are surmounted? Student pilots need an official doctor's note certifying that they are indeed deaf, and must present it to the FAA medical examiner. They must take a special medical test, administered by an FAA inspector, to satisfy the FAA that being deaf doesn't affect their ability to fly an airplane.

Like driving a car, piloting a small aircraft is done visually and by feel. It takes skill—some have it, others don't. It's not easy. But those who have succeeded testify that there's nothing like the thrill of lifting off in your own plane. Quite literally, the sky's the limit.

* Kisor, a veteran journalist, author, and private pilot, is DPA's Vice President for Outreach and editor of the **DPA Newsletter**.

▲ ▲ ▲

A Deaf pilot gets grounded

Even pilots who hold current and valid licenses can run into unforeseen difficulties—not air turbulence, but attitudinal barriers. Oregon pilot Bruce Brennan's lawsuit against the Knoxville Flight Training Center is a fairly well-known example. Essentially, it's a story of the dire consequences of misunderstandings—or leaping to conclusions.

In July 1994, Brennan came to Knoxville, Tennessee to participate in DPA's Annual Fly-In, held in conjunction with the NAD's biennial conference. At 2 p.m. on July 6, after the Fly-In, Brennan, an experienced pilot, went to KFTC and requested a check-out flight for a Cessna 172 with a certified flight instructor—standard procedure. He presented his credentials and filled out the necessary forms. The counter clerk, Heather Allen, told him to come back in two hours, when the instructor would take him on the check-out flight.

It was at this point that Brennan wrote Allen a note saying that if KFTC didn't let him have a check-out flight, he would sue them. He already suspected discrimination.

When Brennan returned at 4 p.m., Allen gave him what he perceived as a runaround. She told him that the owner, John McConkey, was the "sole decision-maker" regarding check-out flights, and was on vacation and wouldn't be back for 4 more days, but that he could rent a plane from Campbell's Aero. As Brennan later alleged in his suit, Allen implied—wrongly—that no insurance coverage was available for a deaf pilot, and that he was a safety risk. Brennan retorted that if a hearing pilot had come in, they would have given him the check-out flight just like that. Allen didn't reply.

Frustrated and furious, Brennan left KFTC and went straight to a lawyer. The next day, he went to Campbell's Aero, and got a check-out flight without any difficulty.

KFTC's version of events was that Allen, a part-time employee, initially wasn't sure if deaf pilots could get licenses. She learned that they indeed can, and that there is insurance coverage for them, provided they're currently licensed with proper medical certification. After Brennan left the office at 2 p.m., she contacted the insurance carrier, and got confirmation that Brennan was indeed covered.

So why was he denied the check-out flight? Brennan claimed that KFTC discriminated against him because he was deaf. KFTC claimed that it was because he threatened to sue them if he didn't get the check-out.

What Brennan didn't realize at the time was that the certified flight instructor, Richard Copeland, an independent contractor, had just returned from a round-trip flight to Georgia and came into the KFTC office around 4 p.m. to do his paperwork. When Allen told him that there was a deaf pilot who wanted a check-out flight, he told her he had no problem with that. But when she added that he threatened to sue KFTC if they didn't rent him a plane, Copeland said that he wasn't going to fly with anyone who threatened to sue. After completing his paperwork, he left the office without talking to Brennan. He maintained that he refused to fly with Brennan solely because of his threat.

On December 1, 1994, Brennan's lawyers filed suit against KFTC, alleging violations of the ADA.

KFTC's position was that Allen only had the authority to make appointments and conduct rentals. Once Brennan presented her with his credentials, she had done all she could do. She had no jurisdiction over Copeland, an independent contractor who exercised his discretion to accept or refuse checkouts as he saw fit. So KFTC was not at fault.

Brennan contended that KFTC couldn't deny that it was in the business of renting airplanes, and that the private contract between KFTC and Copeland was not publicly displayed, nor was he advised that KFTC had such a contract with Copeland.

When the suit reached court, Judge Robert P. Murrian granted summary judgement in favor of KFTC. Basically, he argued that it was irrelevant that the contract between Copeland and KFTC wasn't publicly posted or that Brennan hadn't been informed of it. As an independent contractor, Copeland had the right to provide flight check-out services, or to refuse to provide them, at his own discretion. Since he was not an employee of KFTC, Allen had no authority over him. Judge Murrian dismissed Brennan's suit.

Brennan's lawyer, gravely disappointed by the summary judgement, filed an appeal, but died before any further action could be taken. His partner negotiated with KFTC (and with the appellate court) to offer Brennan a modest monetary settlement ($2,500) and a letter of apology. The lawyer urged Brennan to accept the settlement, since an appeal could end up costing him thousands of dollars, and was risky—he might very well lose. He told Brennan that the apology should be considered a "priceless victory."

So Brennan accepted the settlement. In Fall 1995, he received the full $2,500 from KFTC's insurance company, plus a one-sentence letter of apology from McConkey.

Ironically, in his Memorandum Opinion, Judge Murrian used the offensive terms "deaf mute" twice and "deaf mutes" once, in reference to Brennan. (We've got a long flight ahead, folks . . .)

While the lawsuit was proceeding, another deaf pilot, Jack Kelsey of Knoxville, came to KFTC to rent a plane and was given "red-carpet treatment." By that time, Allen was no longer working there. We don't know if Copeland gave Kelsey his check-out flight.

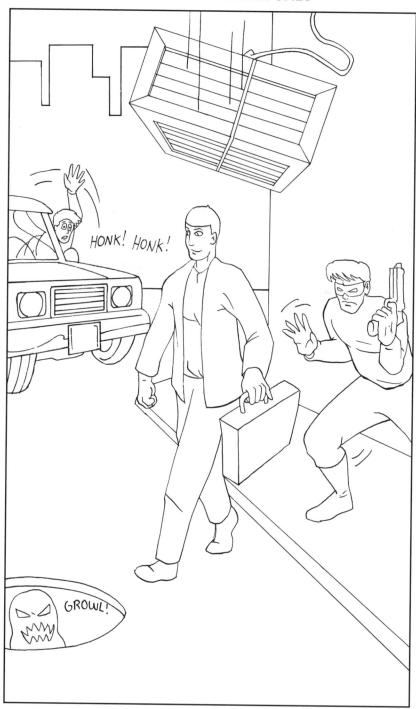

Chapter 73

Aren't deaf people more prone to accidents?

n the last century it was commonly, and mistakenly, believed that deaf people had shorter-than-average lifespans. Insurance companies considered them high risks—more accident-prone than hearing people—and accordingly charged them more.

It is true that deaf persons are more vulnerable in *some* circumstances. Every so often, you read a newspaper item about a deaf man or woman who was shot to death in a mugging or store robbery. Too often, the criminal orders the victim to do something—"Don't move!" or "Lie down!"—without realizing that the deaf person can't hear the command. Especially from behind. When the deaf victim fails to comply, s/he gets killed, and another tragic crime story ends up in the newspapers. The effect of such stories, unfortunately, is to reinforce the stereotype of deaf people being helpless, pathetic, and easily victimized.

Sometimes it *can* make a difference if a victim is able to inform the assailants that s/he is deaf. In **I Didn't Hear the Dragon Roar**, Frances M. "Peggie" Parsons tells of how she narrowly escaped being knifed to death in Mozambique. Having disregarded a warning not to walk alone in the dark, she went downtown, took a "wrong exit" from a department store, and was attacked in a narrow alley by "three surly young men with tribal scars across their faces." One brandished a knife. She struggled to get one hand free and gestured that she was deaf. The man with the knife signed, "You deaf? Me have deaf sister." He ordered his accomplices to release her, helped her to her feet, returned her purse, asked her what she was doing in Mozambique, and kissed her hand in parting, saying, "You saint. No walk alone!"*

As for fires: deaf people, particularly impoverished children and the elderly who live in unsafe buildings without proper smoke-alarm hookups, are indeed vulnerable. Smoke alarms are available with flashing "strobe" signals that are virtually impossible to miss, even if you're asleep. Some single persons and families have a hearing-ear dog—a dependable mongrel or pedigree working-breed who is specially trained to respond to noises and alert its owners. (A good dog is priceless. How many lives—whether deaf or hearing—have been saved by "ordinary" family pooches?!)

Some news stories identify accident victims as deaf—even when their deafness has no relevance to the accident. Deaf people have automobile accidents involving locked brakes, hydroplaning on icy and flooded roads, avalanches, hurricanes, and unpreventable collisions, just as hearing folks do. To read some of these stories, you'd think that these folks had accidents simply because they were deaf. Makes us wonder if the reporters believe, deep down inside, that all deaf folks ought to stay home, since it's so hazardous to venture outside!

In some ways, deaf people may have definite advantages over their hearing counterparts—e.g., job safety. Alert deaf people keep their eyes open and their reflexes sharp. However, it must be said that not all deaf people *are* alert. Some are careless, lethargic, and clumsy. These become the "accident-prone" folks of the stereotype. (Some forms of deafness also affect the center of balance in the inner ear, which entails both impaired hearing *and* balance.)

Hearing people who work with deaf people often develop a knack for warning them of danger situations: an oncoming ambulance or car, a lowering crane, any unusual noise or alarm. These warnings are always appreciated. We haven't quite reached the point where we can take them for granted. Hearing workers don't invariably think of their deaf co-workers during fire alarms. There have been occasions when hearing workers responded to an alarm by fleeing and leaving their deaf co-workers behind.

A $36-million lawsuit filed in 1998 against the B. Manischewitz Company, one of the world's largest suppliers of Passover matzo, alleged discrimination against 10 deaf bakers, all immigrants from the former Soviet Union. According to the suit, Manischewitz and the Bakery, Confectionery, and Tobacco Workers International Union failed to provide sign-language interpreters, making it impossible for deaf workers to participate in contract negotiations. More dire was the allegation that during a major fire and blackout in 1994, all of the hearing employees evacuated the premises. One worker had to run back inside to inform a deaf baker that there was a fire and get him safely out. No flashing alarms had yet been installed. Manischewitz considered the suit "without merit," and insisted that it was committed to meeting the needs of its deaf workers and resolving any concerns they might have.

If you work with a deaf person or happen to meet one at work, and encounter a danger situation, you can warn her by gently patting her shoulder twice, quickly, jabbing your hand, palm down and fingers together, against your forehead ("Know-this?"), and pointing to the source of danger: the ambulance, crane, or source of noise. If there's an alarm, you can simply indicate, "Come with me" or use the signs for "fire" or "emergency." If it's a *real* emergency, yanking him by the sleeve or grabbing his arm and pulling him with you are acceptable, if abrupt, means of warning. Don't bother thumbing through your ASL phrasebook; just grab him and run. Deaf people understand. Safety comes first; the explanations can wait.

Deaf people are not more prone to accidents just *because* they're deaf. A multiplicity of factors are involved.

* Frances M. Parsons, **I Didn't Hear the Dragon Roar** (Washington, D.C.: Gallaudet University Press, 1988), xii.

Chapter 74

How can deaf people be bothered by noise if they can't hear?

wo reasons, essentially: (1) because a number of us possess some degree of residual hearing that registers very loud noises, and (2) because of the vibrations accompanying them.

One of the more common misconceptions in current circulation (yet another one!) is that deaf people aren't bothered by loud noises. The common phrase "stone-deaf" (which some deaf people perceive as an insult, and others accept) suggests that profoundly deaf people are impervious to noise.[1] This is not strictly true. Even they may be bothered by extremely loud, high-pitched, screeching noises (e.g., the siren of an approaching ambulance, police car, or fire truck), since these are accompanied by high-frequency vibrations that can cause acute physical discomfort. The inner-ear mechanism might not register the sound very well (or at all), but those vibrations are nonetheless bombarding our inner ears and our skulls. Noise affects many of us in more of a tactile than an aural way. We might not *hear* the sound so much as *feel* it.

Other particularly distressing noises include jet planes (especially noticeable if you live directly underneath the descent path of an airport), pneumatic drills, truck motors, and (for some) shouting, screaming, and yelling. If it's loud enough to make hearing people cringe and cause damage to their inner workings, chances are it's going to bother us too. Deaf people tend to be more sensitive to these vibrations than hearing people. Some hearing people don't understand this. A hearing college student with a new deaf roommate, for instance, may *think* that it's okay to play blasting-loud heavy-metal music. If your deaf roomie asks you to turn down it down because the bass is much too loud, s/he's not faking deafness or being a spoilsport. The thumping, booming bass section (to say nothing of the percussion) typically reverberates through the room—and beyond. It may be "fun" for the music-lovers to "get into" the mood of the music by feeling it rumbling through their bones and guts, but for those who are trying to focus on studying or writing, it's extremely annoying.

This, of course, is an understatement. Music—however it's defined—can be used, unwittingly or not, as a weapon of mental cruelty. It is certainly used deliberately as a weapon of psychological intimidation by gang members, to cite one example. Playing booming-loud music of a certain kind at all hours is a remarkably effective way of asserting domination, letting your neighbors on the block know who rules the territory. Non-gangsters can be incredibly inconsiderate of their neighbors' need for quiet at night, and people are constantly suing each other over loud music and other forms of noise pollution.

Even bilaterally deaf people may have different degrees of hearing loss on either side—which means that one ear picks up more sounds than the other. If they wear one or two aids, the aids act as an auditory "vacuum-cleaner"—amplifying *all* sounds within range. (Sophisticated digital models allow the user to program them for sound selectivity, but digital aids are incredibly expensive. Analog aids are still prevalent.) Some severely/profoundly-deaf people wear aids all day, since they want to be attuned to environmental sounds wherever they are. So, of course, they're sensitive to certain loud, disruptive noises.

Some years ago, I (MSM) went to a small-town concert with my family during a festival. There was a band or orchestra standing on a platform that had been set up on the main street. The audience stood around.

Everything was fine—until the musicians hit some high-pitched notes. It bothered the heck out of me! I just couldn't stand it. These high-pitched sounds were screeching through my head. And I'm a profoundly deaf person! I was standing there with my family, and you can imagine how they felt when they saw me with my face scrunched up in agony, pointing to my ears, signing that the noise was causing me pain. So I left. My family were baffled. But seeing me leaving, they also left.

The audiological lobby (most prominently Better Hearing Institute, Deafness Research Foundation, the American Academy of Otolaryngology-Head and Neck Surgery, and the relatively new Deafness Education and Awareness For Rockers) has mounted anti-noise public-service campaigns. They encourage hearing youngsters and teens to reduce the volume of noise in their lives—the kind that they can control. Instead of "playing it loud," they're urged to "turn it down." The goal—a sensible one—is to help younger people conserve and safeguard their hearing. But we, as deaf people, also have an interest in this campaign. Noise bothers us, threatens us, and has a negative physical effect on us. So we have every right to get involved in the campaign against noise pollution. It's our business, too.[2]

Back in the not-so-distant days when printing was the top profession for deaf men, many of them were hired as Linotypists and spent long years in the composition rooms of newspapers across the nation. This was considered a desirable match, supposedly because operating a Linotype machine was an extremely noisy business, noisy enough to deafen hearing operators, but if you were already deaf, you wouldn't be bothered by the noise. Nowadays, we are more apt to think twice about on-the-job noise hazards, and to use protective earplugs.

Despite the stereotype of deaf people as totally unaware of and unconcerned about the noise they make (q.v. Agnes Thatcher, the shrill, loud-snoring, drawer-slamming roommate from hell in M. E. Kerr's **Is That You, Miss Blue**?), deaf people are often sensitized to others' needs, and can be quite considerate. When staying in buildings with wooden floors, they will caution each other to be quiet—i.e., no stomping, since it creates vibrations that might disturb others. (Stomping is considered okay on concrete floors, though, but not as a means of getting someone's attention.) If one housemate is leaving for work early in the morning while others are sleeping, s/he doesn't slam doors, because a slammed door can shake the whole house. When there's a deaf baby around, adults will say "*Shhh!*" to each other—i.e., don't stomp, don't make noises that cause vibrations that might wake the baby. (But talking is okay.)

Loud music, however, does have a place in Deaf culture. Years ago, a friend laughingly told one of us (LL), a newly-arrived NTID student, that the student hangouts in the "Tunnel" (the maze of interconnected corridors, rooms, and facilities underneath the residential-hall complex) featured bright lights—so that everybody could see each others' signing clearly—*and* loud music, so that hearing students couldn't use their voices to communicate with each other, but had to rely on, and thereby improve by practicing, their signing skills. (This has already been noted in Chapter 69.) Deaf parties (as noted in Chapters 64 and 65) typically feature loud disco music, so that attendees can benefit from the bass section, dancing to a good strong beat. Whether or not you consider this "noise pollution" depends on your view of discos. In the right place, and at the appropriate time, it can be fun. If you dislike discos, you'll shun them.

For many deaf people, the everyday preference is for a quiet environment. The stereotypical view of deaf people is that we "live in a world of silence," which is untrue. Our auditory perceptions, are, of course, radically different from those of hearing people, but we do not exist in a "silent" world. There's plenty of visual color. And yes, it's possible to have an environment free of noise pollution that *isn't* boring.

[1] The common phrase "stone-deaf" (or "stone deaf')" is more or less synonymous with what the audiologists call "profound-plus deafness." Now, some deaf people consider "stone-deaf" a rank insult. (See notes to Chapter 37.) Others aren't bothered by it at all. The word "stone," used colloquially as a modifier, has taken on connotations of "absolute" or "utter"—e.g., "a stone rip-off." The phrase "stone-deaf" suggests that the degree of hearing loss is absolute. But even those with a total or near-total loss can be sensitive to certain noises, especially those are physically harmful.

[2] Should deaf people wear ear protectors in noisy workplace situations? It's a good idea, since a number of us possess some degree of residual hearing that registers very loud noises. Some deaf people, even though the auditory hair cells in their cochleae, or their auditory nerves, may be nonfunctional, are nonetheless sensitive to bothersome noises. Most of us still have good bone conductivity.

Chapter 75

Why do some deaf people
want or need hearing dogs?

—Elizabeth A. Brietkrietz, Cottage Grove, Minnesota

 ogs provide companionship and comfort, and trained dogs provide an additional measure of reassurance. They free deaf owners from having to depend exclusively on electronic signaling and other safety devices.

Humans usually can't smell smoke when they're asleep. A dog's sense of smell is much more acute than ours, and a dog can respond quicker than a smoke detector. Even though deaf people may benefit from having strobe-light smoke detectors, there's always a possibility that these may fail—or that sleepers may be lying with their heads tucked into their arms or the pillow, effectively shielding their eyes from the strobe. It makes sense to have a trained dog.

The most familiar companion dogs are "seeing-eye dogs" or "guide dogs for the blind," used primarily in public settings, where traffic and obstacles (broken sidewalks, potholes, construction areas, etc.) pose particular hazards to blind people. These dogs are rigorously trained to guide and protect their owners in public.

"Hearing-ear" or "hearing" dogs are trained to respond to specific sounds, such as a doorbell, telephone, alarm clock, smoke alarm, crying baby, someone calling the owner's name, and/or intruder. When the dog hears a sound, it goes to the deaf owner, makes physical contact by pawing the owner's leg if they're standing or sitting, or, if they're asleep, by nuzzling the owner's hand or face, or jumping onto the bed, and then the dog takes the owner to the sound. Some respond to visual commands as well as voiced ones. Some deaf owners use visual/ASL commands exclusively.

Seeing-eye dogs are usually "on duty" in public. Hearing dogs are usually on duty at home. Home is where most of *our* hazards are. Some deaf people don't take their hearing dogs out in public, unless it's for the company and exercise. Others prefer to take their dogs with them wherever they go—shopping, jogging, business forays, social gatherings, libraries, conferences, vacation trips, even dining out. These dogs are legally entitled to the same privileges accorded seeing-eye dogs. Hearing-ear dogs wear a distinctive safety-orange collar and leash in public. (Unlike seeing-eye dogs, they don't wear harnesses.) An official photo-identification card is attached to the dog's orange leash, and owners often carry a certificate and explanatory booklet with them, just in case they run into ignorant folks who cause difficulties for them. Having the documentation handy forestalls nasty scenarios.

Not all deaf people who have dogs have "hearing" dogs. Some of our dogs are just ordinary pets with no special training. (These, of course, can often do a good job of alerting and protecting their owners in an emergency.) But some folks feel that as long as they're getting a dog, why not have one *trained* to respond to sounds? Some owners train their own dogs from puppyhood. But most people prefer to obtain one from a specialized training center or agency. According to Robin Dickson of Dogs for the Deaf, based in Central Point, Oregon, "There is no charge from the legitimate nonprofit training centers."

Obtaining a certified hearing dog isn't a quick one-day affair like going to a shelter, choosing a pooch, and bringing it home. As with an adoption agency, there may be a waiting list of clients. Training and placement take time. Says Dickson: "The dogs are in training for 5-6 months. In addition to the sound training, they are also thoroughly obedience-trained and socialized. This is necessary so that they will behave in public and be able to cope with the world.

"The matching process is very important. When the dog is

about 2/3 of the way through training, the trainer begins looking for the right applicant for that dog. We match the dog's strengths with the person's lifestyle, activity level, and expectations. Some dogs are better in a quiet environment with one person; others do better with lots of activity and distractions. So it is a very careful practice to find the right place for each dog so that the dog and person will receive maximum benefit from each other."

How effective the dog is depends on the dog's personality and how well it's trained, as well as the owner's needs, and whether the dog is treated as a pet or a worker. One professional hearing-dog trainer told us that she once placed a dog with a deaf couple who had a new baby. The dog was trained to alert the parents when the baby cried. Unfortunately, the dog was *too* effective—every sleep-whimper, every burp, every sneeze, and the dog dashed off to notify the parents. After enduring several days of an ongoing barrage of "false alarms," the exhausted and frazzle-nerved parents called the trainer. She took back the dog and de-trained it. Meanwhile, the parents installed an electronic "baby-cry" signaler, and finally got some peace. They kept the dog as a pet.

Say "seeing-eye dog," and we tend to visualize the familiar German Shepherd or Golden Retriever—good hefty working-breed dogs. Hearing dogs don't have to be of any particular breed or size, although some breeds, of course, work better than others. We've seen Golden Retrievers, Labrador Retrievers, Shelties, and a goodly proportion of mixed breeds on duty. (A nervous, yappy type like the Chihuahua is obviously a poor choice.)

Many excellent hearing dogs are simply abandoned, unwanted, or stray puppies or adult mutts adopted from a local pound or animal shelter, who might otherwise have been destroyed. The main criteria are intelligence, trainability, and good temperament.

"Our trainers are specially trained in what to look for at shelters when they are looking for dogs," says Dickson.

"Basically, they are looking for dogs that are 2 years old or younger. (We will take dogs up to a maximum of 3 years, but prefer 2 or younger.) They also look mainly for dogs that are small to medium-sized—35 pounds or under—because this is what the majority of our applicants want. We can find larger dogs if someone wants a bigger dog. Then the third thing is the dog's personality and temperament. We want dogs that are friendly, bouncy, energetic, playful, and *not* aggressive. We want dogs that are eager to please and want to be loved. Our trainers regularly go to shelters on the West Coast looking for suitable candidates."

Currently, owners of seeing-eye dogs get financial aid and tax breaks for their upkeep and medical care. Owners of hearing dogs don't. Consequently, many deaf people who'd like to have a hearing dog can't afford to. Seeing-eye-dog training and placement programs have been around for quite a while. Hearing-dog programs are a relatively recent innovation. Several of these nonprofit agencies operate around the country to find, train and place hearing dogs, and raise funds to help defray the costs. The goal: that *all* deaf persons or families who want or need a hearing dog should be able to have one—and get the best one for them.

As Dickson notes, "There are several training centers, plus private trainers who train Hearing Dogs. People need to know that there is a great difference between many of these as far as methods, charges, quality, etc. Those interested in obtaining a Hearing Dog should research carefully and make sure they are getting a well-trained dog. Cost should not be a factor; there is no charge for our dogs, and we are the oldest and largest training center in the country. Our quality of training and service is the very highest.

"Deaf people need to check carefully to make sure they are getting a dog that will benefit them. They also need to realize that having a Hearing Dog involves a lot of work. This is not a robot or something you tie to a tree in the back yard. These dogs need love, care, and reinforcement of their training if they are going to truly benefit the person."

Deaf Awareness 5-Minute Quiz

Chapters 61—75

Answers are on the bottom of the page, upside down.

True or False:

1. The role of Belinda in *Johnny Belinda* has long been a favorite of Deaf actresses.

2. The concept of "Deaf literature" is contradictory, since ASL is not a written language.

3. Deaf moviegoers in the U.S. have traditionally enjoyed subtitled foreign films.

4. A number of deaf people have had distinguished careers as professional dancers.

5. As a career, recreation, form of entertainment, or means of self-expression, music is, unfortunately, entirely off-limits to deaf people.

6. Deaf people are immediately recognizable as "Deaf" because of their facial expressions.

7. Even if they're from mainstreamed backgrounds, many deaf people prefer sleeping in complete darkness.

8. Deaf people are prohibited from becoming commercial (airline) pilots, but can operate small commercial aircraft such as cropdusters.

9. Since driving is primarily an auditory activity, deaf people have had a tough time getting licenses and insurance.

10. Some of the best hearing-ear dogs are former stray mutts or abandoned pets who would otherwise have been destroyed.

Over a decade of promoting Deaf Awareness

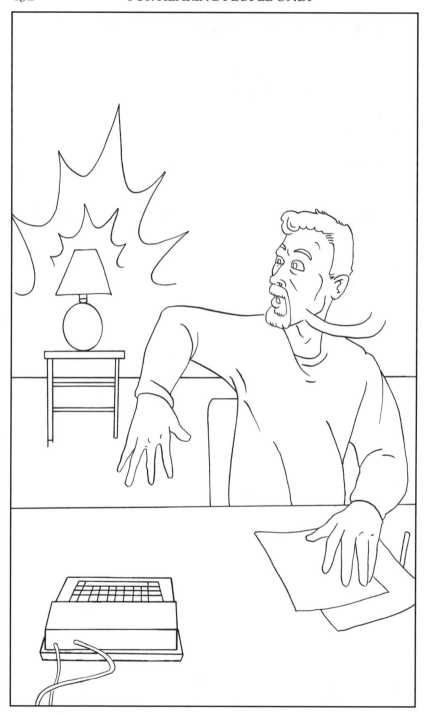

Chapter 76

How do deaf people use telephones? What about doorbells and alarm clocks?

o reiterate a trite but important fact: the deaf and hard-of-hearing population includes persons with very different communications abilities, needs, and preferences. Each person is different.

Telecommunications: The telephone, as we've already mentioned, provides one useful line of demarcation between the audiologically "hard-of-hearing" and "deaf." Hard-of-hearing persons can carry on telephone conversations with a voice handset; deaf persons cannot.

Thus, you'll find that many hard-of-hearing people function nicely with a conventional voice telephone, possibly with an amplifier. But some hard-of-hearing and most deaf people prefer to use a TTY and relay services, rather than rely on direct voice communication. With a relay service, some hard-of-hearing, late-deafened, and oral-deaf persons prefer using *voice carryover* (VCO). With VCO, users read the incoming message as a regular typed TTY readout, but, using a separate or built-in microphone hookup, can speak directly to the other party. For those who have clear speech, this is a useful option, as it saves time.

Keyboarding: As for TTYs, there is a variety to choose from. Many portable models are battery-operated/electric. They are *not* cheap. The most basic models (without a printout) cost well over $100. (Some states provide them free to qualified residents.) The more costly models boast an array of sophisticated features.

Some computers have built-in TTY capacity, and there are TTY modems (to transform a computer into a usable TTY), as well as pocket-sized and cellular-compatible TTYs. There are also combination TTY/voice phones, so all members of an "intermodal" family or staff can use the same device.

TTYs have been augmented or even supplanted, to some extent, by real-time chat/message programs and E-mail. There's even a toll-free Internet-relay service that connects Internet "callers" with voice-telephone parties. Wireless communications, such as text pagers, are becoming increasingly popular, although cellular phones are considered an impractical luxury. TTYs are still a necessity.

Gizmos galore: Deaf people, as we all know, use lights to substitute for auditory signals. Flicking the lights in a room or area on and off to call a deaf person is one of the commonest applications.

What with the ADA, the making and selling of electric and electronic signaling, visual-alerting, and assistive devices is a booming business. There are a bewildering array of gizmos and doodads—e.g., phone and doorbell flashers, baby-cry monitors, fire and smoke alarms—on the market.

Travelers' rest: Since the passage of the Americans with Disabilities Act, hotels and motels (to cite one sector) have scrambled to comply with the law by making their accommodations accessible to deaf and hard-of-hearing "guests." They proudly advertise their compliance with the ADA.

As might be expected, the concept of compliance has been interpreted in various ways, so it's a good idea to check ahead. Travelers should be on the lookout. A hotel may offer each deaf guest an "ADA compliance pack" that includes a portable TTY and visual fire alarm (if these aren't already installed in the room). Or it may have one solitary TTY on the premises. If someone else has borrowed it, and you haven't brought one with you, you're out of luck.

Flashing-light signaling/warning systems: Flasher systems alert users to a doorbell, ringing phone, or incoming fax by causing a dedicated electric light or all the table lamps in a particular room or area to flash. The whole apartment or house can also be rigged up. (These require standard incandescent lightbulbs, by the way. Compact-fluorescent bulbs don't work with these systems.)

Baby-cry monitors work rather like nursery intercoms, but convert sounds into light flashes.

Some signaling devices (e.g., phone-flashers or wake-up alarms) use strobe lights, but some deaf people dislike the intrusive and startling flickering—and strobes have been known to trigger epileptic seizures, so many of us prefer to avoid them. (They are used in some classrooms—cautiously, we hope.)

When we see a light flashing, how do we know whether it's the door or the TTY? And what if we have several TTY lines in the house? Signaling systems can be rigged up so that lights flash in a certain pattern for the doorbell, another for the TTY, and each TTY can be connected to a specific light or lights, so that they flash in every room or particular rooms. They can also use differently-colored bulbs to indicate which TTY is "ringing." For example, our doorbell flashes in a series of quick, repetitive "buzzes" each time it's pressed; our TTY in longer, slower pulses. One TTY line has a white lightbulb, another yellow.

You can plug in a relatively inexpensive signal light, connect a couple of lamp-flashers, or have a sophisticated house-wide system professionally installed. It depends on what you need and (of course) how much you're willing to spend. Having some electrical know-how is a definite plus.

What all of this means is that we, just as our hearing counterparts, can have our domestic tranquillity shattered by an unignorable ringing phone—or rather, a flashing one. But these systems can be switched off if we don't want to be disturbed.

Smoke alarms: Deaf people probably spend more money on smoke alarms than the hearing do. Hearing people can manage with an audible smoke alarm in, say, two strategic areas, but deaf people need to install a strobe smoke alarm in each room. (A few years ago, a new smoke alarm hit the market. It released a pungent odorant when activated, and was claimed to be effective at rousing sleepers.)

Vibrotactile doodads: Then there are vibrotactile devices—e.g., the buzzing pager. Some persons use vibrotactile alerting devices (which can be worn on the wrist or belt) while going out in public. Because they "sound" when another person approaches, or when a loud noise (e.g., an ambulance siren) activates it, they confer a measure of security. Wearers remain aware of what's going on around them without constantly having to turn around.

Buzzing awake: As for the challenge of getting up in the morning: battery-operated and wind-up alarm clocks are virtually useless for many deaf people. Sometimes a clock radio, with the volume turned up high, does the job, but it disturbs other people within earshot. An electric bed-vibrator is reliable but heavy and bulky (i.e., it doesn't travel well), and requires careful installation and a metal bedframe. It also has an exposed cord.

Some deaf people prefer a light-flasher or strobe timer-alarm, but we've found that it's all too easy to "hide" from a flashing light by turning away and pulling the blankets over our eyes!

As for impromptu approaches: I (LL) used to pin a wind-up traveling alarm clock in a tank top and wear that over a nightshirt, to ensure getting up on time for college classes. It worked most of the time. A vibrating timer, small enough to wear on a Velcro wristband, can also be used for this purpose, but it's still fairly easy to sleep through.

Vibrating alarm clocks are popular for deaf people and are catching on for non-deaf who need to get up earlier than their bedmates do. A compact battery-operated vibrating clock slips under the pillow. Unlike conventional battery-operated alarm clocks, it doesn't emit a polite "beep" when the alarm is triggered, but 60 strong vibrating blasts. (Try sleeping through *that*.) Since the alarm isn't audible, it won't bother anyone else.

The disadvantage of a battery-operated alarm clock is that when the main batteries wear out, the clock will not keep proper time or rouse the user. Vigilance is a must. We use rechargeables, with a spare pair.

To sum up: the wonders of technology make it possible for us to enjoy accessible communications and a degree of security—at a price.

Chapter 77

Why do deaf people live where they do?

here deaf people live, and why, is a subject in itself. (The following assessment is, of necessity, *very* general.)

Deaf people are attracted to the big cities for the same reason hearing people are—greater opportunities. When considering Deaf demographics, though, there are a couple of unique factors. To understand why the deaf population is distributed the way it is, one needs to understand something of our history and language, as well as the crucial importance of the residential schools for the deaf.

Affiliation with the Deaf community has traditionally begun at school. As we have already pointed out, deaf people prefer to associate with other deaf people because of the shared bond of language and experience. We feel most comfortable with those we can communicate freely and fluently with. We establish firm, loving friendships in school, and seek to maintain them after graduation. Schools for the deaf are the heart of our communities; the campuses are hubs.

Some campuses are located in the countryside, others in bustling urban areas. When these schools were being set up across the nation during the 19th century, the land appropriated for them was sometimes situated in out-of-the-way domains, as if to keep the campuses and their inhabitants tucked discreetly out of sight.[1] Not always, though. The American School for the Deaf was originally located in downtown Hartford; the Lexington School for the Deaf on Lexington Avenue at 68th Street in Manhattan; the Pennsylvania School for the Deaf in Philadelphia. The Indiana School for the Deaf in Indianapolis was previously located on the old National Road, a major Midwestern highway.

All these campuses became the hubs of Deaf communities. Graduates sometimes settled nearby; families were established and grew up, so to speak, in the shadow of the schools. Deaf alumni maintained their association with each other through school publications (the "Little Paper Family") and organizations that met regularly. Deaf clubs were set up locally. These filled the need of Deaf residents to socialize with each other, relax in a congenial environment, share the latest news and gossip, and, when technological advances permitted, to enjoy silent/captioned movies.

Wherever you have a school for the deaf, you will generally find a Deaf community grown up around it. This is especially true of "the Big Three"—Gallaudet University, NTID, and CSUN. There is a huge Deaf community, with Gallaudet as the hub, in the Washington, D.C./Potomac/Chesapeake area—which includes Silver Spring (site of NAD's headquarters), Beltsville, Lanham, Laurel, Bowie, Greenbelt, Gaithersburg, Hyattsville, New Carrollton, Potomac, Rockville, Bethesda, Baltimore, and Annapolis in Maryland, as well as Columbia and Frederick, where the two MSD campuses are located. It extends to Arlington, Alexandria, Springfield, and Richmond in Virginia. Likewise, the Rochester-Henrietta-Brighton-Pittsford, New York area contains a large population of NTID graduates and deaf faculty and staff. Much the same goes for Northridge, Riverside, and Fremont in California—sites of CSUN and the two CSD campuses.

The relationship between the Deaf community and schools (especially community colleges) can be symbiotic. Many community colleges offer ASL and interpreter-training courses; these are often situated in cities that have large Deaf communities. The bigger the community, the better chance of finding skilled Deaf teachers for these courses. Likewise, schools for the deaf offer more and better positions to Deaf teachers, administrators, and staff (e.g., Texas and North Carolina). So having a "good" community there is a definite plus.

More public high schools and "mainstream" colleges are offering ASL and Deaf Studies curricula, which also attract skilled Deaf teachers and their families. Good schools attract good teachers, which in turn attracts students. The community benefits. (This, of course, is the ideal.)

The school factor is immediately apparent. A bit harder to explain, because it involves a situation that existed over half a century ago, is the concentration of Deaf communities and sports events in the Great Lakes states.

As noted above, deaf people have gone where the opportunities were—particularly situations they had been trained for in school, and industries that welcomed them.[2] (And places where there were other deaf people!) In New York and Washington, for instance, the great daily newspapers employed them as Linotypists and printers. In Flint and Detroit, they worked on the auto-assembly lines. They worked in Savannah and other Eastern shipyard centers. They still work for the U.S. Postal Service and in factories across the nation in large numbers.[3]

During the two World Wars, deaf citizens were exempted from serving in the armed forces. So they joined the war-industry workforce, where they were welcome—and badly needed. The situation parallels that of the many women who found rewarding work—at least temporarily—in the war industries. Indeed, the great rubber companies based in Akron, Ohio—Goodyear and Firestone—mounted organized campaigns to recruit deaf workers—women no less eagerly than men. As a result, they moved *en masse* to Akron during World War I, and Firestone even established a colony there—including social and sports facilities—to accommodate the large population of Deaf workers and their families. They (and the companies) prospered. They enjoyed good wages, good working conditions, and, best of all, the company of other Deaf workers. It's a fascinating chapter in our history.

In many ways, to be sure, it wasn't such a wonderful time to be deaf. Virtually all schools in the States followed a rigid and repressive oral/aural curriculum. Sign language wasn't officially accepted or recognized anywhere, except in the Deaf clubs and churches. Joblessness and discrimination were perpetual concerns. Yet, in some ways, the World Wars benefited the Deaf community. Those living in Akron's Deaf colony set up clubs, mini-theaters, and organized athletic competitions (e.g., the "Akron Goodyear Silents").

After World War II ended, the Deaf colony disbanded. Rosie the Riveter was forced to relinquish her job to Johnny the Veteran. Deaf joblessness increased. The population of deaf card peddlers mushroomed. But many Deaf families, having set down roots in these cities, remained. So did their cultural life and sports clubs. One legacy of the war-industry experience is the institution of the Central Athletic Association of the Deaf, which predated the founding of the American Athletic Association of the Deaf (now the U.S.A. Deaf Sports Federation), and is its oldest regional affiliate. CAAD comprises the states bordering Lake Erie—Ohio, Illinois, Indiana, Michigan, Wisconsin, and the areas of Buffalo, New York, and Erie and Pittsburgh, Pennsylvania, plus Kentucky. (There are large Deaf populations in Cleveland and Columbus, and Cincinnati lies on the northern Kentucky border.) This encompassed the Deaf populations of the chief automobile, rubber, and steel cities.

On April 13, 1945, representatives of a number of deaf clubs met at the Akron Club of the Deaf and formed what is now the USADSF. The next day, the first national deaf basketball tournament was held in the Goodyear Gymnasium; Buffalo defeated Akron.

Also worthy of mention is the Great Lakes Deaf Bowling Association, which **Deaf Heritage** calls "the oldest and largest bowling tournament in the country."

Ohio, by the way, still has a reputation as welcoming deaf workers because of its exemplary experience with them during the wars. That's possibly why Ohio automatically issues all deaf residents a "Handicapped" parking-space permit. This could be construed as patronizing and insulting—or as a gesture of thanks. ("Here, take the best parking spaces.")

Today, the deaf population is scattered throughout the States. But you will still find large concentrations of Deaf population in the "magnet" cities. As long as the residential schools are strong, there will be strong Deaf communities.

The growing trend towards mainstreaming, however, means that more deaf children are growing up without a strong sense of belonging—no affiliation with other deaf children, no "Deaf" communal identity. It's not unrealistic to predict that, if this trend continues, within a few generations (say, 50 years), Deaf communities will have lost their "hubs." Instead of carrying a strong sense of place, of identity, we'll be lost in the multitudes.

[1] The Governor Baxter School for the Deaf in Maine is one of the most remote. It's located on an island (Mackworth) off the coast of Maine. In contrast, Rochester School for the Deaf is located north of the North Loop, Rochester's central business district.

In some cases, the land surrounding the original campus became so valuable as commercial property as businesses moved in and built up, that it was more feasible for the school to sell the old campus, relocate, and build a new campus from scratch—as happened with the American School for the Deaf and the Indiana School for the Deaf. ASD's original campus is now the site of an insurance company; ISD's old campus is a small public park.

[2] Agriculture was at one time an important feature of deaf-school campuses, which typically contained full-fledged herds of cattle, milk cows, barns, dairies, bakeries, and cultivated crops of corn, wheat, and other staples. The Kentucky School for the Deaf in Danville was one of the last schools to de-agriculturalize.

The vocational departments of these schools also typically contained printing presses, machine, cobblers', and textile shops.

[3] There is a link between industry and the location of schools. Three state schools (originally, two for whites in Morganton and Wilson, and one for blacks in Raleigh) were set up in North Carolina to accommodate the large deaf population attracted by that state's industries.

Chapter 78

Why do so many Deaf people work in printing, post-office, or factory jobs?

or many years, printing was considered the ideal job for a deaf man. Most residential schools for the deaf had their own print shops and published newsletters, newspapers, and journals—the legendary "Little Papers." Printing paid well, even during the Depression. And it offered prestige. In the Deaf community, printers were "the elite." Many deaf men became skilled Linotypists. (As we've noted, deaf Linotypists presumably could better concentrate on their work without being bothered by the extremely noisy machines.) But with the revolution in cold type and desktop publishing, and the phasing-out of Linotype machines, printing has ceased to be the "natural" choice. Nonetheless, it's still a popular one.

The second most common traditional vocation for deaf boys—shoemaking—is history now.[1]

For deaf girls, very few of whom entered the printing field (not that they were encouraged to!), dressmaking/ seamstressing was considered the ideal ticket to financial independence in the event they couldn't snag a husband. In the days before off-the-rack clothing offered a wide variety of sizes, it was, no doubt, an indispensable skill.

Teaching the deaf was a respected profession for Deaf adults—that is, until the "victory" of oralism more than a century ago. As a result of the schools' mass switch to the oral method, Deaf people were gradually forced out of the profession. Even today, the overwhelming majority of teachers of the deaf are hearing.

Many deaf people still work in blue-collar trades. They tend to seek jobs known to be "open to the deaf." The U.S. Postal

Service is the nation's largest single employer of deaf people. Factories (at least until the latest series of recessions) always needed workers. Deaf people like to work with other deaf people. And there is peer pressure to conform. Certain jobs are "socially acceptable." Others aren't. Members of the local Deaf community may look askance at a deaf person who "steps out of line."

Moreover, one has to consider the relatively poor English skills of a number of deaf people—whether they're from the traditional schools for the deaf, oral schools, or mainstreamed public-school programs. You don't need good English skills to work at the Post Office in the capacity of a clerk or mail carrier, on an assembly line, or burger-flipping. You can get by with other skills.

As a result of many factors, relatively few deaf people have ventured into non-traditional ("white-collar") careers. Progress has been notably irregular. The doors of opportunity, which were not exactly flung wide, are slowly opening. Slowly. Deaf children are still subjected to low expectations—"A pilot? Don't be silly. Deaf people can't be pilots!" "You can't be a TV producer—you're deaf!" "An Olympic athlete? Sorry, but the Olympics are for hearing athletes."

As young adults, they continue to face discrimination, blatant and subtle. By this time, many have developed a self-image problem. They may see their own choices as limited. If others believe they can't do something, and they likewise believe that they can't, how can they? Even if they have a good attitude, a potential employer may have already soured on the prospect of having a deaf worker. How many employers refuse to hire a third deaf person because of bad experiences with the first two?

Even bright, highly motivated, enthusiastic Deaf people may be badly educated and ill-prepared. And in today's fiercely competitive job market, "fighting spirit" alone isn't quite enough. Support, networking, and mentors are still in short supply. And many Deaf people seem quite content with the "old ways." Fewer risks mean less frustration, pain, and disappointment.

In the early 1980s, a hearing oralist administrator expressed this common view:

> "We all talk," said George Pratt, president of [Clarke School for the Deaf]. "It's unlikely to me that the rest of the world is going to learn sign language just to accommodate to the deaf. The deaf have to accommodate to the hearing." (...)
>
> "My daughter is deaf. She is now thirty-five years old. An architectural draftswoman at Kodak in Rochester. She's the only woman in the office and the only deaf. If she couldn't talk, she'd never be able to have that job."[2]

Fortunately, this arrogant attitude isn't true anymore. More employers are willing to take a risk by hiring a deaf worker. Spurred by the ADA, more deaf job-seekers will surely venture into new territory. Good speech is no longer seen as the main criterion of a deaf person's success in the Hearing world. Talent is, along with responsibility, imagination, the ability to learn, and, most of all, a good attitude.

Nowadays, more options are available to deaf students. Thanks to Section 504 and the ADA, more fields are open— and opening—to deaf people. More community colleges offer Deaf Studies programs and provide good support services to ensure equal access to information, and equal participation in discussions and all class activities.

The picture is changing. While the old frustrations are still with us, and some challenges will always be with us, new opportunities are emerging on the horizon.

[1] For a biography of one such Deaf man, see Harvey Barash and Eva Barash Dicker, **Our Father Abe: The Story of a Deaf Shoe Repairman** (Madison, Wisc.: Abar Press, 1991).

[2] Arden Neisser, **The Other Side of Silence: Sign Language and the Deaf Community in America** (New York: Knopf, 1983), p. 126.

▲ ▲ ▲

NTID and the "techie" option

Higher education for deaf people became a reality in 1864, when President Abraham Lincoln signed the charter for what is now Gallaudet University. Gallaudet was, and still is, the only 4-year liberal-arts college for deaf people in the world.

While many hearing people know about Gallaudet (which seems to capture the lion's share of publicity), not too many are aware of the existence of the National Technical Institute for the Deaf (NTID), which is one of 8 colleges of Rochester Institute of Technology. NTID was founded specifically to address the problem of deaf people's under-employment in skilled technical trades. Such a college was originally proposed by Peter N. Peterson, a deaf teacher at Minnesota School for the Deaf, in 1930. P.L. 89-36, the law creating NTID, was signed by President Lyndon B. Johnson in 1965, and just in the nick of time, too. The first students were admitted in 1968. A nationwide rubella (German measles) epidemic during the mid-1960s resulted in an unusually large number of deaf and multiply-handicapped babies. By the time these children of the "rubella bulge" were ready to enter college in the summer of 1984, NTID was prepared for them.

NTID attracts deaf students from across the nation, and accepts Canadian and foreign students. The average deaf student population during the academic year is between 1,000 and 1,100. They come from residential schools, oral schools, day programs, and mainstreamed public schools. In short, a wide diversity of backgrounds.

Rochester, New York, is universally known as the home of Kodak. It's also the original home base of Bausch & Lomb (the giant optical company), IBM, and Xerox, which still maintain a presence there. NTID's host institution, RIT, maintains close ties with corporations like these. Largely because of

NTID, Rochester also boasts the largest per-capita deaf population of any city in the U.S.

Students have a wide array of majors and several programs to choose from, and NTID boasts that 95% of its graduates find appropriate employment. Many of the careers are in non-traditional, "bankable" fields. Majors in the Associate Degree Technical Programs are: Accounting Technology, Administrative Support Technology, Applied Computer Technology, Art & Computer Design, Automation Technologies, Business Technology, Computer Aided Drafting Technology, Computer Integrated Machining Technology, Digital Imaging & Publishing Technology, Laboratory Science Technology, and Ophthalmic Optical Finishing Technology (making eyeglasses). NTID students can also cross-register into RIT's other 7 colleges, taking advantages of the available support services (interpreters, notetakers, and tutors).

No institution is perfect. The concept of full access and the availability of support services for cross-registered NTID/ RIT students has been rather too often more of an ideal than a reality, but it can justly be said that NTID has opened up many new careers for deaf students and has, in its own way, helped combat stereotyping and negative beliefs. Students are reminded that upon graduation they may conceivably become the first deaf person hired by their company, and that their employers may well judge all deaf people by their behavior. It's a burden, yes, but also an opportunity to break new ground—and to excel.

NTID isn't the only "techie" option, of course. With the phenomenal growth of the Internet and advances in technology, more deaf students are choosing technology-related careers—information and imaging science, for example. The emphasis in career preparation at schools and programs for deaf students has been changing to reflect this. Today, being "smart-deaf" means becoming computer-literate and comfortable with a multiplicity of communication modes and media.

Chapter 79

Why is employment for deaf people limited?

ctually, it's not. Or it shouldn't be. Ever since the passage of the Americans with Disabilities Act of 1990, employers are required to make "reasonable accommodations" for deaf workers. (Small companies are exempt, but larger ones aren't.) Ideally, this gives deaf jobseekers an equal shake. In real life, the situation's a bit more complex.

With the ADA guaranteeing equal access to education and employment, this technically means that we are free to choose whatever field we can excel in (or try). The boundaries—the limitations—are still ambiguous. No, we cannot serve in the armed forces, and therefore cannot enjoy the benefits accorded to those who do. Yes, we can join the Coast Guard and work at NASA. Can we be astronauts? Is there a definite "yes" or "no"? The lawsuits of David Schultz and Stacy Adam versus the YMCA brings a troublesome issue out into the open: just which jobs require hearing, and which jobs don't? When is a hearing requirement sensible, and when is it discriminatory?

Obviously, it isn't practical for deaf persons to seek to become disk jockeys or air-traffic controllers. How about audiologists? If monitoring sounds can be done visually (as with an oscilloscope readout), would that field be off-limits to us, or negotiable?

Breaking into "unthinkable" fields is by no means a recent phenomenon, although the ADA has certainly given it impetus. The surprising thing about deaf people's choosing "untraditional" fields is that if you study history, you'll find that deaf people have been doing seemingly impossible things for centuries. Science, literature, business, invention, aviation, dance, music—deaf people have entered, struggled, and scored achievements there.

Without a doubt, the picture has improved markedly during the past few decades. Without a doubt, much more needs to be done before we can consider ourselves as having attained equal treatment.

We've already pointed out that certain blue-collar trades are traditionally favored by deaf workers—e.g., U.S. Postal Service, factories, printing. As we've also noted, teaching the deaf was once the most prestigious Deaf profession, until the oralists took over the schools and forced deaf people out. Only a mere fraction of current teachers of the deaf are themselves deaf. One could justly say that the demand for good teachers outstrips the supply. Teaching ASL to hearing high-school and college students is a promising field, but some Deaf teachers—i.e., qualified, skilled native-ASL users—have found that less-qualified hearing teachers have been given preferential treatment. Otherwise, it's still relatively rare for a deaf teacher, especially an ASL-Deaf one, to teach hearing students (with an interpreter on duty during the class session). Deaf persons with good speech skills have always been able to handle the lecture aspects. It's the dialogue part that causes difficulty. However, this is not necessarily an insurmountable obstacle. It depends on the classroom, the subject, the chemistry, and the ambiance.

What influences our choice of career? In the old days, it was relatively simple: you entered your family's trade—whether it be farming, printing, mining, or weaving. If you attended a school for the deaf, you'd be trained in a particular trade there. If you were Black and/or female, your choices were further limited. The establishment of Gallaudet University expanded those horizons considerably. But a number of deaf persons wanted a mainstream education. They took the risks, and some succeeded. Others weren't allowed the opportunity, so they chose alternate paths.

One obstacle to entering a profession is getting access to the education and training. Deaf people began entering "mainstream" colleges, universities, and graduate programs long before the days of professional interpreters. They were exceptional, but if they could persuade the admissions people to give them a chance, they were at least allowed to enroll. That was the first hurdle. They compensated for whatever they missed in class by making arrangements with classmates to copy their notes, scheduling appointments with their teachers, getting tutoring, and/or by doing extra reading. Passing the exams was the next hurdle. Of course, discrimination was—and is—rampant. But deaf people—a scattering, perhaps, but a significant scattering—have succeeded. If one can, so can others.

The worst barrier of all is (big surprise!) people's attitudes. Even if young deaf people are told that they "can do anything—except hear," there are many factors that determine what avenue they will choose, and which avenues they will reject. These factors reflect social realities. Gender bias, for example. Fewer girls than boys—deaf or hearing—choose science careers. Racial bias is another factor. And the fact that while hearing students, depending on luck, have access to "gifted" programs, there are virtually none for deaf students, because of our small numbers. The relative scarcity of deaf mentors is another negative factor. Communication problems are yet another.

Obviously, not all career possibilities are equally feasible. Everyone has talents. Everyone has limitations. Everyone has abilities. And everyone has disabilities. Nothing is accomplished without risk and sacrifice. We deserve the right to fail as well as to succeed. The opportunity is not always there; sometimes it's denied. The goal of the ADA is to equalize the odds. We have to decide what course to pursue, if it's worth the risk, and if we encounter a bad enough obstacle, push forward or take legal action. Or a detour.

Chapter 80

"Should my office clerks be given different, lesser duties because they are deaf?"

Two deaf clerks work for me. One was born deaf, we'll call her "D." The other had spoken and knew English before becoming deaf; we'll call her "L." "L" is obviously intelligent. She often intimidates "D." Perhaps it's "L's" culture, but she even "said" to me, "I demand . . ." "D" has her good qualities but is not "obviously intelligent." She forgets easily. For instance, we get batches of work in the unit. They are numbered with batch numbers. They are supposed to be logged onto a log each day. "D" often forgets to. We have work to control onto computer terminals; neither "D" nor "L" remembers all steps even though they have books and their own notes.

"D" does not understand English very well. I can't sign. "D" is the permanent clerk, "L" is the "helper." However, "L" interprets for "D" and often acts superior.

I know I must learn to sign. This doesn't happen overnight. I sometimes get very frustrated.

Should these clerks be given different, lesser duties because they are deaf? Does being deaf hinder them from performing daily tasks the same as the other clerks?

Any understanding you can give me will be greatly appreciated.

—Suzanne Shearin, Cumming, Georgia

o start with, let's do a bit of sweeping-up of some "sweeping generalizations." We can start with such nuggets of wisdom as 'Deaf workers can't handle abstract thinking as well as hearing can'; 'Deaf workers have difficulty remembering daily tasks'; 'Deaf workers just aren't as attentive to detail'; 'Deaf workers can't understand English', *etc., etc., etc.* That's bad logic and bad politics.

Is it a matter of intelligence? Education? Aptitude, perhaps? We *will* venture to say that deafness is most likely *not* to blame. This may not be much of a consolation, but it's probably the truth. Deafness has nothing to do with disorganization or forgetfulness.

Your two troublesome clerks, "D" and "L," could just as well be hearing. ("But of course," you may say, "if they were hearing, there'd *be* no problem!") Let's hypothesize. We all know of office clerks with perfect hearing who are unsuccessful at carrying out their tasks—poor performers, sloppy, careless, forgetful, mentally disorganized, bad attitudes—or any combination of these. I'm sure that plenty of supervisors have gotten two under-performers who work (and forget) together and set up a pecking order of sorts. Can we blame their incompetence on the fact that they're hearing?

Now, you suggest that "D" and "L" have some good qualities—enough to make you hesitate before booting them down the ladder. However, the current situation is hurting the company—work not logged in, directions forgotten, tasks not completed properly. What to do?

Attack the memory problem first. Evidently "D" and "L" have difficulty remembering/completing tasks, even with their own notes. Take a positive approach. Since Deaf people tend to have a strong visual sense, you might try making a few "constant reminders"—bold, colorful flow-charts or stand-up/flip-over desk cards, listing your workers' responsibilities ("Every day: Log on such-and-such"). This could be a stand-alone setup with punched holes, rings or spirals, and a stable easel or backing, a bit like the colorful dessert menus displayed on each table in some family restaurants. Office- and art-supply stores sell presentation binders whose covers convert to display easels. These might be ideal.

Once you have the reminders designed, with everything set down that you want them to remember, post them in full sight of their workstations. You could even make big laminated ones that they *have* to check off, task by task, using water-soluble or china markers. Or try small markerboards. See if that helps.

Anyone can spout off the standard rhetorical blather about intercultural sharing, cross-cultural communication, mutual respect, open-mindedness, etc., to the point of exhaustion, but the everyday reality is something else again—physically, mentally, and emotionally draining. The breakdowns in comprehension and the failures to "get across" are terribly frustrating for you. It must be frustrating for "D" too, as "she doesn't understand English very well." She's in roughly the same position as a native speaker of Chinese whose grasp of a second language, English, just isn't very advanced. And your grasp of her native language—well, it isn't there yet. Since "L" is "postlingually deafened," her frustrations are different. In a sense, she's "stuck" between you and "D."

We encourage you to start learning sign language as a step towards establishing a truly bilingual workplace. Seeing that you're making a genuine commitment to learning Sign will undoubtedly help "D" and "L" understand and cooperate. Your positive motivation will encourage them. If you can't learn Sign fast, use plenty of body language. Point with your finger. Be expressive. Be visual.

In response to your final question, we want to stress that deafness need not be a hindrance to clerical competence, a retentive memory, abstract thinking, quality performance, or excellence in general. What deaf people are fighting for is not preferential treatment, unearned breaks, or the soft life. Our goal is to be capable of functioning in the world, in whatever path we choose, doing our best at what we do best, judged by our true abilities, and standing on our own strengths. We expect no less of ourselves than the world expects of any professionals. That's our idea of *real* equality.

Chapter 81

Can deaf and hearing people work together, or is it better for deaf people to work only with each other?

ork is a pretty huge word. It encompasses so much. "Workplaces" include factories, warehouses, shops, kitchens, offices, schools, colleges, and homes. Many ASL-Deaf people prefer working with other ASL-Deaf people because they share a common language, a cultural background, and a feeling of community. Communication, culture, and community are three of our vital concerns. It's possible to enjoy all three in the workplace, but it's still relatively rare.

Many deaf people dislike working in Hearing environments and for hearing bosses for the simple reason that many of these bosses are not particularly aware of or sensitive to their communication needs, and the Hearing office or factory environment is not geared to those needs. One ASL-Deaf man we know (whom we'll call "Steve") works in a small but busy firm (we'll call it "Prism Graphics") where he is the sole deaf employee. Steve is valued for his technical expertise, but he's not treated with the respect he deserves. On occasions, the boss, "Fred," when angry or in a bad mood (or just coping with a hangover), pokes his head over Steve's shoulder while he's at his workstation and yells into his ear. No one we know, deaf or hearing, enjoys having an angry man scream into their ear. It's physically painful. Extremely so. And no, it doesn't help Steve hear. On other occasions, Fred makes jokes to the other workers about the stupidity of deaf people—right in front of Steve. Since Steve can speechread, he recognizes that he's being made the butt of their vulgar and mean-spirited jokes. Yet Fred doesn't realize that he's a bigot. He—supposedly—respects Steve. Steve hates his boss's attitude, but is stuck. He needs that paycheck.

This is but one example. The Americans with Disabilities Act has had varying impact on the nation's businesses—ranging from "none" to "slight" to "profound." Every boss is different; every office is different; every school, every campus, every work situation, to some extent, is unique.

It is certainly possible for deaf and hearing people to work together in harmony, with respect, full and open communication, and equal opportunity. We would imagine that these situations are also rare. Many Deaf people, we're sure, are in situations where they feel squelched, oppressed, isolated, exploited, or even discriminated against. The current spate of ADA lawsuits is just the tip of the employment iceberg. Many deaf people put up with imperfect situations because they feel that the risk of losing their jobs outweighs whatever benefits they might gain by taking legal action.

Gallaudet University has come under fire for not preparing its students to function in mainstreamed situations. The fact is that Deaf people enjoy working with others who can communicate freely and openly with them, without the obstacles, misunderstandings, and frustrations that often attend "intermodal" situations. There are still relatively few all-Deaf companies in the States. But these provide Deaf people with an alternative to mainstreaming. And there are a handful of companies that exemplify the ideals of the Deaf community. They work hard, have teamwork, a common goal, and, deliberately or not, increase the Deaf awareness of the general (and often uneducated) public. Simply by running a thriving business, even a small one, they present a powerful model: Deaf are just like everyone else—they can be smart and successful. Freed from communication conflicts and interactive discords, Deaf people can focus on their work—inventing, designing, developing, manufacturing, publishing, informing.

Is it *invariably* better for Deaf to work with Deaf? We don't think so. For one thing, we've learned that being "Deaf" is no guarantee of possessing a good attitude. You can be impeccably ASL-Deaf but irresponsible, immature, unprofessional, and, most significantly, have a bad attitude—a fundamental lack of respect for other ASL-Deaf people, or other persons in general.

Deaf employees who exhibit annoying tendencies such as snooping, who have bad tempers, who gossip, who cannot follow directions, who goof off when they're not being supervised, who make mistakes because they don't read well or carefully, but who expect to be forgiven because "after all, we're all Deaf together," can hardly be considered assets to a company. A Deaf boss would rather hire hearing employees who can be trusted to take their responsibilities seriously, focus on their work, and do it well.

Similarly, deaf bosses who have contempt for other deaf people and who show substandard communication/people/management skills only perpetuate the negative stereotype of "deaf" as "incompetent."

On the other hand, some impeccably Hearing people make excellent bosses and co-workers. Those who respect Deaf people and the Deaf community, who have good communication skills, who are committed to teamwork and partnership, are the rare jewels of the Hearing workplace. They should be cherished. (And multiplied.) By "communication skills," we mean a willingness to learn and listen—especially if their sign-language skills aren't terrific. After all, the ability to communicate fluently in sign is just one aspect of communication, and one facet of one's personality. If the other factors are favorable, Deaf people will happily accept imperfect signers if they're patient and have a positive attitude, especially if they're committed to improving their signing skills to facilitate on-the-job communication.

Given our choice of working with ASL-Deaf people with bad attitudes or hearing people with good attitudes, we'd choose the latter.

Chapter 82

If a Deaf worker gets laid off because s/he can't use the telephone, isn't that plain discrimination?

fter nearly a decade working at Prism Graphics, Steve has been laid off. Business has been slowing down, the boss explained, and the company is downsizing. Steve has been a dedicated, skilled, productive worker, but he's deaf. The major reason Steve is being laid off is his inability to use the telephone.

Prism Graphics has a main voice number and mini-switchboard (Centrex or multi-line) system. Clients use this number to call the company at all hours. Prism's small staff takes turns answering the phone during lunch hour. Steve couldn't do this; he had to skip his turn.

Couldn't Steve have used a TTY—with relay—when he was on lunch-hour duty? Ostensibly, this was possible, but in practice, it was utterly infeasible, especially with a Centrex system.

The possible & the probable: Most of the clients weren't familiar with the workings of the relay system, and even if they were, certainly didn't want to bother using it to contact Prism (assuming they knew that Steve would be on duty, which they didn't). It took too much time and involved too much bother. Calls from clients are often of a technical nature, with a lot of printer's jargon being exchanged. With a relay call, there is the omnipresent probability of misunderstandings creeping in: garbled phrases, missed or misconstrued words, erroneous transmission of numbers, scrambled data, *etcetera*. Such misunderstandings may be harmless or a minor annoyance in an informal chat, but dangerous in a technical conversation between client and company.

The main barrier, though, was technological. There is, at present, no *automatic* way to hook up a voice caller and TTY callee with a relay service.

"Forgetting": Steve brought a TTY to work and hooked it up to a modem line so he could communicate with a few deaf friends and colleagues. Calling them was easy. But whenever one of Steve's deaf friends contacted him at work, and Steve didn't answer the TTY (if he was in the washroom, darkroom, or anywhere out of eyeshot of the flasher), they had to call again, going through Prism's main phone number, via relay, and leave a message for him, asking him to watch out for the light or to call back. And whichever staffer answered the phone tended to have a remarkably casual attitude about giving Steve the message. More often than not, they didn't bother passing the message along. They "forgot."

The wonderful world of telephony: Steve's problems with the telephone didn't end with his layoff. When he was applying for unemployment insurance, he ran into another frustrating telecommunications situation.

The local unemployment office, operated by the State Department of Labor, utilizes a new toll-free "Tel-Claims" system—a maze of recorded messages instructing callers to press a variety of buttons to proceed through various categories, like a telephonic flow chart directed by robots.

After being laid off, Steve stopped by the unemployment office downtown, picked up an application, and asked if there was a TTY number. There wasn't. Instead, a staffer gave him a leaflet with information about calling the Telephone Claims Center to file a new UI claim.

The first relay call went fairly smoothly. He was connected with two staffers, assigned a Personal Identification Number, and answered a list of questions about his Social Security number, background, earnings, and work history. At the end of the transaction, he was told to call Tel-Claims on Sunday. And he received claim information in the mail.

He followed instructions, and used relay to contact Tel-

Claims—or, more accurately, he tried to get through. The relay agent kept redialing, getting a busy signal, and then got a series of recordings, but invariably didn't have enough time to press the specific button required to proceed to the next step. If you don't press one of the correct buttons promptly, your call is terminated—you get automatically disconnected. No matter how often she tried, the relay agent could not get through to Tel-Claims. After over a half-hour of this catch-me-if-you-can-while-you're-running-around-in-circles escapade, Steve gave up.

The next day, Monday morning, he drove back to the unemployment office, bringing the TTY printout with him. He showed it to a caseworker so she could see for herself that access was impossible. She appeared flustered, and asked, "Why don't you have your friend call for you?"

In the "Information for Claimants" booklet published by the State Department of Labor, is this dire warning: "You could lose up to 20 weeks of benefits if you allow someone else to call for you." When Steve called the caseworker's attention to this passage, she responded by pointing to a passage in the Tel-Claims leaflet: "Those having a language difficulty, or a speech or hearing impairment may request that a friend or relative assist in the telephone claim process." She then advised him, "Why don't you press #5 for general information? Don't press #1, press #5." She also gave him a fresh copy of the Tel-Claims leaflet.

Steve returned home and tried again. He says, "I thought I'd get a live person, but I didn't." When he pressed #5, he ended up getting another recording (a TTY user can recognize a voice recording by the pattern of flickering on the modem light), and got automatically disconnected again. When he put a call through via relay, he got the recording and cutoff again, but this time the relay agent was able to tell him what the message said: "We could not recognize your response, therefore your call is being terminated." Still hoping to reach a live person at that station, he tried again, and got another recording: "Press #1. If no response, press #0. Your call is being terminated." The relay agent told him, "There is no time to respond. I pressed #1 for 'yes' and it still disconnected." Steve thanked her and asked her to post her agent's code, time, and date, so he could use the printout as evidence.

He then returned to the unemployment office, and showed the caseworker the new "runaround" TTY printout. Genuinely puzzled, she asked him (in writing), "Why didn't your friend call for you?" Steve replied, "All my friends are deaf. Can they help?" The caseworker gulped, then made the necessary call for Steve. It took only a couple of minutes.

In short, this kind of system is simply not set up to accommodate deaf callers who use relay. What would have taken a hearing caller perhaps 15 minutes to accomplish took Steve around 6 hours—3 days, 3 round trips, including miles of driving, the bother of finding a parking space, and waiting.

What would solve the problem? Having a multi-lingual UI Website! It would be equally accessible to most claimants, except (possibly) blind ones, if they have access to a computer. Steve discussed his dilemma with the caseworker. "I asked her, 'Why not Internet?' She replied, 'The Federal budget doesn't have the money.' I told her, 'It costs you more to have these pamphlets printed in three, four, or five different languages [than it would to set up a Website]. If you had the information on Internet, it'd save a lot of paper, the cost of printing, *and* the phone bill!' She replied, 'Well . . . '"

Tele-screening: Nor was that the end of it. Since UI applicants are required to continue searching for work, Steve made several calls to other firms asking if there were openings. He called via relay, of course. And he was invariably told that there were no openings. None. No one wanted to talk to him.

Now, had Steve recruited a hearing friend to call the same firms directly, immediately after getting rebuffed, and had that friend been told, "Yes, we have an opening; come on over," *and* had Steve recorded these interchanges, then he might have a *bona fide* discrimination case.

Our wish: If TTY-compatible programming technology were available, this might have solved 85% of Steve's problems with "not being able to use the telephone." We would love to see the telephone companies offer a new option, "TTY standby calling," which would automatically connect a voice caller to the local relay service as soon as (but not until) the TTY callee picks up the receiver. This way, hearing callers who don't realize that the number they're calling is a TTY number would be automatically connected with relay. Relay "stands by" while the TTY rings and as soon as the deaf callee picks it up, shows up. TTY standby calling would encourage easier, unobtrusively relayed deaf/hearing telecommunications.

If all telephone companies installed programming that automatically recognized a TTY signal, this could be a reality. As it is, it's just a wish.

Were such a program available, Steve could have served his turn during lunch hour, communicating with clients without either party's needing to dial the relay service first. There might have still been problems with transmission and garbling (since a relay service would be involved), but if a client wanted to leave a simple message, "I'll come by at 3:30 to pick up the proofs," Steve would have gotten that message to the boss.

Real life: Laying off deaf workers because they can't use the telephone—isn't this situation grounds for an ADA job-discrimination lawsuit? In Steve's case, no. But had he worked at a large company, corporation, or institution, he might have had a good case. A deaf worker employed in a small company or facility that uses a Centrex system doesn't have much of a case. Prism Graphics, being a small firm, didn't make much effort to be ADA-compliant. The boss could claim that by letting Steve set up a TTY, he was making "reasonable accommodations," and to go further would constitute an "undue burden." That's not rank discrimination, it's real life.

Chapter 83

What are some of the problems deaf people have with telephones?

eaf workers have much the same problems with telephone access throughout the country (and, we imagine, the world). Some workplaces, of course, are more accessible and communications-friendly than others. Prism Graphics was by no means the worst.

Broadly speaking, there are four kinds of telephone systems in common use at workplaces:

1.) A Centrex system: the modern version of the old-fashioned switchboard. This system uses a "central" telephone number, a receptionist or operator, and extensions. Incoming calls are answered by the receptionist, who forwards important (or all) calls, and takes messages. Some receptionists will not divulge extensions, but will simply ask the caller which extension s/he wants. This is a convenient system for hearing staff, who may enjoy some degree of freedom from having to deal with bothersome calls coming into their offices at inconvenient times. But it is very difficult for deaf people to deal with a Centrex system, since it's technically incompatible with a TTY.

Actually, considering the variety of Centrex setups available in the United States, the ease of getting through depends on several factors—what kind of equipment is used, how advanced it is, if there's a computerized "backup" system, and (of course!) if the receptionist has a TTY. A modern multi-line system that accommodates intercoms, call conferencing, and pagers creates another obstacle: auto-answer TTYs can't be used with this kind of system.

How do deaf workers cope with Centrex/multi-line systems? A TTY user working at a facility with a Centrex can hook up a TTY, but can't use a "B-jack" connection, because Centrex systems use multi-lines. This means that s/he must pick up the telephone handset and place it on the TTY cradle each time a call comes in (or each time s/he wants to make an outgoing call). S/he can make outgoing calls by dialing the prefix #9, but cannot hook up an auto-answer TTY.

A few Centrex systems do have "direct" extension capability without the need for a receptionist's intervention. But each call still requires physical intervention by the TTY user.

If a deaf caller wants to contact a deaf employee in a Centrex-based facility, that's a problem, since relay can't connect two TTY users. The receptionist can probably recognize a TTY signal and (with luck) guess which person the call is for. This is an easy matter if there's one deaf person on staff, but trickier if there are more than one. Should there be more than one TTY user on staff, the receptionist runs the risk of connecting the caller with the wrong person.

Kate, one of Steve's deaf friends, works at a state-funded psychiatric hospital. Since the budget is tight, the telecommunications equipment used there is old, if not downright outdated. (The building is modern, the telephones aren't.) A receptionist handles all calls—no recordings, no computerized shortcuts. When Steve wants to call Kate, he dials the Centrex number directly (without going through relay), and hits the TTY's space bar repeatedly until the receptionist transfers him to Kate's station. If he's lucky, that is. Sometimes Steve gets transferred to the wrong one, since there are two other TTY users on staff.

Steve can use relay to call the hospital receptionist, but since Kate uses a TTY, Steve can't proceed with the call. How can he avoid having his call transferred to the wrong station? One solution would be to make a double call: first use relay to communicate with the receptionist: "I'm going to call Kate Anthony directly via TTY as soon as I hang up. Can you transfer the call to her?" He then exits relay, hangs up, and redials. Another possibility: dial Operator Services for the

Deaf, relay the call to the receptionist, then get connected to Kate, at which point the OSD operator exits the conversation. But this would cost extra. Steve would be paying person-to-person rates for the OSD call, even though it's a local call.

Deaf callers who know how to navigate the Centrex can save themselves a good measure of time and trouble. Occasionally, a facility has two numbers: one being the "public" number (answered by a live receptionist), and the other being the "private" (unpublicized) number for friends and family to use. This connects with a computerized setup utilizing a recording instructing the caller to press specific buttons or dial the extension. It's a shortcut if you already know the number you're after.

Laurie, another friend, is the sole deaf staffer at Rockbridge Associates, an engineering firm. Its Centrex setup is more sophisticated than the one in Kate's hospital. Callers who dial the "private" number get a computerized recorded message like this: "Thank you for calling Rockbridge Associates. If you are dialing from a Touch-Tone phone, please press #1 now. To listen to a directory, please press the star button now. To return to the main menu, press #1 at any time, or you may hold the line to speak to the receptionist. Please hold while I transfer you to the operator." (Piped-in music starts playing.) If the caller holds, the phone rings once, then the receptionist answers: "Good afternoon, Rockbridge Associates . . ."

These recordings include beeps signaling when to press a particular button. But exactly when is "now" if you can't hear the beeps? By using relay a couple of times and asking the relay agent how long the interval was between the recorded instructions and the beep, Steve was able to make a direct TTY call to Laurie at work, bypassing the receptionist. The relay agent told him that the beeps indicating when to press button #1 and dial the extension he wanted were 5 seconds apart. So he dialed the number himself, counted 5 seconds, pressed #1, counted 5 seconds more, then dialed Laurie's extension, #234. It worked every time.

This is a "secret" trick Steve has learned: asking a Centrex receptionist if the facility has another telephone number— that is, a "secondary" or "unpublicized" number in addition to the main one, or if there's a second phone extension that can be dialed directly. This information will not usually be volunteered by the receptionist; the caller needs to ask.

2.) Dedicated lines and direct links: This system uses numerous dedicated lines instead of extensions. Since a dedicated line (as opposed to a multi-line) can accommodate a TTY, deaf workers can link up with the phone system by hooking up a TTY with a B-jack. NTID/RIT has one of the best, most accessible telecommunications setups we've seen— a thousand (or more) dedicated lines! Deaf employees are provided with TTYs. It's exceptionally easy for deaf callers to get through. Steve can call just about anyone who works at NTID/RIT, directly, without bothering any receptionists. If he wants to call Dr. Wise, and she's not in her office, her TTY line rings 6 times, and the call is forwarded to a receptionist, who takes a message. Dr. Wise's TTY can be programmed to start an auto-answer tape after the fourth ring.

This is a fabulously expensive system, but it guarantees easy access for deaf callers and callees. We realize that it's probably more of an exception than the rule.

3.) Recordings: A fact of life for all of us, and an especially frustrating, barrier-ridden technological advance. We're thinking of the maddening situations we get when we use relay to dial an institutional, governmental, public-facility, or theater number, and get a recording instructing us to press #1, #2, #3, #4, or #5 when the beep sounds if we want to be routed to a specific department or category of information. They're frustrating because the relay agent always has to wait until the recording ends, then redial and go through the whole *shpiel* from the start, then leave our message. (They customarily tape recorded messages, then replay and transcribe them for the deaf caller.) Since TTY typing is slower than speech transmission, and these recordings (and the short interval between instructions and beeps) go fast, there's simply not enough time to get the message down on tape the first time around. And we can never really be sure if our message gets through safely. Many don't seem to.

Trying to get through to a live staffer through the barrier of a recording menu can be nigh-impossible, since typing takes much too long for the system. By the time the deaf caller understands which button needs to be pressed for which station, more than 5 seconds have elapsed; it's too late. The caller gets automatically disconnected.

5.) Tapping a modem line: Some employers have a true commitment to providing ADA-mandated access to their deaf workers. Others are indifferent or unwilling. Most bosses (especially those who use multi-line systems) balk at the prospect of setting up a dedicated phone line for a TTY-using employee. It means additional expense for them. Smaller businesses can probably cite the "undue hardship" clause of the ADA.

However, most companies in the U.S. have one or several extra dedicated lines set up for fax machines and Internet modems. Because these are dedicated lines, they're TTY-compatible. Most bosses will allow deaf workers to "tap" these lines for their TTYs, enabling them to "get around" the Centrex system—as long as they don't interfere with fax and Internet traffic. This is a low-cost, no-hassle solution to the telephone-access problem—albeit only a partial one.

Up and coming: Some of the options offered by local telephone companies, such as call forwarding, work with TTYs. Others, such as call waiting, (enhanced) 3-way calling, and voice mail, don't. Since they are all voice/auditory-based, they're impossible for deaf workers to use.

As E-mail, instant-message, videophones, and wireless systems become more widespread, our communication options continue to expand. But on the whole, despite the incursions of the ADA and other legislation, the situation is far from perfect or even tolerable. The ideal is not yet the reality.

Chapter 84

Do deaf people face discrimination, and how often?

—Elizabeth A. Brietkrietz, Cottage Grove, Minnesota

lmost as soon as the Americans with Disabilities Act became law, deaf people began filing lawsuits against various city, county, and state agencies, public facilities, *and* companies, charging them with discrimination. This doesn't mean that these deaf citizens were merely waiting for the first opportunity to stir up trouble, but that they now had the opportunity to press for the kind of changes they wanted—their rights.

Yes, deaf *and* hard-of-hearing people have long been discriminated against, and still are. Our history is one of injustice. Living in the modern era hasn't magically nullified this injustice. Discrimination takes blatant and subtle forms. Blatant discrimination is when a firm refuses to hire a deaf job-seeker "because we need someone who can use the telephone." Fifteen or twenty years ago this *might* have been a legitimate concern. Now, with around-the-clock relay service in all states, and the greater ease of making interstate and international calls, to say nothing of affordable TTYs, fax machines, modems, and the boom in Internet and real-time-message programs such as ICQ and AIM, it's no longer a good excuse. Wireless pagers and Internet relay are yet another great equalizing medium.

Subtle discrimination is more difficult to catch. ASL-Deaf people used to shun many prestigious jobs because employers didn't want to hire non-speaking deaf, claiming they "wouldn't fit in" or "wouldn't be comfortable there" or "might have too much difficulty communicating." Many highly-qualified Deaf people still get passed over in favor of non-disabled *or* disabled hearing persons. That way, the employer can comply with the ADA while avoiding the messy problem of hiring Deaf people.

Today, deaf college graduates are venturing into new and untraditional fields. This is encouraging, but the majority still face the traditional barriers of underemployment, lack of mobility, substandard salaries, and prejudice. Deaf people, especially those for whom ASL is their first language, are still hampered by the old English-literacy problem and lack of access to the same information their hearing peers take for granted. Technological advances like computer-assisted notetaking (CART), real-time captioning, Internet, and E-mail make it easier, but the literacy/communication barriers are still formidable. Many of our readers agree that deaf people do *not* get salaries commensurate with those of equally-qualified hearing workers.

We have gotten awfully mixed messages from our society. Let's consider how society responds to the needs of other sectors of the disability lobby. People who use wheelchairs are told, "We'll install ramps, curb cuts, and lowered drinking fountains, and we'll modify public-toilet cubicles and other facilities to make them accessible for you." Blind people are told, "We'll install Braille signage and other tactile aids for you to enable you to navigate buildings and facilities more comfortably." When it comes to our needs as deaf people, we get this kind of message: "Why don't you get yourselves fixed?"

Sign language has emerged from the Dark Age, when it was virtually outlawed in schools for the deaf and in public places, and is now shared and celebrated openly, but the old prejudice against it is still formidable. Despite encouraging attitudes on the part of some broad-minded professionals, the medical/audiological sector remains a bastion of ignorance and deeply-entrenched negative attitudes towards signing. We believe that the traditional medical attitude influences social attitudes towards accommodating our needs as

Deaf people. Instead of gaining respect for our preferred mode of communication, our language, we're told to "read lips" and get our defective hearing repaired or mitigated. Refusal to do so entails social and cultural isolation, or simply invisibility.

Still, we've come a long way from the days that Senator Tom Harkin recalled in his speech at The DEAF WAY in July 1989: his deaf brother Frank had been told he had *three* career choices: printer, baker, or cobbler. We haven't yet reached the point where we have Deaf mayors and congresspeople, or Deaf administrators of Hearing institutions. (It's enough of a challenge getting qualified deaf people to represent a deaf constituency.)

When parents and administrators boast about the success of their oral-deaf children and students, we feel that there's a subtle backlash at work. The message seems to be: Get your kid fitted with a cochlear implant, send her to an oral school or mainstream her, prevent her from "falling back on" sign language, and voilà!—instant success. As long as a deaf person acts "hearing," the Hearing world will accept her. Huh?

Education and employment aside, do we face discrimination in our everyday lives? We certainly do. When a popular public lecture series neglects to arrange for an interpreter, offering feeble excuses for not having one. When we can't find captioned videos or cable programming. When multi-billion-dollar corporations refuse to spend a few thousand bucks to advertise in Deaf publications or closed-caption their commercials. When community services are inaccessible to us. When we explain to a store clerk, "I'm deaf. Could you please write that down for me?" and the clerk walks away. When we can't get through to a business via relay, because the staffer who answers the phone hangs up before we can even say hello. Whenever deaf children, expressing their ambitions, are told, "You can't do that, you're deaf!" And so on.

Chapter 85

I've noticed that successful deaf persons are always put down by other deaf people, by means of lack of support and gossip—back-stabbing, name-calling, nasty rumors. Can't deaf people appreciate successful achievers who benefit their community?

he operative word here is "jealousy." Deaf culture embodies a "closed group"—small in numbers, linguistically unique, and mindful of their differences. Deaf people have traditionally tended to band together; thus the Deaf club, which has proven not just a vital social institution and positive means of sharing information and experiences and garnering support ("networking"), but less admirably, a hotbed of gossip, destructive rumor-mongering, and character assassination. Despite recent incursions from home-centered TVs and VCRs, the Deaf club is still a mainstay of the Deaf community. So is gossip. While the influence of the Deaf club seems to be steadily waning, gossip shows no signs of abating. Indeed, the Internet brought a new form of cyber-pollution: "flaming," e.g., sending the chosen victim insulting, anonymous E-mails—the most cowardly form of attack.

Oppressed in blatant and subtle ways from a very early age, Deaf people have traditionally reacted by huddling into something like solidarity: "Let's endure this together; are we all here?" This group loyalty has in turn fostered a rigid conformist mentality. (It is more prevalent in some schools, the ones that foster gossipy cliques instead of encouraging leadership.) If I'm oppressed by the Hearing culture, and you're oppressed, we can help each other out, but if you do something to rock the boat or break loose from the group, even if it will ultimately benefit me, you've disrupted the order of things and behaved disloyally to your Deaf culture. I feel threatened by your success, and I'm jealous.

The situation is analogous to that of black students in inner-city high schools who are serious about their schoolwork and trying to excel in academics—the kind of young I-really-want-to-go-to-college achievers everybody wants to encourage. Everybody? What kind of peer pressure are *they* experiencing? How much support do they get from the others? In the early '90s, we saw a *World News Tonight* segment on the plight of these students, who complained about being verbally and physically harassed—even beaten up—by other black students because they were seen as "nerds" or "trying to act white." They were under tremendous pressure to be part of the gang, and when they refused, the gangies vented their wrath on them. It sounded eerily familiar.

Many Deaf people don't understand what "dreams" and "ambitions" are. They are schooled in lowered expectations almost from the start. (That is undoubtedly one reason why some parents of deaf children prefer the idea of mainstreaming, and not without reason—many residential schools for the deaf don't offer the same quality of academic challenge as public schools.) They have been conditioned to take the least challenging path: seek out a factory job, buy a house and car, and settle down, "just like everyone else." That's what's acceptable. Those who cherish a different dream—taking risks, moving into non-traditional (Hearing) professions, rejecting the club mentality—may find themselves becoming targets for the most vicious imaginable brand of gossip.

What starts as a cultural issue shades into a moral one. Gossip says plenty—about the jealousy, bitterness, and weak characters of those who spread it. Well-adjusted, happy, mature individuals do not feel the need to project their own inadequacies onto others.

Still, one can participate in slander without even realizing the moral dimensions. Ray Luczak's ASL play, **Whispers of a Savage Sort**, was first staged at the New American Deaf Play Creators Festival in Fall 1996, at NTID's Panara Theater. This stark drama was given an appropriately stark, propless staging, with strong performances by Deaf stars and students. Clever use of lighting evoked the various settings: a bowling alley, a bank, a park bench, a couple's bedroom.

Whispers focuses on the destructive effects of gossip in the Deaf community. The willing participants consider it harmless recreation: "We don't gossip. We share *news*." Ironically, several of the Deaf performers *and* members of the audience disliked the script and felt threatened by the play, because it tore open the covers and spilled out one of the community's dirtiest, darkest secrets.

The Deaf community is like a small town where everybody knows each other. Once a person acquires a bad reputation, rightly or wrongly, s/he is apt to be gossiped about, and this kind of character-smearing can have terrible repercussions. Innocent people get hurt, and badly, too. The sheer viciousness of Deaf-against-Deaf hostility has to be experienced to be believed.

Why is this a Deaf problem? If a hearing person becomes the target of slander, s/he can move to another city and make a fresh start. But even if a Deaf person moves to a new city, s/he's still in the Deaf community. In a sense, s/he's stuck. As long as s/he remains in that community, there's no escape. As I (MSM) am fond of saying, "A Deaf person can't get a divorce from the Deaf community."

Crab theory is considered a prime "moral illness" in our community. Deaf leaders have even convened discussions and led workshops on what to do and how to combat it. It's a problem that successful Deaf achievers, the kind of people who are most likely to become targets of slander, have to cope with every day. No cure's in sight.

Chapter 86

At the airport, I was approached by a deaf person selling manual-alphabet cards. Should I buy one?

NO! NO!

Many people in the Deaf community know some-one who sells "ABC" cards for a living. That certainly doesn't stop us from feeling angry and resentful about it.

    A peddler appears to be uneducated, un-skilled, and unemployable, a pitiful victim of society. In truth, some of these peddlers are not uneducated, nor unskilled, nor unemployable. They're clever. By preying on the gullibility of hearing people, a successful peddler can earn $200—or more—a day! Card-peddlers like to frequent heavily trafficked places like airports, where a continuous stream of foreigners, newly arrived in the States, are getting their first glimpse of Ameri-can society—and the first deaf person they meet is, for all practical purposes, a beggar. Small wonder that Deaf people, the majority of whom are hard-working taxpayers, bitterly resent the stereotype that these peddlers perpetuate.[1]

    Deaf people have invested considerable time, energy, and passion into educating the Hearing public and attempting to undo the cumulative damage of centuries of negative, de-meaning, and offensive perceptions of the Deaf. It's an ongo-ing process. Along comes a peddler with a stack of cards, each one stating: "I AM A DEAF-MUTE." Is this how we want hearing people to see us? In their own humble way, such individuals threaten to undermine all that Deaf people have labored to achieve, and all for the sake of monetary gain (their own or the head honcho who collects kickbacks). Who knows how many thousands of hearing folks without any prior knowledge of deafness have encountered these peddlers? Ambassadors of Deaf culture, indeed! Imagine the fear that strikes the heart of a mother or father whose child has just been diagnosed as deaf and who recalls encountering a peddler: Is my daughter or son going to become one of *them*?

There is a difference between voluntarily buying a trinket from a peddler at a sidewalk table or cart, and being psychologically pressured into "paying any price you wish" for a fuzzy ABC chart by someone who comes up to you in a shop or café. At least the stereotypical blind man selling pencils for 5¢ apiece at the street corner is offering something useful for the money.[2] We've noticed that none of these kind-hearted folks who bought ABC cards ever bothered to use them. (If they did, we'd have a legion of hearing people who could fingerspell!) ABC cards aren't a legitimate product like pencils or pot-holders. They're a gimmick. Selling them is a psychological con game. Hearing people who really want to learn the manual alphabet and to communicate with Deaf people shouldn't have to pay through the nose for it.[3]

In buying an ABC card, hearing people feel they're doing a good turn by helping a less fortunate person. One peddler's solicitation card (attached to a keychain) reads: "$1.00 contribution will be appreciated," implying that their money is going towards a non-profit cause. It isn't. The money they give peddlers is money that could be, but isn't, used for a really positive cause.

If you truly want to "help deaf people," there are many good and enjoyable ways to do it—e.g., buying a ticket to a National Theatre of the Deaf performance, a beautifully handcrafted item made by an NTID student, a calendar or box of holiday cards designed by students from the nearest school for the deaf. You can show your support of Deaf people by patronizing Deaf businesses and school/organization fundraisers. Purchase items from campus bookstores or giftshops. Buy books by Deaf authors and works of art by Deaf artists—for yourself and to give as gifts.

Just in case you need another reason not to shell out, we'd like to note that a good number of these "deaf" peddlers aren't even deaf. They're hearing persons faking deafness.

There's one thing that these peddlers can't seem to handle. When approaching a potential "soft touch" who asks them sternly in fluent ASL, "Why are you doing this?", the only thing they can do is mutter "Oh, sorry!" and make a quick escape.

Not all members of the Deaf community despise peddlers. Some feel that card-peddling should be tolerated, as it's part of our culture. It may not be the most prestigious way to make a living, they feel, but peddlers shouldn't be vilified. They are certainly accepted in the Deaf-club milieu. (A few even pay taxes on their earnings.) Some Deaf people resent them for "giving deaf people a bad name." But others admire them for wreaking revenge on the Hearies who exploit Deaf people. The bosses who operate peddling rings may exploit other Deaf people, but the peddlers themselves target hearing strangers exclusively. In other words: "You cheat ours, so we're gonna cheat yours." Unfortunately for this logic, the *real* exploiters and oppressors aren't the ones who get defrauded by the peddlers.

---

[1] See **Deaf Heritage,** pp. 255-259, for a historical survey of peddling that includes the poignant "Profile of a Deaf Peddler." There was an upsurge in deaf peddlers after World War II, as deaf factory workers were replaced *en masse* by returning war veterans. Deaf organizations tried to combat the peddling "epidemic" as forcefully they could.

[2] Peddlers don't necessarily limit themselves to ABC cards. They can push small items like Band-Aids, combs, or keychains—all in return for a "suggested contribution" which is much more than the items are worth. The cute little "greenback" keychain we saw, for example, was selling for a "suggested contribution" of $1.00. Not a bad profit for an item which cost the peddler perhaps 10¢.

[3] For example, NTID publishes an attractive brochure, "Let's Communicate: Basic Signs & Tips for Communicating with Deaf People," which contains clear illustrations of the manual alphabet, the numbers 1-10, and an assortment of basic signs. It's free for the asking.

The plight of the Deaf Mexicans

Their plight made front-page news and received prime-time coverage throughout the nation. A group of 51 Mexicans, all deaf, had been held in bondage by a deaf Mexican family, the Paolettis, in Queens. The "slaves" were forced to peddle trinkets—flag pins and keychains with miniature baseballs and bats, thousand-dollar bills, and tiny screwdrivers—on the streets and subways of New York. They lived (so to speak) in two bunkbed-crammed apartments. Each night, they packed their backpacks with trinkets and keychains, each one tagged with a slip requesting $1.00 and (falsely) stating that they were earning their livings selling them.

They were forced to start work early each morning, and were told not to come back until they had earned their quota of $100 a day. If they didn't meet that quota, they were beaten or tortured with a stun gun. If they came back too late, they were locked out for the night. They were treated brutally by their "masters" and their "assistants."

But the people of New York, so hard-bitten and supposedly unsympathetic to peddlers and "illegals," were notably kind. Some customers gave them $2 instead of the single dollar the tags requested. (The peddlers could pocket the extra dollar, but that was risky—they were sometimes searched and punished if secreted money was found.) The owner of a coffee shop gave them free bagels and coffee each morning.

They walked through the subway cars as they rumbled forward, shyly laying down a trinket next to each rider, avoiding eye contact with them, then coming back to collect the money and unsold trinkets.

And because New Yorkers had a soft spot, they brought back a lot of money—all of which went into the Paoletti family's cashboxes, and ultimately into their bank account in Mexico City.

The New Yorkers who bought their keychains and trinkets,

when interviewed, expressed their outrage at learning about their true circumstances as slaves in a bondage ring, and said that they deserved the chance to make an honest living. They were working hard, pacing the subway trains and streets all day, risking abuse and muggings. Had they been allowed to keep the profits they had made, New Yorkers wouldn't have complained. But, we wonder, had they known that the money was going to the Paoletti family, would they have refused to buy the trinkets?

Each trinket sold brought the peddlers one dollar nearer to meeting their daily $100 quota, and that meant that they could return to their "quarters" sooner. But it didn't guarantee them a decent meal or a comfortable night. The Paolettis kept them living in fear. Only when they became desperate enough to do something did they go to the local police station and tell their stories. The news broke on July 19, 1997.

During the exposé, some grim facts emerged about life for deaf Mexicans. They receive a sporadic, substandard education. They have few prospects for higher education or jobs. If they're lucky, they can scrape out a living in a menial trade. Or earn a bit of money by peddling trinkets on the streets. They were eager to come to the United States, illegally, because they were promised good salaries and easy work by the Paolettis and their agents, who recruited and smuggled them in. Organized bondage rings were broken up in several other cities. Most involved deaf Mexicans.

The City of New York, represented by Mayor Rudy Giuliani, responded with compassion and generosity. After the trial of the Paolettis and their cohorts, those who wanted to stay were given temporary visas and the promise of full citizenship; those who wanted to return were flown back to Mexico. Several of them expressed fear of retaliation; others had grown to like life in the city. But all were unanimous in one respect: none of them wanted to peddle again, ever.

Chapter 87

Do advertisers recognize a "Deaf market"?

rom our own experience as consumers and being in the media business, we'd have to give a *very* mixed answer to this question. There is no denying that Deaf people, as consumers, have been making substantial gains, especially since the passage of the Television Decoder Circuitry Act, the ADA, and the legislation pertaining to telecommunications and emergency access. On the other hand, we still have a major visibility problem. Too many advertisers just don't *see* us.

What is important in the advertising world is numbers. Numbers are powerful. Numbers get respect. Numbers cannot be ignored. Do Deaf consumers have numbers? In some respects, they certainly do. Consider the oft-brandished statistics about there being some 22 (or 25, or 28) million persons in the United States with some degree of hearing loss, ranging from hard-of-hearing to profoundly deaf. Is this an important market? Yes—if you're selling TTYs, assistive-listening devices, and hearing aids, you pay attention. But suppose you're selling cola, fast food, running shoes, polo shirts, perfume, cars, air conditioners, or insurance? Do you recognize this market?

One of the major media victories won by ASL-Deaf people was breaking into TV commercials. Audree Norton, a founding member of the NTD, was the first Deaf performer to be featured on a TV commercial. This paved the way towards more prime-time, national, mainstream commercials exploiting the beauty and novelty value of ASL. Among our favorites: Marlee Matlin's Whiskas spot, Bell Atlantic's E-911 spot with children from California School for the Deaf, and Jackie Roth's spot for Bayer Aspirin. Care was taken in casting and in getting the ASL just right, and the results were delightful—and effective. All received enthusiastic responses.

Then came the monkey wrench in the machinery. Saturn Corporation was doing an admirable series of "real-people" TV spots and print-media ads (no professional performers need apply) and recruited an ASL-Deaf teacher—or so they thought. Holly Daniel's TV spot was hailed as a breakthrough . . . until the word got out that Daniel was a hearing woman impersonating a Deaf signer. And her signing on the commercial was farcical.

What worried us was the possible "fallout" effect—that Saturn would not be willing to make a replacement spot with a genuine ASL-Deaf Saturn-owner (and we knew that there are plenty of them out there), and that other companies, mindful of the bad publicity and embarrassment Saturn experienced, would be reluctant to develop their own ASL-Deaf ads. Since the "Holly Daniel hoax" broke, we have seen no new ASL commercials or ads. (Saturn ditched the "real-people" series in favor of a campaign focusing on the technical aspects of the car, not on the owners, so the issue quickly became moot. We'll never know . . .)

Another thing we're concerned about is the willingness of advertisers to reach out to the Deaf market. Do they make a commitment with rhetoric, or with their advertising dollars? We have seen that many companies are willing to set up TTY lines or hire a few deaf people, but a lot of them don't go further than that—if even that far. Some companies, like the telecommunication giants, often co-sponsor Deaf-oriented events. That's good PR and shows community involvement. Some companies simply issue press releases about their "newly-accessible" services and TTY lines, and that's good PR, too. But do they advertise to ASL-Deaf people just as they do to hearing people? Ah, there's the catch.

Getting back to numbers: The advertising world recognizes the burgeoning Hispanic-American market. Several large companies have ad agencies specializing in this market, in addition to their English-speaking target market. The important African-American (Black) market is also recognized. The Asian-American market is beginning to gain recognition. And the teen market is big bucks. But what about the ASL-Deaf market? Do you ever see ads for Coca-Cola, Pepsi, Smirnoff or Absolut vodka, Velveeta cheese, Hershey's chocolate, Levis, Nike, Macintosh computers, microwave popcorn, automobiles (we're not picky), or perfume (any brand will do) in *any* Deaf-oriented publication? We don't mean little text boxes with TTY numbers in them, we mean *real* full-page or double-page or multi-page ads, the kind you see in **People Weekly**. Have you ever seen a Coca-Cola commercial in ASL?

What does it take to convince the business world that Deaf people make a viable market? That it's worthwhile for companies to target them? That they deserve a modicum of respect as a cultural/linguistic group? As consumers? As people? That those fancy commercials could be closed-captioned for a tiny fraction of what it costs to produce them and buy air time? The DPN uprising propelled our concerns onto the front pages and prime-time slots for a week or so. Memory fades quickly, though. Within a couple of months, it seems, the mass media went right back to using terms like "deaf mute" and "hearing impaired." (Compare the terminology used in the 1988 coverage of DPN with that afforded the illegal deaf Mexican immigrants in 1997 and you'll see what we mean.)

It would be terrific if advertisers, with their multibillion-dollar budgets, recognized that Deaf consumers are a desirable part of their demographics. And that Deaf people buy a lot of things besides TTYs and ILY keychains. But we haven't yet reached that point. When corporations put their money where their PR rhetoric is, then we'll *really* have something to celebrate.

Chapter 88

Aren't deaf people complaining too much about being mistreated by salesclerks? After all, hearing customers get treated rudely, too!

he case of Mike Gannon, the deaf man who was viciously beaten by a Radio Shack salesclerk in Virginia after making a credit-card purchase of hearing-aid batteries, may be an extreme example, but it underscores the lack of communication awareness (even in stores that supposedly serve deaf and hard-of-hearing customers) and the importance of sensitivity and decency.

Malls, supermarkets, stores, shopping arcades, ticket counters, and sidewalk bazaars are often the main public interface between us (deaf people) and them (hearing people). Every time deaf people enter a store, they're entering a battleground; they're taking risks. They may encounter salesclerks who know nothing about communicating with deaf people, and who may not even have the patience (or decency) to look them straight in the face while speaking to them. And, since a number of deaf people have clear speech and may "pass" as hearing, the salesclerks may assume that they *are* hearing. So requests to repeat a question, or statements to the effect of "I didn't understand you; I'm deaf," can get spontaneous reactions of snickers, sneers, or rude retorts such as "Oh, you're deaf, huh?" The underlying thought is: *Yeah, sure you are. You trying to fool me?* We have found ways to deal with insulting remarks—by making snappy comebacks, for one. Others say nothing, leave the store, or take various after-the-fact actions: writing a complaint to the owner/manager, and, in extreme cases, filing a lawsuit (as Terrylene Sacchetti did against Burger King after being refused drive-through service).

All of us have shopping horror stories, just as we have restaurant horror stories. There is simply no way to predict whether the clerk or ticket agent we're dealing with is going to be a good one or a bad one.

To be perfectly fair, we acknowledge that a number of salesclerks are thoroughly decent persons who approach their job with a good attitude, try to serve the customers, and show respect for deaf and disabled people. They may not be "educated," but they possess a modicum of common sense. (Or, we should say, *uncommon* sense.) These are the clerks who keep us coming back to the stores. Unfortunately, they are all too rare.

Mike Gannon's lawsuit against Radio Shack emphasizes the importance of corporate policy. We saw for ourselves how a burger joint near Gallaudet University kept a 3" x 5" pad of paper and a pen on the counter so deaf customers could jot down their orders and thereby avoid confusion and its consequences: delays, disputes, and traffic snarls. This doesn't apply to drive-through orders, which have traditionally been placed through a sound-based electronic hookup. Customers (i.e., deaf people) who wanted to place orders but who tried to circumvent the inaccessible microphone system didn't get served. One Gallaudet student was so dissatisfied with the treatment he received in the drive-through line that he sued McDonald's and ultimately won a modest financial settlement and a political victory for other deaf customers. McDonald's agreed to make its drive-through service more deaf-accessible.

We agree that it's good for clerks, servers, waiters, ticket agents, cabbies, tellers, etc., to know fingerspelling and some basic signs, and judging from the booming popularity of sign-language classes and our own encounters, we are pleased to see them, have always expressed our appreciation for their efforts, and wish to encourage them to keep practicing. It's good to see a hearing person communicating with us in our language (or trying hard to communicate as best they can). But we are pragmatic enough to realize that the majority of clerks, servers, cabbies, tellers, etc., are not sign-literate. Although certain employers (e.g., USPS) have set up sign-language classes in one or two cities, these are strictly voluntary, and involve a tiny number of total employees. We don't believe that hearing merchants and clerks should be *forced* to learn sign language to accommodate deaf customers. It should be a matter of free choice, motivated by enthusiasm—a desire to bridge the communication gap. A pad-and-pen setup will do nicely for everyday transactions. If a store can afford to set up a ramp, it can spend a couple of dollars for a pack of memo pads and some pencils or pens, to be kept handy at all times. The store can have its pencils or pens imprinted, so that when customers walk off with them, as customers will, the store can consider it a PR freebie. Since many stores already distribute promotional freebies like pens and memo pads, this can hardly be accounted an "undue burden!"

Sensitivity training would make things so much easier for us, and could be accomplished at little or no additional cost, but too many corporations treat deaf customers as invisible. They don't recognize the importance of clear, unimpeded communication. They just don't acknowledge our existence. They are simply not interested. (Until, that is, they get hit in their wallets.)

We are aware that the caliber of salesclerks seems to have declined precipitously over the past decades. We recall clerks in long-since-vanished department stores and small, friendly, locally-owned shops, the kind we knew by name and who knew us by name, and whose judgment we could rely on. They would give their honest opinion if they felt a garment didn't look good on us—even though it meant losing out on a sale and a possible commission. The growth of shopping centers and malls, which spelled doom to the old-fashioned department stores and small shops), brought a new impersonality into the experience of shopping. So we have also known many clerks—of the "modern" school—who stood by apathetically while we struggled or tried on items that looked absolutely dreadful. Training? Or attitude?

Here are a few experiences that come to my mind (LL):

> While looking for a replacement part for an iron, I asked the clerk in the appliance/repair shop to write down what he was saying, in my memo book. He did—that the store didn't carry that particular part. He then said something else, and, on being asked to write that down too, merely underlined what he had already written.
>
> I recall (all too vividly) a later encounter with a haughty bridal-store clerk who refused to help me with an outfit I was considering buying there. Recognizing a snub, I excused myself, walked out with all the dignity I could muster, and never returned.
>
> One of my worst encounters (circa 1970) was with a sneering, obnoxiously rude Long Island Railroad ticket clerk: "You didn't hear me, huh?" Nowadays, I'd be less likely to endure such treatment silently; I'd politely ask for his name and/or code number, and, if he refused to cooperate, I'd note the date, time, and his ticket-window number, and send a formal complaint to his supervisor.
>
> A similar experience occurred when I tried to get Amtrak information via relay (circa 1990). The communications assistant connected with a ticket agent who had a very bad telephone manner. When she requested the ticket agent's number (as a preliminary to making a formal complaint), the agent refused to give it and said, "I don't have the patience for this," and hung up without giving me the ticket information I needed. But I appreciated the way the CA stood up for my rights.

And here's one particularly shocking example that happened to me (MSM) in April 2002 :

> I ordered a quantity of imprinted T-shirts from a favorite local silkscreen studio that I had done business with in the past. When I placed a call via New York Relay to find out if the T-shirts were ready for pickup, my call was answered by an exceedingly ignorant receptionist named Margaret. After Margaret picked up the handset, the CA told her (in accordance with NYRS policy)

that she had a relay call. Margaret blurted out (apparently to a nearby staffer), "F--king relay call for the deaf! I hate them!" She was unaware that the CA was faithfully relaying her outrageous remark to me (since a CA is supposed to relay all such "background" remarks and "asides" to the caller). I played it cool, giving no indication that I knew what she'd just said, merely asking when I could pick up the T-shirts and being told they were ready. I casually asked—twice—to whom I was speaking, and Margaret finally gave me her first name before she hung up. I tore off the TTY printout of this conversation and brought it to the silkscreen company. The boss was out at the time, but a staffer (*not* Margaret) made a photocopy for him. This staffer read the transcript and was not at all pleased by this example of rude and unprofessional conduct. I, of course, was furious.

When the boss returned, he gave Margaret an official reprimand and recorded the incident in her personnel file. He also sent me a formal (and forceful) letter of apology. I was satisfied with his response.

We have the right to be treated with respect, no less than hearing customers do. If the respect is not forthcoming, we have the right to express our displeasure (in a tactful way), complain to the management, and (if it's warranted) to weigh our legal options. It's not something to take lightly. In our lawsuit-happy society, people go around threatening to sue (and do file lawsuits) for the most ridiculous reasons. But we recognize the seriousness of the situation. Indeed, our problem as a community of consumers isn't filing frivolous lawsuits, but in not complaining loudly enough, or high enough, or persistently enough, when a complaint is truly warranted.

Do customers (deaf *or* hearing) have to accept and endure rude treatment or snide comments from store employees? We say no, but we believe in exercising a bit of diplomacy before contacting our local ADA-compliance watchdogs. Education is needed everywhere, including the retail battlefield. It *is* possible to score a point in the battle without creating new enemies. And it *is* possible for both sides to win.

Chapter 89

What concerns, problems, or suggestions do deaf people have that are directly related to law enforcement?

—Deputy Julie Linder, Bakersfield, California

everal issues that concern us are: 911 access; being able to establish clear communication with police and other law-enforcement authorities when giving testimony as crime victims or eyewitnesses, or being questioned, detained, or arrested (and being provided with a sign-language interpreter if the occasion warrants); getting fair treatment by highway police and county prosecutors; confidentiality of TTY transcripts used as evidence; and equal access as participants in courtroom proceedings—whether as plaintiffs, defendants, witnesses, attorneys, or jury members. (Equal access means having qualified interpreters and a video-monitor/real-time-captioning setup.) We are also concerned about the isolation and mistreatment of deaf prison inmates, whether in jail or state or federal prisons. We are, in effect, hammering out the fine points of the Americans with Disabilities Act as we go along.

Deaf people are still being arrested and mistreated because police and other authorities don't believe them or don't recognize the importance of providing interpreters or other reasonable accommodations. That situation is improving, to some extent, anyway. But deaf and deaf-blind victims of mistreatment have some shocking stories to tell.

Most newspaper and TV stories have focused on deaf victims or deaf perpetrators of crimes. True, deaf people have been victimized far more often than they have committed crimes. And a few courageous deaf persons have chosen law-enforcement careers, although prejudice against deaf cops is still formidable.

These are some of our concerns, with some actual cases involving deaf persons on both sides of the law.

Fatal signs: Everyone knows the horror stories (unfortunately true) about deaf people shot by burglars or muggers because the perps didn't realize their victims were deaf. There have been several verified reports of gang violence against innocent Deaf people because the ASL signs used by the victims resembled handsigns used by rival gang members. (Gangs have appropriated signs and fingerspelling for their own purposes.) In 1995, for example, Latell Chaney, a deaf man in Minneapolis, was viciously attacked on a city bus by gang members. He survived, but lost an eye.

During the past few decades, a number of lawsuits involving deaf people have made headlines. **DEAF LIFE** has cited and reprinted several newspaper reports that underscore the complexities of the fair-access-to-communication issue and the urgent need for better police/Deaf-community relations.

Deaf criminals: Some deaf people who have committed crimes have been known to use their deafness to try to get their sentences reduced. In the 1990 Rewolinski murder case, a Deaf man convicted of first-degree murder argued that had sheriffs not confiscated a printout from a TTY call he made in the sheriffs' office shortly before he strangled his girlfriend, he would have been convicted of manslaughter (murder without premeditation). The TTY tape showed violent intent. Was it private or public property? Rewolinski's lawyers argued that it was private. Prosecutors argued that it was public. The state of Wisconsin made every attempt to accommodate him and give him a fair trial. He lost his bid to have his conviction reduced to the lesser charge of manslaughter.

Courtroom injustice: While some deaf persons have tried to get "special consideration," others—especially impoverished inner-city Blacks and Hispanics—have been victimized by police and court systems. In her autobiography, **A Loss for Words**, Lou Ann Walker, who worked as a courtroom interpreter in some harrowing situations, describes the tragic case of a young inner-city Black Deaf woman who killed her sister's abusive boyfriend in self-defense, and was given a harsh prison term for manslaughter. Had she been hearing, she might have been acquitted.

In other cases, deaf defendants have gone through their trials, uncomprehending, without the slightest notion of what was going on or being said. The celebrated case of Donald Lang, the languageless deaf man accused of murdering two prostitutes and represented by the brilliant deaf lawyer Lowell Myers, was an extreme manifestation of this.

In still other cases, as with Rewolinski's, every possible measure has been taken to guarantee Deaf defendants a fair trial: shifts of skilled interpreters, privacy screens so that the defendant can have confidential signed conversations with lawyers, and a real-time-captioning (CART) setup. These real-time systems have gained widespread acceptance in courtrooms, and are welcomed as an enhancement rather than a distraction.

Bondage rings: Deaf people have traditionally been vulnerable to exploitation, being cheated and robbed with impunity because of the communication barrier. That, of course, has been changing. The 1997 scandal involving bondage rings—the wholesale enslavement of dozens of deaf Mexicans by other deaf Mexicans—shows that law-enforcement agencies can act in a humane fashion towards the deaf victims while carrying out justice against the deaf perpetrators.

Doing time—with fair access? What happens when deaf people break the law and are justly convicted of a crime? For deaf prison inmates, there are often terrible frustrations of not having easy access to a TTY or interpreter. Prisoners have forfeited most of their rights as U.S. citizens, but the ADA applies to deaf inmates—or doesn't it? Prisons have been, as a rule, notoriously slow to grant deaf inmates equal telecommunications access or provide interpreters. Hearing inmates can often use pay phones in their cellblocks at any time, while deaf inmates have to put in requests for TTYs several days in advance—and don't always get them. They may or may not be given interpreters when they go before the parole board for a review. They may have access, or none, to life-skills classes and other valuable services offered to inmates. They may be subject to mistreatment or simply ignored. There is widespread sentiment in our society against "coddling criminals," but even state prisons have certain standards of humane treatment.

Are deaf inmates entitled to fair access to the same programs and services provided to hearing inmates? Most of us would agree that they are. Deaf inmates are currently scattered among hearing inmates in state and federal prisons. Should a separate "Deaf prison" be established to serve the particular needs of Deaf inmates? There is no consensus on this.

Shut up and quit fidgeting: Deaf people under arrest are sometimes mistreated because police and other authorities don't believe them or don't recognize the importance of providing interpreters. Consider a nightmare situation (Fall 1997) involving a young woman with Usher's Syndrome who had just moved to San Francisco and who unwittingly took an escalator out of a prestigious department store she had never visited before, while holding merchandise she hadn't yet paid for, which she was—so she thought—taking to a lower floor. To her surprise, she realized that the escalator was going out into the mall. Before she could find an escalator going back into the store, she was grabbed, arrested as a shoplifter, and taken, none too gently, to a police station for questioning. Her explanations were scoffed at, and an extremely bright, painful light was shone straight in her face while her mug shot was being taken. (This despite her protest that she had US and that the lights might permanently affect her already-limited vision.) She was kept in jail until late at night, and although she asked for assistance in summoning a taxi to get back home from an unfamiliar, dark, and dangerous section of the city, she was given none. Although the store dropped the charges against her, she still had a police record, lost out on at least one job offer because of it, and was considering suing the store and the city police for their mistreatment of her.

You want an interpreter? What's that? One of the biggest problems we face is not being able to secure an interpreter when we need one. The agencies that have the responsibility to safeguard the public haven't always been responsive. In 1992, an innocent Deaf man, James Kennard Thompson of Nashville, was arrested on an outstanding-rape warrant and jailed for a week before the sheriff's office realized they had the wrong guy. (They were looking for a criminal named James Edward Thompson.) Thompson brought a $1 million lawsuit against the city for not providing an interpreter in night court.

Deaf people have become more assertive about filing lawsuits. When Paul McComb of Bakersfield, California, a respected Deaf advocate, was injured in a run-in with the Kern County Sheriff's Department in February 1995, nobody who knew the McComb family believed the "official" Sheriff's Department story that Paul McComb punched and kicked the deputies. (Some of these Deaf Californians had had runins with impatient and insensitive deputies themselves.) The community was horrified to learn that McComb had been hurt and his family, even their dogs, had been pepper-sprayed. And why? The deputies wanted to question McComb's son, Leonard, who's hearing. McComb refused to cooperate unless an interpreter was present so he could understand what was being said. The police refused to bring in an interpreter, drew their guns, charged into the house, and beat McComb on the back of his legs with their batons. Because Leonard refused to cooperate with them, they arrested him, handcuffed and dragged him off while other officers pepper-sprayed Paul's wife, Lu Ellen, and their daughter Beth.

The deputies made conflicting claims that Paul McComb punched a sheriff's sergeant in the head as Leonard was being dragged away, so they wrestled him to the ground, hit him on the legs with their batons, and handcuffed him. He was booked for investigation of assault on a peace officer. The Sheriff's Commander told reporters that deputies were under no obligation to provide McComb with an interpreter because he was neither a witness, suspect, nor a victim of a crime. Instead, McComb "had an obligation to cooperate" with the deputies. McComb insisted that he had a right to know what was being said. The Deaf community agreed.

In its coverage, the **Bakersfield Californian** interviewed officers of the Sheriff's Department, publishing their allegations as though they were facts, but did not contact McComb to get his story.

The charges against him were soon dropped, but McComb, who worked as Outreach Coordinator for the Greater Los Angeles Council on Deafness in Kern County (B-GLAD), filed a multimillion-dollar lawsuit in Federal District Court against the Sheriff's Department, charging excessive force. A public rally, sponsored by GLAD, was held to demand an end to police insensitivity and mistreatment of deaf citizens.

Such suits underscore the urgent need for better police/Deaf-community relations. We've seen an upsurge in the number of lawsuits filed under the Americans with Disabilities Act and other civil-rights legislation against businesses, cities, and law-enforcement agencies, by deaf people who have been victimized or discriminated against. Some of these cases have set precedents. Despite the recent proliferation of frivolous lawsuits in our suit-happy society, we see this as a healthy trend. Deaf people are refusing to be intimidated. They are serving notice that mistreatment that might have been silently endured a few decades ago, for lack of recourse, will no longer be tolerated. Most Deaf citizens are law-abiding taxpayers. They are demanding respect as first-class citizens.

Bullies with badges: Trouble is, a lot of law-enforcement officials still haven't gotten the message. All deaf people, it seems, have their "cop horror stories": encounters with impatient, nasty, and brutal police officers, especially on highway patrols.

In Spring 1997, for example, "Alan," a Deaf man who had recently moved to Indianapolis (which boasts a large Deaf community and a number of police with signing skills) and was still finding his way around, was driving home late one night from a bowling tourney with a friend and inadvertently made a wrong turn in a dark tunnel. The "NO LEFT TURN" sign that was supposed to warn him wasn't clearly visible. He was treated to a terrifying outburst of anger (and a $95 ticket) by the traffic policeman who stopped him. Although Alan immediately rolled down his window, and gestured that he was deaf, and that he wanted to get his pad and pen, he was afraid to budge. The police officer behaved in a threatening manner, shouted at the Deaf men, seemed infuriated by Alan's attempts to explain to him that he was deaf, ignored his questions, and refused to write down the reason why he had stopped them. Alan was afraid to reach into the glove compartment for the pad and pen he kept there, since he suspected that the furious cop would interpret the gesture as reaching for a gun, and shoot him without further ado.

Finally, Alan was allowed him to get the pad and paper. The officer snatched them roughly away, and scribbled illegibly on the pad. Alan handed his license to the officer, who returned to his police car. Fifteen or twenty minutes later, he came back, scrawled a terse explanation about the "NO LEFT TURN" sign, then rudely thrust the pad, pen, license, and a $95 traffic-violation ticket at Alan. He asked the officer *where* the sign was, but the officer walked off without saying another word, got into his car, and drove off. The flabbergasted Alan drove around until he located the sign, which was too dark to read. He formally protested the fine and the way this officer had treated him.

This was *not*, alas, an isolated incident. Alan did everything he could to cooperate, but wasn't shown the slightest bit of civility. Other drivers have had bad run-ins with rude or brutal traffic cops who denied them the simplest courtesy of an explanation.

It should be stressed that Deaf people, in general, behave respectfully towards police officers. If they're stopped and pulled over by a traffic cop, the first thing they do is to let the cop know they're deaf, hand over their license, and try to communicate. Or to find out why they've been stopped. Sometimes they haven't a clue. At the very least, they deserve the basic courtesy of communication—an explanation of why they've been stopped, an answer if they have a question.

When Joseph Kolash, Outreach Manager of the New York Relay Center, was stopped in Green Island, New York, in August 1994, he tried to communicate with the officer, explain that he was deaf, and find out just why he was stopped. He was given no explanation. Instead, he was screamed at and treated as though he were drunk. After he handed the officer his license and stepped out of his car, a breath-analyzer tube was pushed into his face. Kolash wrote: "You are supposed to have communication with me first, before I do anything. You have violated my right to communicate." The officers persisted, giving him one handwritten note ("Blow in tube"), and he submitted to the test, which showed that no alcohol was in his system.

The officers involved denied that they had been rude or refused to communicate. Kolash contended that the town was not complying with the ADA. He attempted to meet several times with the mayor, but was rebuffed. The mayor insisted that Green Island was already complying with the ADA.

One of the main problems involving Deaf people's relations with law enforcement is that a number of law-enforcement officers are simply brutes. Attorney Lowell Myers told us, "Brutal and sadistic people are attracted to police work like flies are attracted to honey." And all the sensitivity training and Basic Survival Sign courses are not going to root this out! If the problem is one of cultural sensitivity, that can be addressed and remedied fairly easily. It only takes a bit of patience and sensitivity to avert miscommunication. But if the problem is inherent cruelty on the part of law-enforcement personnel, the only thing Deaf victims can do is fight back through the court system.

Close call: Not all ADA lawsuits involving police mistreatment of deaf citizens make it to court. On January 3, 1997, Jason Kaldani, a Deaf driver, was stopped for speeding by California Highway Patrol Officer Richard Gibson. Kaldani was dissatisfied by the "unprofessional" way Gibson behaved and mistreated him (conducting a search of his vehicle without his consent, grabbing his wallet, refusing to answer his questions, etc.), and filed a citizen's complaint against CHP. Shortly afterwards, Gibson notified Kaldani that he had filed a counter-suit against him for defamation of character, and threatened to sue for damages in Small Claims Court. The American Civil Liberties Union filed a federal lawsuit against Gibson, alleging that his threat was in retaliation against Kaldani for exercising his civil rights, and was also in violation of the ADA. The ACLU sought an injunction against

Gibson to prevent him from proceeding with his suit.

On April 29, 1998, the ACLU announced that a settlement had been reached. Both parties agreed to drop their respective claims. Kaldani would dismiss the federal lawsuit against Gibson; Gibson would not pursue his defamation claim against Kaldani. Both were pleased with the outcome.

Mistaken identity: Sometimes our difficulties with police go beyond rudeness and mistreatment. Consider the experience of 17-year-old Edward Rowe, a student at Alabama Institute for the Deaf and Blind, who was held at gunpoint by Talladega police who mistook the car he was riding in for a getaway car containing three dangerous criminals. Rowe's mother, Rita Hendricks, and her fiancé, Kelvin Colbert, both soldiers at Redstone Arsenal, were driving him to school on February 28, 1999 when their car was stopped by police. They had posted a lookout for three black armed robbers whose car was similar to the one driven by Hendricks. (She, Colbert, and Rowe are black.) The three were forced out of the car and to their knees; Hendricks and Colbert were handcuffed immediately. Hendricks yelled, "My son is deaf! My son is deaf!" Rowe was terrified—shivering with fear—when an officer held a gun to the base of his skull. "I didn't know whether they were going to shoot me," he recalled, signing through an interpreter. He wanted to ask his mother what was going on, but she was handcuffed and he couldn't move.

The three testified before City Council about their ordeal and received an official apology from the Police Chief Joe Hare, who acknowledged that it could have been worse, "referring to a case in California where officers shot a deaf man as he reached for [an identity] card." He promised an investigation of the incident.

Hendricks wasn't satisfied with the city's response and was considering filing a lawsuit. She also wanted police to be trained in dealing with deaf and disabled persons. An AIDB teacher offered to provide basic-sign classes to emergency personnel at little or no cost to the city.

The scary thing about stories like this is the knowledge that it could happen to any of us.

As for the deaf man in California: we have read of other instances in which a deaf person was shot by police while reaching for an ID card (containing proof of deafness) or a pad and pen. The officer who did the shooting presupposed that the person was reaching for a hidden weapon (a not-unreasonable assumption), and acted quickly. For us, it's a *very* real fear. We speak from experience.

Know their rights—and your signs: We believe that all law-enforcement personnel, anyone who has contact with the public, and *especially* anyone working in a city with a sizable Deaf population, should have a working knowledge of at least a dozen or two basic signs, plus fingerspelling. There is no ideological excuse. All personnel should be required to gain a basic understanding of Deaf culture and communication. (E.g., eye contact, social space, body language, the need for any officers questioning a Deaf person or taking a deposition to keep their faces in full view and as well-lit as possible, and, if they can, to remove their sunglasses so the Deaf person they're talking to or questioning can have an unobstructed view and can read their faces more easily. The same courtesy accorded to Spanish-speaking citizens can be accorded to ASL users. And even if officers don't know how to communicate with Deaf people via ASL, a modicum of patience and sensitivity can make a big difference.

Suggestions: What can be done? Plenty! William B. "Duke" Whiteside, Community Policing Project Coordinator at the National League of Cities, has written an instructive article, "Bridging the Gap: Community Policing and Working with the Deaf and Hard of Hearing." For the following list, we've borrowed a suggestion or two from Duke Whiteside (who has borrowed one or two from us).

Twelve things law-enforcement officers can do to improve relations with the Deaf community (and prevent costly lawsuits):

● Learn at least a dozen or two basic signs and phrases: *hello, what's wrong?, where?, who?, name, right, wrong, right, left, problem, sign, license, car, drive, road, ticket, speeding, law, drinking, fight, gun, arrest, jail, safe, safety, emergency, danger, warn, rights, crime, hurt,* etc.

● Learn fingerspelling, which is a tremendously useful thing for *anyone* to know (e.g., being able to communicate cogently with someone who's choking).

● Understand our need to have fair and accessible communication, a right accorded to hearing citizens. Be patient when dealing with persons whose primary mode of communication is American Sign Language. Be willing to use pad-and-pen to communicate.

● Support legislation that enables deaf drivers to have a voluntary code added to their licenses. When the license is checked and run by a police officer, the code automatically shows up. This enables officers to know that the driver is deaf *before* approaching his or her car, and gives them a chance to contact an interpreter or to be prepared to use an "alternative form of communication"—i.e., writing.

● Be responsible enough to summon a qualified sign-language interpreter when the situation requires it. (Of course, not all situations permit, but most of the time, it's feasible.)

● If Deaf suspects need to be physically restrained, conventional handcuffs should not be used, except as a last resort. Handcuffing a Deaf person who relies on ASL to communicate is like gagging a hearing person. An alternative form of restraint that allows the detainee sufficient freedom to sign is preferable—at least in most cases.

● Deaf detainees need fair and prompt access to an interpreter and a TTY. If TV is available in jail, deaf inmates should have access to captioning. Much of this is common sense, but not common practice.

● In cities or regions with sizable Deaf populations, *all* law-enforcement personnel who have contact with the public should take a "Basic Sign Skills and Deaf Communication" course, and to keep their skills sharp with periodic refresher courses and practice—and contact with Deaf people. All officers-in-training should have some Deaf-communication/sensitivity training.

● There should be an official liaison to the Deaf community.

● All police departments should have copies of valuable resources that are produced and made available by other police departments: e.g., videotapes/DVDs and pamphlets on communicating with deaf people.

● Beware of bad attitudes and brutes on the force. If officers don't have respect for the citizens they're supposed to protect, if they can't reciprocate the basic courtesy shown to them, if they are the furious, impatient, Raging Bull type, they shouldn't be out on patrol.

● Encourage deaf people to get involved—by volunteering on citizens' neighborhood patrols, working as police auxiliaries, and even entering the police force. Visit high schools and programs for the deaf. Present a positive image—and an open door. Law enforcement should be a viable career option for deaf people. There is much that they *can* do.

When dealing with authority figures, deaf people tend to be respectful, polite, and patient. They will do what they can to facilitate communication. They are demanding respect as first-class citizens—and the basic courtesy of having that communication reciprocated.

None of us know when we'll become crime or disaster victims, or witnesses, or have run-ins with the police. The prospect can be terrifying. ASL-Deaf, oralists, hard-of-hearing, Usher's Syndrome, deaf-blind—we're all affected. The ADA helps, but isn't a cure-all. The U.S. law-enforcement and court systems are far from perfect. Sometimes they are unbelievably bad, just as bad as those in "uncivilized" or "nondemocratic" countries whose "barbaric" standards we look upon with scorn.

On the bright side, Deaf people, as we have pointed out, have been making slow but steady progress in exercising their right to serve on juries. They are eager to serve, and a growing number have done so, quite capably. Not long ago, two Deaf citizens were elected jury foremen. And, yes, both did fine. With interpreters and a CART setup to guarantee access to the proceedings, we can rise to the challenge.

The battle for equal rights, equal protection under law, and equal participation as first-class citizens has not yet been won. But suit by suit and case by case, progress *is* being made. Law-enforcement personnel can be part of the problem—or partners in progress.

▲ ▲ ▲

Jury duty: no exemptions requested

Deaf people were traditionally exempted from jury duty—even though there was no law on the books prohibiting them from serving. But after the passage of the ADA, that began changing. Stories about Deaf people serving on juries began cropping up in newspapers across the country. These folks let it be known that they wanted to serve, and eagerly seized the opportunity.

Charles V. "Chuck" Williams, teacher, administrator, and advocate, who was appointed to the Gallaudet University Board of Trustees in 1994, was the first deaf juror in Ohio and served as foreman of the jury panel—possibly the nation's first. In Fall 1995, Tommy Donnelly, a construction analyst with the U.S. Department of Agriculture and a Deaf-community activist, became the first Deaf juror in Wake County, North Carolina—and, possibly, the second Deaf man in the nation chosen as jury foreman by his hearing peers.

Donnelly uses ASL as his first language. Ten years previously, before the ADA was passed, he had reported for jury duty, but was summarily excused for two reasons: 1) he couldn't hear, and 2) a thirteenth person was not permitted in the jury room, even if that thirteenth person was a certified interpreter bound by a strict code of ethics not to interfere in any way with the deliberations.

There never has been a law against Deaf people serving on juries. Appellate-court decisions in other states have found that it was not against the law to bring an interpreter into the jury room. But most Deaf people, when summoned, asked to be excused from serving, fearing that they'd obstruct the proceedings or be forced to pay for the interpreter. The ADA guarantees deaf citizens the same access to facilities and services that others have free access to, and that includes jury duty, one of the privileges of U.S. citizenship. And Deaf citizens welcome the opportunity to exercise that privilege.

In Fall 1995, Donnelly reported again for jury duty in Raleigh. This time he was seated. The trial involved a civil lawsuit over injuries sustained in an automobile accident. It wasn't front-page material, but in its own modest way, made history. Neither the plaintiff nor defendant, nor their attorneys, challenged Donnelly's selection. No one raised any objections. Fellow jurors showed their confidence in Donnelly's ability by electing him foreman. There were difficulties, though: during arguments, the interpreter had a hard time keeping pace, and some jurors addressed her instead of Donnelly. But it worked out well.

The **Raleigh News & Observer** carried an upbeat article headlined, "Jury box one less barrier for the deaf community," with a "teaser" caption above a large photo of Donnelly signing: "FIRST DEAF JUROR SAYS IT'S AN HONOR TO SERVE."

As for the outcome, both parties were found at fault; neither was awarded any damages. After the verdict had been announced and the jury dismissed, Donnelly told a **News &** **Observer** reporter that the jury experience "renewed his faith in democracy." He was even thinking of getting involved in politics.

Both of us (MSM and LL) have at different times reported for jury duty. Neither of us reached the interview stage, so we know that our dismissal wasn't due to making a poor impression on the court officials. It was an interesting experience for us, though. It involved a lot of waiting in a large room with many other potential jurors, an open-captioned video that provided a brief history of public justice (especially as practiced in England) and the evolution of the concept of trial by jury there and in the States, the modern court system, and some key terms, such as *voir dire*. We had arranged for interpreters, and that turned out to be the best part!

When I (LL) answered the summons, there was another Deaf man there, and two interpreters. After we'd filled out the paperwork and watched the video, we waited. We'd brought books to read, but ended up talking with the interpreters. Even though they were technically on duty (and were breaking the rules by talking with us), we had a good discussion about the jury-selection system.

A Deaf friend of ours, "Dan," who had made it to the interview stage, told us that he and another Deaf man, "Jack," had been asked (separately) what they'd do if they were chosen to be part of a jury, and all the other jurors held one opinion while they, Jack and Dan, dissented. Jack said, "I'd give up." Dan said that if he believed strongly that he was right and the others wrong, he'd try to persuade the other jurors of the wisdom of his viewpoint. The jury-selection teams want people who can think independently and express their opinions with assurance—something to keep in mind if you receive a summons!

Deaf Awareness 5-Minute Quiz

Chapters 76—89
Answers are on the bottom of the page, upside down.

True or False:

1. Deaf people only need one visual smoke alarm for the entire house.

2. Schools and colleges for the deaf serve as "magnets" or "hubs" of deaf population.

3. Many deaf men traditionally worked as Linotypists. They were considered to be ideal candidates for this deafeningly noisy job.

4. Communication access isn't everything. It's not invariably better for a Deaf worker to have Deaf bosses or co-workers, if they have bad attitudes.

5. While Centrex and multi-line systems are technically incompatible with TTYs, creating difficulties for deaf staffers, dedicated fax/modem lines can easily be "tapped" by TTY users.

6. The implementation of the ADA has effectively put an end to discrimination against deaf people.

7. Having experienced considerable prejudice from the majority culture, deaf people are remarkably empathetic towards and supportive of mavericks and achievers within their own community.

8. Some members of the Deaf community approve of manual-alphabet-card peddlers, since it's part of Deaf history and culture.

9. The best way to get clerks to treat deaf customers with a modicum of respect is to compel them to take sign-language classes.

10. There is an old law on the books prohibiting deaf people from serving on juries.

10. False.
1. False; 2. True; 3. True; 4. True; 5. True; 6. False; 7. False; 8. False; 9. False;
Answers:

Chapter 90

Why don't some deaf people trust hearing people?

et's rephrase the question: *Why don't some black people trust white people?* The memories of slavery, oppression, violence, discrimination, denial of opportunities are still vivid. Racial injustice is still a reality in the United States. Through the centuries, deaf people have likewise been victims of oppression, although, we admit, we have never been kidnapped from our native countries and forced *en masse* into slavery. The discrimination we have faced is of a subtler variety, although more ancient.

Another substitution: *Why don't some American Indians trust white people?* Like American Indian children, our Deaf ancestors were dispossessed of the rights of citizenship, denied access to their native language, and forced to assimilate into an alien (majority) culture. Even if they tried to behave and talk like the majority, they weren't really accepted. Not completely.

Traditionally, Deaf people have been looked upon as "different." They might be feared, but they weren't respected. As with any cultural minority, perhaps more so, there has been a strong "huddling instinct"—Deaf people banding together and giving each other support and sympathy, keeping ASL alive, and not having any more to do with the outside (Hearing) culture than is necessary. You don't have to be a whiz in sociology to recognize that Deaf people have been oppressed for centuries. Negative views of deafness (and the abilities of deaf people) are at least as old as Aristotle—no doubt older. (Aristotle is credited with the first recorded false assumption, vintage 355 B.C., about the intellectual abilities of deaf persons: "Those born deaf become senseless and incapable of reason.") And with such oppression have come ignorance, misunderstandings, and hostility, all of which are, unfortunately, still far too prevalent.

To understand the educational/communicative/political rift between oralists and signers, Deaf Power advocates *versus* the Hearing Power incumbents, you need to understand the bitter ideological feud that began with Edward Miner Gallaudet and Alexander Graham Bell—two powerful hearing leaders who have had so much influence on deaf people's destinies for more than a century. Although Gallaudet disagreed with Bell on several key points, he deferred to Bell's view that deaf people should not be allowed to teach other deaf people. Having its finest deaf alumni teaching deaf children and adults had been one of the community's most cherished prerogatives. Now that, too, was taken away.

Although Gallaudet managed to keep his new college alive, and maintain it as a bastion of sign language, hearing oralists nonetheless came to wield tremendous influence there. When William Stokoe arrived as an English professor in the early 1950s, oralists were treated with deference. Textbooks used in teacher-training classes—for those who planned to work with deaf students and supposedly serve their interests— adhered to the pathological view of deafness, portraying deaf subjects as deficient and intellectually abnormal.

It is one of the ironies of history that after publishing his discovery that ASL was indeed a full-fledged language, Stokoe was widely regarded as crazy. It took a while for the Gallaudet College community to readjust its perceptions. Even so, Gallaudet remained firmly under hearing leadership, and those hearing administrators, feeling threatened by the political ramifications of Stokoe's research and his undeferential attitude, ultimately closed down his Linguistics Research Lab and sent him packing.

We have already mentioned several times the old campaign against ASL in the deaf schools. The tide is turning, but immeasurable damage has been done. Deaf adults still recall some of their teachers, the oppressive influence of these powerful ambassadors of Hearing culture. They look back with anger. As recently as our grandparents' and parents' generations, deaf children were taught that deafness was bad, signing was not socially acceptable, something that had to be hidden, as if it was shameful and dirty, and that, if they wanted to achieve Acceptance, Happiness, and Fulfillment, they should act as "Hearing" as possible. *Don't let anyone else see you signing.*

Having received an inadequate education from those well-trained hearing teachers, they were often ill-prepared to cope with the challenges of living independent lives among the Hearing. Some older Deaf people have vivid memories of being taken advantage of by unscrupulous hearing salesmen and agents who sold them appliances, furniture, or automobiles on the installment plan and "conned" them into signing contracts whose fine print they didn't understand. The result? The items they thought they owned were repossessed. All that was gained was a bitter education in the less admirable ways of the Hearing world.

These negative attitudes have largely given way to more positive views, but the memory remains. In some cases, oppression of deaf children isn't just a memory; it's still happening. Certain groups of hearing people (or individuals) still oppress Deaf people. They want to suppress ASL. They threaten the Deaf community. They would like to see it dissolved.

Old prejudices and cultural attitudes die hard. Most Deaf people *are* willing to meet the Hearing community halfway. If the Hearing community really wants to establish mutual trust, it must be able to convince the Deaf community that it has its welfare at heart. But there must be open communication and genuine respect. No more "plantation mentality;" no more paternalism. The ongoing threats of closing Deaf schools, which strike at the very heart of the Deaf community, do not bode well.

Chapter 91

What do you mean, "An interpreter is a person who earns money off Deaf people's language"?!

ntil the 1960s, there was no such thing as a professional interpreter. Interpreting was not a profession; it was a favor hearing children did for their
deaf parents, or hearing parents did for their deaf
children. A skilled hearing relative or neighbor
could be pressed into service when needed—if a deaf person
had to consult with a lawyer or doctor, etc. It was an amateur's
field. There was no code of ethics or certification process.

In 1964, the Registry of Interpreters for the Deaf, the national certifying body, was founded. With the recognition of
interpreting as a profession, our social status has changed
tremendously—for the better. To keep pace with the increasing demand, more and more interpreters are being trained
and certified. (The Americans with Disabilities Act will certainly encourage the profession even further.)

Interpreters have become a fact of life, a part of the American scene. Switch on the evening news, and wherever you see
a Presidential candidate or governmental bigwig addressing
a crowd, there's usually an interpreter just to the side of the
lectern. Some hearing theatergoers, even those who feel that
theatrical interpreters are distracting, a visual annoyance,
may find themselves taking a peek—they're curious, even
fascinated. The public visibility of interpreters has certainly
fostered new awareness of Deaf people, their language, and
their needs.

Interpreting has become a respectable, if tough and occasionally hazardous, profession. Its rigid code of ethics was
designed to protect the privacy of both parties, but it can work
against the Deaf client. In a courtroom setting, an interpreter

is forbidden to explain *anything* to the jury, even if they're unfairly prejudiced against the Deaf person. We've read Lou Ann Walker's harrowing account of her stint as a city-appointed interpreter in a courtroom and at a psychiatric clinic. She felt terribly constrained by the code of ethics. Although she wanted to, she was forbidden to explain to the jurors why her client, a young, poor black woman who killed her sister's vicious boyfriend in self-defense, was behaving the way she did. She "didn't know how a person was supposed to behave in front of a jury." Although she should have been acquitted, she was found guilty and sentenced to prison. Walker, who sympathized with the woman, was helpless to aid her in court: "I was a robot."

In the days of "Mom 'n' Pop" interpreters, the deaf client wasn't expected to pay a fee. You didn't pay for a favor. With the rise of professional interpreters, a deaf person who needs an interpreter (say, to consult a lawyer) often has to foot the bill. The cost of an interpreter is as high as $50 an hour. Who pays? We do, often. A good number of deaf people cannot afford to hire an interpreter.

Where do interpreters learn their trade? They take courses. Who teaches them? Very often, native-ASL users, Deaf people. How much do these teachers earn per hour? We have it on good authority (from an actual sign-language instructor) that a high-school teacher may earn as little as $5-$7 per hour while a college-level teacher will do better—$15-$30 per hour. (It depends on the setting.) And how much do interpreters earn? Unlike teachers, they have the power to set their own fees. They generally earn $30-$50 per hour. Well, you may say, interpreting is a physically and mentally challenging, frequently exhausting, field demanding a high level of skill. Well, we reply, the same can be said of sign-language instructors. So why do interpreters earn $30 to $50 an hour while the people who teach them earn $5 to $15 per hour?

Could it be that teaching just doesn't command the same prestige as interpreting? Teaching is expected to be a "labor of love." Interpreting is a profession. Most interpreters enter the profession because it's a good career, not necessarily because they love ASL or cherish Deaf culture. The more professional distance between the interpreter and client, the better. Some deaf people, seeing how much money interpreters make (especially compared to their teachers), resent it. Imagine how you'd feel, knowing that your students will always earn more—in some cases, a lot more—than you who teach them. How many administrators are willing to pay a teacher $30 or $50 an hour? Yet an interpreter can demand—and receive—high fees.

Any hearing person can become an interpreter. The job market is open to all hearing people. It is *not* open to all deaf people. (They are severely limited in the kind of interpreting they can do: sign-to-sign.) So you have a corps of hearing people earning money off Deaf people's sign language—a profession more or less off-limits to Deaf people themselves.

An interpreter who "slips" can create costly misunderstandings or cause considerable damage to the client. An interpreter who makes a mistake while interpreting a Deaf person's testimony in court can have a destructive effect on his or her life. A *few* interpreters like to play God over their clients. They're power-hungry; they enjoy the feeling of controlling Deaf people.

That said, we'd like to emphasize that there are a few truly superb interpreters. They respect Deaf people; they have a good attitude towards Deaf culture. They charge reasonable rates. In return, they are respected and esteemed by the Deaf community. *And* there are a few truly bad interpreters—the ones who cause trouble for their profession by "giving interpreters a bad name." The majority of interpreters are in between. They're in a career; they earn money.

If you have difficulty understanding why we made our statement about interpreters in the first place, why not ask a Deaf person how s/he feels about interpreters? Chances are, they'll echo some of the things we're saying here.

Chapter 92

What exactly is the interpreter's role? Who does the hiring? Who pays?

here are several different kinds of interpreters, the most familiar being the sign-language inter- preter, who translates spoken English into Sign English, PSE, or ASL—depending on what is being communicated, the deaf client's preferred recep- tive-communication mode, and the interpreter's skills. Sign- language interpreters often function as reverse interpret- ers—translating a deaf client's signs into spoken English for the hearing party. There are also oral and cued-speech inter- preters, and those who work with deaf-blind clients. Inter- preters may have specialized training (medical, legal, class- room, etc.).

With the implementation of the ADA and the increased participation of deaf people in business, government, and "non-traditional" professions, there is an increased demand for interpreters that outstrips the present supply. So inter- preting is a field that is definitely growing. The demand is steadily increasing, and promises to continue.

Interpreting, as a profession, is a relatively recent offshoot of the Deaf civil-rights movement. In the not-so-good old days, deaf people had to depend on volunteers (their hearing parents, children, relatives, friends, even neighbors) to inter- pret for them—e.g., on the telephone, at the Division of Motor Vehicles, the bank, job interviews, in court. The agencies, stores, banks, offices, and government facilities in question accepted no responsibility for making communication acces- sible; the burden rested solely on deaf persons, and if they couldn't find someone to "help" them when they scheduled an interview with the loan officer, well, so much the worse.

Those days are now history. Interpreters are professionals who operate under a strict code of ethics.

This means that deaf people no longer have to rely on the good graces of amateur volunteers (which could be a humiliating and very risky business), but *somebody* has to pay for the interpreter. Getting access to communication is our right, but it isn't necessarily "free." Although interpreters can and do volunteer their time (usually for nonprofit, community-oriented events), they expect to be paid for services rendered to individual clients. The ADA puts the responsibility on the service provider, employer, or facility.

Of course, this has met with resistance. "Reasonable accommodation"—how much, how far—is a hotly-debated issue. We've begun to see a spate of lawsuits filed against medical clinics, hospitals, and other public facilities that refuse to foot the bill. And the facilities are fighting back.

According to the ADA, the employer is supposed to pay for the interpreter. This is, of course, a legitimate business expense that also falls under the category of "reasonable accommodation." Some employers, naturally, balk at having to do this. Critics of the law claim that this creates an "undue hardship" for smaller, financially-strapped companies, and the ADA exempts the smallest companies from this requirement; while they're encouraged to provide interpreters, they're not compelled. This could mean that small companies may not be as welcoming towards deaf workers, who bring with them their requirements for accommodation, as larger ones. It's a complex situation—with no "quickie" solutions.

As for locating and hiring an interpreter: Sometimes the new deaf employee recommends a good interpreter; sometimes the employer contacts a community agency, Vocational Rehabilitation, or college for a referral. Interpreters can work independently as freelancers, or in conjunction with an interpreting agency/service—or both. The employer contacts the interpreter directly, or calls the service and arranges to have an interpreter come at a specified time, or regularly, depending on the situation. Arrangements need to be made in advance, usually 48 hours. (Interpreters in great demand have incredibly busy schedules.) Logistics (traveling time, bad weather, etc.) all have to be worked out. Interpreters get flat tires and run into traffic jams and other disasters just like the rest of us. For an unplanned session or emergency, the interpreting service can send an interpreter "on call." Employers hiring freelancers should have a backup.

Suppose, then, the employer agrees to provide an interpreter? That hurdle's surmounted. We then have to consider the caliber of the service itself. In return for a paid professional service, the consumer—let's say a deaf employee—has every right to expect a certain standard of quality. Confidentiality is—we hope—assured. Interpreters should provide a complete translation of the spoken English into sign language, faithfully rendering the nuances of emotion and emphasis. They're not supposed to interject their own feelings or bias into their work—e.g., a distaste for one party, communicated through a sour facial expression. Although the deaf client depends entirely on the interpreter's skill to get a clear picture of what is being conveyed, the interpreter is supposed to remain neutral—to function as a proficient, but objective, conduit for communication. The aim is to eliminate the barrier between the hearing employer and the deaf employee—to give that deaf person the exact same quality and quantity of communication as s/he would have received had s/he been hearing, and to enable him/her to communicate just as freely with his/her co-workers, supervisors, boss, or interviewer.

Hearing—and deaf—clients, especially those working with one for the first time, sometimes don't understand what interpreters are "about." They need to be educated. In real-life situations, this can be tricky, since an interpreter is restricted by the code of ethics, which prohibits them from adding personal comments or explanations while on duty. We've read of a judge who halted proceedings and reprimanded an interpreter for using foul language in court, when all she was doing was giving a faithful rendition of the testimony of a deaf witness—the real "culprit." Other interpreters have similar stories—some funny, some not—about the confusion and incomprehension of clients unfamiliar with their role.

It's not always the *client's* fault, though. In the mid-'80s, an educational interpreter with religious scruples against using profanity refused to translate "bad language" while on duty. The deaf students who were her clients insisted on their right to know *everything* that was being said, profanity included, and the dispute ended up in court.

Many interpreters are native ASL users—that is, they had Deaf parents and grew up in Deaf families. But having a native's knowledge of ASL does not automatically qualify one to be an interpreter, nor does it guarantee that one will be a first-rate interpreter. Indeed, some excellent interpreters learned ASL in college.

The interpreter plays a vital role in facilitating communication. That is indisputable. But there is a wide variance in skills. All interpreters are *not* equally qualified, nor equally good. For one thing, some of them are just not properly trained. The RID and the NAD maintain their own lists of qualified interpreters, with varying levels of certification. But that doesn't stop Jo or Joe Shmo from taking a couple of sign-language classes and then setting up a "practice" as a "professional interpreter." Some states don't require interpreters to be properly certified, so if you live in one of those "lenient" states, the interpreter hired by your firm may turn out to be a "Jo Shmo." It's a real problem.*

Having an under-qualified or unqualified interpreter can have dire consequences, as we've already noted. Imagine you're a hearing juror listening to the testimony of a deaf witness—or a deaf defendant—and the interpreter isn't really doing a good job of conveying what that person is saying. How can you render a just decision with defective input?

Qualifications alone don't guarantee optimum service. An interpreter can possess the highest qualifications—and still have a bad attitude. Aside from signing skill, attitude is the most important consideration (and one that may well make or break an otherwise adequate interpreter)—how interpreters treat their deaf clients—if they put the client in the spotlight and make her/him feel important, become that person's best, most expressive and fluent voice, throw themselves fully into their work, instead of having a patronizing "help-the-poor-deaf-person" attitude.

And one final, *very* important consideration: allowing the deaf consumer to be the boss. An interpreter with a good attitude is a rare jewel indeed. Such a one can make a tremendous—and positive—impact on the entire workplace.

* See Chapter 94.

Chapter 93

I plan to hire interpreters for my deaf employees. What are the do's and don'ts? What do I need to know?

et's say you're an employer, executive, personnel director, or assistant, and have been given the responsibility of finding an interpreter for one or more deaf employees. You're starting from scratch. Your first responsibility is scheduling an interpreter to cover a meeting, to be held at the conference table.

Preliminary considerations: Some deaf employees may not be experienced in the fine points of using an interpreter. Others are veterans. You may get a mixture at the same time. Ask them if they've used interpreters before, and how frequently. What has their experience been? Are they new to it? Get their input.

No "Amateur Hour": Don't ask a hearing co-worker who knows some sign language to function as an "interpreter." This is the domain of the professional. If you maintain a professional standard of quality in your workplace, use professional interpreters. Certification provides some reassurance that the interpreter is qualified, skill-wise. But "qualified" and "certified" are not synonymous. "Uncertified" is not necessarily "unqualified," either. The deaf client may prefer an independent interpreter who doesn't hold RID, NAD, or any other State Quality Assurance certification.

Mode: Ask your deaf employees what their communication preferences are. Chances are, there'll be a diversity of preferences—e.g., one worker may prefer Sign English or PSE; another, ASL. These differences will have to be worked out. Deaf people are usually good about compromising. A skilled PSE interpreter is generally understandable to all users.

"Pooling": Next, ask the deaf employees if they have a favorite or preferred individual interpreter or service. Experienced clients maintain their own listings of interpreters they like and trust. Make use of these lists. You can then try to obtain an interpreter from the "preferred pool." Make sure you have alternates, so if the #1 interpreter on the list cannot come, you'll have a dependable backup.

Shifting responsibility: Although earning one's living by sitting and signing someone else's dialogue, testimony, or lectures full-time sounds like a breeze, it can be exhausting. Deaf people do not customarily stay in one place and sign continuously for hours at a time, but interpreters are expected to do just that. It puts a particular physical strain on the hands, wrists, arms, and shoulders.

How many interpreters will be needed? If the session is going to be reasonably brief, one interpreter can handle it. But what if the scheduled half-hour briefing turns out to be not so brief—more like an hour's session?

An interpreter can usually work for 30 minutes, *possibly* up to 45 or 50 minutes, without a break. For anything longer than that, request two interpreters. A single interpreter cannot be expected to carry the sole burden of interpreting a long meeting. Long lectures, presentations, or depositions require at least two interpreters who work in half-hour shifts; this gives each one time to recuperate between stints. If the meeting is lengthy (or if you suspect that it may turn out to be), you should schedule two interpreters so they can take turns, alternating shifts.

Therefore, if you're planning a 2-hour meeting or presentation, you should schedule two interpreters. What about a one-hour meeting? Two interpreters are likewise a good idea here, since what is scheduled for an hour may end up running to an hour and 15 minutes, or even an hour and a half.

Even after you agree to have two interpreters, make sure to allot sufficient time for them, should the meeting run overtime, as meetings frequently do. You don't want the interpreters to have to stop in the middle of a crucial (or lively) discussion, pack up, and exit, since their allotted time is up. This leaves the deaf clients stranded. Be prepared for the unforeseen.

Strategic planning

Timing: So you've scheduled two interpreters for your 2-hour session, and agreed to factor an extra half hour of discussion time into the interpreters' schedules? Excellent! Now, to the details.

Lighting: Before the meeting starts, check to make sure that the lighting is adequate. The deaf employees can help with this. Is the conference room well-lit, with even lighting? Are there high-contrast shadows cast on faces? (This will be visually annoying.) Will the lighting be dimmed at any point? (This will cause "readability" problems.) You may need to set up a pole-mounted or high-intensity lamp on a small stand for darkened rooms where videos, slides, films, or overhead projections are shown on a screen. (We're assuming that these are not captioned. Overhead projections will be readable, but any spoken commentary must be interpreted.) If any audio-visual presentations are planned, you need to work out the lighting details beforehand so the interpreter and clients can follow what's going on without any interruptions, panicky searches for portable lighting, or frantic scramblings to get a better view.

Chairing: Consider the seating arrangements. (This sounds ridiculously obvious, but make *sure* there are enough chairs for everyone, including the interpreters!) The interpreter needs to sit (or—less commonly—stand) near you, for optimum visibility. Make sure to have an extra seat located conveniently nearby, for when the interpreters switch shifts—so that the interpreter who is "tired" can quickly and quietly change places with the "fresh" one, with a minimum of distraction and visual disruption. Will everybody have a good view? The deaf employees will want to sit where they can get a good view of you and the interpreter together—a vantage point.

Final details: It's a good idea to have the interpreters arrive early so that they can work out the final details of seating and lighting arrangements, etc., with you. They may notice something you've overlooked, and which may present a potential problem. Once the meeting starts, the interpreters will be comfortably settled, and everything will flow much more smoothly.

During the meeting

Everything rolling? Relax, focus on your task, and, as much as possible, try to forget that an "outsider" is there.

Points of protocol: Be aware of proper etiquette. Speak directly to the deaf employees—not to the interpreter. (Never say, "Tell her that . . ." or "Ask him . . . " This is a mistake commonly made by novices!) Face the deaf employees when you talk to them; face them when you're listening to what they're signing. Talk *to* the deaf persons (just as if they were hearing), not *about* them. The interpreter will sign *everything* you say, even when you talk to her/him. S/he will also be as unobtrusive as possible; the deaf person's signing will "become" the interpreter's own voice. With a bit of experience, you'll get used to it.

A small caveat: Some of the hearing attendees, especially those who have never before had the opportunity to see a "live" interpreter close-up, may be fascinated by the interpreter's signing. They may pay more attention to the interpreter than to the speaker! It's normal for hearing audiences to be intrigued, even mesmerized, watching an interpreter work. Keep this in mind, and take it in stride. Consider it a beneficial cross-cultural/educational experience for them.

Voice, yes; opinions, no: An interpreter is bound by a strict code of conduct and ethics. S/he is there to facilitate communication, not to participate in the discussion, give feedback or advice, express opinions, etc. If you need to discuss communication issues, you should schedule a private meeting with the interpreters and the deaf employees, well in advance of the company meeting, or afterwards.

Orderly conduct: If possible, make sure that only one person at a time "has the floor." Interpreters cannot magically unscramble and interpret meetings where two or more persons are arguing a lively point at the same time, or a "rapid-fire" discussion is erupting in several places around the table. Keep proceedings orderly.

Break time? Check with the interpreter on duty, periodically, to see if s/he needs a break. If so, let the entire group have a stretch—even 30 seconds.

Assignment: completed

Mission accomplished: Remember to thank the interpreter at the end of the session.

Don't forget that interpreters work confidentially. After the meeting is over and the interpreter packs up, everything that has been discussed is "forgotten." Erased.

After the interpreter has left, privately ask your deaf employees if they were satisfied with the interpreter's work. You may want to schedule an informal follow-up meeting for this purpose. Were they satisfied? Did they understand everything under discussion? Do they have any feedback? Criticisms? Suggestions? The deaf client is the best judge of an interpreter's effectiveness.

N.B.: Despite the best intentions, things can, and do, go wrong, and scheduling an interpreter is no exception. Good planning, however, can increase the odds of success.

Final note: Interpreting is a challenging, tough, physically and mentally demanding job, but can—and should be—a rewarding one. For the interpreter, the client, and the hiring party, there's often an element of surprise: you never really know what you're going to get. Think adventurously. Do what you can to make it a rewarding, positive experience for everyone there.

EARLY SEPTEMBER:
TAKING A
BEGINNING SIGN
LANGUAGE CLASS.

MID-DECEMBER:
HANGING THE SHINGLE.

Chapter 94

If I take one or two sign-language classes, will that make me a qualified interpreter?

—Holly P. Roth, Columbia, Maryland

ardly. But you'd be surprised how many people have little—or no—idea of just what it does take to make a qualified interpreter.

After "one or two sign-language classes," you can expect to know maybe 20 signs—which certainly does *not* qualify you as an interpreter! (An analogy: Is someone qualified to practice neurosurgery after taking one or two pre-med or freshman-biology courses?)

Exactly what constitutes a *qualified* interpreter? To backtrack a bit, we can define an interpreter as a facilitator of communication between Deaf/hard-of-hearing and hearing persons. Common settings are "educational, occupational, legal, medical and mental health, rehabilitation/social services, religious, television and artistic performances, platform interpreting, and business, industry, and government." The goal is to give all participants equal access to the same information. This is a demanding task calling for a professional. Nobody becomes a professional at *anything* after taking one or two courses. Getting to the top of the interpreting profession (or any profession, for that matter) takes skill, dedication, discipline, training, years of hard work, *plus* a good attitude.

The Registry of Interpreters for the Deaf, based in Silver Spring, Maryland, is the national certifying/membership body for interpreters, teachers, and students. RID provides "a nationally recognized credential that assures quality to con-

sumers"—the RID certificate of transliteration, interpretation, or both. These are awarded after the interpreter takes
and passes a written test (with ethical-standards and knowledge portions) *and* a performance test in the area(s) of trans-
literating spoken English into ASL or signed English, or
translating a form of sign language into spoken English.

To become a *qualified* interpreter, you need to go through a
good interpreter-training program (ITP). According to
Bethany L. Stancliff's RID pamphlet, "Sign Language Interpreting: A Career Information Packet," "there are currently
73 [sic] interpreter-preparation programs in the United States
and Canada. Some programs offer a certificate in interpreting, some offer a 2-year associate's degree, and a few offer a
4-year bachelor's degree. To date, only Gallaudet University
offers a master's degree in interpreting. Programs range in
size from 5 to 50 people and practicum hours vary from 0 to
528. Some programs require only admission to college, while
others have a rigorous interview process. Because of the
growing demand for interpreters, new programs are developing, and these statistics continue to change."

So if you're just breaking into sign-language studies and are
considering becoming an interpreter, you need to choose a
college that offers an ITP. Not all ITPs are equally effective.
There is no universally-accepted standard as to what constitutes an adequate ITP, but RID is working on that.

As Stancliff puts it, "There are several skills or qualities that
are advantageous to have as an interpreter: flexibility, objectivity, self-discipline, punctuality, responsibility, a professional attitude, exemplary spoken/written English, ability in
American Sign Language and/or signed English, good inter-
personal skills, maturity, and a recognition of persons who
are deaf as capable human beings." ITP students, she suggests, should "take classes in other related areas"—anthropology, public speaking, and English—to enhance their cultural perspective and communication/performance skills.
"Because interpreters can be asked to provide services in

every discipline, from scientific to medical to legal, it would be helpful to build up one's general knowledge; the greater the 'knowledge base,' the better."

In 1988, RID began awarding the CI (Certificate of Interpretation), which applies to ASL/English, and the CT (Certificate of Transliteration), which applies to signed English/spoken English. CLIP (Conditional Legal Interpreting Permit) and CLIP-R (Conditional Legal Interpreting Permit-Relay) are advanced specialist permits. CDI-P (Certified Deaf Interpreter-Provisional) is for Deaf and hard-of-hearing interpreters, and replaces the old RSC (Reverse Skills Certificate), which, along with the CSC (Comprehensive Skills Certificate), TC (Transliteration Certificate), and IC (Interpretation Certificate), are no longer offered. These "defunct" certificates (and others, like the Oral Interpreting and Performing Arts certificates) are still valid for RID members. (See list below.)

Deaf people can become interpreters with CDI certification. Incidentally, we have been informed that deaf people have served on RID's board, committee, and leadership positions "for years and years."

As we've already pointed out, the quality of currently-active interpreters varies in the extreme. While it does provide some assurance of skill, certification alone doesn't guarantee a first-rate interpreter. (Same situation with teachers. A teacher may have "proper" certification, but in practice, be semi-literate or otherwise incompetent.) And then there are interpreters who lack any certification at all. Some students, after taking a few sign-language classes, emerge, egos puffed up, with the attitude: "Look at me, I'm an *interpreter!* I want to *save* deaf people. I want to *help* them, because I know some *signs!!!*" There are some people out there who *think* they're good interpreters (but aren't), and who lack the necessary qualifications. Call them "amateurs;" call them "non-professionals;" call them "Brand X interpreters." They are not answerable to the RID or its Code of Ethics. In hiring them and using their services, the client and consumer have no "guarantee," no "service warranty," no official recourse. They won't get the same quality of service they expect from a certified interpreter.

Since RID has no real authority to enforce its standards, anyone can call her/himself a "qualified interpreter." This, by the way, is not illegal. Quality-assurance testing systems do exist in some states—but not all. Some states don't require or recognize RID certification. Which means that, if you live in such a state, are involved in courtroom litigation, and need an interpreter, the court district may hire an uncertified interpreter. (Certified interpreters charge more than uncertified ones.) If you're a key witness in a murder trial, would you want *your* ASL testimony to be rendered into spoken English by someone who's taken a couple of sign-language classes and then hangs out an "Interpreter" shingle? If you're a Deaf member of the jury, would *you* want to depend on the signing skills of such an interpreter? A scary thought for many of us.

And who should have the authority to determine standards of qualification—RID, the NAD, or the states? It's a real headache—for Deaf consumers and interpreters as well. The Deaf consumer should beware—and be aware.

CURRENT CERTIFICATIONS

In 1988, RID began offering two types of certification, under a new testing system, both of which are full, independent, generalist certificates:

Certificate of Interpretation (CI): ability to interpret between ASL and spoken English both sign-to-voice and voice-to-sign.

Certificate of Transliteration (CT): ability to transliterate between signed English and spoken English in both sign-to-voice and voice-to-sign.

DEFUNCT CERTIFICATIONS

These full certifications were awarded prior to 1988:

Comprehensive Skills Certificate (CSC): ability to interpret and transliterate between ASL and English.

Reverse Skills Certificate (RSC): ability to interpret and transliterate between ASL and English; the interpreter is Deaf or hard-of-hearing, and transliteration/interpretation is rendered in ASL and spoken, signed, or written English.

Two types of partial certifications were offered during that time:

Transliteration Certificate (TC): ability to transliterate between spoken English and a signed code for English.

Interpretation Certificate (IC): ability to interpret between ASL and spoken English.

Between 1975 and 1988 two specialist certificates—Legal (**SC:L**) and Performing Arts (**SC:PA**) were available to interpreters who held either a CSC or an RSC. These indicated that the holder had completed specialized training or demonstrated a satisfactory level or performance in the specific area tested.

Three certificates were granted in interpreting for oral-deaf persons from 1979 to the mid-80s:

Oral Interpreter Certificate: Spoken-to-Visible (OIC:S/V): ability to paraphrase and transliterate a spoken message from a hearing person to a deaf or hard-of-hearing person.

Oral Interpreter Certificate: Visible-to-Spoken (OIC:V/S): ability to understand the speech and silent mouth movements of a deaf or hard-of-hearing person, and to repeat the message for a hearing person.

Oral Interpreter Certificate: Comprehensive (OIC:C): ability to paraphrase and transliterate a spoken message from a hearing person to a deaf or hard-of-hearing person, and the ability to understand the speech and the intent of the speech and silent mouth movements of the deaf or hard-of-hearing person.

The above 9 certifications are no longer awarded under the current testing system, but are valid as long as the interpreter holds a current RID membership card.

Chapter 95

Is it important for interpreters to socialize with the deaf community?

—Sherry Pifer, Hutchinson, Kansas

ign-language interpreters, by the nature of their job, are in a complicated position. Deaf people are their clients, their constituency. But can Deaf people be their friends as well?

There is no law against interpreters having Deaf friends, or even socializing with their clients. The formidable RID Code of Ethics is designed to protect the privacy of the client and to safeguard the confidentiality of what transpires while the interpreter is on duty. What is discussed during that transaction is not to be disclosed to anyone else afterwards. And, because the Deaf community is relatively small (everyone seems to know everyone else), this can be a real problem for interpreters and clients involved in "sensitive" transactions such as psychiatric, drug-rehabilitation, or sexual-abuse counseling.

Off-duty, interpreters are free to associate with whomever they please. Some are active in the Deaf community, socialize with Deaf people, and have Deaf friends. They are liked and respected, and are always welcome—for themselves.

The term "interpreter" can encompass anyone from a seasoned, highly skilled veteran to the rawest of fumbling freshmen. While a number of interpreters have native fluency, many don't. Some, after all, don't have any exposure to ASL or signing before college. Suppose the interpreter in question is an ITP student whose background in signing is relatively limited? Many are inexperienced, "green," and may never have interacted with Deaf people before taking their first ITP classes. What about *their* relationship with the Deaf community, which traditionally looks on "arrivistes" and strangers with suspicion?

We referred the question to a veteran interpreter, Helen Young, whom we consider one of the very best. She replies:

> This is a subject for controversy. My feelings are: "It depends."
> Some [ITP] students and [other] hearing people have grown up in the deaf club. They would feel comfortable because they would adhere to the "social norms." These people can move about without disrupting [the social flow]. New signers would not know these things, except what they've gleaned from teachers and textbooks.
> There are two very distinct social happenings at the deaf club. [First,] there are the sit-down-and-talk kind of happenings where deaf people can catch up on the news, discuss ideas, and converse freely [about] their thoughts and ideas.
> Then there are the "events" such as fundraisers, Timberfests, picnics, or boating. These are fine for students to attend because they can volunteer to run a booth, set up children's games, or serve food. That's what we call responsibility. Everyone will benefit in some way.
> The first situation, to me, would be very obtrusive [for an inexperienced ITP student to try and participate actively] and would perhaps lead to some bad feelings towards students who come to practice signing skills.
> There are other ways of doing this, such as becoming a "Big Brother" or "Big Sister" to a deaf student, [or] adopting a deaf grandparent in a nursing home. You can be creative.
> By doing the latter, you are giving something back to the community and you are gaining knowledge of a very diverse group of people, without intruding on their social life.

In other words, "green" interpreters have to proceed cautiously when it comes to entering a Deaf social milieu. If they plunge into the wrong social climate (an intimate gathering at a Deaf club) before they develop strong signing skills, they could very easily end up in an awkward or embarrassing fix, getting snubbed (the cold-shoulder treatment) or insulted (a nasty confrontation). Entering a "closed" social milieu suggests a pushy type—someone who's trying to get something (exposure to everyday ASL to improve their sign skills) without having first earned the trust of the community.

If, however, they volunteer to help out at a public event such as a festival (where help is always needed), or perform a vital service like mentoring or tutoring, they are "giving something back to the community." They're giving valuable commodities—their time and energy—in return for valuable commodities: gaining exposure to ASL and learning some fine points of social interaction while making new friends.

There are many interpreters who earn money from their work, but have never earned the Deaf community's respect. What differentiates those who earn respect from those who don't? Ms. Young's comments provide the clue: it's all in one's attitude. Respect must be earned, and making a real commitment takes time and effort. But respect is the best payoff imaginable. When an interpreter cultivates a good relationship with the Deaf community, the harvest is mutual respect. That's the highest compliment that can be accorded to an interpreter: good skills, a good attitude, and one who has earned the respect of the Deaf community. Socializing *can* play an important role in that relationship.

Chapter 96

What are some of the difficulties faced by Deaf people in mainstreamed support groups?

DA or no ADA, it's been nigh-impossible for Deaf people to get full access to and benefit from peer-support/therapy groups for battered women, survivors of sexual abuse, substance (alcohol and drug) abusers, and people with HIV/AIDS. But, you might ask, doesn't having a good interpreter solve the problem? Not entirely.

Support groups are characterized by free, uninhibited emotional interchanges between members. There's a lot of talking, and participants often reach a high pitch of emotion. It's not uncommon for them to break down and sob, and to wildly hug each other. The point is to be able to express feelings openly, to share pain and hurt, in a supportive environment.

Whenever you have an interpreter working with a Deaf client in this kind of environment, something's lost.

It's difficult for an interpreter to keep track of the sometimes rapid-fire interchange, and to convey, in sign, the nuances of feelings in participants' voices. Sure, the Deaf client can see the expressions, but it's a challenge for the interpreter to keep pace with them. It's like the problem of real-time captioning on the news, in which radically edited segments may be as brief as a few seconds and transition between clips is rapid: by the time the caption hits the screen, the scene has been switched and someone else has begun talking. There's a crucial lag between the action and our comprehension.

Neutrality is a bigger problem than speed. Professional interpreters are bound by a strict code of ethics that prohibits them from injecting personal feelings in their work, and from interacting emotionally with their clients. In other words, the dividing line between Interpreter and Client is kept sharp. This is fine for cool, non-emotional situations involving lectures and business meetings. But if the Deaf client is in a support group, her/his needs are markedly different from those of, say, an employee or student. In therapeutic situations, this may work against the client—and the interpreter too.

Emotional catharsis—expression and purging of pent-up emotions in a non-destructive manner—is a vital part of the healing process. During an emotional outpouring, the Deaf client may want to hug the interpreter, to feel a sense of connectedness, to derive comfort and support. But the Code of Ethics forbids the interpreter to reciprocate, to react in any way. She must sit there, dutifully signing, with no flicker of personal emotion. The division between Interpreter and Client must not be blurred. The barrier must not be transgressed, no matter what. So the Deaf client cannot interact with her as with another member of the group, nor can she show normal human feelings. If she has the urge to respond (interpreters are, after all, sensitive human beings with a full range of emotions), she must repress these feelings.

One can imagine that after the day's work is done, the interpreter goes home and attempts to effect some kind of catharsis for the reactions *she* repressed on the job! Were the interpreter allowed to share in the emotional give-and-take, it would be beneficial for the client, and easier on her, too. But that's not provided for by the Code of Ethics.

Another big problem is scheduling. Arrangements are made in advance with the interpreter-referral agency to have the interpreter cover the group session, say, from 1 to 3 p.m. or from 7 to 9 p.m. The governmental agency paying for the interpreter stipulates that he cover that particular session. But what about the freewheeling conversation before and after the session itself? Communication, at least for the hearing members, is going on, but without the pressure of the group session and possibly without the leader. Nothing prevents *them* from talking while they're waiting for the session to start—but the Deaf participant may be excluded from these proceedings. Why? The interpreter isn't there. Or if he has already arrived, he is enjoined from covering the informal chat, because it isn't yet 1 p.m. or 7 p.m.—the time that the formal session is supposed to start, the agreed-upon time he goes on duty as an interpreter. A few interpreters *will* cover the before-and-after conversation. A very, very few. Most won't. The result? The Deaf patient cannot participate in beneficial between-session therapy—or share in the communication.

As a result of these factors, it can be exceedingly difficult for a Deaf patient to keep pace with his or her hearing counterparts. This prolongs the recovery process for them. It can certainly make it more frustrating.

Now, if you have a counselor or caseworker (*etcetera*) who's fluent in ASL, this obviates the difficulty. The role of a counselor or caseworker isn't as strictly circumscribed as that of a professional interpreter. While it may be forbidden to hug your interpreter, it may be okay to hug your caseworker. However, very few mainstream programs serving a Deaf minority boast ASL-fluent staff.

The obvious solution is to set up programs specifically for Deaf patients. This isn't quite as easy as it sounds. Money, or lack of it, is a major obstacle. In areas where there are relatively few Deaf people, it isn't economically feasible as it would be in areas with large Deaf populations (e.g., the Beltway, Twin Cities, and Los Angeles). There are still relatively few such programs, and as much as we dread repeating the obvious, more—much more—needs to be done.

Chapter 97

Are Deaf people more prone to AIDS and other diseases because they don't understand how to protect themselves?

n a sense, they are, because they lack access to information and services that hearing people take for granted. In 1984, when the media finally caught on to the AIDS epidemic, we witnessed the first outpouring of publicity. It did *not* reach the grassroots Deaf population.

Deaf people have long been isolated from the information stream—TV, radio, newspapers, magazines, books. The growth in prime-time and real-time TV captioning over the past few years doesn't magically solve this problem. Much of our everyday information comes from newspapers—a medium that many Deaf people avoid, as the small print and technical vocabulary are daunting. Radio is still, and will continue to be, totally inaccessible.

Deaf people whose primary language is ASL often have rudimentary or substandard English reading/comprehension skills. As has been endlessly repeated as though it's a measurable statistic (which it isn't), the "grassroots" norm is said to be third-grade-to-fifth-grade level. Many of us certainly know Deaf people who have difficulty reading. Much of what is published and disseminated in the Hearing community just doesn't reach them. It's incomprehensible. Some oral-deaf people are just as vulnerable because they depend exclusively on speechreading and audiometrics; their English skills may be just as poor as those of their ASL-Deaf counterparts.

It's not just a media problem, either. Relatively few public-health programs (hospitals, clinics, hospices, *etcetera*) have been accessible to Deaf people. Relatively few doctors, nurses, and paramedics have sign-language skills. Hospitals will often not bother to contact an interpreter.

Deaf schoolchildren, as a whole, don't get good sex educations—but the same could be said for many hearing children. Deaf children whose hearing parents and siblings cannot communicate with them are, of course, at a tremendous disadvantage. Traditionally, young Deaf people have gotten much of their information about sexual relationships from each other. It's common practice for Deaf friends to get together, describe their escapades and affairs in unblushing detail, and compare notes. Misinformation is also spread this way.

Here's an example of how misunderstanding can lead to tragedy. A Deaf man, "Tim," worried about his symptoms, goes to a clinic. He gets tested, and the diagnosis comes in. The doctor tells him, "You're HIV-positive." Tim is delighted. "Positive" means good, clear, all systems okay. He goes happily back, convinced he's gotten a clean bill of health, and continues having unprotected sex. "Negative," in our parlance, usually means bad news. "Positive" has a good connotation. This example (which is, alas, based on fact) underscores the urgency of our plight and the need for HIV/AIDS services to be accessible to us. Had all the doctors been able to explain to all the Tims why "HIV-positive" is very bad news indeed, the lives of more Deaf people could have been saved. Unfortunately, we are too often the last to find out what others have known for years.

We know of some Deaf people who've contracted AIDS through drug abuse, but by far the majority contracted it through sexual activity. We are all familiar with the "It can't happen to me" attitude. Some Deaf people still feel that because they're already deaf, nothing further can happen to *them*. Many straight Deaf men were convinced, "Oh, it's a gay disease—won't affect me." Or Deaf women thought: "Oh, it's a man's disease—I'm safe." AIDS has become more and more a "hetero" disease. It has spread rapidly through the Deaf community. Deaf people have been dying of dying of AIDS at a disproportionately high rate. All of us are affected. All of us know people who have HIV, are dying, or have already died of AIDS.

All of us who have attended local exhibits of the NAMES Project Memorial AIDS Quilt during its many travels have seen panels commemorating Deaf people and ASL interpreters whom we personally knew. Some of us have even contributed to those panels, or even made them in memory of friends. The Deaf Community has lost some of its brightest lights.

One encouraging sign is that more and more educated Deaf people are getting actively involved in AIDS prevention, outreach, counseling, and volunteer services. They are setting up and taking over AIDS services aimed at the Deaf community. One excellent example: AIDS Education/Services for the Deaf, under the auspices of the Greater Los Angeles Council on Deafness (GLAD). The National Coalition on Deafness and HIV/AIDS represents deaf, hearing, and multicultural/ethnic communities, as well as people with HIV.

Chapter 98

Are deaf children more apt to be abused because their abusers assume they can't tell anyone?

buse is the deliberate infliction of pain or hurt by those who have power, onto those who are weaker, younger, smaller, or powerless. Sexual, physical, and emotional abuse of schoolchildren by staffers and older students is not a new problem. It is probably an ancient one. Nor is it limited to schools for the deaf. But deaf children have traditionally been more vulnerable to abuse, and seen as the "perfect" victims, because of the communication barriers between them and the hearing community.

The sexual predator thrives on secrecy. *We're friends. This is our special secret*, he tells his victim. *Don't tell anyone.* The physical abuser often uses threats to enforce the victim's compliance (and to guarantee silence). *If you tell, I'm going to come after you and REALLY give you some punishment.*

With deaf children, there is an added plus for the victimizer. In some cases, young children may not have the vocabulary to describe what's going on or what has been done to them, they may not be able to articulate their experiences in sign, and, anyway, whom can they tell? Even if they are articulate and do tell a trusted adult, who's going to believe them?

A school for the deaf, with its dormitories filled with vulnerable deaf children, has long provided a near-ideal situation for sexual predators and sadists. During the heyday of oralism, few, if any, of the teachers or staff could sign. And sign language was officially suppressed. Even today, teachers of the deaf may not be fluent in ASL. There is no official requirement in any state or Canadian province, so far as we know, that a teacher of the deaf must know sign language. And if teachers and staff can't communicate fluently with the students, how can the students make themselves understood?

Since many deaf children had hearing parents who couldn't communicate with them well and/or didn't see them often, that avenue of disclosure was effectively sealed off. If parents can't communicate with their kids in the first place, they can't give the kids warnings, lectures, and instructions on how to protect themselves. There's no real dialogue, no heart-to-heart talks, and no exchange of confidences.

And if the administrators and officials can't communicate with the kids either, don't listen to them, don't believe them, and don't want to admit that anything's wrong (it would be too embarrassing and might even cost them their jobs), the victims are trapped. Silenced. At least for the time being.

As for physical coercion, public attitudes have changed over the past decades. What was called "discipline" in the 1960s and '70s is now called "abuse." As the concept of safeguarding children's rights has evolved, we've seen greater awareness, more open discussion, more publicity, and more lawsuits. Court cases involving accusations of abuse of one kind or another by students against teachers and staffers or fellow students have become almost commonplace. This also applies to residential schools for the deaf. As awareness has grown, the public complaints have increased.*

Perhaps the most well-publicized deaf-school scandal of our times is the revelation of pervasive and long-continuing sexual and physical abuse inflicted on students at the Jericho Hill School for the Deaf in Vancouver, British Columbia, Canada, during the 1960s, '70s, and '80s.

For more than a decade, officials denied that there was anything wrong. After a long cover-up, the government finally admitted that the students at Jericho Hill had, indeed, been abused. The first victims were identified in 1982, and the wheels of justice began to turn . . . slowly. The revelations, when they were finally made public, were shocking. One former student testified that a notoriously brutal female dorm counselor slapped the boys' faces for a slight offense, but for more serious offences, forced them to strip, and beat them on their buttocks with a two-by-four. When they were lined up, naked, for their nightly showers, she would shove them under the faucet—where the water might be freezing cold or unbearably hot. A male counselor grabbed naked boys by their genitals, watched them shower, or took them for "trips" on his day off. A male relief worker deliberately locked a teenage girl in the weightlifting room with a group of 15 teenage boys, telling them to "have some fun" with her. She was gang-raped.

As the scandal was publicized, more victims came forth. The first criminal charges were made. Ultimately, B.C.'s Ministry of Attorney General set up a special Jericho Individual Compensation Program to offer financial compensation to the victims, who were now adults coping with the horrible, and unpurged, memories of what had happened to them during their school years. The task of calling forth the victims, reaching those who had not come forward, and investigating and filing criminal charges against other abusers, continues.

Such compensation, however, was offered at a price: anyone who agreed to accept the compensation had to drop any plans to pursue further legal claims against the province. This "compensation plan" has stirred up a measure of opposition among deaf victims and advocates, who want full justice, not a cut-rate deal.

The now-notorious Jericho Hill School was finally closed, and the students were transferred to new programs set up in two schools in Burnaby, South Slope Elementary and Burnaby South Secondary. Plans were made for the establishment of a new residential school. Steps were taken to ensure that the tragedy would not repeat itself. Students at Burnaby's new Jericho Hill K-12 program receive instruction in living skills that includes abuse prevention. Sign-language classes have become increasingly popular with hearing students. ASL has gained more official and popular respect as a language.

Numerous proposals and recommendations were made. It's too soon to see whether all of these will be adopted. Among them: all staffers and personnel associated with schools for the deaf were urged to learn ASL and develop a better understanding of the communication issues involved. Other recommendations: that ASL be recognized as a foreign language for university admittance, offered to hearing students in junior- and senior-high school, and, in general, the promotion of more awareness and understanding of ASL.

What does sexual abuse have to do with one's communication mode? Plenty. One reason why the Jericho Hill nightmare continued unchecked for so long was that few hearing persons in "positions of authority" understood ASL, which was the first language of the victims, some of whom were as young as 5 or 6. They had no one to confide in but each other. They saw their families during Christmas, Easter, and summer vacations. Then there was the officials' tendency not to believe what the students were saying because of the pervasive suspicion that all deaf children lie and fabricate stories and accusations. According to a 1991 newspaper article indirectly quoting Dulcie McCallum, B.C.'s ombudsman, "Even after social workers and officials at the education ministry began investigating charges of abuse, the children were not seen as credible witnesses."

What happened at the Jericho Hill School is not unique to Canada. Similar cases have been reported, investigated, and prosecuted (with varying degrees of rigor) in the United States. Sometimes the police investigate, but no criminal charges are filed (as happened with Jericho Hill). Sometimes the abuser is forced to resign (which leaves him or her free to take a new position at another school); less frequently, s/he is arrested, put on trial, convicted, and serves time.

The repercussions to the victims, needless to say, are horrendous. The cost in emotional trauma, pain, and stunted lives, cannot be calculated. Victims of abuse carry the emotional scars for years, sometimes for the rest of their lives. A few become abusers themselves, perpetuating the terrible cycle. Some parents of victims carry tremendous anger and guilt for forcing their children to attend the school where they were abused.

Deaf activist Roger Carver, writing about the Jericho Hill tragedy, argues that to eliminate the abuse, we have to eliminate the root cause: the long-standing control of deaf institutions by hearing administrators, and let deaf people regain control of their own schools. He sees the Jericho Hill scandal as symptomatic of a general failure to give deaf children the decent education they deserve.

Having deaf administrators does not automatically eliminate abuse, as the reports show. But if it's part of a systematic program of all-round education, accessibility, improved communication, and empowerment, that's all for the better. More understanding of, and respect for, ASL will facilitate the process.

Incidents of abuse have been reported at a number of schools for the deaf in the U.S. Does this mean that any school in which abuse occurs should be closed down? Some extremists, seizing on these disturbing statistics, go so far as to urge the abolition of all schools for the deaf. But is this the solution? Forcibly mainstreaming all deaf students into public schools would isolate them further and make them even more vulnerable. And—guess what!—plenty of sexual and physical abuse has been reported in public schools, too. Predators have long found haven as teachers, coaches, and scoutmasters. Abusers prey on children who are isolated and lonely, who have no "support network" of friends.

It's not just a school problem either; it applies to deaf children and their families. **The Province**, a major Vancouver newspaper, cites the case of a deaf girl on Vancouver Island who was being sexually abused by her hearing father. Her teacher recognized the symptoms and sent her to the doctor—with her father serving as interpreter. (He was, after all, the only person who could interpret for her.) He told the doctor that she had suffered a bout of flu, but was recovering.

Is the supposed lack of words in ASL the problem? No. ASL has, in fact, a rich and vivid vocabulary of sexual and socially restricted signs, some of which have several regional and ethnic variants. (**Signs of Sexual Behavior** is one such well-illustrated compilation.) The challenge is for the adults in positions of authority—parents, teachers, doctors, adminis-trators, lawyers—to know these signs, too. The major prob-lem isn't vocabulary; it's attitude.

As tempting as it sounds to opponents of Deaf Culture, closing down schools for the deaf is not the solution to abuse. What *would* help? Making it tougher for abusers and preda-tors to take positions as dorm counselors or coaches, *etcetera*, where they have easy access to victims. Implementing more stringent screening procedures for applicants to staff posi-tions. Doing intensive background checks. Networking. Es-tablishing an international database listing known abusers of deaf children. Safeguarding the rights of deaf children and teenagers in medical and legal situations by guaranteeing them first-class interpreters. Teaching young children about the dynamics of abuse. Giving them a better sex education and an opportunity to express their concerns and to report abuse promptly. Making it easier for youthful abusers to receive effective, accessible treatment—and removing them from the dormitory milieu.

First and foremost, parents should be able to communicate with their deaf kids, to instill self-confidence, to teach them that their bodies belong to them and that they don't have to share them with anyone else, and to answer their questions about their private parts, using the correct anatomical terms.

Yes, it's possible to teach 3-year-olds how to protect them-selves. Victimization thrives on ignorance, which is fostered by those favorite old-fashioned attitudes: "Oh, no, it's much too soon to discuss these things with them. Wait until they're 12 or 13." Or: "I don't want to discuss *sex* in my classroom!"

Or: "I just don't want to deal with this!" If deaf children are more vulnerable to abuse than their hearing peers, why should they be kept more ignorant? It doesn't make sense.

It is tougher to abuse an educated child, one who knows how to say no, how to assert herself, how to act on his gut feelings. A brutal counselor will have a tougher time getting away with abusive behavior if the children know how to say, "You don't have any right to treat me like that, and I'm not going to let you get away with it." A sexual predator will not find it easy going with a child who can say, "No, you're not my friend, we don't have any secrets, and I'm not going to let you touch me. Leave me alone!"

Parents should be able to ask their young children, "Has anyone ever touched you where you didn't want to be touched, or touched you in a way that made you feel uncomfortable or afraid?" or "Has anyone offered you a treat or a present or a favor in exchange for doing something you didn't want to do?" or "Has any teacher or staffer punished or hurt you for no reason, and made you promise never to tell anyone?" If the children understand the questions and can respond honestly, and the parents can explain the difference between "good" touching and "bad" touching, the tactics used by abusers, and what steps to take, that may "catch" present abuse and prevent future abuse. But if parents can't and won't, then the task is left to the teachers (some of whom may be squeamish about discussing such things), or a guest speaker. Or someone else. Or nobody.

Knowledge may not always confer power. But ignorance is definitely not bliss.

* In January 2002, a major scandal rocked the international Catholic community: revelations of the Church's official cover-up of sexual abuse of children and teens by pedophile priests who, instead of being defrocked and prosecuted, were transferred to new parishes. The scandal was given considerable front-page, cover-story, prime-time publicity in the national media. Two facts are obvious: abuse is a widespread problem in our society, and no institution is immune— not even the family.

The old days

The new days

Chapter 99

Why does the younger generation of deaf people have such poor manners compared to the older generations?

onsider the familiar lamentation: "*What* is the world coming to? I just don't understand what it *is* with these young people. They seem to have no concept of manners at all." The national decline in manners is a general sociological phenomenon— it's not confined to the Deaf community. But it affects us too.

The church was once an active presence in *all* schools— before the Supreme Court's 1963 ban on school prayer put an end to daily Lord's Prayer recitals and Bible readings. In some ways, this was good. No longer could teachers force their religious biases on their students with impunity; no longer would Jewish and other non-Christian kids be compelled to recite portions of the New Testament in class. But many people feel that something has been lost—a certain wholesome moral, spiritual, and social influence. We've gained freedom—but have we lost our manners?

Many schools for the deaf were founded by Catholic priests and Protestant ministers, and had an explicitly religious mission: to teach deaf people so that they could understand the Word of God and attain salvation. The National Institute in Paris, founded by the abbé de l'Epée, was, of course, Catholic. Thomas Hopkins Gallaudet was a Congregationalist minister. The Hartford Asylum was unabashedly Congregationalist. With the growth of deaf education in the States came a number of Catholic residential schools—some signing, some oral. Most of the state residential schools were mainstream Protestant. Being state-supported didn't necessarily mean secular or pluralist—until recently.

Religion was thus an integral part of the residential-school experience. Students attended chapel on campus every Sunday *en masse*, or went to a Deaf church or interpreted services in the community.

Anyone who has ever seen religious signing done well knows that it's exceptionally beautiful. For deaf people, chapel was an enjoyable and uplifting experience. The soaring, graceful, dramatic signs, the visual calm, were certainly inspiring—and conducive to good manners.

Until fairly recently, at many state schools for the deaf, grace was said before meals. This meant that a certain measure of decorum was imposed on the children: a moment of solemnity and self-discipline before eating. After grace was abolished, the kids simply sat down and tore into the edibles. No pause, no thanks to God. Pass the mustard, nitwit!

It's obvious that the church no longer plays the influential role it once did in deaf people's lives. It's not entirely the fault of the Supreme Court ruling, however. It's the price of technological progress. Life at residential schools used to be a full-time experience. The relative difficulty and expense of transportation forced many deaf students to stay at school all week. Some didn't go home more than once or twice a year; some less frequently than that. Teachers were always there to supervise the students on Sunday or interpret for them at off-campus churches.

When students began going home for the weekend, this tradition was broken. Assuming your (hearing) family attended church on Sunday, you'd likely accompany them. And—nine times out of ten—there'd be no interpreter, so you'd be reduced to fidgeting and daydreaming in your section of the pew until the dreary business was over. Or, if your family didn't attend church or left you at home while *they* went, that was that.

Even if they went home for the weekend, deaf children of deaf parents often attended their parents' Deaf or interpreted church/synagogue, so they maintained a strong Deaf identity, a cohesion. This has been one factor in influencing "Deaf-of-Deaf" students to become leaders in the community. While many deaf children of hearing parents have become progressively more secular and mainstreamed (and disaffiliated), many DODAs have benefited from solid religious and family influences that promote good leadership qualities. They recognize the importance of good protocol, of courtesy.

Since religion is now de-emphasized at schools for the deaf, many deaf children grow up with minimal religious teaching or influence. Freedom of religion often means no religious contact at all. Growing up without any religious identity isn't always a boon. With the loss of religious influence comes the breakdown of discipline—it's hard for a secular school to instill old-fashioned values of morality, decorum, respect.

This parallels a nationwide falling-off in religious commitment. Despite periodic and limited flare-ups of fervor, the student population is arguably much more secularized than it was a generation or two ago. Case in point: the U.S. Catholic Church. During the '60s, once-thriving congregations dwindled. Funding dried up. Parishes consolidated; venerable old churches, once the pride of their communities, were vacated. Parochial schools, once plentiful, closed by the thousands; Catholic students were transferred *en masse* to public schools. Several Catholic schools for the deaf were closed, secularized, or broadened their focus to include physically and mentally handicapped students.

However, the pendulum has a way of swinging back. Note the current trend towards conservatism: etiquette classes for young children, imposition of uniforms or restrictive dress codes in public schools, and the "comeback" of the academically demanding, well-disciplined parochial schools. Can this be seen as the backlash of freedom—or the inevitable reaction to decades of deteriorating values? Will school prayer make a comeback? (Early-morning "flagpole" prayer sessions are already being conducted—legally—at some public schools.) No doubt, residential-school administrators and faculty are watching the trends with keen interest.

Chapter 100

In our city it seems that the churches are beginning to reach out to the Deaf community. Is this the case in other parts of the U.S.?

The National Information Center on Deafness referred this question to Duane King of Deaf Missions (Council Bluffs, Iowa). His response:

es, more hearing churches do seem to be reaching out to deaf people. That is certainly not to say that enough of the reaching-out is done in the right way. Even so, it is encouraging to me to see the reaching-out happening.

As you must know, a very large percentage of the culturally-Deaf people are virtually untouched by most of the reaching-out that is done by hearing churches. The ordinary interpreted service does not appeal to a person for whom English is a foreign language. But I feel that, more and more, the hearing churches are beginning to realize the need for Deaf people to have worship and study and fellowship that is led by Deaf people, and primarily prepared for Deaf people. It might be [possible] someday (far in the future, I'm afraid) that you would ask another question: "Do more Deaf churches seem to be reaching out to hearing people?!"

Even though more hearing churches do seem to be reaching out to Deaf people, an ironic turn of events seems to be making it so that some Deaf people (often influenced by hearing people who are strongly supportive of Deaf culture) are refusing to be touched, even though someone is reaching out to them. The current trend toward separation of cultures, or at least the restoration of Deaf culture, naturally leads one to the conclusion that to reach people of the Deaf Culture, we must train a Deaf person who will be accepted by the culture. Whether or not this is right, it is a fact of the 1990s.

Of course, this is one person's point of view. There must be many other opinions!

▲ ▲ ▲
A few comments of our own

The relationship between churches and deaf education is quite old. The earliest deaf children known to receive an education were from wealthy and aristocratic 16th-century Spanish families whose parents sent them to monasteries to keep them out of society and to prevent them from reproducing. Some of these deaf boys received an education so they could inherit the family fortunes. The law of the land allowed deaf heirs to inherit, provided they could read, write, and speak. Benedictine monks taught several generations of young deaf noblemen. Our commonly used manual alphabet is based on the one they used. Fray Pedro Ponce de León (1510?-1584) is credited with being the first teacher of the deaf.

The abbé de l'Epée and T. H. Gallaudet both had religious missions—to educate the deaf to enable them to attain salvation. Gallaudet's eldest son, Thomas, became an Episcopalian priest. He founded the first Deaf congregation in the United States, St. Ann's Church for the Deaf in Manhattan, and is credited with introducing signed religious services. Largely because of his work, the Episcopalian Church took the lead in Deaf outreach.

By offering signed Sunday services in schools for the deaf (which were attended by both oral and manual students), Protestant and Catholic churches helped keep ASL alive during the "Dark Age" of oralist repression.

Today, the U.S. Catholic Church has a Deaf-outreach program, administering several schools for the deaf. (Some are oral; some signing.) Father Tom Coughlin, the first ordained

Deaf Catholic priest in the U.S., has founded a house for deaf men and women with religious vocations.

There are a few Jewish synagogues for Deaf congregations, primarily in California, Chicago, and New York. The Hebrew Theological Seminary for the Deaf is located in Chicago. Because of relatively tiny Jewish deaf population (and de-emphasis on missionizing), outreach is on a much smaller scale than among Catholics or Protestants. One noteworthy program is Our Way, under the auspices of the National Conference of Synagogue Youth, a division of the Union of Orthodox Jewish Congregations, possibly the largest Ortho-dox organization in the States. They serve Jewish students and young adults from a variety of backgrounds, some of whom have never received even a rudimentary Jewish edu-cation. The Chabad Lubavitcher Chasidic movement has also done *some* Deaf outreach, as have the Conservative and Reform Jewish branches. The are clubs and other organiza-tions for Deaf Jews (such as the National Congress of Jewish Deaf), but no Jewish day schools that use sign language.

The efforts of mainstream churches, offering summer camps and social programs for Deaf youth and adults, are com-mendable. Fundamentalist churches also engage in Deaf outreach. There is one branch of a certain fundamentalist Christian church that specializes in missionary outreach to deaf people. Some of us find this practice disturbing, as this church places great emphasis on "hell" and "eternal damna-tion." The missionaries seek to collect as many Deaf souls as they can, so they can gain credit for "saving the Deaf." They prey on naïve deaf people who have never had a religious education and who join the church out of fear. Once in the church, they are effectively brainwashed. This church preaches a gospel of narrow-minded intolerance towards Jews, Catho-lics, and all others who are perceived as non-Christians according to their doctrines. Yet it maintains an active pres-ence in our community. We consider this spiritual exploita-tion—ancient oppression in new religious trappings.

Chapter 101

Do Deaf people understand boycotts?

eaf people have long been politically weak—which is one of the reasons that the success of DPN was, and is, astonishing. Make no mistake about it— Deaf people have fought valiantly for what they believe in, and not alone. But we have been relatively small in numbers and, until fairly recently, lacked political sophistication. In the early years of the 20th Century, deaf people successfully fought for the right to drive cars—although in some cases it took several years before statewide bans were rescinded. (They were not as successful in preventing the takeover of deaf schools by oralists.) In 1977, Deaf leaders played important roles in getting Section 504 of the Rehabilitation Act enforced—e.g., the synchronized sit-ins in HEW Secretary Joseph Califano's office and VR offices across the nation.

If there's one thing that provokes different reactions from deaf and hearing citizens, it's a boycott. Deaf people, on the whole, simply don't respond the way hearing people do.

In Hearing culture, if a person commits a wrong, s/he is ostracized or shunned by others in the community. In the closely-knit Deaf community, this usually doesn't happen. Supposing a Deaf club-member does wrong—abuses or exploits others, betrays friends, borrows money repeatedly and doesn't repay, lies, steals, etc. Instead of being expelled from the club, s/he will most likely be treated as though nothing had happened.

Consider an actual incident in a Midwestern club where a Deaf man, "Leland," pressured several other club members into loaning him money—loans that he never repaid. Some 30 years passed before the club's officers finally voted to expel him. In any other ethnic/religious/social club, the culprit would have been expelled within a matter of days.

A main factor is the relatively closed social milieu of the Deaf community. Deaf people set up clubs to give themselves an opportunity to socialize freely with others they can communicate with. Because of the formidable communication barriers that still exist between deaf and hearing, Deaf people's opportunities to socialize are severely limited. They do most of their socializing among themselves. Relatively few hearing people can sign well enough to carry on rapid-fire social conversations. In a sense, Deaf people are in social captivity; they're compelled to stay within that small circle. They simply have no choice but to retain the same acquaintances, however dubious their ethics may be, unless they wish to take the risk of breaking away and isolating themselves. They don't easily cut their Deaf friends and acquaintances—especially when those friends and acquaintances grew up with you and attended the same school you did. It just isn't done. Other members will talk among themselves: "Oh, I've known him 20 years," "We go way back," "We went to the same school," *etcetera*. This group loyalty serves to protect the wrongdoer. If two Deaf people went to school together, they've developed close bonds that, in some cases, go deeper than conventional morality. You don't see justice done on your schoolmates. You excuse them. You don't snub them.*

A Deaf club-member can move from friend to friend—forming and destroying sequential friendships with a series of other members, moving on to a new victim every couple of years when the previous relationship breaks down.

As a result, some Deaf people can commit all sorts of wrongs and get away with it. Not perpetually, but as in the case of "Leland," the deadbeat borrower, it took his clubmates several decades to expel him. When the majority is finally motivated to act, *everyone* is compelled to vote unanimously against the wrongdoer, and dissenters are ostracized. Even the deadbeat's wife, "Millie" (who retained her membership), was forced to vote to expel him. That way, she couldn't later claim that she supported him. The evidence would be on record: she voted with the rest.

There are two things that serve to unify Deaf people: 1) when deaf schools are threatened; and 2) blatant oppression by hearing authorities. Then you will find Deaf people banding together with remarkable solidarity.

Every time a school for the deaf or an effective public-school "magnet" program is attacked or threatened with closing, the community is galvanized and goes into action—e.g., forming *ad hoc* committees, picketing, petitioning, lobbying, holding press conferences, mounting letter-writing and fundraising campaigns. These don't always succeed (e.g., the closing of the Boston and Nebraska schools for the deaf), but legislatures have learned that the Deaf community, organized, can be a potent political force (e.g., the saving of Central North Carolina School for the Deaf in Greensboro and the deaf program in Manhattan Beach, California).

What happened in Texas in 1991 with Gayle Lindsey, an unpopular hearing administrator, is instructive. An angry group of Deaf Texans rallied and organized, then literally hooted her out of office. (Unfortunately, this doesn't work with corrupt and ineffective Deaf leaders. We have a harder time getting rid of *them*.)

DPN aside, most deaf people have never learned to become politically powerful because they've grown up in institutions where they've been taught how to be obedient, passive, and quiet, not to stand up for themselves, and certainly not how to communicate their needs. "Be quiet!" "Stop that!" "Get in line!" "Stay there!" "Put your hands down!" Many schools actively discourage deaf kids from asking questions: "Do it. Don't ask questions. Just do as I say!" Needless to say, children who are encouraged to ask questions, and whose questions are taken seriously, learn to think for themselves sooner—a good foundation for becoming politically savvy. Those who are shepherded into unquestioning obedience have a more difficult time acquiring power, sharing it, and wielding it responsibly.

It remains to be seen if the Deaf community can present a unified front—to make our shared concerns and needs known—in the coming Presidential campaigns.

* However, community loyalty doesn't apply to those who simply attend the same college together, nor to contemporaries who aren't schoolmates. Deaf people from mainstreamed backgrounds aren't accorded the same consideration given to those who are products of schools for the deaf. Hence, they are vulnerable to attacks from other deaf people. Those who are late-deafened and are likewise from "hearing" backgrounds are also easily made targets. They don't have the cultural "shielding" that protects those who are "native products."

It's difficult to oppose someone you see, and interact with, socially every day. It's easier to oppose someone who never comes to your club—and whose communicative values don't jibe with yours.

▲ ▲ ▲

A sidenote on boycotts

When a corporation or business is behaving unethically, concerned citizens launch a boycott—an organized nonviolent protest aimed at hurting the offenders financially, and, ideally, forcing them to comply with the demands of the citizens. A boycott is the most popular means of social action undertaken against corporations. Everyone in the community can get involved. The object is to compel the targeted company to improve its policies by hitting it where it hurts most—by making a dent in its profits. Companies are embarrassed by bad publicity, which also has a negative effect on the shareholders.

In the past decades, there have been numerous boycotts by

all manner of groups, and these have had varying degrees of success. Some of us recall the boycotts of non-union California iceberg lettuce and grapes in the early '70s; the boycott of orange juice after Florida Citrus Council spokeswoman Anita Bryant launched an anti-gay crusade (1977); the international boycott of the Nestlé Corporation, which was unethically promoting infant formula in Third World countries (early '80s); and the furious reaction (Spring 1985) to Coca-Cola's marketing "New Coke," which forced the company to reinstate the old formula, renamed "Coke Classic."

Successful protests by the African-American community prevented the marketing of a new brand of cigarette ("Uptown," 1990) and a potent new malt liquor ("PowerMaster," 1993), both of which were to have been promoted exclusively to Black consumers.

The recent actions against Nike (for its practice of employing Third World children in sweatshop conditions and paying them tiny salaries), and the resultant bad publicity it generated, certainly bit into Nike's profits. The campaigns to gain better working conditions for global-corporation and migrant workers, such as strawberry pickers, continue.

The 1992 boycott instigated by the Deaf community against Columbia Pictures' *Calendar Girl* (in which a hearing actor with no previous experience in signing was cast as an ASL-Deaf character, bypassing Deaf actors) started out promisingly, but was rendered moot when the film was pulled from distribution; it was a clunker.

Occasionally, though, a boycott of a film or book has the opposite effect of what it's intended to do—e.g., the Christian Coalition's boycott of Martin Scorsese's *The Last Temptation of Christ* (1988). The movie's instant notoriety helped boost box-office sales. Likewise, The 1989 Iranian *fatwa* (religious edict, in this case a death sentence) decreed on author Salman Rushdie forced him into hiding, but helped propel **The Satanic Verses** onto the best-seller lists, a ranking it might not otherwise have achieved.

Chapter 102

Do we need another
"Deaf President Now" revolution?

he "Deaf President Now" movement of March 1988 was the single most astounding event in Deaf history. DPN was not the first organized Deaf protest. It *was* the most successful, and has served as an inspiration, if not a blueprint, for subsequent protests. The founding of the National Institute in Paris, "Old Hartford," Gallaudet University, NTID, and NCOD were all seminal events. But in terms of sheer impact, DPN was, and remains, unique.

What happens at Gallaudet University has profound repercussions at the other "sister schools," NTID and NCOD/CSUN. NTID students were electrified by news of DPN. Several busloads of students sped to Washington to join the protest—which, by the time they arrived, had become a victory celebration.

Afterwards, they looked around and were, understandably enough, inspired to *think* about replicating DPN, a prospect that made the administration queasy. RIT had no deaf Board members. NTID was headed by a hearing administrator, Dr. William Castle, who was a past president of AGBAD, an oralist—signing, to be sure—but a controversial figure in the Deaf student/faculty/staff community. There were not enough interpreters or notetakers for cross-registered RIT students. Equal access (TTYs, relay services, captioning of RIT instructional films, etc.) was more of a dream than a reality. There had already been a few small-scale, low-key organized student protests. Nothing that would be considered front-page stuff.

When Dr. I. King Jordan visited NTID in November 1988 to relate his experiences and take questions from a large and enthusiastic audience, one student stood up and said that some of them were considering pulling off their own DPN-style protest to put pressure on the administration to appoint a Deaf director and administrators, and didn't he think this was a good idea? Dr. Jordan tactfully replied that it wasn't. DPN was a revolution, a "once-in-a-lifetime" event, and any attempts to duplicate it would backfire. He explained that he was a traditionalist, a conservative, and believed in working through the official channels first. Real change, he said, would take time.

It was sage advice. There was no "NTID DPN." It turned out not to be necessary. Had NTID students attempted to pull it off, it would have been an embarrassment—for them.

After Dr. Castle, who had been NTID's director since its founding, announced his retirement in November 1994, a search process was initiated. It resulted in the appointment of NTID's first deaf director, Dr. Robert R. Davila. He was considered a "prize catch" and received a joyous welcome.

What DPN accomplished noisily, with a week-long strike, marches, rallies, press conferences, extensive TV and print-media coverage, and hot controversy, NTID accomplished quietly, through official channels, but no less effectively.

Still, change comes slowly at times. RIT appointed its first deaf Board member in 1989. Attorney Bonnie Poitras Tucker, an expert in disability law, is a staunch oralist who uses a cochlear implant, refuses to sign, and opposes separate schools for the deaf. She does *not* consider herself part of the Deaf community.

In Fall 1991, the NTID Student Congress organized a "Campus Access Now" protest to address the issues of accessibility, communication barriers, and support services. It was *not* conducted through a campus siege. Nor were there quick solutions.

After Dr. Albert J. Simone became president of RIT in 1993, he began learning basic ASL from NTID's Sam Holcomb, included brief signed remarks in his inaugural address, and later that year, at NTID's 25th Anniversary celebration, gave a complete speech in sign to alumni. None of RIT's previous presidents had seen the need to learn sign language. Dr. Simone *wanted* to communicate directly with deaf people, to acknowledge that NTID students, faculty, and staff were an important part of the RIT community. The NTID community was delighted.

In some situations, quiet diplomacy works best. In others, community-wide protest can have a swift and positive effect. Three years after DPN, the Deaf community of Texas rallied against the reappointment of Gayle Lindsey, a much-resented hearing member of the Texas School for the Deaf Governing Board. On May 1, 1991, they marched on the State Capitol, and that day, Lindsey agreed to resign.

The protests that started on April 25, 1994, against the appointment of a hearing CEO, Max Gould, for the Lexington Center were most directly reminiscent of DPN.

The Connecticut community likewise rallied to oust an incompetent hearing political appointee, Valerie Marino, who had headed the state Commission on the Deaf and Hearing Impaired for two years, even though she knew nothing about Deaf issues and publicly declared that she didn't need to, either. After giving her an opportunity to settle in, attempting to work with her, politely expressing their concerns, and getting rewarded with two years' worth of steadily deteriorating services, the community took action and rallied at the State Capitol on February 7, 1997. Marino was reassigned to another department the following July, vacating the post of CDHI Executive Director.

DPN taught us something about change. There are many constructive ways to effect change. Sometime it needs to be done clamorously; sometimes quietly. But the motive is the same. Deaf people demand a say in matters that affect their destiny—and a chance to show that they are capable. That, after all, is what our struggle for civil rights is about. It's not yet over. Indeed, it's scarcely begun.

Over a decade of promoting Deaf Awareness

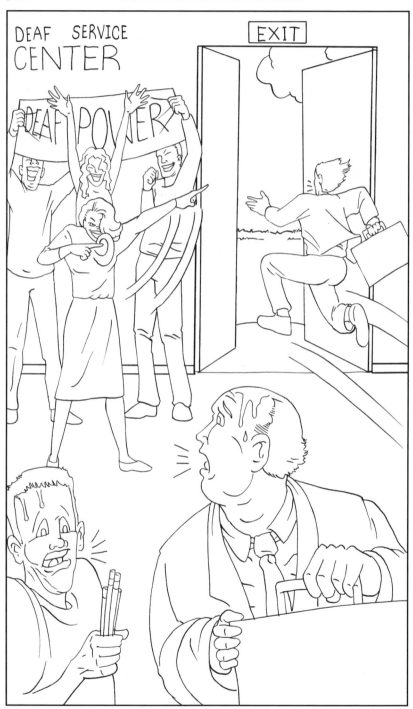

Chapter 103

Should *all* deaf institutions and agencies be headed by deaf people?

We know that this is a controversial chapter. Please read it with an open mind.

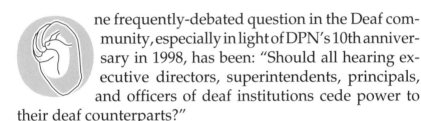

ne frequently-debated question in the Deaf community, especially in light of DPN's 10th anniversary in 1998, has been: "Should all hearing executive directors, superintendents, principals, and officers of deaf institutions cede power to their deaf counterparts?"

Is this what we *really* want? Or need? Will it benefit us?

In a "Guest Column" published in the **Greensboro News & Record** a week after DPN ended, Dr. Elisabeth Zinser made a provocative comment: "As the civil rights of deaf people are assimilated fully in our society, it will be as conceivable to have a hearing president of Gallaudet, once again, as it will be to have a deaf president of the University of North Carolina. We are not there yet. Not now."

We agree. In an ideal world, the Deaf and Hearing communities work together towards their mutual advantage. There is no discrimination, political game-playing, power struggles, or crab theory. All candidates are judged solely on their merits. In the real world, of course, dirty games are played everywhere. Discrimination hasn't been magically vanquished by DPN or the passage of the ADA. Each faction looks out for its own interests. But . . . why should the goals of either community *have* to be in conflict with each other?

Consider the distinguished careers of hearing people who devoted their time, energy, and sometimes their lives, to the cause of deaf education and advocacy. The abbé de l'Epée was one of the first to break free from stereotypical views, to approach deaf people as a student, to learn their language, and to see it as a valuable mode of communication. Many of his successors at the National Institute in Paris were patriarchal oppressors, to be sure. But a few were our friends and allies. The founding of the American School for the Deaf is a story of cooperation, shared civic responsibility, and acceptance of risks. There was a common desire to achieve a goal: bringing education to the deaf population of the United States.

In his **History of the Kentucky School for the Deaf**, published in honor of KSD's centennial (1923), Charles P. Fosdick makes an arresting comment about KSD's fifth superintendent, David C. Dudley: "Mr. Dudley had grown up among the deaf, was entirely at home with them and thoroughly devoted to their interests." This sentiment is echoed by George M. McClure, writing about KSD's eighth superintendent, Augustus Rogers: "The deaf had no more loyal friend than he."[1]

Can a hearing administrator wielding power over deaf people be a "loyal friend" of the Deaf community? Of course. Relatively few deaf people headed schools for the deaf until the last few decades. But not all of these hearing superintendents ruthlessly imposed narrow, distorted, paternalistic-oppressor views about language and deaf people's capabilities onto their charges. Some advocated on behalf of Deaf rights. Harvey Prindle Peet and his son Isaac Lewis Peet, who both headed Fanwood, were "giants in the field."

Philip Gillett, who headed the Illinois School for the Deaf, recommended legislation to have fingerspelling taught in all public schools in Illinois. (A *very* advanced idea!)

And consider two eminent contemporary superintendents: Oscar Cohen of the Lexington School and Winfield McChord, Jr., formerly of ASD. Our community just wouldn't be the same without them.

Superintendents of schools for the deaf aren't the only luminaries. Dr. Edward Allen Fay, scholar, researcher, and longtime editor of the **American Annals of the Deaf**, grew up at the Michigan School for the Deaf, where his father was superintendent, and supported the right of deaf people to be educated through sign language at a time when it was feared that sign language would be swept away by the oralist tidal wave.

Take away our hearing friends, supporters, advocates, students, and teachers, and you end up with a Deaf history riddled with holes. There simply can be no Deaf history without Hearing leadership and support. The Irish Republican motto, "Sinn Fein"—"Ourselves Alone"—has always troubled us. We believe in coalitions, not battle lines; bridges, not barriers.

To paraphrase the question we asked our readers in 1993: if there are two equally qualified candidates for a position, one deaf and one hearing, should the job be given to the deaf candidate? During much our history, this question was never asked. Deaf administrators have grappled with the same problems besetting their hearing counterparts. And, of course, not all deaf "supers" have necessarily done a better job than their hearing predecessors.

Replacing a hearing administrator with a deaf one makes sense *if* the deaf candidate is qualified and the hearing administrator isn't acting in our best interests or is voluntarily stepping down. And is it fair to replace a deaf administrator with a hearing one? If the hearing administrator does a better job than the deaf one, surely. Being deaf or hearing should not be the issue. Ability should.

It all comes down to a question of interest: Can a hearing person in a powerful and influential position have the Deaf community's best interests at heart?

Certainly. When we feel outrage at the shenanigans of hearing profiteers, thieves, exploiters, autocrats, and other scoundrels who victimize deaf people, we remind ourselves that every community is like a barrel of rubies intermixed with rotten apples. The small number of rotten apples shouldn't make us lose sight of the rubies.

White Hats, Black Hats

It's tempting—and too easy—to see hearing people in terms of black and white: the bad guys and the good guys.

But it's pretty easy to determine whom the community's staunchest allies, supporters, and advocates have been. Their actions have been in accordance with their opinions.

Here's an admittedly biased sampling of a few notables, in and outside of the educational field:

● Auguste Bébian was the teacher of the great 19th-century French Deaf advocate Jean-Ferdinand Berthier. According to William Moody's **Gallaudet Encyclopedia** entry, they "argued that LSF, the 'natural language of signs,' should be recognized as the primary language of instruction for deaf students."

● Dr. Powrie Vaux Doctor, a long-time professor at Gallaudet College, and a colorful character. His memory is honored by the endowment of the Doctor Chair of Deaf Studies.

● The Rev. Thomas H. Gallaudet held a rigorously Congregationalist view of sin and salvation, but his influence on Deaf history, through his work with Laurent Clerc and the Hartford Asylum, was positive.

● Joanne Greenberg wrote a realistic novel about a Deaf couple and their relationship with their hearing daughter, **In This Sign**, part of which was adapted as a TV-movie, *Love is Never Silent*, which won an Emmy for Julianna Fjeld, the co-executive producer. Fjeld had successfully held out for getting Deaf performers Phyllis Frelich and Ed Waterstreet in the roles of Janice and Abel Ryder. The result? Sparkling performances by Deaf actors, rave reviews, an Emmy, and enthusiastic audiences.

● Senator Tom Harkin of Iowa, considered one of the best friends of the Deaf community on Capitol Hill. His brother Frank is deaf. At The DEAF WAY Conference and Festival in July 1989, Harkin told a huge audience how Frank had been informed that because he was deaf, he could become a cobbler, a baker, or a printer. That was one of Tom Harkin's first realizations that there is injustice in the world.

● Dr. Ray L. Jones, who oversaw the National Leadership Training Program at CSUN.

● Harlan Lane, professor and scholar, author of **When the Mind Hears** and the perennially controversial **Mask of Benevolence**, has been one of our staunchest supporters.

● Edna Simon Levine, a noted psychologist at New York University, and Broadway actress Anne Bancroft used their connections and clout to try and obtain grants to launch the NTD. Dr. Levine and Jerome D. Schein created the renowned NYU Deafness Research & Training Center.

● Elizabeth Peet was a legendary professor and Dean of Girls at Gallaudet College, and a superb signer. She was also the daughter of Isaac Lewis Peet and granddaughter of Harvey Prindle Peet, both of them distinguished superintendents of Fanwood. She encouraged Martin Sternberg to compile an ASL dictionary, which he did. It took 19 years. Sadly, Dr. Peet didn't live to see the published book, but she knew it was being done. The **American Sign Language Dictionary** is now a definitive work, and a popular CD-ROM.

● Dr. Harold Quigley was a respected and loved superintendent of the Rochester School for the Deaf.

● Susan M. Schaller has done much to focus community and national attention on the plight of languageless deaf people. She is author of **A Man Without Words** and founder of a nonprofit organization, NaDA.

● Mary E. Switzer, the visionary Commissioner of the Office of Vocational Rehabilitation, helped launch the NTD, RID, Captioned Films for the Deaf, and CSUN's National Leadership Training Program, among others.

● Helen Young, who operates an interpreter service in Arizona, exemplifies the highest standards of her profession: skilled signing, respect for the client, and respect of the Deaf community. A joy to work with.

● Dr. Elisabeth Zinser, whose appointment as Gallaudet University's 7th president focused world attention on the Deaf community as nothing had ever done before. With grace and dignity, she transformed an impossible situation into a personal and political triumph—for herself and the DPN advocates. She was an honored guest at the DPN+10 festivities.

● Parents of deaf children who approach the Deaf community with an open mind, bringing their questions and concerns, seeking guidance, and establishing rewarding cross-cultural friendships. By taking a broad view of "normality" and "different-ness," they acknowledge that their child is a unique person with individual needs. Parents who invest time and energy into learning how to sign so that they can share a language with their deaf children. Parents who support their deaf children in fighting for their rights to get accessible communication and to obtain the best possible education.

● The many anonymous hearing supporters and local businesspeople who donated food and other provisions to the DPN protesters. They sympathized with the students' desire for justice, or maybe had a soft spot for the underdog. They played an important role in the protest's success.

● Administrative assistants, secretaries, PR people, librarians, and outreach directors at schools for the deaf who facilitate research and interviews, answer questions, and provide information. (What would we do without them?)

While we admire Thomas Jefferson for his views on democracy and government, and are in awe of the inventive amplitude of his intellect, we cannot muster any enthusiasm for his astonishingly narrow-minded attitude towards deaf people. When offered the opportunity to move John Braidwood's oral school from Cobbs (the Bolling plantation) to the University of Virginia in 1816, he replied that he had no interest in promoting a "mere charity." This is especially ironic in light of the fact that Jefferson was distantly related to the first generation of deaf Bollings.[2]

Dr. Mason Fitch Cogswell and the city fathers of Hartford, Connecticut, won everlasting glory by sending Rev. Thomas H. Gallaudet abroad, and giving Laurent Clerc a hearty welcome. And Virginia did get its school for the deaf 23 years later, 13 years after Jefferson's death. Jefferson had nothing to do with its establishment. Had his attitude towards deaf education been more enlightened, the history of the Deaf community in the United States might well have taken a radically different course!

What about Alexander Graham Bell? Oralists praise him; ASL-Deaf people execrate him. It can be argued that his influence on Deaf history has certainly been negative, but not completely so. Without the invention of the telephone, would we have had the TTY? Without telephone lines, could we possibly enjoy the benefits of the Internet? Bell's theories about deafness have not stood the test of time. As for his obsession with making deaf people talk, we can be grateful that he never lobotomized any of his students, to eliminate the deaf part of their brains!

Bell aside, we have much to grateful for in our relationship with the Hearing community. We shouldn't forget those who gave generously of their time, energy, and concern, to the furthering of our interests. What benefits us benefits us all.

---

[1] McClure quotes Rogers' final annual report (circa 1928): "I wish to say that money expended in the education of the deaf brings as large, if not larger, return than that spent for hearing children . . . I am sure the state gets a larger return on the money expended here than in any of its other institutions, no matter how important or worthy they may be."

[2] See John Vickrey Van Cleve and Barry A. Crouch, **A Place of Their Own: Creating the Deaf Community in America** (Washington, D.C.: Gallaudet University Press, 1989), Chapter 3, "Braidwood and the Bollings," pp. 26-27. Jefferson's sister Martha married John Bolling, the uncle of John, Mary, and Thomas Bolling, Jr., the first three deaf Bollings.

Chapter 104

What problems, difficulties, or challenges would a "hearing and deaf" couple face as they relate to one another (i.e., dating, marriage)?

hen we originally published this question in **DEAF LIFE**, we received three intriguing responses from readers who were partners in deaf/hearing relationships and marriages.

I (LL) happen to be a survivor of a failed deaf/hearing marriage. My progressive deafness was certainly a factor, although by no means the only one. I've long been interested in learning how both partners make their intermodal marriages (my term) work.

In her autobiography, **The Feel of Silence**, attorney and law professor Bonnie Poitras Tucker, herself a survivor of a bitter divorce from a hearing man, makes some acerbic observations about deaf/hearing marriages. She cites a report that indicates that while quite a few prominent deaf men have hearing wives, practically no prominent deaf women have hearing husbands. Intermodal marriages benefit deaf men far more than deaf women. Deaf men in such marriages typically derive immeasurable support from their hearing wives, who assist them in their work and show enduring loyalty, compassion, and commitment—qualities that our society expects of wives. On the other hand, deaf women with hearing husbands have been in a much less favorable position. They haven't received the same kind of support and encouragement from their hearing husbands that hearing wives have traditionally accorded their deaf husbands. It's not just a Deaf-community problem; it's a problem affecting our entire society.

▲ It is not easy to be a "hearing and Deaf" couple because there are so many things involved. Deaf and hearing people usually think and express their ideas in different ways. Communication is the biggest problem because of hearing people's signing skill is not often very good in general. It would be too difficult to talk with each other if they are not able to talk to each other effectively and at fast rate. So they won't talk to each other as much.

Also, it depends on the hearing person's involvement in the Deaf community, and understanding of Deaf culture and customs. I dated a hearing person once, and I learned a lot from this mistake. The person was not really willing to learn ASL (and knew only little) and expected me to use my voice, but it is much easier for me to use sign language. He also refused to be involved in the Deaf community, that is where I always am, so we did not see each other very much. I don't feel too comfortable being around hearing people for too long because of communication barriers even if we could write back and forth, but it is a boring and long task, as is speechreading and speaking for most deaf people. He didn't care about Deaf culture or why my customs are different in some ways.

All of this was causing too many conflicts so I decided it was not worth it to date him any longer.

I feel that the best hearing candidate is a person who has a strong skill of sign language or even a strong desire to develop his/her signing skill, is willing to be involved in the Deaf community, and understands the differences in Deaf and hearing people and their world. The [hearing] person also cannot expect the Deaf person to be like a "hearing." All of these can be applied in a marriage between a Deaf and hearing. But the ability to communicate is much more important in dating, including the ability of making some adjustments.

All of the above is important because the couple will be in the Deaf world more often than the hearing world (except when the couple is in a public university where the contact with the Deaf community may be limited). The person must be serious about accepting the challenges of dating and marrying a Deaf person because he/she will be partially leaving the hearing world.

Daphne Goodall
Rochester, New York

▲ I am deaf and my husband is hearing. We met each other from our old job. One day he asked me many interesting questions about Deaf People like how to use special TDD and how come deaf became deaf? He also wanted to learn sign language. I taught him a few signs that relate to work, he became more interest and wanted to learn more signs, he went to night school to learning more signs. We are still working together to develop better communication skills. I taught him more signs everyday. Of course we had a lot of notes that we wrote each other to keep up with our communications.

After a few months he asked me to go out on a date. I was very shocked because I never thought about this happening in my life. He was very patient with me and he kept working on sign communications. He told me that he felt that sign language is very important and beautiful for deaf people to use. He felt it was really worthwhile for him to learn many new signs.

Later on we got married—in May, 1991. We are very happy marriage. Right now he is an interpreter, he enjoys it very much and he met many different deaf people. Now we don't write each other notes any more, WHEW!!!

I know it is really hard to learn sign language for hearing people, but it will take time and a lot of patience. It is really worth the challenge to learn new things. Most of my friends won't accept my husband because he is hearing. That is very wrong, to discriminate. People have to understand that no one is perfect. I know most hearing people think that deaf are dumb because hearing people don't understand the deaf people. I hope hearing people will understand about deafness people someday.

People should not to be discriminate—everyone is the same if you are deaf or hearing people. Just let love be in your heart. GOOD LUCK!!!

Sarah A. Burden
St. Clair Shores, Michigan

▲ My fiancé and I are a hearing and deaf couple. We both agree that communication and culture are two factors that can influence our relationship a lot. There are two different languages and two different cultures that need to be taken into consideration at all times. We have grown up in our own culture with our own language and sometimes it is difficult to always be sensitive toward the other one's needs. But it is vital if the relationship is to last.

Societal pressures as to educational issues, communication issues, etc., also influence our relationship. We each have our own opinions on certain issues and we discuss them.

They keys to any successful relationship are honesty, trust, and communication. If those are intact then any problem or challenge can be conquered.

Mechelle Disch
Fitchburg, Massachusetts

William Hayes
Rochester, New York

Deaf Awareness 5-Minute Quiz

Chapters 90—104

Answers are on the bottom of the page, upside down.

True or False:

1. Aristotle believed that born-deaf people could learn to think and communicate just as well as hearing people, given encouragement and a good education.

2. Some Deaf people are angry about the radical disparity between the salaries of interpreters and the Deaf people who teach them.

3. A single interpreter can work for an hour or two without a break.

4. The Comprehensive Skills Certificate is no longer awarded by the RID.

5. The Code of Ethics prohibits interpreters from socializing with their clients when they're off-duty.

6. In many ways, deaf people have been at a tragic disadvantage when it comes to getting information about AIDS that could have saved their lives, but wasn't accessible or understandable to them.

7. Pervasive sexual and physical abuse in deaf schools and programs has much to do with the victims' mode of communication.

8. The earliest schools for the deaf, whether Catholic or Protestant, had an explicitly religious mission.

9. Deaf people's social opportunities are unlimited. Members of a club typically stay within a small, closed social circle for sentimental reasons.

10. Very few hearing administrators and teachers have cared about the interests of the Deaf community they've supposedly been serving.

10. False.

1. False; 2. True; 3. False; 4. True; 5. False; 6. True; 7. True; 8. True; 9. False;
Answers:

Chapter 105

My wife is deaf. I'm hearing. When we enter the deaf community, why do I feel like I'm from an alien nation? I want to fit in . . . but how?

e'll start with the assumption that this relationship is basically strong and healthy. No amount of advice is going to save a relationship that isn't. We also assume that this question refers to social (club-type) situations.

As you undoubtedly know, intermodal (Deaf/Hearing) relationships and marriages are fairly common. And yet, judging by the statistics, these tend to be more risky (and unhappy) than Deaf/Deaf ones. Even so, some prominent Deaf advocates and "leading figures" have hearing spouses. How do they reconcile "marrying out" with their philosophy of Deaf Pride?

In a word, love. In another, commitment.

Obviously, Deaf and Hearing partners find each other attractive at least partly because of their differences. Disparate backgrounds can doom a relationship—or add zest to it. In a successful partnership, the differences are balanced with a degree of commonality—shared values and interests. These could include children, religion, social activism, commitment to improving the educational and legal rights of deaf people, an ASL background, love of a particular sport (e.g., skiing), or a particular passion (building a family, restoring old houses, horseback riding, collecting books or antique paperweights, gardening, breeding Siamese cats, training companion dogs, operating a business, etc.). Partners in successful relationships often have wildly divergent interests and a few shared ones. Or vice versa.

So what happens when the partners leave their home or business environment and venture together into, say, a Deaf club or social group, where one of them "belongs" and the other is an "alien"?

Communication is the most formidable barrier, followed closely by *attitude*. Obviously, it helps for the hearing spouse to know sign language. Then s/he can communicate on a reasonable level with most Deaf folks. But in these Deaf-culture enclaves, hearing interlopers are apt to be viewed with suspicion, if not outright hostility. We've heard, and read, stories from hearing and late-deafened persons about how cruelly they were treated when they ventured into Deaf society. This, unfortunately, is to be expected. There are a considerable number of Deaf snobs—and just plain nasties. A hearing spouse has to learn how to handle these people when they perform their "if looks could kill" or "what the hell are *you* doing here?" routines. (Suggestion: shrug it off with an expression of exquisite boredom and go elsewhere. Revisit the punchbowl or join a livelier group.)

One thing to keep in mind about "hostiles": most Deaf couples with kids have hearing children (and raise same), so what's their beef against hearing people? On what basis is a person to be rejected just because s/he is hearing? Let *them* answer that.

The "alien" partner should count on getting moral support from the "belonging" one. So, Deaf folks, if your hearing spouse is being cut down by your Euchre League buddies, *you* should be prepared to deal with it tactfully but forcefully.

One thing Deaf people resent—understandably—is when a hearing person tries to "elbow in" on a Deaf group. There is a fine distinction between being assertive and aggressive. The situation's a bit like that of the new kid on the block. You may need to make the first move. If you have something to offer the group—your skill as a magician, juggler, or cardplayer; a mini-van; choice captioned or foreign videos; a basket of home-baked goodies—these can help ease the shock.

You might consider inviting the group (or a select part of it) to your territory for a party, dinner, buffet, or cookout. This can serve as an effective icebreaker.

Everyone likes a neighbor who can "make good things." If you can make terrific doughnuts, pies, cakes, cookies, or pizza, that's a "marketable" skill. If not, you can buy ready-made, or commission custom-made, goodies—and cater a cheesecake-variety party, an ice-cream-and-cookies social, a pizza fest, or a barbecue with home-baked pies or a variety of fresh-fruit dishes for dessert.

You could also throw a seasonal or theme party for your Deaf acquaintances. This need not be fancy or expensive. It need not even feature alcoholic beverages. It requires planning (designing and sending invitations), forethought (establishing a comfortable, well-lit environment with plenty of chairs), and imagination (making it an event worth going to). If you lack indoor space, it could be a poolside or backyard gathering. Have a lawn picnic. Rent a tent.

These suggestions do involve some measure of time, trouble, and expense. Consider it an investment in your social life and the community. The payoff—more cordial relationships with some good folks—could be handsome.

First and foremost, be comfortable with yourself. Greet your guests by namesign; make them feel valued and at ease. Then relax. You've done your fair share. You'll be showing the Deaf folks that you're willing to take the first step; the next step is up to them.

Some Deaf persons may warm up to a new arrival quickly. Others may keep a wary distance at first, but will gradually "come around." Still others never will. (You don't have to invite them back.) You, in turn, have to have a genuine commitment to the group (doing what you can to help out and participate) and a measure of indomitable good will (without losing your self-respect).

And best of luck with the doughnuts.

Chapter 106

If there's a hearing person with minimal or no signing skills in a group of deaf individuals who all are skilled signers, should the deaf people write notes back and forth with the hearing person? So many times I have seen deaf individuals demand to be included in the conversation of a group of hearing people, but completely ignore a hearing person in a group of deaf people.

—Gary Crawford, Crookston, Minnesota

ustice, like communication, is a two-way street. If you accept the pronouncements of oralists and anti-ASL propagandists, signing deaf people constitute a tiny minority of communicators. We recognize that the majority of hearing people don't know how to sign, and that many are not motivated to learn. Does this give deaf people free license to ignore the occasional hearing person who wanders into our midst? We do so at our own peril.

Two key points:

1.) It's exceedingly rare to find a solitary hearing person at a Deaf gathering who doesn't know sign language and cannot communicate with Deaf people at a basic level. The

reverse of our deaf-person-at-a-hearing family-gathering scenario is a sole hearing relative in a Deaf family. But then, we
have to ask, how can a hearing person have lots of Deaf
relatives and not know how to sign?

2.) Moreover, it is true that some Deaf people will ignore the
solitary hearing person at the gathering. They prefer to focus
on their own conversations and concerns; they don't want to
bother with stray hearing strangers. Some Deaf people have
the scornful attitude: "Hearing people, look at them—*they're*
the ones who have a communications handicap."

Says one Deaf man:

> Keep in mind, Deaf people—88%, 99%—grow up feeling left
> out, excluded, all their lives. All *our* lives. So when a hearing
> person shows up at a Deaf gathering, our feeling is, "Let them
> have a taste of their own medicine for one day!"
>
> Most Deaf people don't carry pads and pencil—it's a question
> of pride. Can't find paper? Then use gestures! The underlying
> motivation is to force hearing people to learn sign language.

Conversely, at virtually every Deaf gathering, there *are*
bound to be people who don't mind, and may even enjoy,
making the extra effort to connect. You will always (or almost
always) find some friendly Deaf people who are willing to
invest a bit of time and energy into establishing some sort of
basic communication. And a number of Deaf persons are
highly motivated. They capitalize on these encounters as a
mutual learning experience, a positive communicative, educational, and social challenge. They discern a prime opportunity to reach out to a hearing person, to teach him a few things
in a friendly way, to influence her perception of Deaf people,
possibly even motivate him to learn how to sign. They want
to be good ambassadors for the Deaf community.

A good number of Deaf people (including the Deaf man
quoted above) have tutored and taught hearing students,
formally and informally, at some point in their lives. These
will be the ones who tend to be especially patient and

empathetic. They understand how it feels to begin learning a new language from scratch. They've been through it with their own students.

Although the barriers to fluent communication may be considerable, we are a resourceful lot. We can usually find a way. Writing notes back and forth is the most common way. Paper is easy to come by—we've even used public-wash-room paper towels and paper restaurant napkins. A chalk-board, magic slate, even a computer keyboard and monitor (if they're handy), can be pressed into service. One of us (LL) has visited friends who used two sets of Scrabble tiles to spell out names and key words on the dinner table!

Some deaf people carry 3" x 5" spiral-bound memo books or small pocket-sized pads of paper. These come in handy for impromptu conversations with salespeople, business con-tacts, or the inevitable hearing stranger who approaches us asking directions to City Hall. They're also good for extended chats. Of course, these are also handy for hearing people (who account for the majority of memo-pad sales anyway).

We consider the old-fashioned method (favored by the sign-illiterate) of scratching block letters into our palms an insult to our dignity. As an absolute last resort, it will do, but it's the lowest possible recourse! And as for "tracing" letters in the air—forget it. As we've already pointed out, it doesn't work.

We would counsel a hearing person in this situation to be assertive. Go into the midst of the clusters of people who are standing around and signing, and say, "Hello. My name is such-and-such and I can't sign well." Use body language and gestures. Be positive. Be confident. If hearing people are assertive and self-assured, most Deaf people *will* welcome them.

Chapter 107

Is it polite for a hearing family or group to talk among themselves at the table when there's a deaf person there? Is it okay for a deaf guest to read a book at the table?

n the Deaf community, it is considered exceedingly impolite for hearing people (whether family, friends, or acquaintances) to knowingly exclude a deaf person from following what's going on. This dinner-table scenario occurs most frequently in hearing families with deaf children. But it happens to late-deafened adults as well. Social gatherings and cozy family dinners can be a brutal ordeal for late-deafened people, who are often forced to sit in a fog of bewilderment and haze of isolation, while the talk, now incomprehensible, swirls around them.

Not all dinner-table scenarios are equally stressful. If the family is just eating quietly, there's no real problem. But if there is conversation of any kind, the hearing members *should* make a genuine effort to include the deaf person. If they know sign, or even fingerspelling, so much the better. But since so many families don't, they need to find *some* way—a gentle pat on the shoulder, pointing to whoever's talking, repeating, jotting down conversational notes—doing whatever they can to include the deaf person in the action.

We recognize that, all too often, hearing families will *not* make the effort. They "don't know how," they're "too busy," "too tired," "too old," or "it's not important enough," or whatever excuses they rely on. They should realize that talking around and through deaf people hurts them. With children, it may have a detrimental and lasting effect on their emotional health. Adults have feelings, too.

Thus, if hearing family or hosts are unwilling to make any effort to include the deaf person, s/he ought to be allowed to read a book at the table while the others are talking. In hearing culture, this is considered inexcusable bad manners. In Deaf culture, the isolated deaf person has the right. By excluding a deaf person from participating in the interchange, the hearing family has forfeited its claim to good manners—it is behaving rudely in the first place.

One of the most common traits shared by deaf people is the experience of being excluded at social gatherings, holidays, and dinners. (This includes picnics and cookouts as much as formal occasions such as tea parties, birthday celebrations, and Thanksgiving feasts.) Recounting, analyzing, and comparing these experiences are part of Deaf culture. Every so often, deaf people get together and discuss their experiences of family exclusion:

"Yeah, that happened to me too. Mother, father, guests yak-yak-yakking, I couldn't speechread, forced into isolation. What could I do? Sit there gaping."

"I visited my family for our annual Christmas gathering, but the next day, I didn't go with them to my uncle's dinner party because I dislike being left out of the conversation. I stayed behind at Mom's place, went online, and cyber-chatted with a few friends."

"I got into a squabble with my hostess's elderly mother when she tried to confiscate the book I was reading at the table."

These tales are all true.

Often, deaf kids or adults will see others (parents, sibs, relatives, guests) telling an anecdote or joke, and will ask, "Mom, what's he saying?" Mom will summarize it *very* briefly. Jokes and funny stories, which are subtle social interactions, are particularly frustrating to miss out on. Much of the charm, the impact of "table humor" is in the shared reaction of the audience—everyone bursting into laughter simultaneously. Suppose there's a deaf child at the table who misses the joke. "Mom, what's so funny?" Mom holds up a finger, finishes laughing herself out, and regains her breath. She then proceeds to retell the joke—but it's not funny anymore. Something—the timing, the spontaneity, the sparkle—has gotten lost.

A good solution (and more socially acceptable than bringing in a book) is to allow the deaf child or adult to bring a signing friend—deaf or hearing—to the gathering or to dinner. At least two deaf or sign-fluent people should be at the table—the more, the better! This way, they can communicate with each other, and the single deaf person won't fall into the "isolation" trap.

Over a decade of promoting Deaf Awareness

Chapter 108

How do Deaf people cope in situations where they're with hearing people who can't sign?

ll of us interact regularly with hearing persons representing a diversity of communication skills, from native-ASL fluency to hopelessly inept rubberlippers. (We won't even *mention* the nasty ones with the *really* bad attitudes!) Depending on our jobs and social lives, we have all sorts of encounters every day (or almost every day). How do we cope? We use our ingenuity, our imagination, our persistence, and our patience.

We acknowledge that deaf/hearing interaction *can* be frustrating. It doesn't always work. But there are rewards. And this much is obvious: when two persons want to communicate badly enough, they usually find a way.

Scratch pads? As noted in Chapter 106, some of us carry jotbooks, 3" x 5" spiral-bound memo books, or small pads and pens; others don't. This can be a political mini-issue. One of the **DEAF LIFE** crew (MSM) says, "I don't believe in carrying a memo pad. I want the burden of communication to be on the hearing person." But another (LL) says, "I'd feel undressed if I left the house without my jotbook." I use it to record book titles I'm interested in, ideas, URLs, shopping memoranda, and as a conversational aid. Those who don't carry paper items employ body language, simple signs, gestures, mime . . . whatever works.

Faking it: Okay, we all know that faking it (i.e., bluffing or pretending to understand unintelligible talk) isn't good practice. It can get us into all sorts of dreadful, embarrassing, mortifying, even dangerous situations. However, there are times when it is the only reasonable expedient. Case in point (as recounted by MSM):

I took a mid-December flight from Rochester to Indianapolis, and was seated next to one of those Sweet Little Old Lady types. And she began chattering to me. She was excited about something, and found me (so she thought) a willing audience. I politely pointed to my ear and shook my head—the universally-understood gesture for "I'm deaf," but she was oblivious. I just couldn't make her understand. She kept babbling on and on, animatedly patting my forearm every so often for emphasis. I imagine she was talking about her family, whom she was going to visit, and her grandchildren and great-grandchildren, and how lovely and cute and smart they all were, and what a lovely house they had, and what a wonderful holiday they were going to have together. This is mere conjecture, because I understood nothing of what she was saying. So I just looked alert and interested, and at strategic intervals I'd give her a nod and smile, as if I were absolutely delighted to listen to her. And that was how I coped with that!

Got the time? And what about hearing strangers who approach us for directions or the time? It depends on how rushed we are, or if there are others around us who can deal with it. Sometimes we don't want to go through the ordeal of starting a time-consuming and misunderstanding-riddled exchange, only to have the other party say, "Oh, never mind!" or "Forget it!!!" and abruptly take off, directionless. That's where a jotbook comes in handy. Most (if not all) hearing folks are good about that. Once we understand what they're looking for, we can determine if we can help.

Being upfront: This isn't *always* feasible, but it's generally a good approach. Telling another person, "Sorry, I didn't understand you; I'm deaf," or "Would you write that down for me, please? I'm deaf," can spare us both tremendous discomfort. We can even tell the other party before they start talking to us, preferably with the universal-gesture-sign for "I'm deaf." We don't have to apologize for being deaf. We just need to inform others who don't know us that we are—the sooner the better. Otherwise, misunderstandings can creep in. And misunderstandings are the bane of our everyday lives.

Real life: We personally know of very few deaf people who use Cued Speech, and we have never seen anyone using it in public, nor have we seen speech-decoding eyeglasses or any other experimental deaf/hearing interface in use.

Is improving our speechreading skills The Answer? Some of us are skilled speechreaders; others try to speechread strangers but end up getting ensnared in miscommunication. Some of us who have taken speechreading training have benefited from it. Others haven't. But learning to pick up "associational cues" (posture, facial expressions, environmental clues) is a good skill to have. Most of are already alert and observant. We *need* to be. But being alert and observant doesn't guarantee that we'll be able to instantaneously decode mumblers and word-slurshers. Sometimes we have to guess.

The important thing is not to be afraid of telling others we're deaf. How they respond to this information gives us vital clues as to what kind of person they are. (I.e., if they're embarrassed, or, heaven forfend, mock us, or respond in a emotionally or physically hostile manner.) In some cases, it will spell the end of the conversation. In a few cases, it will provoke an interesting conversation. In others, the conversation will get off to the wrong start, but will end up proceeding in a positive direction. Some hearing people don't have the patience. Some are simply mean. Some are dumb jerks. And a few are vicious. (Luckily, as decent, law-abiding citizens, we have the law on our side—well, most of the time, anyway.) We can't tell until we assay.

Granted, people in general are an unpredictable lot. So the best approach is to be prepared for the unexpected. These interactions can be quite educational—we gain a better understanding of how hearing people see deaf people, what kind of images or preconceptions they have. Most of us already have a pretty good idea, though. That's why Deaf people tend to be patient. We do our best ... and are prepared for the worst.

Chapter 109

When dealing with strangers, how upfront should deaf people be about being deaf?

n the whole, we feel that deaf people should be honest when dealing with strangers. That means identifying ourselves as deaf immediately. Being forthright has definite advantages.

The oralist position is that deaf people should act as hearing as possible—in other words, to pass, whenever possible, as hearing. While this may work splendidly for some people at least some of the time, it creates certain hazards. But even oralists can be upfront.

Bonnie Poitras Tucker's **The Feel of Silence** is a fascinating account of a profoundly deaf woman's struggle to succeed in the Hearing community. As she has made clear in the book and in numerous interviews, Tucker, a noted attorney and expert on disability law, has never learned sign language, and refuses to do so. She advocates oralism, although she admits that it may not work for everyone as well as it has worked for her. She feels that the Deaf community is "segregated," restrictive, and prefers to work within the broader parameters of the dominant (Hearing) community.

This is not to say that the Hearing community has made it easy for her. She hasn't had a particularly easy time at all. **The Feel of Silence** contains some bloodcurdling anecdotes about the treatment she has experienced from hearing people. For example, needing to get her refrigerator repaired, warning the repair office that she wouldn't be able to hear her home phone ringing—and having the repairman not show up because he called twice and didn't get an answer. Getting into a crowded dry-cleaner's drive-in pick-up line during the Christmas rush, not realizing that her automobile horn was blaring. Then off to the post office, where everyone waiting in the long line had to take a numbered slip and the numbers were called out by the clerks—and she couldn't speechread it when it was called.

If a deaf person notifies others (or whoever's in charge) by saying, "I'm deaf, and I won't be able to hear my number over the P.A. What should I do?", will s/he get some elementary accommodation? Maybe. A big maybe.

For ASL-Deaf people, being upfront means signing openly, proudly, wherever we are. Should ASL-Deaf people use sign when they're among hearing (or deaf) nonsigners? Well, that depends on the situation and the people involved. Some oral-deaf people, like Tucker, do not like to communicate with Deaf people who are signing, as it distracts them, making speechreading more difficult. They want to focus their attention on the face, not the signs. Some Deaf people always sign—say, in restaurants—hoping that the hearing person may possibly understand a little. When ordering from a menu, a deaf person can simply point, or scrawl a note. If s/he wants to be very political, s/he can do what Alan R. Barwiolek did—make the server write down all the specials, if they're not posted. (Al B. invariably ordered from the regular menu.)

Deaf people should be allowed to sign in any situation—i.e., they should not be told, "Use your voice," if they are not comfortable using speech. It should be their decision. Using one's voice to order something can be useful in a pinch, but can get a deaf person into all sorts of difficulties.

Bernard Bragg has a story he likes to tell, "The Beefeater Catastrophe." (It's recounted in **Meeting Halfway in American Sign Language**.) He was visiting friends (Tom Posedly, deaf, and Penny Posedly, hearing), and they went to "a posh restaurant." Feeling a bit cocky, Bragg declined Penny's offer to interpret orally for him and said, "I will speak for myself." Whereupon he told the waiter that he wanted a "Beefeater martini up with a lemon twist." When the drink arrived, "it was in a very tall glass and was orangish-pink in color with a slice of lime and a cherry stuck on the top. I must have looked horrified because the waiter asked 'What's wrong?'" Penny told Bragg that she couldn't possibly fingerspell the ingredients the waiter rattled off. Bragg didn't even dare to taste it.

Similarly, Tucker (who always uses her voice) recounts her difficulty in ordering steak:

> I like my steak rare. Very rare. [But] nine times out of ten I get it cooked "well." Despite my best efforts, somehow my *r* sounds like a *w*, and thus when I say 'rare' it comes out sounding like "well."
>
> I've got a new trick. Now I order my steak "rare" and continue by saying, "That means bloody—almost walking." Usually it works.

Deaf folks who don't feel over-confident about using their voices have found that writing down their choices on a slip of paper (preferably in neat printing, one slip per person) and giving it to the server is a practically foolproof approach. This leaves no room for misunderstanding. It makes life a bit easier for the servers, too, since it frees them from the onus of deciphering the unclear speech of deaf customers in what may be a noisy environment, or trying to decode confusing gestures.

Some of the stickiest situations arise from travel. (Surprise!) When she's commuting by air, Tucker tries to get a front aisle seat. Southwest Airlines doesn't assign seats, but issues numbered boarding passes on a first-come, first-served basis. Those with numbers under 20 board first and get first choice of seats. This necessitates getting to the airport very early. On one occasion, even though she arrived early, Tucker received pass #48—too far in back.

> I explained to the ticket lady that I was totally deaf and a lip-reader and needed to sit in a front aisle seat so that I could lipread

the flight attendant in the event of an emergency. "No problem,"
said the ticket lady. "Just listen for the preboarding announcement and tell the agent you are deaf and wish to preboard."
 I sat in the back.

As soon as we board a plane, we communicate to the
attendants that we're deaf. A bit of body language (pointing
to our ear and shaking our head emphatically) and mouthing
(optional) does the trick; we don't necessarily have to use the
ASL sign, which is less easily understood. We (usually) get
respected as deaf people. If the crew knows that there's a deaf
passenger aboard, they won't assume that s/he hears a P.A.
warning. Some attendants will be very helpful—writing
notes, for example. An occasional attendant may know how
to fingerspell.

 However, notifying the attendants that one is deaf does not
necessarily prevent misunderstandings and the resultant
disaster. A truly horrifying anecdote in Tucker's book describes a communications mishap involving a carry-on week-
ender bag (which contained three days' worth of clothing for
a business trip, a portable TTY, and a vibrating alarm clock).
During the 2-1/2-hour delay before the plane took off from
Phoenix, she told one attendant, then another, that she was
deaf and asked them both to "relay any broadcasted messages" to her. Both promised to do so. She received no
messages. When she was leaving the plane at Washington
National Airport at 3:30 a.m., she discovered her bag was
gone.

> Overhearing my query to the stewardess about the whereabouts
> of the bag, the pilot replied, "I put it off the plane, of course; it was
> in the space reserved for *my* bag." Gritting my teeth, I asked the
> pilot why he hadn't simply moved the bag to another location on
> the plane. He replied, "That's *your* responsibility. I got your name
> from the label on the bag and called you over the loudspeaker
> several times and told you to come move your bag. You ignored
> me."

Worse was to come. Almost 20 hours later, the bag was finally located—"stashed . . . in the pouring rain. The bag and its entire contents were soaked."

Would Tucker have fared better had she written a message to the attendants, instead of using her voice? Maybe, maybe not. The point is that she *was* upfront.

It's easy to take a smug attitude, to say that Tucker has made her choice to "live in the hearing world" and has to take her lumps, but the fact is that all of us are subject to being misunderstood or treated with boorish obtuseness, even hostility, because we're deaf, no matter how we try to forestall it. Oral-deaf, ASL-Deaf—it can happen to any of us.

While it is true that deaf people are the victims of prejudice in subtle and blatant forms, most of the time there is nothing to be lost by saying, "I'm deaf." In most cases, it benefits us— and those we're communicating with. And when it doesn't— well, we have to consider the options. Is it worthwhile to ignore other people's boorishness? To explain? To protest? To demand a formal apology? To take legal action? That's something each of us has to decide for ourselves. Nobody ever said that it was easy.

Chapter 110

What are some of the differences between "Deaf" and "Hearing" etiquette?

ere's a brief guide to a few of the most important "social" differences. (And keep in mind that there are many variations of "accepted" social behaviors!)

▲ Deaf people don't wait to be asked how they're feeling. They volunteer that information first.

▼ Hearing people will ask (and wait for) "cue" questions: "So how've you been feeling lately?" "How are you?" "How's it going?" or "What's new with you?"

▲ It's acceptable for Deaf people to talk (sign) while they're eating with others.

▼ Hearing people are taught to avoid talking and eating at the same time. ("Don't talk with you mouth full!")

▲ It's difficult for Deaf people to carry on signed conversations while cutting up food.

▼ But . . . hearing people can carry on conversations while cutting up food.

▲ But . . . Deaf people can sign while they're drinking.

▼ Hearing people can't talk while they're drinking.

▲ Deaf people are more physical than hearing people. They will pat another person's shoulder or arm ("social space") to get attention.

▼ Hearing people are apt to feel intruded on when their "personal space" is violated this way.

▲ Carrying on lively social conversation, Deaf people are very animated, flinging their signs around, nodding, supposedly grimacing. The repertoire of expressions includes those normally linked with extreme anxiety, dismay, sneering, anger, or pain (creased eyebrows, pursed lips, and apparent scowls, for example) or facial twitches (signifying agreement). These intense expressions are a normal part of the grammar and color of ASL.

▼ Hearing people interpret this level of involvement and expression as "having an argument."

▲ Deaf people usually don't interrupt each other on the TTY (even though new technology makes interrupting possible). They wait until they get the "GA" (go-ahead) signal. (On older TTYs, interruption is still impossible.)

▼ Hearing people routinely interrupt each other on the phone—that is, it has always been easy to do. Some persons, of course, don't habitually interrupt the other party. Others do it often, or depending on the situation, call, or caller.

▲ Even when they're angry, Deaf people usually pay attention and wait until the "other person" is done signing before having their say. This is carryover from the "GA" habit. They wait until they get a "signal" to proceed.

▼ When they're angry, hearing people often interrupt and yell at each other. Ever lived in an apartment building and been forced to listen to a Hearing argument taking place in the apartment just above yours? ASL users can be just as angry—but easier on the neighbors. (Of course, if *they* stomp and throw things, there's little advantage to having a Deaf neighbor.)

▲ Signers also have a tendency to repeat questions, statements, directions, etc., without being asked: "Where'd you go? Where'd you go?" This helps assure comprehension. If you don't catch it first time around, you will on the second.

▼ Hearing people usually don't repeat questions unless they're asked.

▲ Deaf people maintain a greater social distance than hearing people (3 feet or more), to give themselves space to sign and to read others' signing clearly—unless they wish to sign privately to each other. Persons who are signing privately may move closer to each other, but will more likely use a "private" style of signing.

▼ The Hearing social distance varies from culture to culture. (Hearing people can move very close and whisper to each other, too, but "secret" signing is relatively rare.)

▲ Deaf people who sign to each other in public places know that their conversation is visible to everyone. To safeguard their privacy, close friends adopt a "disguised" style of signing that they understand perfectly but which makes "eavesdropping" more difficult (and obviates the need to move close together); use a jacket or overshirt as a shield; or go to a hidden place to talk privately.

▼ Hearing people can have intimate talks in crowded restaurants by whispering or shielding their mouths.

▲ To communicate at optimum level, Deaf people have to maintain near-constant eye contact. Even strangers.

▼ In U.S. culture, hearing people are taught "not to stare," and may feel uncomfortable with this. They tend to drop or avert their gaze fairly frequently in normal conversation. Strangers are not supposed to stare at each other. A fixed, maintained eye contact may have threatening or sexual overtones—in Hearing culture. In Deaf culture, it doesn't.

▲ In the past, it was acceptable for Deaf people to pop up at a friend's house unannounced, as the lack of telecommunications made it virtually impossible to let the friend know they were coming. Although TTYs have partly put an end to this practice, some people (changing plans after leaving the house) still occasionally do that.

▼ It's considered bad manners for hearing people to show up without calling first.

▲ When stopping by and finding nobody there, Deaf people tend to wait for the absent friend to come back.

▼ When stopping by, if the friend isn't home, hearing people leave immediately.

▲ When toasting each other at a wedding or anniversary party, Deaf people don't clink their glasses; they gently knock the backs of their hands together. Many of us can't hear the pleasant clink of glasses, so we've devised an "alternate practice."

▼ When toasting each other, hearing people don't physically touch.

▲ Deaf people like to congregate in well-lighted rooms (even nightclubs and restaurants), so they can see each other better.

▼ Hearing people prefer dimly-lit nightclubs and restaurants for "evenings out," since these have a cozy, romantic connotation.

▲ When dining out, Deaf people relocate or remove vases displaying flowers, tall candles, and vertical menu displays, since these obstruct a full view of each other's signing.

▼ Hearing people usually don't have a problem with these items, and we've rarely, if ever, seen them rearranging their tables after sitting down.

▲ Some Deaf people, carrying on an animated conversation with friends in a restaurant, use their normal conversational habits—whacking, rapping, knocking, slapping, or banging the table for emphasis—as a way of punctuating their conversation or reacting to what another person is saying. The noise can sometimes be heard by other diners, and can be annoying—or momentarily distracting.

▼ It's considered bad manners for diners in restaurants to thwack or rap on their tables, or to make any sort of noise that can be overheard by other diners. (All of us have, however, witnessed nasty, and loud, squabbles between two hearing persons in restaurants, diners, or coffeeshops.)

▲ Many of our readers are already familiar with "flying hands"—ASL applause. An audience being addressed by a Deafblind person (i.e., with Usher's Syndrome) signals its appreciation by stomping. (They can also use "flying hands" if the speaker has enough remaining vision to perceive it.)

▼ Hearing audiences signal their appreciation by clapping their hands and/or cheering—the louder the applause and cheers, the more enthusiasm expressed.

Well, you get the idea. Most of these social-cultural differences, as you can see, are based on our need to communicate visually. A newly-arrived person who is familiar with Hearing behavior, but not Deaf, can suffer acute "culture shock" when entering a Deaf milieu. But after you've absorbed some of it, you can see that there's logic behind the apparent oddness. The purpose of "Deaf" customs is to facilitate communication. Our communicative values and needs may be different from "Hearing," but the basic social values—politeness, sharing, paying attention, taking turns, etc.—are much the same.

▲ ▲ ▲

We'd like to clarify a point. The 16th item originally read, "Deaf people like to congregate in well-lighted areas" and "Hearing people prefer dimly-lit areas." This applies to cozy, intimate social situations that take place during the evening— not regular business/daylight ones!

Here's a letter we received from a disgruntled reader.

Throwing *all* hearing people into one category?

I am writing in response to the *For Hearing People Only* column in the May 1997 issue of **DEAF LIFE**. While some of the comparisons between "Deaf" and "Hearing" etiquette are accurate, I believe the writer was presumptuous with particular statements of how hearing people feel in certain situations.

I am a hearing person that works in a state office for people who are Deaf and Hearing Impaired. I am somewhat involved with the Deaf community and have very good friends who are Deaf and use sign language. I must say that I disagree with the statement regarding "personal space." Personally, I do not feel intruded upon if a Deaf person is physical and wants to get my attention, nor do I interpret lively social conversation among Deaf people as "having an argument." I resent the implications that "Hearing people routinely interrupt each other on the phone," and that "Hearing people often interrupt each other when they're angry and yell at each other." I do not believe I am the exception as implied in these statements. It should be noted that how a "hearing person" reacts in a particular situation is a matter of character and personality. Some people are not polite and are very comfortable interrupting you, whether you are hearing or Deaf.

Two of the most intriguing comments were that "Hearing people . . . tend to drop or avert their gaze fairly frequently in normal conversation," and "Hearing people prefer dimly-lit areas." Personally, when I communicate, I prefer to maintain eye contact at all times which shows the other person that I am genuinely interested in what they are saying. It does not matter to me whether the person I am communicating with is hearing or Deaf. I treat them the same. In addition, I cannot say I have a propensity for dimly-lit areas either.

I am uncertain where the writer of this article got their information, but feel it is unfair to throw all hearing people in one category. It should be noted that the statements made in this article are 1) a matter of the writer's opinion; and 2) based on the personal observations and experiences of the writer when interacting with hearing persons.

My advice? Why not leave the comparisons between Deaf

and Hearing people out of the article and focus entirely on the differences within the Deaf community as it relates to "etiquette"? A simple overview of things a hearing person may encounter when interacting with people who are Deaf should suffice (i.e. People who are Deaf offer much detail when communicating; may chew loudly while eating, and might bang on a table, stomp their feet, and/or tap the shoulder of another person to get their attention, etc.).

Respectfully submitted,

Denise D. Reihart
Mechanicsburg, Pennsylvania

The Editors reply: Our examples weren't meant as blanket categorizations—we know that one's communication "quirks" vary considerably according to personality and other factors—but to give an idea of some of the important Deaf/Hearing differences. We drew on our own experience and observations.

Since you've already had some exposure to Deaf communication, you are most likely sensitized to the need to keep steady eye contact. Frankly, we've met a number of hearing people who have atrocious "eye manners." These are the ones we were thinking of.

Some hearing persons, if a stranger approaches them and taps them on the shoulder . . . are liable to jump out of their skins!

Many restaurants and nightclubs catering to hearing clientele are dimly-lit. And think of the cliché of a "romantic dinner by candle-light." Hearing culture equates intimacy and romance with dim lights.

As for interrupting each other on the phone—we didn't mean to imply that all, or even most, hearing people do this—but that it is far more common for hearing persons to interrupt each other on the phone than it is for TTY users. It's easy for them to do so. It isn't customary for us. New technology makes interrupting possible, but it hasn't been around long enough for us to take it for granted!

As for table-banging . . . we'll be doing a separate feature on practices like that and their effect on hearing strangers. [See page 618.]

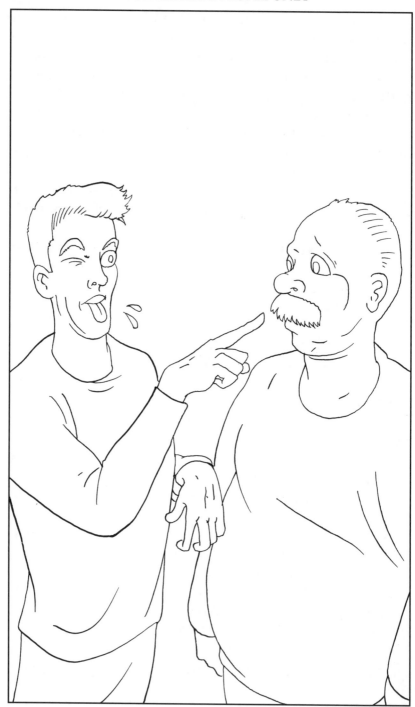

Chapter 111

Are all Deaf people really so tactless? For example, my friend, describing someone he knows, will mime, "so-and-so, fat" instead of just using her name. If they don't like what you're wearing or how you look, they'll tell you so. Why is that? It bothers me that they treat hearing people that way.

common complaint about deaf people is that they lack politeness. They insist on remarking upon details that hearing people tactfully leave unmentioned. If they run into a man wearing an especially loud or grotesque necktie, they'll say, "Ugly tie—why?" If they're introduced to a woman with a prominent mole or scar on her face, they *have* to ask about it: "Mole on face—why?" "Scar—how?" If they encounter an old friend or acquaintance who's noticeably put on weight: "Fat—what happened?" If they meet a man who's lately grown a mustache: "Grown a mustache? I don't like!—Shave!"

As with so many seemingly illogical practices in the Deaf community, there's a good reason for at least some of these responses. Deaf people are *very* attentive. Their perceptions are emphatically *visual*. Suppose your deaf friend asks you, "How's Paul doing?" You look puzzled and say, "Which Paul do you mean?" Your friend then launches into what looks like a vividly satiric 3-second pantomime but is actually an objective description (in ASL) of the salient points of Paul's appearance: "Tall; fat; thick, sweeping mustache; prominent mole on his right cheek." Seeing this description, you now know exactly *which* Paul is meant. No insult is intended.

It's true, though, that deaf people often don't attempt to hide their reactions of surprise or dismay. Supposing you encounter an old deaf friend—you haven't seen her for 10 years. After greeting you, she looks at you with astonishment, shakes her head, and tells you (perhaps with a little headshake), "Wow, you're fat! You've really gained weight!" She doesn't consciously intend to jeer at you, she's simply comparing the reality of your present appearance with the recollections of your former one. Some people *are* sensitive about their obesity; others have a self-accepting or even devil-may-care attitude. But your deaf friend is blithely blunt about it. It can be hard to take.*

On the other hand, if you've lost a noticeable amount of weight, are sporting a smashing new coat or outfit, spiffed up your previously drab appearance, gotten a flattering new haircut, etc., your deaf friend won't let *those* details go unnoticed. In that case, you may find yourself appreciating her bluntness!

In the case of hearing men growing new mustaches: it may be looked on as an obstruction to communication and therefore something that ought to be eliminated quickly—or simply as an aesthetic blunder. Deaf men certainly grow mustaches and beards in a variety of styles, but most take care to keep them neatly trimmed. Those who don't are seen as communicative poor sports and menaces. They're hindering other deaf people from getting a clear, unobstructed view of their faces, and deaf people look at them with distaste and resentment.

In real life, deaf people can be quite tactful. Consider the scenario of the oddly-matched couple: e.g., a good-looking man who marries an especially plain or tacky-looking woman. (Or *vice versa*, we hasten to add.) Now, imagine you are the husband of such a one. You run into an old deaf friend at a party. Your wife is talking to someone else. Your friend points to her and asks, "Your wife?" On his face is the slightest shadow of a dubious and hesitant expression. ("You *married* that dorky-looking woman???") You say, "Yes." Your deaf friend politely nods and says, "Oh." He quickly composes his face to register diplomatic acceptance of the fact. ("*Best not to say anything.*")

Some deaf people are exquisitely tactful, attuned to the nuances of their friends' moods and feelings. Others charge forward like bulldozers—blunt, tactless, and rude.

---

* Consider the nuances of English synonyms for *fat*: e.g., *overweight, heavy, portly, obese, pudgy, roly-poly, stout, round, large-sized, big-sized, plus-sized, gargantuan, grotesque, gross, bloated, paunchy, adipose, barrel-shaped, bulging, fleshy, chubby, tubby, full-figured, matronly, lard-bucket, tub of lard, out of shape, porcine, corpulent, beefy, buxom, embonpoint, zaftig, fatso.* A few of these are clinically neutral; some insulting; some considered crude slang; some euphemistically polite, some humorous, even affectionate.

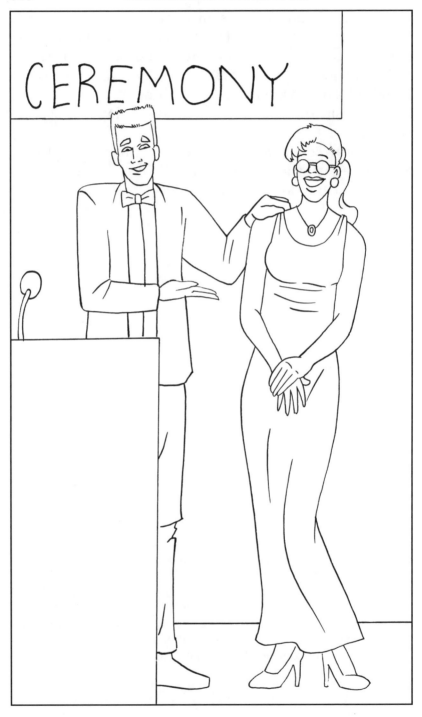

Chapter 112

Why don't deaf people use terms like "Ms." or "Mister" when addressing people?

Calling a teacher by his last name is considered rude and inconsiderate in Hearing culture. My first teaching experience was at Rochester School for the Deaf, and I could not understand why my students would not use "Mister" when addressing me. I was always called "Palmer." I thought this to be rude and inconsiderate, being naïve of Deaf Culture at the time.

—inspired by Carl Palmer, Rochester, New York

ertain social customs (or behaviors) considered indispensable in one culture are so much excess baggage in another. In the case of terms of address (hereinafter, simply "terms"), hearing people have been using the polite terms "Miss," "Mrs.," and "Mr.," for a couple of centuries. "Ms." is a more recent addition, although it's based on an old usage. Like "Mrs." and "Miss," it was originally an abbreviation for "Mistress," a respectful term of address (back then, at least) and the female counterpart of "Master." Other common terms are "Doctor," "Captain," "Sergeant," "Sister," "Brother," "Father," "Mother," "Reverend," "Cardinal," "Senator," "President," "Officer," and "your Honor." In England you will also find a complex system of terms for the nobility and royalty: "Sir James," "Lady Sarah," "Your Grace," "Your Eminence," "Your Highness," and "Your Majesty," for example. All this protocol can get complicated, which is why we have etiquette books, charts, and guides for travelers. Other cultures have their own standards of protocol. Terms, of course, vary from language to language: Señorita/Señora/ Señor, Fraulein/Frau/Herr, Mademoiselle/Madame/Monsieur, etc.*

There is one culture that dispenses with terms almost completely, and that is Deaf culture. Nowhere do you find terms employed in everyday communication. When Jan Jones is introduced to a Deaf group, her name will be spelled out by whoever is introducing her, or she'll do it herself and show her namesign (e.g., "J" on the left wrist, where she wears a gold wristwatch). She will never be addressed as "Ms. Jones," just by her namesign or a fingerspelled "Jan" or "Jones."

This isn't rude or thoughtless, just practical. Terms like "Mr." and "Ms." serve nicely for hearing communication, but they're absolutely superfluous in ASL conversation. For one thing, they'd need to be spelled out every time they're used, which wastes time and energy. Sign language is an admirably concise form of communication. True, ASL users could undoubtedly have devised a system of abbreviations (a special cheek-pinch to indicate "Mr." or "Ms."), but they have found it easier not to bother using terms at all. There are, of course, signs for "lady," "gentleman," "captain," "doctor," "president," "judge," and "police," for example, but these are used descriptively like other occupational nouns—e.g., "teacher," "superintendent/boss," or "performer." There is no ASL equivalent to "Ms." or "Mr." If a Deaf ASL user wants to specify whether a certain person is a single or married adult, descriptions, not terms, are used: "Man, name S-A-M S-M-I-T-H, around 35-old, marry-finish . . ."

Hearing persons use terms to indicate respect or, more commonly, as a matter of automatic everyday politeness ("ma'am" and "sir"). How, then, do deaf people show respect if they don't use the common terms of politeness that hearing society takes for granted? They do so physically—through touching, patting, hugging. Bonnie Brown, who's introducing Jan Jones, clasps her warmly by the shoulder. Sam Smith, introducing Jack White, gives him a friendly shoulder-pat, or a one-armed hug. Both communicate: "This person is esteemed/liked by me." Needless to say, these usages are more or less nonstandard (or downright taboo) in polite hearing society, where touch and physical contact are restricted.

There are two exceptions to the no-term rule in Deaf culture: onstage and at meetings. During staged performances and events, the master or mistress of ceremonies (a splendid term, that) will formally address the audience and the guests/performers: "Ladies and gentlemen, I would like to introduce Jan Jones, a lady of accomplishment . . ." At meetings, where the rules of parliamentary procedure are followed to a lesser or greater extent, the presiding speaker will use similarly formal terms: "President White, Vice President Black, Executive Director Gray, Chairman Brown, and members of the Board, I wish to introduce a gentleman, Sam Smith, whom some of you have already met. . ."

In written communication, of course, terms of address *are* used: "Dear Ms. White . . ." Deaf people generally know how to negotiate them.

If you're baffled by Deaf people's apparent rudeness in the matter of terms of address, and their stubborn refusal to stop calling you by your last name only, take heart. If Deaf people *really* want to be rude and inconsiderate, they'll refuse to communicate with you at all. Pay attention to the substance, not the apparent lack of social niceties.

---

* In some cultures, people are commonly addressed by their last names—i.e., enlistees in the military, students in English boarding schools, and (also in England) higher-ranking servants and governesses. An exception: in contemporary British culture, valets and chief ladies-in-waiting are addressed by their first names.

Chapter 113

Why do deaf people always tell me what they're planning to do? Why do they go into lengthy explanations of their plans, complete with details? And why are they always telling me their life stories by way of explanation for showing up late?

t's a holdover of an old practice in the Deaf community. Like so many other "odd" practices, it was based on necessity. Until fairly recently, deaf people had virtually no access to telephones (unless they could find a ready recruit or volunteer in the family, or had an understanding neighbor). Without TTYs and relay services, they relied of "word-of-eye"—person-to-person communication. Instead of phoning her friend Joe to tell him she was on the way, Jan had to plan ahead with Joe, well in advance. Deaf people therefore developed, to a high degree, the art of explaining one's future schedule. Dan tells Kim: "First I'm going to the store, then I'm going to visit a friend, yak-yak, then I'll stop and get the car fixed," *etc., etc.* That way, should Kim need to locate Dan, she knows where he is going. She may even be able to locate him, should she need to. This practice spares deaf friends the frustration of waiting in vain for someone.

Deaf people—particularly older ones—are used to coping with this kind of frustration. In the not-so-good old days, deaf people who wanted to visit deaf friends and couldn't arrange an impromptu "volunteer-relay" call simply showed up without calling ahead—an unpardonable gaffe in Hearing culture. If the friends were home, they visited. If not, the family either waited or turned right back without the visit.

The generations of Deaf adults who attended residential schools during the '30s, '40s, '50s, '60s, and even the '70s, when telecommunications access was restricted, developed the habit of sequential explanation. Even though the telecommunications situation has drastically improved over the past few decades, the habit remains. It's just something deaf people do and take for granted. It does, after all, have a practical purpose. But it can be perplexing (if not slightly annoying) to hearing co-workers, bosses, and friends.

Likewise, when a deaf person shows up late, s/he tends to launch into a precise chronological account: "Had trouble starting the car, then went over to visit a friend, yak-yak, stopped to get car fixed, oops! I arrive late, sorry." A hearing person in the same situation would simply say, "Sorry I'm late," and let it go at that. Again, this is a holdover from a time when deaf people simply weren't able to contact others to inform them promptly. When they arrive late, they fill their audience in on the details. It makes sense if you're deaf. Unfortunately, this kind of behavior is looked at askance in the hearing/professional world.

By the way, the old custom of showing up at a friend's house without calling them beforehand is dying out—thankfully, to many of us. Now that a large number of deaf people have TTYs, and each state has full-scale relay services (and a number have TTY-loaner programs), there's technically no excuse to pop up unannounced—although some deaf people continue to do it once in a while. And while it looks as though it's simply done out of laziness or habit, there's a reason: the long-standing telecommunications barrier. If Kim leaves the house, drives to a fast-food restaurant or hardware store, and decides to stop by to visit her friend Jan, in most cases she can't call from a public phone. (Most deaf people don't have portable TTYs or access to public TTYs. There are simply not that many TTY-equipped payphones.) So she has to hazard an unplanned visit. Jan, of course, understands.

Before the advent of the telephone, deaf and hearing people were on a more equal footing. Politically (or rather "techno-politically"), there was no significant "difference" between them. Hearing people had no real communication advantages over deaf. Both deaf and hearing could use telegraphy, mail, and handwritten notes. The telephone changed all that. Deaf people became communications-disadvantaged. They've been catching up. There are now cell phones that work with portable TTY hookups, real-time-chat programs for those with computers, and the increasingly popular wireless pagers—but the situation for many of us is still far from ideal, especially with public facilities.

Chapter 114

Why do Deaf people always hug each other when they greet? Why do they always pat their friends on the shoulder just before they leave?

eaf people have social rules and etiquette, of course—but some of the "Deaf" rules may be unfamiliar, even bizarre, to hearing onlookers. Not surprisingly, Deaf social communication works differently from its Hearing counterpart. Many of our "social quirks" serve a vital function in Deaf interaction, but are baffling to hearing people. For example, the custom of Deaf people hugging each other by way of greeting. Is this really necessary? In Western culture, hearing people typically make do with a handshake. (And a simple handshake carries a whole vocabulary of nuances and messages!) Deaf people often go beyond the handshake. Hugs are a friendly, physical, but nonthreatening way of expressing equality between two persons on reasonably friendly terms. After the hug has been completed, the two disengage and move backwards, for better visibility and to give each other signing space, and the conversation commences.

Deaf people are a bit more physical than hearing people. They have a different vocabulary of physicality. Their usage of touch differs from Hearing norms. It's acceptable practice to pat another person's shoulder or arm (the accepted "social space") to get attention—even if that person is a stranger. Some hearing people, as we've mentioned, are apt to feel jittery or threatened when their "personal space" is violated this way, especially by a stranger. Of course, hearing strangers occasionally tap, pat, poke, or whack another stranger on the upper arm or side, gently or roughly (the "Move over, I'm getting off the bus" or "You're in my way" types of nonverbal messages), depending on how rude or polite they are. Deaf people's taps are more standardized and emphatic: "May I have your attention?" or "You there! I need your attention, right now!"

This attitude towards touch encompasses Deaf-Hearing interactions as well. For a waiter to touch a hearing diner's shoulder to get her attention is an unpardonable blunder in Hearing culture, an infraction of the unwritten rule against physical contact between a server and a customer. But for a waiter to do the same to a Deaf diner is perfectly acceptable—in Deaf culture.

As for the "goodbye pat," this serves a useful function: notifying the others in the group: "Goodbye, I'm leaving; I'm not slipping out on you." This forestalls a time-wasting, futile search for someone who has slipped away. Taking "French leave"—exiting a social gathering without saying goodbye—is, in certain situations, acceptable behavior in U.S. Hearing culture, but usually not in Deaf. (It depends on how crowded or impersonal the gathering is, of course.)

The goodbye pat also affords the leave-taker an opportunity to exit the gathering in a friendly way. If s/he won't be back for a while (going abroad, cross-country, on a long vacation, off to college, moving away, or starting a new job in another city), all parties present take advantage of this last opportunity to interact until the next get-together, and they make the most of it. Everyone hugs the leave-taker.

Even after everyone has left their seats and relocated to the driveway or sidewalk as a prelude to seeing their friends off, they keep chatting away, reluctant to part. So there may be multiple farewell hugs all around. Deaf people are notorious for taking long, protracted farewells of each other. There are jokes about how Deaf people are incapable of saying goodbye. Deaf goodbyes often go beyond "lingering" to "marathon!"

In Hearing culture, dinner or party guests who overstay their welcome by lingering in conversation and postponing their departures are a major annoyance to hosts. We've read numerous complaints about them, along with some amusing advice on how to get them going without being overtly rude. Deaf hosts can likewise have a problem getting rid of guests who tarry into the wee hours, yakking about their personal tribulations. But in many instances, the reluctance to part is mutual.

Deaf people have devised other social practices that seem peculiar, unnecessary, or tacky to the uneducated—such as announcing to others in the room, "I'm going to the bathroom" (*"me-go-toilet"*). Why do they do this? So that the others won't search in vain for the bathroom-goer after s/he leaves the room. It forestalls frustration ("Where did Jan go?"). Hearing people usually see no necessity of doing this. (They can yell upstairs or through the closed bathroom door, "Jan? You in there?") But for Deaf people, this "odd practice" shows consideration. Actually, it's quite logical—by Deaf standards.

As we've pointed out in Chapter 110, there is an underlying logic behind all of these "quirks." The instinctive goal is to communicate visually and kinetically, share information, show respect for others' communication needs, and interact on an equal level.

In Chapter 10, we touched on the topic of regional sign accents. Every deaf person has a unique style of communication—an accent in body language, so to speak. ASL users have idiosyncrasies—e.g., a repeated "hey there!" hand-flutter (used to get someone's attention) even when the other person is attentively facing the "speaker." There are persons who punctuate their signed conversations by periodically tapping or whacking the other person on the arm, much as certain hearing persons punctuate their conversations with habitual phrases like "See?", "y'know," "don't you know," or "really." In any case, it can be annoying, certainly. Or one simply gets used to it.

Chapter 115

Last June I (hearing person) went to a Deaf Club meeting. My Deaf cousin was there and we chat[ted] for a while. Then later he wanted to kiss me on the lips for goodbye. So my question is: is a kiss on the lips for goodbye part of Deaf Culture? If so, why?

—Sherry Pifer, Hutchinson, Kansas

very culture has norms—standards of behavior that are acceptable. Behavior that falls outside of these norms is socially unacceptable. And the fascinating thing about human behavior is that these norms vary widely from culture to culture. What is normal and acceptable in Culture A is offensive in Culture B. If you've ever taken an Introduction to Anthropology course, this is one of the first thing you learn.

We've already pointed out that different cultures have radically different norms regarding touch and physicality, and this includes kissing.

What's in a kiss? Kissing is a physical expression of feeling that has a wide range of meanings or connotations, many different shades of significance ranging from the purely social or friendly to the purely sexual. And in some cultures (traditional Japanese, for example), kissing on the lips is not an acceptable form of public behavior.

In Russian and French culture, for example, it is perfectly acceptable for a man to publicly kiss another man on both cheeks. This is a well-known friendly or honorific gesture, not a sexual one. In U.S. culture, it's common for women, especially in social situations, to give each other a polite peck on the cheek. Similarly, it's acceptable for men and women who are not "romantically linked" to give each other a polite kiss on the cheek, although in some American religious communities, such as Orthodox Jewish, this is not permitted. Our culture, however, is still uncomfortable with the sight of two women or—even more so—two men kissing each other on the lips.

In Western culture (and this goes for Deaf culture, too), kissing on the lips is usually reserved for those who have romantic feelings towards one another. And those feelings ought to be mutual, or else the kiss shades into harassment. Kissing on the lips, then, is a socially-restricted gesture.

As we've pointed out, the way hearing people communicate with their eyes, faces, and hands is different from the way ASL-Deaf people do. We use our hands as hearing people do their voices—as instruments of communication. In Deaf culture, you don't find as much emphasis on handshakes as you do in Hearing culture. As we've already noted, the use of facial expression and eye contact are also different, since the face is used grammatically in ASL and other sign languages.

Now, in Deaf culture, hugging pretty much takes the place of handshakes and formal greetings and leave-takings. As we have already noted, Deaf people often hug each other when exchanging greetings or saying goodbye. Hugging is generally done between social equals, friends, or those who claim to have friendly feelings. It can be used, however, between two persons who have just met each other or who don't know each other well. An affectionate smooch on the cheek or brow is appropriate when the huggers are close friends who haven't seen each other in a long time, or when one of them is moving away. But Deaf people tend to avoid kissing on the lips unless there's a serious emotional relationship involved.

From a purely practical point of view, kissing on the lips is awkward and interferes with communication. The physical closeness required for "lipping" deprives the kissers of the wide field of view required for good receptivity. You can't see well and communicate properly when another person's face is in your own. Truth be told, Deaf culture doesn't have much use for lip-kissing.

If your Deaf cousin wanted to give you a goodbye kiss on the lips, he was doing so because he wanted it, not because it's part of Deaf culture, because it isn't. We suspect that he may have been taking advantage of your inexperience with Deaf people. In that case, he wasn't acting as a representative of Deaf culture, but as a man who wants to grab a kiss he wasn't entitled to.

That sort of behavior is by no means limited to the Deaf community. Men have been doing that for ages—in all cultures. And, Deaf or hearing, all women have the right to refuse. You had, and have, the right to draw back out of kissing range and say something like "No, thanks, I prefer to hold the kiss until we know each other better." If your cousin respects your feelings, he won't make an issue out of it. If he doesn't—well, you know you're dealing with a difficult guy!

Chapter 116

If there is a Hearing speaker, the Deaf audience claps their hands. If there is a Deaf speaker, the Deaf audience waves their hands. But if there is a Deaf speaker and a Hearing audience who know little or nothing about Deaf culture, what should they do?

—Holly P. Roth, Columbia, Maryland

 embers of any audience where there is a Deaf speaker or performer *should* applaud by waving their hands, "Deaf-Culture" style. It's a matter of simple courtesy. If they applaud by clapping their hands in the conventional Hearing fashion, the Deaf speaker will probably *see* it and appreciate the thought—but waving-hands applause will have so much more impact and be all the more appreciated. If the intention is genuine, why not choose the vehicle that can express it most powerfully? For us, waving hands carries better. And it's not difficult to do.

When we wish to honor people of a different culture, we do it by expressing our esteem for them in their own language—or, at least, in terms they can understand. By waving their hands, hearing audiences show that they recognize and respect the Deaf speaker as a person.

How to do it? You can hold your hands upright, palms facing the stage, and gently oscillate your hands, as though there are little motors in your wrists. Or you can move your hands back and forth in a synchronized single or symmetrical double arc, as though they're windshield wipers sweeping across an invisible windshield. Or you can simply hold your hands up and wave in the style you're accustomed to. Variously known as "Deaf applause," "visual applause," or "flying hands," this charming practice is gaining in popularity.

An audience's waving hands, hats, or handkerchiefs to signal its appreciation of a deaf person is really an old practice, undoubtedly invented and reinvented through the centuries on the spur of the moment. There are published allusions to it going back to the early decades of the 19th century—and we may possibly uncover even earlier ones. We see these as a tribute to human ingenuity in overcoming a communication barrier.

The audience that attended the premiere performances of Beethoven's Ninth Symphony in 1824 waved their hats and handkerchiefs in acclamation when he faced them and bowed. This is the earliest recorded reference (as far as we know) to visual applause, and one familiar to any student of music history.

In **DEAF LIFE**, we've noted an 1892 description of spectators at a Washington, D.C. baseball field, delighted by the exploits of Deaf center-fielder William Ellsworth "Dummy" Hoy, rising up *en masse* and "wildly waving hats and arms." Readers have shared with us a mid-19th-century reference to an audience's waving their handkerchiefs to the late-deafened Czech composer Bedřich Smetana;* a 1912 report in **The Silent Worker** of an audience at the Chautauqua Institute applauding a Deaf presenter by similarly waving handkerchiefs (the "Chautauqua Salute"); and a firsthand account of a Deaf slo-pitch softball team from Edmonton, Alberta, who waved hotel dinner napkins at an awards banquet (1980), sparking a visual-applause trend in Canada. Participants in the National Festival of Arts of the Deaf, also in Alberta (1984), were even issued "clapkerchiefs"—little pieces of imprinted cloth to be used for applauding. Those who forgot to bring them waved their hands in the air.

Likewise, "waving hands" seems to have caught on in France around the same time and spread through the Deaf community there; some U.S. visitors, notably Gerald "Bummy" Burstein, saw it in 1985. He taught it to participants at the Youth Leadership Camp that summer, and the YLCers brought it back home with them, taught their friends, and instigated a happy epidemic. By the time of The DEAF WAY International Conference and Festival (Washington, D.C., July 1989), everybody seemed to be doing it. It spread like the proverbial wildfire because it was easy, fun, and foolproof. It makes a striking, even beautiful scene. On occasion, the waves have been synchronized so that they "break" or "ripple" from one end of the audience to the other and back. Spectacular!

Deaf applause suits our visual orientation precisely. It doesn't demand unusual exertion (unlike clapping and shouting, which can leave you with sore hands or a hoarse throat). Any audience can clap politely (even if they're bored), but waving hands does demand kinetic participation—you *really* have to get into it, show spirit. But what better way to do it? To a Deaf person facing such an audience, a forest or ocean of waving hands is a glorious sight.

References:
"The Colorful Legacy of 'Dummy' Hoy," **DEAF LIFE**, November 1992, p. 22. The reference is to a remark by Henry Furness in **Sporting Life**, 1892: "When outfielder Hoy made a brilliant catch, the crowd arose *en masse* and wildly waved hats and arms. It was the only way in which they could testify their appreciation to the deaf-mute athlete."
Bummy Burstein, "The Saga of the Waving Applause," **DEAF LIFE**, July 1992, pp. 26-27. Bummy is a noted Deaf advocate and parliamentarian.
"Waving hands: a Canadian perspective," letter by Roger J. Carver, M.Ed., **DEAF LIFE**, October 1992, p. 6.
"The 'Chautauqua Salute,'" letter by Harry Lang, **DEAF LIFE**, December 1992, p. 4.

*Smetana's first name is pronounced "**be**-der-zhik." The diacritical mark above the *r* is called a *hachek* (haček).

Chapter 117

Why do Deaf people always hang around after a play (or any other event) and stand together and talk?

or Deaf people, going to the theater or stadium isn't just an opportunity to see a play or a game, it's a cherished social opportunity as well.

In mammoth, spread-out cities like Los Angeles, Deaf residents don't get to see each other all that often. When a public event does bring them together, they take advantage of it—customarily hanging around afterwards, catching each other up on what's been happening in their lives.

Hearing people can do this on the telephone. Chatting, exchanging news, or yakking, is easily accomplished—just reach for the phone and dial a number. Deaf people, who depend on TTYs and other keyboard devices, prefer to save the intimate chat for person-to-person encounters. They consider the TTY a cold, impersonal medium. Hearing people can convey emotions through the intonations of their voices, which carry over the phone. TTY users can't do likewise. They communicate through an electronic readout or printed scroll, which cannot spontaneously convey their feelings as a voice telephone can. The nuances and subtleties are hard to convey. That's why TTY users will sometimes punctuate their conversations with helpful parenthetical expressions like (Hahaha!) or (Smile!), or use typographical "smileys" like :-) or :-(. Deaf people are visually oriented. We can't, after all, sign to each other on the TTY. We can't see each other's faces or the nuances of expression or gesture. Videophones are not yet in widespread use—indeed, many of us have never seen one up close. Chatrooms and instant-message

programs afford more enjoyment than TTYs, but not everyone has access to them, or likes them.

Moreover, TTYs and phones are expensive to use. Time
spent on the phone costs money. So Deaf people, being
practical, don't use their TTYs all that much, and rarely for
social chats.

Thus, many Deaf people "save it" until they have a chance
to get together. When the opportunity arises, they seize it. We
are intensely social creatures. We *need* to be with other Deaf
people. And if we don't get to see other Deaf people terribly
often, all that accumulated and suppressed craving for socializing comes out in a torrent! (And, considering the high cost
of telecommunications, this is a *positive* way to save money.)

This means that after the game is over or the curtain
lowered on the final curtain call or the cinema screen goes
dim, Deaf people congregate in the lobby and strike up
marathon signed conversations. Long after the hearing folks
have gone home, clusters of Deaf people are still standing
there carrying on dozens of simultaneous conversations. The
well-known "NTID Street" outside the Panara Theater in
NTID's LBJ Building (a broad corridor/lobby) has been sen-
sitively designed to accommodate these social clusters while
leaving room for traffic to pass through (or to detour by the
staircases). It's bright and spacious—good visibility and room
for everybody.

Nonetheless, this Deaf custom of thronging lobbies after the
play is over can create a nuisance for theater managers who
want to close up. Deaf folks, deeply involved in their conversations, may not pay much attention to the passage of time.
Once they get together, they can keep at it for hours. But
theaters do close for the night. Staffers want to go home.
Custodians want to sweep away the debris and mop the
floors. Owners want to lock up. In which case, someone has
to flick the lights off and on to warn the Deaf chatters that it's
time to relocate. Or—if the signers are blocking passage-
ways—a staffer can approach the clusters and politely ask

them to move aside to a less-trafficked area. Or suggest they go across the street to a restaurant or tavern (which will, one hopes, keep later hours). Such a suggestion is usually received enthusiastically. That's what a good restaurant or tavern is—a convenient spot to eat, drink, and carry on long conversations without worrying about being shooed out—at least, not for a while!

A further note: This kind of "lobby-thronging" behavior isn't limited to theatrical events. It takes place at conferences, conventions, and expos, too.

At an expo, Deaf people tend to throng the aisles and strike up long conversations, ignoring the booths. This can cause some consternation to the merchants, since these visitors may be obstructing traffic and decreasing the visibility of their displays, and consequently interfering with their ability to attract customers. In short, spoiling their business. Merchants pay hefty sums to reserve space at these events and to rent the necessary props, and go through considerable trouble to transport their merchandise and set up their eye-catching displays . . . only to have Deaf visitors turn the exhibition hall into a social tearoom! And merchants who try to shoo off Deaf loiterers will bring a community's wrath upon themselves. Depriving Deaf people of the opportunity to chat freely and openly promotes bad feelings.

One solution is for the expo organizers to provide dedicated social space for the attendees—to make such a space attractive by surrounding it with refreshment booths with lots of comfortable seating and good lighting, and to encourage them to go there to chat. Or an empty portion of the exhibition hall can be set aside for socializing. This may—or may not—work. It's worth a try, though. Merchants and marathon chatters can indeed coexist in harmony.

Chapter 118

If two Deaf people are having a signed conversation, is it OK for a hearing person to walk between them?

s we all know by now (don't we?), signed conversations require more space between participants than their spoken/heard counterparts do. Deaf conversationalists need unimpeded views of each other's faces, torsos, arms, and hands. So deaf people step back and leave more space between themselves when they're having a conversation. This can create problems for passersby who literally have to squeeze through the middle of a conversation, physically interrupting it. Occasionally a passerby can make a detour around a group of signers, but suppose (as often happens) the signers are blocking the only convenient passage. Should a passerby feel guilty about cutting through a group of signers? Is this a social blunder? Is it bad manners?

Our answers to these questions are: no, no, and no. Our response to the question of cutting through is: Yes, it's okay. Deaf conversationalists can see someone coming. They'll stop signing when someone starts cutting through, then pick up when the coast is clear.

Often, at large Deaf gatherings (conventions, celebrations, reunions, etc.), deaf people will sit on opposite sides of corridors or hallways, or even steps, to have leisurely chats. They let all the foot-traffic flow between them. Frequently, they'll turn their heads and "duck" around interrupters—it's part of the normal give-and-take of public conversation.

At other times, however, the signers will be standing in a cluster or circle. Even two signers can block an entryway. Our advice to hearing passersby who find themselves in this situation is to (literally) take it in stride. Suggestions: Gently tap the nearest deaf conversationalist twice on the shoulder. (Use the underside of your fingertips. Don't shove.) It helps if you know the sign for "excuse me," but even if you don't, you can hold up a finger to indicate "Wait a moment!" Or say, "Excuse me, I want to go through." And point. This gives the signers an extra moment to "wrap up" and pause. Pass through in whichever manner you normally cut through a crowd. Keep your head up. Whatever you do, *don't* hunch over and try to be unobtrusive. *Don't* stoop. Don't break your back on our account.

Whatever you do, be confident. Consider a pair of windshield wipers in use during a rainstorm. When the wipers arc back and forth smoothly, it's not a visual annoyance. But if the wipers behave in an arthritic, creaky fashion, they *are* disturbing. A driver can have difficulty focusing on the road when the wipers act this way.

The same goes for hearing people who need to pass through a crowd of signers. If they stay upright and stride confidently through the crowd, it's really not annoying. The signers won't mind. However, hearing folks who start, stop, hesitate, re-start unsteadily, then freeze, and start again, are *extremely* annoying. So are the ones who hunch over and try to "tunnel under" the signers. It just doesn't work. Not only do these folks utterly fail to be inconspicuous, they call attention to their interruption in a most annoying fashion.

Be aware, however, that even though the vast majority of deaf people will accept the interruption with good grace, there will always be a sour minority who will get angry and show obvious irritation. Don't let them get you down. After all, *they're* the ones blocking the passageway.

Deaf Awareness 5-Minute Quiz

Chapters 105—118

Answers are on the bottom of the page, upside down.

True or False:

1. Hearing spouses who wish to "break the ice" with a chilly Deaf group can host an informal gathering, such as a cookout.

2. Some deaf people refuse to carry a pen or paper with them, to compel hearing people they meet up with to sign, not write.

3. Occasionally, bluffing is the only reasonable expedient for a deaf person forced to "listen" to a hearing person's monologue.

4. Informing flight attendants that we're deaf the moment we board is a foolproof way to avoid problems with P.A. announcements.

5. It is socially unacceptable for a deaf person to sign while eating or drinking.

6. Since deaf people need a clear view of other people's faces, they're annoyed, even angered, when conversing with a man who has a messy beard or a thick, sweeping mustache.

7. Deaf culture has no use for terms such as "Mr." or "Ms." because deaf people are tactless and rude.

8. Deaf people sometimes pop up at their friends' houses without calling ahead first because they decided to visit after they left the house and couldn't locate a TTY on the way.

9. Many Deaf "social quirks," such as "goodbye pats," serve a useful communicative function.

10. Deaf people like to hang around lobbies after the play or movie is over and chat with each other because they don't have anything better to do with their time.

Answers:
1. True; 2. True; 3. True; 4. False; 5. False; 6. True; 7. False; 8. True; 9. True; 10. False.

Chapter 119

I've noticed that deaf people stare. Why do they do that? Don't they realize that this makes hearing people uncomfortable?

he way we use our eyes is deeply influenced by family and culture. Babies and young children instinctively look at other people with a direct, wideopen, totally uninhibited gaze. As they grow older, they learn "not to stare." This is part of the system of social inhibitions that separates adults from children. By the time they're halfway through elementary school, children have absorbed these inhibitions: don't stare, it isn't polite.

In some cultures it isn't considered polite to maintain steady eye contact (also called a "direct gaze" or "locking eyes)." Locking eyes (in modern Western hearing culture) is something reserved for lovers, sweethearts, married couples, or adoring fans. Or kooks. A deep, direct gaze signifies emotional intimacy, or depth of fervor. Strangers are not supposed to do this. In New York City, for example, strangers try to avoid looking each other in the eye at all. A direct stare can mean trouble, even danger. A woman, especially, may feel threatened if a strange man stares at her. In some religious communities (e.g., Muslim and certain "ultra-Orthodox" Jewish), unrelated men and women are not supposed to look at *or* speak to each other—period.

When two hearing strangers strike up a conversation and "lock eyes," one or both may start to feel uncomfortable. Even when close friends are having a cozy conversation in private, they don't really look at each other. They glance at each other every so often, then look away. Their eyes may wander all over, then rest briefly on the other person, then go off again. Remember, hearing people are often very lazy about *using* their eyes. They don't have to rely on them for spoken communication. They can depend on their instinctive listening skills.

Do hearing people *really* look at those they're communicating and interacting with? Here's a telling anecdote from a book appropriately titled **Reading Faces**. A certain artist (hearing) was curious to see how much people really saw:

> I'd had a well-trimmed beard and mustache for about 6 years. Some friends joined us for dinner at home, people we saw often. Late in the loud, wine-drinking evening, on a whim I went upstairs and shaved off my beard and mustache. After I came down, the party continued, but nobody caught the difference. The last friend to go remarked, "You're looking terrific, pal—stay healthy." Amazed, I said to my wife, "Nobody saw—"
>
> "I did, of course," she said, "but I was waiting for the others to notice. See, people don't really *look* at each other!"*

In other words, the artist's friends looked *at* him. But they really didn't *see* him.

Deaf people depend on their eyes to communicate. We *need* to maintain steady eye contact. It's essential to us. And that bothers some hearing people. They may feel like their "personal space" has been invaded. They don't like to be "stared at." One hearing woman we know, after meeting a Deaf man for the first time, complained that he'd been "staring" at her. We explained that he was speechreading and watching her face for associational cues, so he could "guess" what he couldn't otherwise catch. Some hearing people make a bigger fuss about this than others, of course. In general, the more outgoing a hearing person is, or the more comfortable and secure they feel about themselves, the less they're bothered by "locking eyes" with us.

Even if we're ASL-Deaf and do not have good oral skills, we nonetheless *need* to look at the other person's face during conversations. We need an unencumbered view of the face, and the upper torso, even the whole body, as much as possible, since the posture and nonverbal "body language" of a person gives us useful intelligence (as espionage reports put it). Speechreading (which really should be called "face-reading" or "people-reading") is, as we've already pointed out, a difficult skill to master, but most of us rely instinctively on it to some degree—even if we can't make much sense out of the syllables, the expression of the face provides important clues: what kind of a message is being conveyed, the speaker's attitude, personality, *etc.* Since we depend on visual information, we can't rely on intonation of the voice; we have to take in everything. Consequently, deaf people tend to be alert and observant. Our eyes are our ears. We see with them—and we listen. Our eyes are our ears, and our intuitive channels.

Incidentally, while hearing persons can "rehearse" their voices to conceal their true feelings, deaf people can do likewise with their faces. But it is exceedingly difficult to suppress *all* emotion, particularly from the eyes.

A person's eyes convey more than their speech does. Hearing persons may try to hide their true feelings, but their eyes are usually a giveaway. Deaf people (whether or not they're culturally Deaf) can be adept at reading the subtle intonations of the language of the eyes. An alert deaf person picks up the hidden message, as well as the overt one. If that makes hearing people uncomfortable, well, that's their problem!

---

* Leopold Bellak, M.D., and Samm Sinclair Baker, **Reading Faces** (New York: Holt, Rinehart & Winston, 1981), p. 110.

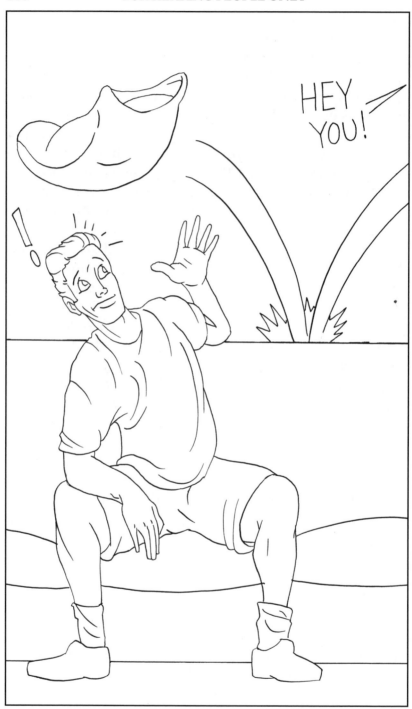

Chapter 120

How do deaf people get each other's attention if they can't yell?

ho says we can't? Some of us respond to a low-pitched, guttural hoot, whoop, or shout. It depends partly on the sensitivity of our residual hearing and on the acoustics of the room we're in, as well as our proximity to the shouter. (Not recommended for outdoor or noisy situations.)

Suppose that yelling isn't an option—what then? Deaf people are big consumers of assistive and signaling devices—doorbell- and telephone-flashers, baby-cry alerters. And, of course, those trusty hearing-ear dogs. But supposing we're in a situation where we can't depend on signalers, flashers, or dogs? How do we get each other's attention when we can't yell and don't have access to technology?

We do our best. A number of modes of direct and indirect attention-getting are commonly employed. (*Direct* means actual eye-to-eye or physical contact; *indirect*, reacting to a vibrotactile stimulus or a roundabout method.) A sampling:

Direct approaches:

1) Signaling with the body: (a) waving the arms and hands in an exaggerated "windshield-wiper" motion; b) creating a light-interference by casting a moving shadow across the other person's field of vision.

2) Toggling the light-switch on and off.

3) Using simple devices: (a) candle; (b) lighter; (c) match; (d) flashlight; (e) portable beamlight; (f) camera flash.

4) "Beanbagging": tossing a lightweight, reasonably soft item (a crumpled piece of paper, pen, padded mailing-bag, or glove) at the person.

Indirect approaches:

1) Sliding a piece of paper under a closed door and swooshing it from side to side.

2) Stomping on the floor. (This depends on how conductive or resonant the floor is. Not recommended for use in upper-story apartments or on concrete.)

3) Kicking or ramming a fist against the door. (This depends on how strong the door is or how careful the knocker wants to be.)

4) Banging an area of a wall against which you know your "signalee's" bed, chair, or couch is placed. (Particularly handy in dorm-room situations.)

5) Using a pet dog or cat to alert its owner. A true story: Jan wanted to visit Jim, but wasn't able to contact him beforehand. His doorbell-flasher system wasn't working. She arrived at his house and jumped up and down on the porch floor, getting the attention of Jim's two cats. (There was a front door with a window that afforded a good view of the front hall.) She waved at the cats and continued jumping. Jim, who luckily wasn't too far from the front door, noticed that the cats were acting "different." He followed them into the hall and caught sight of Jan in the front-door window. Mission accomplished.

6) Using a neighbor's telephone creatively. Suppose Dan gets locked out of the house and needs to summon Kim, a housemate or friend, who is out of eyeshot of the door-flasher. (Or suppose there isn't any doorbell-flasher.) Dan goes to a neighbor, Kat, and dials Kim's phone number—directly. No TTY or relay-service call is needed. Dialing Kim's number suffices. This activates Kim's TTY phone-flasher. If Dan knows which room the TTY is in (and if it's on the first floor), he can run over and get Kim's attention by standing near a window of that room and waving when Kim answers the TTY. (He can also get quick results by using a flashlight when Kim answers the call.)

A more time-consuming approach involves searching/ waiting for someone. If Kim wants to visit Jan, but thinks that she might be working on, say, a backyard garden or farm lot, or strolling in a nearby woods, Kim will walk to the backyard, look around, and wait. Even if Jan has a doorbell-flasher or TTY with flasher setup, these wouldn't be visible from the outside. Kim can't holler, as Jan wouldn't respond. So Kim has to depend on direct eye-to-eye contact.

Deaf people commonly hang around longer than their hearing counterparts would, hoping that the person they're waiting for will show up. Usually they'll wait 15 minutes to an hour—or more, depending on how badly they want to see the other person. Occasionally, this can get them into trouble. If they're mistaken for trespassers, they can be subjected to some pretty rude—or worse—treatment.

Then we have the broader area of observation and deduction. Deductive analysis of details isn't limited to deaf people, but they make good use of it. In their ability to notice and interpret easily-overlooked details, deaf people occasionally rival Sherlock Holmes. Is the hood of a car parked in the driveway warm? Someone has arrived home recently. If it's snowing, and there's a patch of fresh snow where the car is normally parked, someone has left the house a while ago. The thickness of "powdering" indicates the length of time they've been gone. If there are footprints and tire tracks in the snow or slush around the front door, how fresh are they? Has someone just left, or just come back? We can get a fairly good idea. Likewise, we can *always* tell when someone has been to a bar—there's a certain unmistakable smell that clings to one's skin, hair, and garments.

In the absence of high-tech devices, deaf people employ a measure of common sense and a pinch of deductive reasoning. It's a survival skill. Indeed, some deaf folks have an uncanny ability to track down whatever friends they're looking for—*wherever* those friends happen to be!

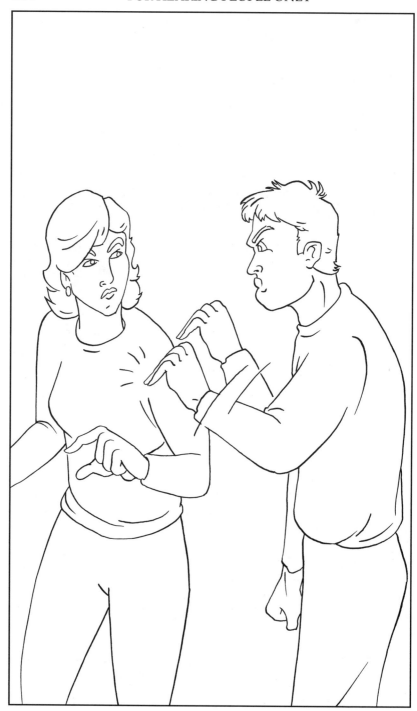

Chapter 121

Is it normal for a deaf people to whack another person on the shoulder during an argument? Isn't that abusive?

lthough Arden Neisser, in **The Other Side of Silence,** has described ASL as "a very cool medium of communication," signers do get angry and need an effective, noncombative medium of conveying their anger. Sign language is that medium. There are certain gestures—attention-getting taps or raps whose physical force (for want of a better description) varies according to the forcefulness of the emotion—and which indicate the signer's intensity of temper and the amount of emphasis s/he places on the message s/he is conveying to the other party. This emphasis parallels the tone of voice used by hearing speakers: from a gentle assertion to an angry shout. These signs are not necessarily construed as "brutality" or "abuse," as long as no physical hurt is inflicted on the signee by the signer. They are not delivered gratuitously, but are a way of emphatically communicating anger and demanding the other person's attention. As such, they serve an important, and positive, purpose in Deaf communication. But signers have gotten in trouble with the law because of it.

Since there is widespread ignorance about ASL, it is possible to misconstrue the signs used by an angry signer, or, even worse, to deliberately take such gestures out of context and use them against the signer by describing them as a physical attack or abuse.

As we all know, when one partner is angry, s/he often uses a harsh voice to emphasize displeasure and to compel the other person to pay attention. In Deaf culture, the tone of voice is more or less replaced with signing, facial expression, and touch. It is correct etiquette to touch another Deaf person on the shoulder or the uppermost portion of the arm to get their attention. If they're sitting, it's acceptable for one signer to touch the other person's knee or the thigh, just above the knee. If the other person looks away, or drops his eyes, thus breaking eye contact with the person who is talking, then she has the right to tap or rap him on the shoulder to get his attention. The amount of force used in this gesture accords with the intensity of the emotions involved. It varies from a gentle, light touch—to emphasize a word or point, or to say "Hey, guess what!"—to a more forceful one: "Look, I'm angry about this!"

When the signer is in a moderately emotional state or has an urgent message, all four fingertips of the palm side of the hand are curled over (palm bent) or held flat, jabbing the shoulder, or, when the signer is feeling intense emotions, delivering a more forceful jab or a relatively gentle whack or slap. This most intense tap is delivered like a regular slap would be, but is more controlled, and is not really painful. The other person feels it—but there is no sting, pain, or red welts. It is meant as a most forceful point of emphasis—not as a blow. Skilled signers can, and do, control the amount of physical force invested in these taps.

There are thus three basic "levels" of shoulder-tapping: 1) a gentle "flag," 2) a moderately emphatic tap, and 3) a forcefully emphatic tap. All are acceptable usage within Deaf culture. The intent—again—is never to inflict hurt but to communicate forcefully to the other person: *"Please pay attention! I'm angry, and I want your full attention now!"*

We present the bitter real-life example of a Deaf couple whose 15-year marriage, under increasing strain, ultimately broke apart. One major issue was quarrels over spending. Another issue, which should never have come up in the first place, was the alleged abuse of the wife by the husband, and the formal complaints she filed with the police against him.

"Bob" was a skilled and versatile blue-collar worker. Quiet, serious, mild-mannered, an East European native, he held a variety of construction jobs, put in overtime, attended advanced-carpentry classes (with a sign-language interpreter) to refine his skills, and saved diligently to purchase necessities like a new van and luxuries like summer vacation trips for the family. He was both thrifty and generous. "Debbie" was pathologically lazy, irresponsible, and spent money—Bob's earnings—like crazy. They had two hearing daughters. During the 15 years of their marriage, they had innumerable arguments and verbal brawls. The issues that provoked these conflicts were never satisfactorily resolved. Despite Bob's patient and sensible explanations about budgeting, the wisdom he imparted to her on "necessities first, luxuries can wait" and "let's start saving money now for next summer's vacation," despite his pleas, appeals, and anguish over the bills that Debbie was running up, she showed no inclination to curb her squandering. She made expensive purchases on the sly, charging them to Bob's credit card (since he had a good credit record), then trying to hide the monthly bills when they arrived. She even illicitly withdrew money from the savings accounts Bob had established for their daughters. Debbie used her reckless spending as a weapon of revenge—a way to rebel against Bob, to exert her defiance of him as provider and "controller." In her view, he wasn't generous enough, so she took what she considered her just prerogative.

It is absolutely normal for couples to argue about money. It's also normal for couples to have angry quarrels—i.e., verbal fights. Sometimes a good quarrel can have a cathartic effect—the proverbial "getting it out of my system." The challenge is to get the anger and frustration out without inflicting harm on oneself or on others. After a "good" argument, both parties feel better, relieved, energized, willing to work towards resolving the causes of the conflict. Peace is restored, and there's a new feeling of vitality. But Bob and Debbie were never able to achieve this; they kept having the same kind of argument over and over again. Debbie's entrenched behavior patterns and inflexible attitudes prevented them from making real progress in their relationship. They were effectively mired.

Bob was not a "physical" person. His concerns about the family finances were legitimate. Had Debbie listened to him, had she tried to understand what he was upset about, had she paid attention to him, he would not have needed to employ any forceful gestures. When it came to *her* gripes, *her* complaints, and *her* demands, she expected Bob to listen to her. And he did. But she wasn't willing to accord him the same courtesy. She argued back. On occasion, she lost her temper and pummeled him with her fists.

What aggravated the situation was that Debbie's parents, "Sally" and "Jim," lived nearby—next door, in fact. Sally and Jim were hearing and mediocre signers, although they could communicate well with Debbie. They did *not* communicate well with Bob. They invariably supported Debbie during their quarrels, even though her irresponsibility was the cause of virtually all of their conflicts, and these same habits exasperated them too. They psychologically bullied Bob, and helped get him into trouble with the court system.

Bob gave Debbie a painful slap on the shoulder maybe once during their marriage (i.e., the kind that leaves a red mark for 10 minutes or so), when he was really furious. However, he never used his fist. He never punched her, slapped her face, or inflicted a black-and-blue mark or bruise. During their regular arguments, he never used anything more forceful than a third-degree "attention-demanding" tap.

So what did Debbie do? She ran off to her mother and bawled, "Bob hit me!" On three such occasions, she officially accused him of assaulting her and got the police involved.

Had Sally asked her to show her the injury, that would have helped Bob's cause. There were no red welts, no blossoming black-and-blue marks. But Sally never asked. And, of course, it was Debbie's word against his. Sally wasn't really interested in the truth, just in keeping Bob under control.

In Hearing culture, tapping or whacking a person on the shoulder, just like that, can be construed as simple assault, and is grounds for arrest. Deaf culture takes a different view.

Granted, there is occasionally a fine line between "forceful emphasis" and an abusive whack or punch that hurts (and is meant to), but sensible Deaf people understand the difference. Debbie either refused to understand, or was persuaded not to. She was *not* a sensible person.

When Debbie went to the local Hall of Justice and accused Bob of abusing her by rapping her on the shoulder, she was taking a Deaf-culture gesture out of context. Ostensibly, she knew better, having a Deaf-school background, but Sally may have incited her to file the complaints out of spite, because she particularly disliked Bob. And the police and judge, being entirely ignorant about the fine points of Deaf communication, bought her story.

Three times Debbie filed an official complaint against Bob. Three times he arrived home from a day's work, where Debbie and Sally were waiting gleefully for his arrival, only to have the police show up. Three times Bob, who was utterly baffled by this turn of events, was forced to gather his clothing and tools and leave the house, escorted by the police. Each time it happened, Debbie decided afterwards that she wanted to "save the marriage," probably because she realized that she, who possessed neither marketable skills nor inclination to find a job, was dependent on Bob's paycheck. But the damage was done. Bob acquired a court record without being able to say a word in his own defense. No one asked him for *his* version of the story.

After their final separation, Debbie spread malicious tales to her bowling-league friends that Bob had abused her. In reality, it was the other way around.

But we wonder how many police officers, court officials, attorneys, and judges realize the truth about Deaf communication?

Chapter 122

Why are deaf people always asking "follow-up" questions— "Did you do this?" "Did you finish that?" It drives me nuts!

his is an everyday situation that occurs within families or between roommates or housemates. We're thinking specifically of households, in which two or more persons, related or not, share the quarters and the responsibilities of housekeeping, and at least one of them is Deaf. Dorm life involves two or more persons sharing a room. (We're using the term "room-mate" to mean "housemate" as well. Even though this term may not be strictly accurate, it's common usage, even among those who share large houses and have their own rooms. It also applies to regular-family-style households.)

Anyone who shares living quarters engages in what is grandly termed social interactions—getting along with each other, and getting tasks done. This inevitably entails asking others to do something for us (or for the household). This can be a point of contention (as when roomies do not get along well), or an opportunity to help keep the social machinery (and the household) functioning smoothly.

When a hearing person asks a roommate to close or lock the door, open the window, draw the blinds, turn on the bathtub faucet or air conditioner, or switch off the TV (*etcetera*), s/he can usually hear it being done. Now, supposing it's a deaf, not a hearing, person who's doing the asking. Example: While washing the dishes, Jan, who's Deaf, asks her hearing room-mate Kim (who's just arrived home) to please lock the front door. Jan slips her hands out of the soapy dishwater so she can sign her request clearly. Kim walks out of the kitchen and returns a few moments later. Jan asks, "Did you lock the door"? Kim says, "Yes." To save time (and as an added courtesy), Kim will go directly to Jan as soon as she returns, volunteering the information: "Done, finished." ("Yes, I did it.") Kim then gets an affirmation from Jan: an "OK" sign or an ASL facial twitch, shorthand for "Thanks!"

Those who are accustomed to Deaf ways become so used to such interactions, they don't think twice about them. They instinctively recognize the logic behind them. Reporting back to a roomie who asks them to do something is a part of friendly everyday communication, just as much as checking the stove and faucets or bolting the doors at night are part of the daily household routine.

But if Kim isn't used to being "quizzed" every time she's asked to do something, she may find it irritating. Replay this scenario with the same roommates. Only this time, Kim is unaccustomed to living with Deaf roomies. When Jan asks her, "Did you lock the door?" Kim is apt to get annoyed: "Why do you ask? Don't you trust me?" Naturally, the expression on her face communicates her annoyance. This kind of response doesn't promote comfortable interactions at all. It may even provoke an argument. And, yes, this does happen—even between friends. Even between siblings.

One Deaf man whose sister graduated from an interpreter-training program says, "When I ask her to do something and she comes back, she never tells me she's done it. I have to ask her. I get *very* pissed off about that, because she really should know."

Some hearing roommates overdo it. Example: Dan (who's Deaf) is vacuuming the front hall when his roommate Jim (who's hearing) comes in. "Please close the door," Dan signs. Jim closes the door in full view of Dan, then says, "Finished!" Dan's dour response is likely to be, "I'm deaf, but I'm not blind. I could see it."

This, by the way, is a habit Deaf people pick up in institutions. A dorm parent or teacher (especially one who's Deaf!)

will ask the student to do something: "Would you close the door?" or "Please turn the light off in the supply closet." When the student returns, s/he volunteers the information: "Done, finished." Of course, s/he could be lying—but that's another issue entirely!

Chapter 123

Why are deaf people so nosy?

earing people—and this goes beyond the obvious—instinctively depend on their hearing, perhaps more than they do their sense of vision. As Frederick C. Schreiber pointed out in an address to International Association of Parents of the Deaf (now American Society for Deaf Children) in 1975, "Hearing children develop language effortlessly." They do much of their learning by overhearing. Instinctively, by chance and accident, they absorb conversations, arguments, the whole array of environmental sounds.

In contrast, deaf children have to be taught language, and this can be a slow, painful process. Why? "This is not because of deafness *per se*, it is a simple physical fact that one hears more than one sees." Communication has to be within eyeshot. On the other hand, Schreiber noted (in a 1972 address) that deaf workers are not necessarily bigger safety risks than the hearing. Years of experience of environmental awareness may even confer an advantage on the deaf. "All our lives we have had to be alert to danger, and it is second nature to us now . . . If a machine breaks down, I can feel it. In a noisy environment, the ability to sense a malfunction is often superior to the ability to hear one."*

So—to restate the obvious—while hearing people can use their hearing as well as their vision to receive environmental cues, we depend primarily on vision and other available senses to receive our essential cues for information and environmental orientation. We "take in" and process our cues differently from the hearing. We become visually aware.

All of us have our petty and not-so-petty horror stories: leaving the faucet running (something that hearing folks are good at preventing); tripping up the car horn; dropping our housekeys on the sidewalk and not hearing the telltale clink that would otherwise alert us; knocking over, crushing, breaking, or spilling something and not being aware of it immediately.

When a deaf person comes home, the first thing s/he does is look around—engage on a little reconnaissance patrol to make sure everything's okay. At periodic times during the evening, s/he'll get up and take a stroll through the house, checking on mate, children, housemates, friends, the rooms, the view through the windows. If we have Deaf housemates, every so often, they'll stop by just to check on us. It's just another detail of everyday life.

Similarly, after leaving a room, especially where there are other people, we often turn and take a quick glance backwards before leaving. It's pretty much instinctive. Our subconscious motive is to make absolutely sure we're not missing *anything*.

Hearing people can have elaborate alarm/monitoring/ paging systems installed. Deaf people can too—if they can afford to. It's not always possible or practical. So we rely on our senses—primarily sight and smell—for cues. We can sometimes feel when a house is empty, or when someone returns; sometimes we can recognize who has come back by the difference in the cadence of footsteps thudding up and down a staircase or vibrating the floor of a room above us, or even the way a door is opened or closed. Certain vibrotactile "patterns" are normal and accepted; something that deviates from this pattern alerts us to possible danger.

There is public snooping, and there is private snooping. By *public* snooping, we mean visual eavesdropping, as when people casually watch other people's conversations. As we've already mentioned, signed conversations conducted in a public area are visible to anyone and everyone. (Gallaudet University's Kendall Green comes immediately to mind, as do NTID's quadrangle and the Tower A lobby.) Students even look down from mezzanines, balconies, and windows to get aerial views of conversations. It is extraordinarily difficult to carry on a private conversation anywhere there are other deaf people, since signing is so visual.

When hearing people are in a thronged restaurant during dinner hour, they can hear the conversations of all the other diners, but the sound will be pretty much an undifferentiated murmur of as many as a dozen or two simultaneous voices, intermingled with the sounds of crockery and glasses clinking, chairs scraping, and the thump of the kitchen doors as the servers carry out the dishes. An eavesdropper would need to "zero in" on one conversation at a time.

Similarly, when entering a crowded roomful of signers, an eavesdropper is greeted by an overwhelming blur of simultaneous motion—the flutter and swoop of dozens of moving hands, rather like an explosion of tidal waves. It's possible to catch a stray sign here and there, but the eavesdropper needs to focus on one signer at a time.

We take a proactive approach when we venture forth in public—we assume that we will be overseen. When we enter a restaurant together, we refrain from signing for a few minutes, taking a quick inventory of the assembled diners to see if there's anyone we know, or anyone else using sign. Once we're sure that we're safe, we can start signing freely. If the coast is not clear, we try to get a table situated out of eyeshot of other signers, or we sign with extreme discretion.

Private snooping is a devilishly persistent and trickier problem to deal with. Snoops—nosy persons—are found in all communities and cultures. We don't have the monopoly on them. However, we've noticed that a good number of deaf people, even those who are otherwise trustworthy, do have a habit of snooping around—reading documents that happen to be within eyeshot, poking around in someone else's room during the occupant's absence, sometimes riffling through a stack of papers "just to satisfy my curiosity."

Curiosity and inquisitiveness are normal human attributes, and essential adjuncts of our need to be visually alert. Bore-

dom is a universal affliction. Deaf people crave information—the kind of input hearing people get "free" from their
noisy environments, radios, background chatter, *etcetera*.
Deaf snoops don't see it in terms of a moral issue. If there's a
letter lying nearby, even though that letter is none of their
business and in no way pertains to them, they're tempted to
take a peek. If there's a printout looping out of the TTY on the
boss's desk when no one else is around, even though they
know they're not supposed to read it, they'll do so anyway.
They're curious, that's all.

In traditional schools for the deaf, the kids share all details
of their lives. One's business is everyone else's business too.
"Privacy" and "confidentiality" are often alien concepts.
Snooping, secret-sharing, and gossiping go together. If one of
them gets a personal letter, why shouldn't the others have a
look, too? It becomes habitual. If the opportunity presents
itself, they take advantage of it.

Human beings, as we know, can be wonderfully logical
creatures—ingeniously concocting justifications, rationales,
and excuses for whatever they desire to do. Some deaf snoops
rationalize what they're doing—e.g., if they don't physically
touch the paper or printout, they don't *really* consider it
snooping.

Needless to say, this can be an exasperating habit in an
office—or anyplace where deaf people are in proximity to
confidential materials or off-limits space.

It's best to be upfront about this. If you're an employer,
supervisor, or boss, *etcetera*, tell your Deaf worker, neighbor,
or friend that you don't believe in nosing into other people's
business and you don't like it when others do it. But a
stimulating environment, such as a busy office or a friend's
colorful, cluttered apartment, is *so* tempting. It can be difficult
to make them understand.

Do warnings help? Doubtful. Threats? Counterproductive.
Problem is, it's difficult to prove unless you catch her or him
in the act. Pilfering items or cash is easier to recognize. But

nosing? Does behavior modification work? How do you reward someone for not snooping when you're not sure they've been cooperating 100%, anyway?

From our experiences, we doubt that nosiness, once it becomes an ingrained habit, can be cured. It can be counteracted, though. The best way to combat it is to remove as much temptation as possible. In the case of a Deaf worker who comes in early and treats herself to a look-around, make sure to put away and lock up whatever stray papers you don't want her to see before she arrives. (Assume that she'll notice everything that's in the open.) Arrange the papers so that they're not easily tampered with, or in such a manner that you can see right away if someone has shifted anything in your absence. (Remember that little trick immortalized in *The Sting* of tucking a small slip of paper into the lower part of the doorjamb?) If you've given your worker explicit directions not to touch certain papers and you find that he has done so, then you can have a serious talk with him about snooping— why it's risky, why it's unethical, why you dislike it, and why it may get him into trouble.

Before doing anything drastic, try a humorous approach— put a sticker-slip on the material the snoop is likely to target. The sticker could read: "Jan, you're not supposed to be reading this!" or "If you can read this, you're snooping!"

---

* Quoted from "Total Communication—As the Adults See It" (1975) and "Potentials for Employment of the Deaf at Levels in Keeping with Their Intellectual Capabilities," 1972; both in Jerome D. Schein's **A Rose For Tomorrow: Biography of Frederick C. Schreiber** (Silver Spring: NAD, 1981).

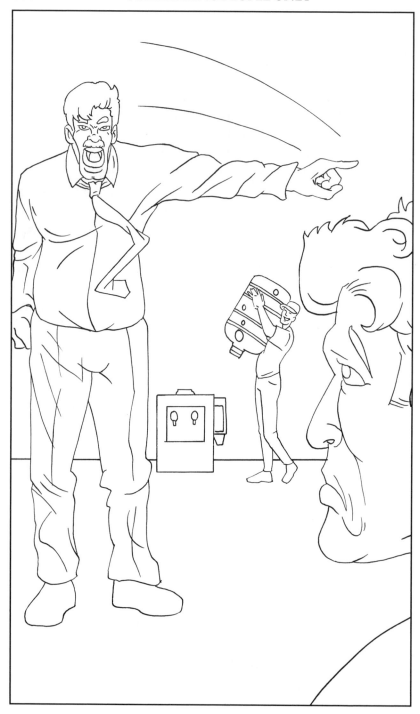

Chapter 124

When I have someone coming in to repair office equipment, my Deaf employee always stands nearby and watches. If I ask him to move off, he gives me a dirty look. Why?

hat do hearing people do to enliven the duller stretches of their workday? They tune into a favorite radio program. Call a client, or even a friend. Or strike up a leisurely chat by the water cooler about the weather, sports, vacation plans, travel, families, pets, cars, hobbies, current sales, international news, finance, new faces at work, or last night's TV-movie. The possibilities are endless.

If you're a Deaf person in an otherwise all-hearing environment, you are pretty much excluded from this. So what do you do to kill time? You observe. You watch people doing things. Especially repair technicians coming in and working on a disabled photocopier, printer, computer, or similar "complex" equipment. Or even a glazier replacing a broken window or glass door. Deaf people aren't necessarily being nosy or meddlesome; they just like to see what's going on. And to understand why it's going on.

Many Deaf people who come from residential-school backgrounds feel that they grew up in a zoo (or the proverbial goldfish bowl), in the sense of being frequently under observation. From the time they start school, they're watched by hearing visitors—legislators, parents, researchers, educational administrators. These observers are perpetually coming into the classrooms to see how they learn, how they sign (or thrive with their speech training). They grow up with someone, usually a hearing someone, stationed behind them and looking over their shoulder. (Deaf kids have their own way of retaliating. If they see hearing kids staring at them, they say, "25-a-look?"—that is, "Pay me 25¢ for the look?"— and shoo them away.) So they feel that it's okay to turn the tables and do a little observing themselves.

Again, this attitude is not to be confused with snooping or a desire to get in the way. It's a normal reaction . . . even a positive one. Curiosity, the hunger to understand, is a desirable attribute. And Deaf people have a notable hunger for information. (We've said it before, and we'll say it again.)

It can, however, cause a bit of trouble on occasion. A real-life example: Steve, the much-put-upon Deaf man working in a small firm, Prism Graphics, where everybody else is hearing, is cut off from virtually all of the everyday interchange that his co-workers have full access to—conversations, radio, overheard telephone talk. He naturally resents this situation, although he's resigned to it.

It so happened that one day, around noon, a bottled-water deliveryman arrived to install a new water cooler. It was a new kind of cooler setup; Steve had never seen anything of the sort before. He had, at that moment, nothing in particular to do. He was intrigued. So he stood by, watching the deliveryman installing the cooler. Along came Fred, the boss, and told Steve curtly, "Move away!" Steve replied, "It's lunch break; I'm leaving." His unexpressed thought was: *Screw you. I want to watch!* But he left.

Is it okay for us to watch? Usually—if we're not deserting our posts or neglecting a responsibility. If it's our workspace or house, of course, we have more independence to decide. If it's an electrician upgrading the fusebox or a worker doing repairs, installation, decoration, *etcetera*, and no huffy boss is around to bother the Deaf observer, the worker most likely won't mind being watched. That way, if we have a question, we can ask right then and there. But if it's a workplace situation with superiors and subordinates, and if we're the subordinates, and the boss is around, s/he may order the Deaf person away. Not that there's a written rule against looking on; there usually isn't. It's more of a social norm. Hearing folks generally don't do that kind of thing. But Deaf people, on the whole, are not inclined to comply. They'd much rather stay and watch—and learn something new.

What's the boss's rationale for ordering the "intrusive" Deaf worker away from the repair technician? "I don't want Steve hovering around the technician because he'll make him nervous." Steve's rationale for staying and watching is: "All my life, I've had hearing people hovering around me, peering over my shoulder. Nobody ever asked if it made *me* nervous. So why shouldn't I give hearing people a taste of what they've given me all my life? If my presence is making the technician uncomfortable, I prefer 'hearing it straight from the horse's mouth.' The technician hasn't complained. Anyway, how else am I going to learn?

"Because if I *don't* watch, and then ask a deliveryman or technician or repairer 'What were you doing there?' or 'What was wrong?' or 'What's that?', I'll get a short, brusque response—maybe a shrug. These guys don't like to be bothered to write something down. I don't want to interrupt them. Even if I did ask them to jot down an explanation for my benefit, I know I'll get a brief, impatient answer, with no details. Hearing people can stand by and ask questions and carry on detailed conversations with these tech people while they work; Deaf people can't do that. If I stay and watch, I'll get the whole picture, or at least something!"

In imperfect situations, how *do* we understand what's going on? We observe. We watch others from the back. We try to make sense of the visual input, whatever clues and cues we can glean. We piece together the fragments and scraps of perceptions as we receive them, reassembling them into a broader picture. Although pieces of the puzzle may be missing, we can try to discern the general outline . . . and try to figure out what's missing and what's there.

Observing and following others doesn't always work. One unhappy recollection (LL):

> Some years ago, I took a dance class at NTID in which the late-deafened teacher had poor communication skills. So I followed my classmates . . . copied what they were doing. But they often made mistakes. It turned out not to matter, because the teacher didn't bother correcting me. He didn't care what moves I made, right or wrong. He simply ignored me. I didn't like being ignored. But he didn't see the point on wasting a moment of *his* valuable time on so untalented a student. He preferred to focus on the others, especially those who could profit from his instruction, and those who were members of his dance corps. Even so, I resented getting less out of the class than my classmates did.

In everyday life, we are faced with choices: to come forward and look on, and risk getting reprimanded, or to comply with the "rules" and stand back, and lose out. To speak out and ask an impatient teacher or clerk or co-worker to repeat or explain something that we've missed—or to remain quiet and try to figure out what's what. Not everyone wants to *bother* jotting something down, either. We run the risk of being misunderstood—or missing out on vital pieces of information—or stepping out of line. It's a gamble.

Since Deaf people are largely cut off from aural sources of information, they lag behind hearing people in terms of immediate access to information (and the benefits of knowing it), if that situation is communicated only aurally. Case in point: a malfunctioning photocopy machine. A hearing worker can call to the repair technician from across the room: "What's wrong?" The technician replies: "Oh, a paperclip got into the drum unit." S/he will get an informative, useful answer. If the Deaf worker asks the hearing worker: "What did he say?" s/he's likely to get a brush-off-type response: "Oh, something needed replacement." Or: "Oh, nothing important." Or: "Nothing you need to know." Or: "He fixed the problem." Or: "I'll tell you later." None of these are proper responses.

A Deaf worker who asks the same questions as a hearing co-worker has an equal right to know the answers, just as much right as the hearing worker does. And s/he may want to know so that s/he'll be able to troubleshoot the same problem, should it pop up again! Many Deaf people tend to remember these details better than their hearing peers, and do a good job of troubleshooting similar problems, say, at home. That's essentially why they don't like to be shooed away. They want to see, to learn, to remember.

Deaf people tend to be respectful of authority, however. If a police officer or firefighter tells a Deaf bystander to leave the area, s/he will comply. Promptly.

▲ ▲ ▲

The Garage Gambit

This situation applies outside of work, too. Lots of Deaf people have cars. And the cars need periodic servicing. A number of deaf drivers want to see what's happening when the mechanic lifts the hood and starts checking the engine. They are likewise eager to see what's doing on the underside of the car. If they have a question or want to describe a problem, they want to be right there.

Some garages are stricter than others about banning customers from the service areas. Some cite an "insurance policy" requiring all customers to wait in a separate area. Instead of patronizing a restrictive garage, deaf drivers will look for another where customers are welcome to look on. They don't like being shunted off to waiting areas. (These typically contain a radio and an old TV set—invariably, one without captioning capability.)

To some people, a garage is a garage, and any one will do. If these car-owners aren't particularly interested in the mechanical details of repair and upkeep, they'll be content to wait in the lobby or waiting room, out of the way. It won't matter if they're shooed away from the garage area. Those of us who are interested in knowing how to fix cars and keeping them running, who are intrigued with the mechanical aspects and enjoy looking on, will be more picky about our choice of garages. Deaf people tend to patronize small service garages, where they get to know the personnel and where they're permitted to stand by watching the mechanics at work.

Steve says that at muffler shops and service garages that do oil changes, he's often told: "You'll have to sit in the lobby." Instead of complying, he drives right off to find another garage. There's a garage in Rochester not far from the NTID/ RIT campus that's popular with Deaf students and alumni. The mechanics may not know how to sign, but they're patient and allow their customers to stand nearby, watching.

And why not? Deaf observers like to station themselves near the mechanics who are servicing their cars. Not too near, but at a comfortable distance. If they stand too far away, they'd have to yell to get the mechanic's attention, and that would scare the mechanic and others nearby—they'd think something's wrong. Exactly the wrong kind of reaction. Instead, Deaf observers station themselves about three feet away, within arm's reach. It's easy for Steve to tap the mechanic on the shoulder or point to something.

Savvy mechanics, those who acquire "Deaf smarts" by experience, learn how to understand their customers' gestures and mannerisms. They know that by having a bit of patience and courtesy, they're bringing in more business. Deaf people tell their friends about their experiences, good and bad, at garages, and recommend garages and mechanics that they like, the ones they consider "Deaf-friendly."

How do you communicate with a mechanic when s/he doesn't know how to sign, and you don't want to bother with writing? You use body language and a repertoire of simple, unambiguous gestures: pointing, the "okay" (#9) sign, thumb up for "good," thumb down for "bad," a shrug with the appropriate facial expression ("I'm puzzled" or "I don't know"), a grimace ("bad problem"). A hearing customer could say, "This part knocks" or "I'm getting a *ping-ping-ping* vibration after the engine warms up." A Deaf customer points and uses mime. Miming a screwdriver driving in a screw means "Can you fix this?" A horizontal sweep of hands back and forth, towards and away from each other, coupled with a tight "negation" expression means "Do not fix this." A beckoning gesture, of course, means "Come here; look at this."

Facial expressions or a slight headshake convey "leave it alone"—"Oh, that's okay as it is." A pushing-forward "stay" gesture means "halt." Other gestures depend on where they're working.

Deaf people prefer to use simple gestures to avoid the necessity of having to write down a question. We would have to go into the car to get paper and pen, if we don't already have them handy, and it takes too long. Meanwhile, we'd miss a couple of minutes—time that we'd prefer to use to observe what's being done on the engine. Gestures make an immediate connection.

Chapter 125

What kind of summer program is best for a deaf teenager?

 hen the winter months melt into spring, and summer plans need to be discussed and implemented, many parents of deaf teenagers start to ask, and worry, "What do I do with my kid(s) when summer starts?"

The Youth Leadership Camp is not the only summer program for young deaf people. We gladly admit that! A number of schools for the deaf sponsor good local summer programs, as do Gallaudet University and NTID. Not all summer programs for deaf kids are sign-language-based, either—e.g., Clarke School's oral program for deaf kids and their hearing siblings, which emphasizes speech-communication skills.

But . . . supposing the Deaf teenager does want a sign-based program? There are Deaf-accessible science, computer, sports, and art camps. There is variety, and there are numerous choices available for a range of age groups.

But the YLC, we feel, is one of the best, if not *the* best, for developing leadership skills in deaf teenagers. Some deaf children are natural leaders—they have the personality traits that can make for effective leaders, if these traits are nurtured—but it can be difficult to develop those traits, especially if the child's major energies are spent in struggling to understand what's going on, in surviving from day to day. A high-stress, low-access environment isn't conducive to developing leadership, creativity, or self-confidence.

One of the most positive aspects of schools for the deaf and magnet public-school programs is that deaf kids have a community of peers they can communicate freely with. Growing up within this community, they don't experience the frustration of having to cope with language/communication/understanding barriers. There is usually (although not invariably) good teacher-student dialogue, too. All of which is excellent for developing self-confidence, at least in communicating. The family environment may or may not be supportive, but if the school fulfills the need to communicate openly and to enjoy unimpeded access to the teaching, the deaf student will thrive—socially, at least. And many young Deaf people who don't thrive academically nonetheless have rich and fulfilling social lives.

Deaf students in mainstream programs are often isolated from their deaf peers. They may have little or no contact with other deaf kids or successful deaf adults—teachers, counselors, and coaches. They may even be "the only deaf kid in school." For those with good athletic skills, this isolation may not present an insuperable barrier. They participate on their varsity teams and win respect by their athletic prowess.

What if your child isn't terribly sports-oriented? Supposing you have a deaf kid who wants something more than athletic competition or the social whirl? That's where a program like the Youth Leadership Camp can make a difference. In the YLC, emphasis is placed on learning, teamwork, decision-making, Deaf mentoring, and acquiring leadership skills. Best of all, deaf kids are with other deaf kids all day long, with Deaf adults directing the program. For some, it can mean temporary sensory overload, even culture shock. They quickly adjust and plunge into the enriched communication environment. And they make the most of it. Shy, reticent students typically gain new self-confidence.

Granted, there are some deaf kids who don't thrive in a camp atmosphere. Their social skills may be so poor that they can't learn to function as part of a team. But participation in a program such at YLC can benefit them, too. It's better for deaf kids to learn to work and play with other deaf kids as equals than to have no contact with them at all.

Particularly important are the friendships made at these camps. Since the YLC attracts teens from across the nation and beyond, it provides a matchless opportunity for deaf kids to meet and become friends with other deaf kids from different parts of the country *and* different backgrounds. Although the daily activities are highly structured, there is time to chat and share experiences. Deaf teens discover that they aren't alone, that their frustrations and joys aren't unique, that other deaf kids have also experienced what they're going through.

Schools and camps present different sets of challenges. Camp is different from school in that the daily pressures are largely absent. The expectations may be higher. "School" connotes regimentation, monotony, discipline, conformity, pressure, endless assignments, and, for some, boredom and isolation. "Camp" connotes fun, adventure, recreation, friendship, learning, exploration, and freedom. Of course, camp can be a dreary experience; school can be rewarding and exciting. Even though a program such as the YLC is highly structured and competitive, much as a school program is, it's an adventure. Campers have more opportunity to do things on their own, to shape their own experience, to take the lead. The more they put in, the more they get out.

Says Dr. Frank R. Turk, co-founder of YLC: "There is something extraordinarily special about this experience which is difficult to describe in words—a family togetherness reminiscent of the greatness of America during its pioneering years."

That quality was community—where teamwork ensured survival and prosperity, and everyone was so busy building their community that nobody had time to feel alone. The best kind of summer programs can give deaf kids a taste of community, the richness of shared communication, a family-like feeling of belonging. Not surprisingly, former YLC participants, after returning to their separate schools across the continent, eagerly maintain contact with each other via E-mail. One summer spent in a good program can have immediate effects and lifelong repercussions. It's an investment we wish all parents of deaf children could make.

Chapter 126

Why do graduates of schools for the deaf hold reunions every other year?

fter you've been around Deaf people a while, you'll notice that their school experiences are much more important to them than the corresponding experiences of their hearing counterparts generally are. Deaf people identify and define themselves by these experiences. They're more involved in each other's lives than public-school alumni tend to be. There's more of a family feeling.

Deaf people are—almost invariably—curious to know how their old classmates, schoolmates, and teachers are doing, and keep tabs on each other. Instead of burying their school yearbooks in the attic, they keep them within easy reach, and whenever the occasion arises—say, a friend comes to visit and mentions seeing a mutual acquaintance from those days— they eagerly search for that friend's picture. These "gossip books" are an omnipresent feature at reunions.

One of the most notable differences between Deaf and Hearing is the closeness that develops between deaf children who attend schools for the deaf. Unless their families relocate to another city or state, these kids characteristically grow up together, and ultimately treat each other as family—or closer than family. It has little or nothing to do with sexual attraction, and goes beyond school spirit. Even in repressive, backwards, academically substandard schools, deaf alumni share a certain bond that is often lacking in hearing kids who attended a series of public schools.

Until fairly recently, when students were given wider choice as to what high school they'd be attending, most hearing people outside large cities attended public school on the basis of geographic location. If they lived in large cities, they could choose on the basis of aptitude by passing specialized entrance exams. But as a rule, if you lived in a certain neighborhood, you went to *that* school, and you attended a succession of different ones (elementary, middle, junior high, senior high) according to age. Every time you'd enter a new school there'd be new teachers and kids—unfamiliar faces—and you'd miss some of the kids you'd made friends with, because they'd have transferred to different schools or moved away. You usually developed some close friendships with some other kids in your class (all roughly the same age as you), but usually not with those who were, say, two or three years older or younger.

With Deaf people, especially those who attended residential schools, it's a different picture. They've often started school as early as age 3, and attended the same campus until they graduated from high school (12th grade). They met lots of other deaf kids, and got to know practically everybody else in the school. If they were residential students, they saw each other in the classroom and in the dorms. They typically formed close, enduring friendships with older and younger kids, as well as those their own age.

While public-high-school alumni hold reunions maybe every 5 or 10 years, deaf-school alumni typically hold reunions every other year. Why?

1.) The graduating classes of deaf schools tend to be quite small compared to those of public schools. While a public-high-school class can number several hundred, or even a thousand or more, the graduating class of a school for the deaf will often number less than 50, sometimes not even a dozen. Deaf-school reunions normally include *all* surviving alumni, spanning a few generations and a sizable range of ages. (Gaps are inevitable.) There are older alumni whose children are grown, and younger alumni who are just starting their families. There are singles. There are friends and spouses who didn't attend the school but met—some of them—through a friend at Gallaudet, CSUN, or NTID. There are those who attended but never graduated.

Once there, they gather into smaller groups encompassing two or three classes together, with the old class presidents or leaders taking an active role. They raise funds for their classes and plan single-year or three-class reunions and other activities a couple years in advance. Parents often bring children to these smaller reunions, where they set up a camp or have family cookouts or parties.

2.) Biennial reunions give the attendees a good opportunity to discuss political strategies. If their school is threatened with major budget cuts or closure (and it's a rare state school that isn't feeling the pinch and the pressure), they can plan activities such as organizing rallies and protest marches, picketing the state capital, mounting petition drives and letter-writing campaigns, and meeting with state or U.S. senators and representatives.

3.) Deaf people are visually-oriented. They much prefer conducting their most important business in person. As we've already noted, many dislike using the TTY for intimate chats. They also tend *not* to keep in contact with friends through letters. So where most hearing people would be content to phone or write others, Deaf people insist on face-to-face communication. Biennial reunions afford them a frequent opportunity to see each other again, share the ups and downs of their lives, and catch up on the latest news. Reunions are a sort of Deaf ham-radio network.

4.) Attending reunions every other year gives the alumni an opportunity to plan an extended vacation during the interval year. These plans could, for example, include a chartered group tour for ASL users, or a family excursion. Participants generally look forward to their reunions, and as soon as one is over, and during the interval year, the planning for the next one begins.

Chapter 127

I've noticed that Deaf people travel a lot—more than hearing people. Why? And how can they afford to? Where do they get the money?

ithout getting into a sociological analysis, we can make a few broad generalizations. Hearing people tend to stay near home base (except for major vacations), but Deaf people travel around frequently. There are the annual or biennial conventions, USADSF/bowling gatherings, class reunions, ASL tours, and other social inducements.

For many of us, opportunities to "go out" are limited. We rarely go to the cinemas to see first-run Hollywood movies, for obvious reasons: no captions. We tend to avoid going to musical concerts, for equally obvious reasons: no access. Sign-interpreted musicals, operas, and oratorios are extremely rare. Most Broadway/off-Broadway plays and theater festivals are still off-limits; there may be special arrangements whereby a single or few performances are interpreted, but that's likewise a rarity. Dining out isn't a major problem, but it can be lonely for single Deaf persons. Nightclubs? Cabarets? Fundraising galas? Most are *not* Deaf-friendly environments. Thus, the more expensive forms of entertainment tend to be relatively inaccessible.

In real life, Deaf people work hard at a variety of jobs (not always the best or most challenging). We don't go to costly, inaccessible concerts or performances; we save our money towards the next travel opportunity. And this is a booming business.

It *is* true that Deaf people are indefatigable travelers. Our enthusiasm for travel originates in the old-fashioned communications embargo. For the better part of a century, Deaf people couldn't contact each other by telephone. Picturephones—a relatively old idea that has been tried and re-tried experimentally—are making a comeback as videophones, but we predict that it'll take some time before they become commonplace fixtures. There are still bugs to be worked out. And they *are* expensive.

Chatrooms? Many of us enjoy them; others don't; and still others don't have access to computers.

That leaves us with TTYs, which are, as we've already pointed out, indispensable, but many Deaf people don't use them for social chats to a great extent, as they don't like carrying on conversations through an LED readout or paper-tape printout. (With a relay service, a one-to-one chat becomes a three-party conversation, one of the parties being a total stranger, *and* with increased possibilities for misunderstandings.) We want the real thing. We prefer to interact personally. This means traveling the distances.

Another basis of this enthusiasm lies in our affinity for other Deaf persons—old schoolmates, friends in other cities, curiosity, the desire to meet other Deaf people, to sample Deaf life in other communities, and explore other cultures. And, of course, our need for accessible communication (ASL in North America). So tours catering to Deaf people include ASL-fluent guides and assistants, and/or sign-language interpreters. Depending on the economics and numbers, these tours can be part of a "mainstream" arrangement or a separate "Deaf-only" tour.

Travel isn't necessarily prohibitively expensive. The key is numbers. Get a group of people together with related interests, charter a plane, cruise, or motorcoach (tour bus), and the costs are kept down. Deaf organizations often sponsor tours that are chartered by commercial travel agencies at group rates. Deaf people, of course, do travel alone or in pairs or as families, but some have found it frustrating. There is strength in numbers—and clout. And, considering the hostility and harassment experienced by single women travelers in some countries, it's safer, if less adventurous, to travel with a group.

Needless to say, we enjoy "seeing the sights" just as much as hearing travelers do. Our delight at seeing the Tower of London, Eiffel Tower, the Sistine Chapel ceiling, the Prado, Parthenon, Taj Mahal, Kyoto, or a tropical rainforest, is ensured by having accessible guidance and communication. It's a frustrating experience to pay a stiff admission charge to an historic site or museum that provides audiocassette "tour guides," or a live guide who communicates in voice only— great for hearing visitors, but not so great for those of us who don't benefit from audio narration, especially when we're the sole deaf person in the group.

Some guides, it should be noted, will give or loan a printout of their script to a Deaf participant. (In that case, it's best to request such an arrangement ahead of time.) The Deaf participant must then try to keep pace with the rest of the group, alternating between reading the script and observing the attractions. It can be tiring. Having a Deaf-accessible tour that includes an interpreter or Sign-fluent docent or guide makes for a less stressful, more relaxing and enjoyable experience.

With Deaf-group tours, there will often be some sort of organized contact with local Deaf groups, and social arrangements, with tour guides or liaisons interpreting between the sign languages. Needless to say, this is a prime bonus of traveling abroad—the opportunity to meet Deaf people in other countries, make friends, and enjoy the kinship Deaf people feel with each other throughout the world. It can be great fun learning to communicate in "universal sign" to other signers, to establish a basis of understanding. That's a thrill worth a dozen top-notch concerts anytime.

Chapter 128

Do Deaf people ever wish they were hearing?

es, primarily because they are disgusted with having to deal with the constant bullshit they get from the hearing world—restrictions, discrimination, *can't* this, *can't* that. *And* the peculiar brand of bullshit found in the Deaf community—the gossip, the backstabbing.

Do Deaf people suffer from sensory deprivation? Most don't. Surprisingly, many born-deaf people don't "miss" sound, music, and spoken conversation anywhere near as much as hearing people think they do. They don't find themselves missing what they never had. (Similarly, many people who are born blind or early-blinded, when asked if they don't miss the beauties of the visual world, colors, rainbows, and sunsets, have said that they can't miss something they've never experienced.)

Late-deafened people are a different matter entirely.* They've lost an integral aspect of their lives they've taken for granted (as do hearing people), and their feelings of loss and pain should never be denigrated. Born-deaf adults, as a rule, tend to be well-adjusted, with a positive view of themselves as Deaf people. They see themselves as whole persons, *not* broken ears, *not* defective hearing machines, *not* deprived of "normalcy." If they don't miss the beauties of music (and, of course, it depends on what you mean by *music*), it's because they have other things going on in their heads and their lives that keep them occupied.

Occasionally, hearing people tell us how much they "envy" the supposed peace and quiet that (they imagine) deaf people experience in their "silent world." An understandable, but patronizing sentiment. Our lives are filled with hubbub and noise—visual noise—*and* we're discriminated against. (We pay a pretty high price for that "peace and quiet.")

A good number of Deaf people don't see the spoken word as the supreme unit of communication. Their early experiences with speech may not be pleasant or productive. They have a fully-developed, expressive, and subtle means of communication—sign language—which suits their needs perfectly. Sometimes they feel a bit sorry for hearing people who can't sign. Signing adds visual and kinetic zip to one's life—why would *anyone* want to be without it?

One of the worst things about being deaf is the isolation we experience—which has nothing to do with the quality of our residual hearing and much to do with the quality of social attitudes. A problem frequently experienced by oral and mainstreamed deaf children is the absence of deaf adult mentors (a.k.a. "role models"). A number of these deaf children honestly believe that they're going to become hearing when they grow up. Since they're surrounded by hearing teachers, therapists, counselors, and staffers, and since their families and all other adults they meet are hearing, they logically assume that there are no deaf adults in the world, and therefore, once they reach adulthood, they too will be hearing. Some of these kids even believe that they will die before reaching adulthood, since they don't see or know any living deaf adults! This is one reason why so many mainstreamed deaf children have "difficulties adjusting." It simply underscores the vital need to bring successful deaf/ Deaf adults into these children's lives. Children who cannot imagine surviving to adulthood as deaf people, needless to say, are in dire need of mentoring.

Anyone who has grown up in the Deaf community knows that Deaf people can be unbelievably vicious to other Deaf people—especially those whose only crime is to be "different," to aspire to something that is not the "norm," to cherish a "hearing" ambition, and to succeed in it. Deaf people trashing other Deaf people is a shameful fact of life for many of us. It originates in jealousy. Instead of encouragement and support, achievers get sneers. Instead of appreciation (let alone admiration), backstabbing. Instead of understanding, hostility.

Add this to the "Hearing" discrimination and incomprehension they are already battling, and you have a pretty heavy burden, one that can be intolerable. Thus, a number of Deaf people have to deal—simultaneously—with bullshit from both Hearing and Deaf communities.

The dilemma facing Deaf people who are victims of crab theory is that they essentially stuck in their community. Hearing professionals who work in Deaf-oriented fields and associate frequently with Deaf people have an advantage: they can retire, quit, defect, pack up and leave, and still have the entire vast Hearing community to navigate. Their social horizons are pretty much unlimited. They need not have any further contact or communication with Deaf people again, if they so desire. They can turn their backs permanently and completely on the Deaf community and take up another endeavor, find a new circle of acquaintances. Deaf people who wish that they could escape the boorishness and nastiness of their communities (the local backstabbers' network) are not in such a favorable position. Their social opportunities are relatively limited. And since everyone in the Deaf community seems to know everyone else, it's nigh-impossible to avoid running into backstabbers or their friends and supporters. Deaf people are effectively stuck in the community, even if they have unjustly acquired a bad reputation.

Small wonder that some creative Deaf people who have labored diligently to increase understanding and acceptance of Deaf culture in the hearing world, or simply succeeding in what they do best and love most, find themselves wishing they were hearing—as a quick solution to an endlessly exasperating problem. Given this double inheritance, who *wouldn't* wish to be free from it?

1950'S

CONTEMPORARY

Chapter 129

Are things better for deaf people now, or did they have it better in the old days?

nterwoven in the tapestry of history is the story of the Deaf community. In some ways, deaf people in the States had an easier time of it back then (say, 100 or 150 years ago); in other ways, our current situation is a vast improvement. Progress involves trade-offs.

Historical novels and movies often portray the past romantically, as a desirable state. If we could transport ourselves back to those simpler times, we might not find them to our liking. In an agriculture-based economy, for example, if your family had a farm, you were needed to help work it. The work was frequently endless and exhausting. Education was of strictly secondary importance—for hearing *or* deaf. Home-schooling was much more common in those days (and much depended on the literacy and attitudes of the parents). Relatively few hearing persons attended college, and those who did tended to be wealthy, or at least financially comfortable. Illiteracy was widespread. Child labor—and child abuse—was rampant. Prior to the establishment of women's colleges, women had a nigh-impossible time obtaining an advanced education. A few of the luckier and more enterprising went to Europe. Without higher education, there was no access to the professions.

Social restrictions were oppressive. Prejudice, ethnic/racial/gender bias, and religious intolerance were epidemic. Virtually everyone believed that blacks were inferior to whites, and a good number of men believed that they had a God-given right to rule (i.e., own) their wives and children. Women in the United States struggled for over a century to gain basic rights as citizens, starting with the right to vote. There was a time when the concepts of women's rights, civil rights, and children's rights were "unthinkable" or "mad folly." It took time for thinkers and doers to articulate, advocate, stimulate public awareness, and rally support for these causes.

Deaf people in the States had the advantage of state schools and a college (what is now Gallaudet University). But if your parents didn't know about schools for the deaf, or lived in a remote area, or had non-progressive ideas about the capabilities of deaf people, you could easily be deprived of even a basic education. Gallaudet University barred women for several years, and there was no law against that. Blacks weren't admitted until the 1950s, a period when social change stirred the national consciousness and rippled through institutions. Until them, segregation and severely restricted educational and employment opportunities were the rule.

Nowadays, deaf people are barred from active military service, as our deafness is considered a hazard on the field. Maybe. But consider the brief but remarkable career of Erastus "Deaf" Smith. During the bloody struggle for Texas' independence, he served as Sam Houston's favorite spy. He had a knack for being in the right place at the right time. He could pass as a Tejano. He captured Mexican military couriers, infiltrated an enemy camp, helped destroy Vince's Bridge, and participated in the climactic Battle of San Jacinto.

So, what's progress? Sam Houston commanded a ragtag, demoralized, and ill-equipped volunteer army. West Point isn't about to admit its first ASL-Deaf cadet. We've had a few pioneering deaf law-enforcement officers, but no FBI agents or Gulf War-type soldiers, so far as we know. Not yet, anyway.

Before the advent of the telephone, deaf and hearing people depended equally on telegrams and letters. The rise of the telephone as the favorite medium of short and long-distance communication changed our lives, to be sure. Deaf people were effectively isolated and denied access to a vast array of jobs and social opportunities. Hearing children of deaf parents, who could use telephones, became liaisons between their parents and the "Hearing world." This placed a burden on the children—and the parents, too. Did deaf people look back nostalgically to the pre-telephone days? Did they find themselves wishing that they could turn the clock back?

Before the advent of the "talkies," deaf and hearing moviegoers enjoyed the variety of silent movies that established Hollywood as a major American and international cultural institution. Deaf people participated in the making of the "silents" and acted in them. Today, we look at the "silents" in their cinematic-historical context as a subject worthy of scholarly analysis, a unique art form, and are committed to preserving the classics of the genre. Many of those who grew up during the "silent era" have looked back at their experience with tremendous fondness, and some have left precious testimonies. Through their eyes—and by seeing the silents as they were meant to be seen—we can recapture some of the freshness, relive the excitement. The "silent era," we agree, was wonderful.

But then, there was no ADA, no civil-rights legislation, no Supreme Court rulings against discrimination.

Then again (going back to the early years of the 19th century), you didn't need teaching credentials to establish a school for the deaf. You rounded up your pupils and began teaching them to read and write. There were no school boards, no tenure, no OSERS. Some schools, like Col. William Bolling's early attempt in Virginia (1812), failed. Others, like the Hartford Asylum and William and Eliza Willard's free-tuition school in Indianapolis, succeeded. And when you went to school, the hours were long and the equipment of the simplest kind. School might be a brutal experience. Teachers, especially in public schools, were allowed, and expected, to mete out physical punishment for infractions of discipline, even for incorrect answers. But—ideally—you learned to read, write, cipher (do arithmetic), and *think*.

What about careers? We learn from the lives of eminent deaf people through the centuries that deafness was not necessarily an impassable barrier for success. Especially in the arts. Deaf Smith may possibly have been an aberration, but we've certainly had an impressive variety of craftspeople, artisans, photographers, and artists. And journalists, poets, teachers, and advocates. *And* scientists. *And* inventors.

As for Deaf arts, they are flourishing like dandelions after an April shower. This—the here and now—is our Golden Age. We have performance artists and writers. We have ASL poetry, drama, comedy, theater troupes, visual arts, and world-class craftspeople.

Well, yes, we're making headway into the professions. Deaf people are entering more untraditional fields, and working their way up.

And yet, competition between deaf and hearing jobseekers is fierce. Faced with a choice between two qualified candidates, one deaf, one hearing, which one will the company hire? The one with perfect speech? Or the one who needs an interpreter? Are deaf people at an automatic disadvantage?

Back then, there were fewer laws. This meant more freedom (at least for some), but also more peril. Rules, regulations, statutes, and laws are a fact (sometimes a nuisance) of modern life. Laws have worked both for us and against us. On the plus side, American Sign Language has gained official recognition in several states. But when new rules unfairly restrict us instead of recognizing our capabilities (as with the YMCA's decertification of veteran lifeguard David Schultz), we challenge them. The ADA is currently being tested in a number of cases. We're glad to have the ADA, although, as we've noted frequently, we know that its passage hasn't miraculously vanquished discrimination. Illiteracy, substandard schooling, legislative pressures to close the schools for the deaf, competition, qualifications, and job-related discrimination are still major problems, and we're going to have to continue grappling with them.

Nostalgia—a fond remembrance of earlier times—isn't necessarily foolish. We should cherish what was good about our past. We should preserve the recollections. We should establish, support, and patronize museums and archives. As for the negative aspects, they too are part of our history. We need to study them, learn from them, and strive to improve the current picture. If this is the best time to be deaf, we have the responsibility to ensure that the future is even better.

Deaf people were excluded from enjoying the "talkies" (except for subtitled foreign films) and using the telephone (unless they had a helpful hearing neighbor or family member), but they had Deaf clubs and flourishing school-based Deaf press—the "Little Paper Family." Technological progress has made these two cherished institutions all but extinct.

Communication is still a major barrier. Computers give deaf people new access to information. But the increasing reliance on voice-recognition technology and the proliferation of uncaptioned video clips (as in news Websites) worries us. We now have widespread relay services. TTYs are still expensive. Videophones are costly. Closed-captioning and open-captioning are a boon, but there's still not enough of it. We have captioned DVDs—and uncaptioned multimedia programs with sound effects. And let's hear it for the latest audiological miracle, the cochlear implant! Three steps forward, one step backwards.

The worst barrier of all, however, is attitude. General attitudes towards us are just as bad as ever. "Deaf can't, deaf can't." "Deaf equals dumb." "You do that really well for a deaf person." Still back in the Dark Ages.

As long as we face these obstacles, we can't say that we've achieved equality. We're fighting to get there, but—as we've noted here frequently—we're not equal yet.

Chapter 130

What things said by hearing people do deaf people hate the most?

e're sure that every deaf person has a few particular favorites, but we'd wager that the following four items are at the top of the list:

1.) "It's nothing."
2.) "It's not important."
3.) "I'll tell you later."
4.) The shoo-off gesture

1. & 2. "It's nothing"/"It's not important": This is what we often get told when we ask, "What are you talking about?" or "What's so funny?" We'd like to know why our family and friends see fit to use these rebuffs—after *they've* enjoyed, laughed at, or responded to a shared joke or story. Why should our access to shared information be denied just because someone else decides it's not important? Obviously, it *must* be more than "nothing;" it *must* have *some* importance. If it was important enough to be shared among hearing folks in the first place, it's important enough to be shared with us too. We resent hearing people's making judgements as to what social communication we can and can't receive. We recognize that a large proportion of all human communication *is* trivial. But don't we have a right to demand a fair share of it? If a joke or story is trivial or stupid, let *us* judge that— after we have access to it!

One Deaf woman told us that whenever anyone used these lines on her when sharing a joke with others, she responded by saying: "Please tell me too. I could use a laugh." It worked!

3. "I'll tell you later." One of us (LL) had a bitter experience with this form of brush-off:

> At a sci-fi convention in Buffalo, Jean A., an organizer from Ohio, told several other attendees an exciting anecdote about how she and some friends had dinner with an English actor we idolized. Basking in the afterglow of a happy memory, Jean described where they'd gone and what they chatted about. Everyone at the table listened with enjoyment. I understood nothing, of course; I watched with yearning and anguish. I wanted—oh, how I wanted!—to get the story from Jean. I don't recall exactly how I broached the subject. Maybe I had said, "What was that again?" and she had replied, "I'll tell you later." Or—more likely—I asked her, "Can you tell me about that later when it's a bit more quiet?" Of course, she had said she would.
>
> When I attempted to 'hold her to her promise' and asked her to repeat what she had told the others, she did so grudgingly, with a sour tinge of resentment in her expression, and the tersest of summaries. I was sorry I'd asked—but I *had* to satisfy my curiosity. Even so, I didn't understand the summary any better than I had the original telling, and I was too embarrassed to ask her to repeat yet again. She didn't like wasting her time on rehashing what she'd already told the others. For her, once was enough. I gave up on her.
>
> I never did find out what transpired at that wonderful dinner, but I told myself that it no longer mattered. That was my last sci-fi convention. I stopped going because I was tired of putting myself in situations like that, of paying full price for a ticket and getting less than half the enjoyment others did.

Why do people say "I'll tell you later" when they have no intention of doing so? It's because most don't like to rebuff others outright, to appear rude or mean. "I'll tell you later" is superficially more polite than "Oh, shut up!" or "Get lost!" People have a tendency to say things "to be polite" that they don't really mean. Or maybe they do mean it at the time—for about a second. We do know that when hearing people say "I'll tell you later," they never do. They **NEVER** tell us later. You can bank on it.

4. The shoo-off: Jan is a deaf member of a hearing family. When she sees that someone's on the phone, she wants to know who the other party is. She approaches and asks the speaker, "Who's on the phone?" This isn't being nosy, it's just asking for a bit of information that a hearing person would have access to (since they can hear the intonations of the speaker's voice and catch names and other clues). In a "bad" situation, Jan's sister, brother, or parents give her the shoo-off gesture. Or shrug. Or say "None of your business." Or ignore her. In an "enlightened" situation, the speaker turns to her and says (in speech, fingerspelling, or sign, or even a jotted note), "Margie" or "Grandmother" or "Cousin Steve" or "Gwen, a friend." Jan is satisfied, nods, and walks off.

How does the scenario play out in *our* families?

The shrug of indifference, the wave of dismissal, the refusal to respond at all, are signs of contempt or (to take a kindlier view) profound laziness. What the shooer-off is saying is "*I'm* not going to bother telling you" or "Don't bother me." The underlying message we're getting is: "You're not important enough to communicate with. You're not worth the effort." To a deaf person, that is the ultimate insult. To be dismissed is to be made invisible. A nonperson. Is there anything that infuriates us more? To be considered unworthy of the effort to communicate?

Getting excluded from social interactions and then brushed off is part of the baggage that comes with being deaf in a hearing group. When a company or facility or nonprofit agency discriminates against us, we can protest, complain to the boss, or contact the Office of Civil Rights. But what recourse do we have when the crime is committed in the bosom of our immediate family?

Yes, it takes time and effort to communicate with deaf people. Yes, it's annoying to have to repeat. Yes, it can be a burden having to translate, interpret, and fill in gaps. But if we are to have justice in the world, and a fairer, more accessible society, this is where it starts.

Chapter 131

What bothers a deaf person the most about hearing people?

▲ What bothers me most is when hearing people think they are complimenting you when they remark, "You are smart for a deaf person," "You did very well for a deaf person," "You speak so well for a deaf person" . . . and other variations of the same. Hearing people never compare hearing people this way. This remark automatically shows the false assumption in our society that deaf people are usually inept, not smart, or not on par with hearing people.

Dawn Skwersky
Northampton, Massachusetts

▲ I can think of many things that are frustrating and irritating, yet I can take them in stride. However, the one thing that upsets me the most is when I am in a group of people, whether friends or family, and a story or joke is told that I cannot understand or has not been interpreted. I ask "What did you just say?", only to be told, "I'll tell you later," with a wave of the hand serving as the only acknowledgement. This not only frustrates me, it makes me feel isolated. This is one of the primary reasons I prefer to be with other deaf people, and those hearing who know ASL & are willing to ensure that all present, deaf or hearing, can be full participants in the group. I have talked with other deaf in my area, and they agree this is also very frustrating. The key here, I think, is to be aware of those around you.

David Evans
Davis, California

▲ What bothers me the most about hearing people is when they are speaking to you and you tell them that you did not understand and mention that you are deaf/hearing-impaired. They would respond with an "Oh, I am so sorry" and start to speak louder and very slow (very articulate). It makes it harder for me to understand them. It would help if they just spoke normally and did not raise their voice. It would also help if those people were educated about the different kinds of disabilities and how to handle any kind of situations with the handicapped people.

Erin M. Strong
Newbury Park, California

▲ As a congenitally deaf physician, I have a pet peeve concerning many of my colleagues who constantly use expressions such as "deaf and dumb, weird speech pattern, deaf-mute, talks with gestures," etc., etc. I take pains to respond to each physician guilty of such entries on medical/surgical charts and/or records and explain that the above-mentioned comments are, at the least, very rude.

I am offering [this example] if you can use it. If nothing else, it makes **me** feel better.

Frank P. Hochman, M.D.
Fremont, California

▲ Easy . . . meeting a hearing person and having their first question be, "Do you speechread?" (of course, expecting me to get that through speechreading). I usually answer, "A little," sometimes answer, "No," and once answered, "I try not to!" (An absurd answer to an absurd question.) It angers me that the attitude is that communication is *my* problem. Without delving too deep—the reason I resist admitting this "speechguessing" ability is that on the occasions before I learned better, I would answer, "Yes" and from then on, they expected 100%, a feat I am not capable of under the best circumstances. Maybe my next answer should be, "Do you sign?" (in sign only!!)

Ellen Kuester
Houston, Texas

Deaf Awareness 5-Minute Quiz

Chapters 119—130

Answers are on the bottom of the page, upside down.

True or False:

1. Even though some hearing persons may feel uncomfortable about it, deaf people *need* to maintain steady eye contact with them.

2. If you can't afford a vibrotactile paging system, it can be really difficult to get another deaf person's attention.

3. Deaf people like to confirm that they've completed a requested task—without being asked follow-up questions—to save their roommates or housemates time, energy, and worry.

4. It's fairly common for deaf people to grow up without a sense of privacy, since they are so often under observation at school.

5. There are too few summer programs that encourage deaf youth to gain and practice leadership qualities.

6. Deaf people tend to be enthusiastic about attending class reunions; they feel strong bonds of affection for their schoolmates.

7. Most Deaf people dislike traveling because of the pervasive communication difficulties and hassles they experience.

8. In the "old days," deaf people might have a certain degree of freedom (to start new schools or serve in a local militia, for example), but they certainly had fewer civil rights.

9. When hearing people tell deaf people, "I'll tell you later," most of the time, they do.

10. What bothers deaf people most about hearing people is that hearing people can enjoy music and they can't.

Answers:
1. True; 2. False; 3. True; 4. True; 5. True; 6. False; 7. True; 8. False; 9. False; 10. False.

Afterword

Here are a few parting thoughts. Above all, please remember that deaf people are human beings who have dreams, desires, ambitions, and feelings, just as you do. If you treat us like human beings, we will surely reciprocate. There's no telling what the rewards may be.

Deaf education (and community) in France began with a priest who had compassion for two deaf sisters. Similarly, the American Deaf community began with a father's concern for his deaf daughter and other such children, and a neighbor's interest. A Deaf teacher in Paris volunteered to come to the States to teach other deaf people. These pioneers helped set into motion a revolution that continues today. They made history. They changed our destiny.

We cannot foresee the possible results of our acts of generosity or simple kindness. Treat a young deaf person with respect, and who knows? Your gesture of encouragement could ultimately result in that person's choosing a career that may have tremendous (and positive) consequences for society. A deaf student could grow up to become the scientist who discovers a cure for AIDS or finds a solution to the ozone problem. Or a world-class artist, performer, crafter, writer, teacher, explorer, or researcher.

Education is an ongoing and lifelong process. We hope that this book has enhanced your awareness of Deaf issues, and that you will want to learn more about them. Our goal has been, and remains, increasing understanding. There can never be too much of that!

Transforming an oppressed minority into a community of first-class citizens is a mutual task. The bottom line is this: to allow deaf people to have their own community, establish their own identity, fulfill their true potential. We invite you to be part of this adventure.

Select Bibliography

General Reference
Carol Turkington and Allen E. Sussman, Ph.D., **The Encyclopedia of Deafness and Hearing Disorders**. New York: Facts on File, 1992.

John Vickrey Van Cleve, ed., **Gallaudet Encyclopedia of Deaf People and Deafness**. 3 vols. New York: McGraw-Hill, 1987.

Deaf Culture, Community, and History
Douglas C. Baynton, **Forbidden Signs: American Culture and the Campaign Against Sign Language**. Chicago: University of Chicago Press, 1996.

Harry Best, **Deafness and the Deaf in the U.S.** New York: Macmillan, 1943.

Horst Biesold, **Crying Hands: Eugenics and Deaf People in Nazi Germany**. Henry Friedlander, trans. and intro. Washington, D.C.: Gallaudet University Press, 1999.

John B. Christiansen and Sharon Barnartt, **Deaf President Now! The 1988 Revolution at Gallaudet University**. Washington, D.C.: Gallaudet University Press, 1995.

Marilyn Daniels, **Benedictine Roots in the Development of Deaf Education**. Westport, CT: Bergin & Garvey, 1997.

Jack R. Gannon, **Deaf Heritage: a Narrative History of Deaf America**. Silver Spring: National Association of the Deaf, 1981.

Nora Ellen Groce, **Everyone Here Spoke Sign Language: Hereditary Deafness on Martha's Vineyard**. Cambridge, Mass.: Harvard University Press, 1985.

Mabs Holcomb and Sharon Wood, **Deaf Women: A Parade through the Decades**. San Diego: DawnSignPress, 1989.

Harlan Lane: **When the Mind Hears: A History of the Deaf**. 1984; rpt. New York: Pelican, 1999. Collingdale, PA: DIANE Publishing, 1998.

—**The Mask of Benevolence: Disabling the Deaf Community**. 1992; rpt. San Diego: DawnSignPress, 2000.

Harlan Lane, Robert Hoffmeister, and Ben Bahan, **A Journey into the Deaf-World**. San Diego: DawnSignPress, 1996.

Harry G. Lang, **A Phone of Our Own: The Deaf Insurrection Against Ma Bell**. Washington, D.C.: Gallaudet University Press, 2000.

Oliver Sacks, **Seeing Voices: A Journey into the World of the Deaf**. 1989; rpt. New York: Vintage Books, 2000.

John Vickrey Van Cleve and Barry A. Crouch, **A Place of Their Own: Creating the Deaf Community in America**. Washington, D.C.: Gallaudet University Press, 1989.

John Vickrey Van Cleve, ed., **Deaf History Unveiled: Interpretations from the New Scholarship**. Washington, D.C.: Gallaudet University Press, 2000.

Richard Winefield, **Never the Twain Shall Meet: The Communications Debate**. Washington, D.C.: Gallaudet University Press, 1987

Sociology & Sociolinguistics

David Goode, **A World Without Words: The Social Construction of Children Born Deaf and Blind**. Foreword by Irving Kenneth Zola. Philadelphia: Temple University Press, 1994.

Paul C. Higgins, **Outsiders in a Hearing World: A Sociology of Deafness**. Beverly Hills: Sage Publications, 1980.

Roy K. Holcomb, Samuel K. Holcomb, and Thomas K. Holcomb, **Deaf Culture Our Way**. San Diego: DawnSignPress, 1996.

Katherine A. Jankowski, **Deaf Empowerment: Emergence, Struggle, and Rhetoric**. Washington, D.C. Gallaudet University Press, 1997.

Arden Neisser, **The Other Side of Silence: Sign Language and the Deaf Community in America**. 1983; rpt. with a new introduction, Washington, D.C.: Gallaudet University Press, 1990.

Carol Padden and Tom Humphries, **Deaf in America: Voices from a Culture**. Cambridge, MA: Harvard University Press, 1988.

Ila Parasnis, ed. **Cultural and Language Diversity and the Deaf Experience**. New York: Cambridge University Press, 1996.

Cynthia Peters, **Deaf American Literature: From Carnival to the Canon**. Washington, D.C.: Gallaudet University Press, 1999.

Steven L. Sachs, **Street Gang Awareness: A Resource Guide for Parents and Professionals**. Minneapolis: Fairview Press, 1997.

Oliver Sacks, **Seeing Voices: A Journey Into the World of the Deaf**. Berkeley: University of California Press, 1989.

Jerome D. Schein and David A. Stewart, **Language in Motion: Exploring the Nature of Sign**. Washington, D.C.: Gallaudet University Press, 1995.

Deaf Education

Thomas N. Kluwin and Michael S. Stinson, **Deaf Students in Local Public High Schools: Backgrounds, Experiences, and Outcomes**. Springfield, IL: Charles C. Thomas, 1993.

David S. Martin, ed. **Advances in Cognition, Education, and Deafness**. Washington, D.C.: Gallaudet University Press, 1991.

Claire L. Ramsey, **Deaf Children in Public Schools: Placement, Context, and Consequences**. Washington, D.C.: Gallaudet University Press, 1997.

Susan Schaller, **A Man Without Words**. Foreword by Oliver W. Sacks. Berkeley: University of California Press, 1995.

Margret A. Winzer, **The History of Special Education: From Isolation to Integration**. Washington, D.C.: Gallaudet University Press, 1993.

Learning Sign Language: Texts and Dictionaries

David F. Armstrong, William C. Stokoe, and Sherman E. Wilcox, **Gesture and the Nature of Language**. New York: Cambridge University Press, 1995.

Bernard Bragg and Jack R. Olson, **Meeting Halfway in American Sign Language: A Common Ground for Effective Communication Among Deaf and Hearing People**. Rochester: Deaf Life Press, 1994.

Rod R. Butterworth and Mickey Flodin, **Signing Made Easy**. New York: Perigee Books/Berkley Publishing Group, 1989.

— **The Perigee Visual Dictionary of Signing**: An A-to-Z Guide to Over 1,250 Signs of American Sign Language. New York: Perigee Books/Berkley Publishing Group, 1995.

Diane P. Chambers, **Communicating in Sign: Creative Ways to Learn American Sign Language**. Introduction by Bernard Bragg. New York: Fireside/Simon & Schuster, 1998.

Elaine Costello, **Signing: How to Speak with Your Hands**. Illus. Lois Lehman. New York: Bantam, 1983.

—**Religious Signing**. Illus. Lois Lehman. New York: Bantam, 1997.

—**Random House Webster's American Sign Language Medical Dictionary**. New York: Random House Reference & Information Publishing, 2000.

—**Random House Webster's American Sign Language Legal Dictionary**. New York: Random House Reference & Information Publishing, 2003.

Ralph Singleton and Judy Singleton, **Underwater Sign Communication: Dance Your Hands!** Union City, CA: Silver Seal Aqua Academy, 2002.

David Stewart, **American Sign Language: The Easy Way**. Hauppage, NY: Barron's Educational Series, 1998.

Martin L. A. Sternberg, **American Sign Language Dictionary, Unabridged**. New York: HarperCollins, 1998.

Anthologies

Trent Batson and Eugene Bergman, eds., **Angels and Outcasts: An Anthology of Deaf Characters in Literature**. Washington, D.C.: Gallaudet University Press, 1985.

Brian Grant, ed., **The Quiet Ear: Deafness in Literature**. London: André Deutsch, 1987.

Jill Christine Jepson, ed., **No Walls of Stone: An Anthology of Literature by Deaf and Hard of Hearing Writers**. Washington: Gallaudet University Press, 1993.

Christopher Krentz, ed., **A Mighty Change: An Anthology of Deaf American Writing, 1816-1864**. Washington, D.C.: Gallaudet University Press, 2001.

Raymond Luczak, ed., **Eyes of Desire: A Deaf Gay & Lesbian Reader**. New York: Alyson Publications, 1993.

Sherman Wilcox, ed., **American Deaf Culture: An Anthology**. Silver Spring: Linstok Press, 1989.

Biographies

Harry G. Lang, **Silence of the Spheres: The Deaf Experience in the History of Science**. Westport, CT: Greenwood Publishing Group, 1994.

Harry G. Lang and Bonnie Meath-Lang, **Deaf Persons in the Arts and Sciences: A Biographical Dictionary**. Westport, CT: Greenwood Press, 1995.

Jane Maher, **Seeing Language in Sign: The Work of William C. Stokoe**. Washington: Gallaudet University Press, 1996.

Matthew S. Moore and Robert F. Panara, **Great Deaf Americans: The Second Edition**. Rochester, NY: Deaf Life Press, 1996.

Jerome D. Schein, **A Rose for Tomorrow: Biography of Frederick C. Schreiber**. Silver Spring: National Association of the Deaf, 1983.

Autobiographies & Memoirs

Anne Bolander and Adair Renning, **I Was #87: A Deaf Woman's Ordeal of Misdiagnosis, Institutionalization, and Abuse**. Washington, D.C.: Gallaudet University Press, 1999.

Frank G. Bowe, **Changing the Rules**. Silver Spring: T.J. Publishers, 1986.

Bernard Bragg, **Lessons in Laughter: The Autobiography of a Deaf Actor. As Signed to Eugene Bergman**. Washington, D.C.: Gallaudet University Press, 1989.

Leah Hager Cohen, **Train Go Sorry: Inside a Deaf World**. New York: Vintage Books, 1995.

Mark Drolsbaugh, **Deaf Again**. North Wales, PA: Handwave Publications, 1997.

Cheryl M. Heppner, **Seeds of Disquiet: One Deaf Woman's Experience**. Washington, D.C.: Gallaudet University Press, 1992.

Leo M. Jacobs, **A Deaf Adult Speaks Out**. Washington, D.C.: Gallaudet University Press, 3rd ed., 1989.

Henry Kisor, **What's That Pig Outdoors? A Memoir of Deafness**. 1990; rpt. New York: Penguin, 1991.

—**Flight of the Gin Fizz: Midlife at 4,500 Feet**. New York: Basic Books, 1997.

Bonnie Poitras Tucker, **The Feel of Silence**. Philadelphia: Temple University Press, 1995.

Heather Whitestone, **Listening with My Heart**. New York: Doubleday, 1998.

David Wright, **Deafness**. New York: Stein & Day, 1969.

By Parents of Deaf Children

Tressa Bower, **Alandra's Lilacs: The Story of a Mother and her Deaf Daughter**. Washington, D.C.: Gallaudet University Press, 1999.

Lorraine Fletcher, **Ben's Story: A Deaf Child's Right to Sign**. Washington, D.C.: Gallaudet University Press, 1987.

Kathy Robinson, **Children of Silence: The Story of My Daughters' Triumph Over Deafness**. New York: New American Library, 1991.

Thomas Spradley and James P. Spradley, **Deaf Like Me**. 1978; rpt. with a new afterword by Lynn Spradley, Washington, D.C.: Gallaudet University Press, 1985.

By Children of Deaf Parents

Charlotte Abrams, **The Silents**. Washington, D.C.: Gallaudet University Press, 1996.

Harvey Barash and Eva Barash Dicker, **Our Father Abe: The Story of a Deaf Shoe Repairman**. Madison, WI: Abar Press, 1991.

Lennard J. Davis, **My Sense of Silence: Memoirs of a Childhood with Deafness**. Urbana: University of Chicago Press, 2000.

Paul Preston, **Mother Father Deaf: Living Between Sound and Silence**. Cambridge, MA: Harvard University Press, 1994.

Ruth Sidransky, **In Silence: Growing Up Hearing in a Deaf World**. New York: St. Martin's Press, 1990.

Peg Strenkowski, **Silent Journey: Life Within a Deaf Family**. Chapel Hill, NC: Professional Press, 1999.

Lou Ann Walker, **A Loss for Words: The Story of Deafness in a Family**. New York: Harper & Row, 1986.

Deaf & Hearing Dogs

Susan Cope Becker, **Living with a Deaf Dog: A Book of Advice, Facts, and Experiences About Canine Deafness**. Ill. Andrew Caylor. Self-published, 2nd. ed., 1997.

Paul W. Ogden, **Chelsea: The Story of a Signal Dog**. New York: Little, Brown & Co., 1992.

Index

Note to the reader

This index was developed in response to feedback and requests from teachers. Our guiding principle has been to devise an index that is easy to use, detailed, comprehensive, and helpful, making the information in this book as accessible as possible to all readers. A few points:

Since this book is *about* deaf people, we have tried to keep the number of entries beginning with "deaf" down to a reasonable level. Instead of "deaf drivers," "Deaf etiquette," and "deaf people: accidents, hazards, safety," there are entries for *drivers, etiquette,* and *accidents, hazards, safety.* We have also decided against making numerous entries with the keyword "hearing" to refer to hearing people's relationships with deaf people, since these relationships are mentioned in virtually every chapter. In some instances, we use the term "intermodal" to refer to deaf/hearing social interactions and romantic relationships.

Major topics (with numerous entries and subentries) include *American Sign Language, captioning, Deaf culture, deafness, discrimination, education of the deaf, interpreters, employment, mainstreaming, misconceptions, prejudice, sign language, schools for the deaf,* and *TTYs.* We have made numerous cross-references to link related topics, and double entries to make the reader's task easier. Thus, education is linked to ASL, literacy, mainstreaming, schools, signing, speech, and parenting topics. The ADA is linked to *disability, discrimination, employment,* and *law-enforcement issues.* And so forth.

Book and periodical titles are in **bold**; plays, movies, and TV series/programs in ***bold italics***. Books and plays are listed both under their authors' names and by title. Schools for the deaf are listed alphabetically under *schools for the deaf.* Colleges, universities, agencies, and organizations are listed by name. Sign languages of other nations are listed under *sign languages.* All locators (page references) indicate pages, not chapters. No distinction is made here between references to the text and to footnotes. We trust that this will not present any particular difficulty, though.

Krentz, Christopher (editor)
A Mighty Change: An Anthology of Deaf American Writing, 1816-1864, 368
Kuranz, Robert, 83
Kurzweil Personal Reader, 54

labels
applied by deaf people, 205–207
"hearings," 253–255
applied to deaf people, 220–243
"disabled" *vs.* ethnic view, 250–251
"hard-of-hearing," 318 *see also* hard-of-hearing: terminology
stereotypes and, 363
Landers, Ann (syndicated column), 221
Lane, Harlan
Deaf-culture scholarship, 329, 334, 585
on pluralization in ASL, 151
The Mask of Benevolence, 585
When the Mind Hears, 54, 58–59, 585
Lang, Donald, 223, 501
Lang, Harry G., 647
languageless deaf adults
advocacy for, 585
Donald Lang's murder trial, 223, 501
fictionalized portrayals, 360
langue des signes français (LSF) *see* sign languages: French
The Last Temptation of Christ (M. Scorsese), 575

late-deafened adults
coping and networking, 321–323
Deaf attitudes towards, 574, 596
definition, 299
enjoyment of music, 382
hard-of-hearing and, 313–314
isolation in family, 603
learning sign language, 80
as part of Deaf community, 206, 309–310
retention of clear speech, 210
susceptible to depression, 359, 701
law-enforcement concerns, 499–512, 665–669
Lentz, Ella Mae, 369
Lessons in Laughter (Bragg), 211
Levine, Edna Simon, 585
Levinson, Ken, 203
Levis (jeans), 491
Leviticus, 305
libraries
college, 183, 187
public, 97–98, 106–107, 155, 183, 241
school, as punishment, 160, 162, 356
Lincoln, Abraham, 448
Lindbergh, Charles, 410
Linden, Joyce, 107
Lindsey, Gayle, 573, 579
Linotypists
"ideal match," 423, 445
at major newspapers, 441
lipreading *see* speechreading
literacy *see also* American Sign Language: English as second language; education of the deaf; Manually Coded English
AIDS crisis and, 551–553
benefits of mastering, 335
choice of career, 446, 476

Notes:

Notes:

If you still have questions...

...send them to us. We welcome your questions and comments.

Our feature, "For Hearing People Only," appears every month in **DEAF LIFE**.

E-mail us at
questions@hpobook.com

An online community forum
http://www.deafnotes.com/

Share your thoughts, opinions, and views on hot topics and controversies— or just join in the dialogue. Our BBS is free, moderated, and open to all. Serious discussions, and fun stuff too.

Like what you've been reading?

Want to order a copy for yourself, or an extra for a friend?

Please print clearly!

Name: _____

Address: _____

City: _____

State: _____ Zip: _____ Phone:(_____) _____

E-mail: _____

Quantity	Price	Postage/ handling*	RUSH**	New York Sales Tax	Total
Single copy	$27.78	☐ Included	☐ $5.00	☐ $2.22	
2 copies	$46.30	☐ Included	☐ $5.00	☐ $3.70	
		Outside USA Postage add		☐ $5.00	
				Grand Total	

*Regular orders take 2 to 6 weeks for delivery.

**RUSH orders will be sent out within 2 to 4 business days after we receive the order. If you want the book(s) sent via overnight (Express) mail, or by UPS or FedEx, contact us for details. No checks for rush orders, please.

**Credit cards (MC, VISA, DC) are accepted ONLY for RUSH orders.

☐ **MasterCard**   ☐ **VISA**   ☐ **DINERS CLUB INTERNATIONAL**

Credit Card #

__/__/__/__/__/__/__/__/__/__/__/__/__/__/__/

Expiration date__/__

Signature_____

Canadian/Foreign orders:

Please enclose an International Money Order (**U.S. funds only**).

A $25.00 fine is charged on all bounced checks.

Send this order form with check or money order payable to:

HPO Book, c/o MSM Productions, Ltd.
1095 Meigs Street
Rochester, NY 14620-2405
FAX (585) 442-6371

For up-to-date contact information (mailing address, *etcetera*), check our Website:

http://www.hpobook.com

Special quantity discounts (20 or more copies) are available. Contact us for details.

Photocopies of this form accepted.

Over a decade of promoting Deaf Awareness